Lecture Notes in Computer Science 14352

Founding Editors

Gerhard Goos
Juris Hartmanis

Editorial Board Members

The series Lecture Notes in Computer Science (LNCS), including its subseries Lecture Notes in Artificial Intelligence (LNAI) and Lecture Notes in Bioinformatics (LNBI), has established itself as a medium for the publication of new developments in computer science and information technology research, teaching, and education.

LNCS enjoys close cooperation with the computer science R & D community, the series counts many renowned academics among its volume editors and paper authors, and collaborates with prestigious societies. Its mission is to serve this international community by providing an invaluable service, mainly focused on the publication of conference and workshop proceedings and postproceedings. LNCS commenced publication in 1973.

Demetris Zeinalipour · Dora Blanco Heras ·
George Pallis · Herodotos Herodotou ·
Demetris Trihinas · Daniel Balouek ·
Patrick Diehl · Terry Cojean · Karl Fürlinger ·
Maja Hanne Kirkeby · Matteo Nardelli ·
Pierangelo Di Sanzo
Editors

Euro-Par 2023:
Parallel Processing Workshops

Euro-Par 2023 International Workshops
Limassol, Cyprus, August 28 – September 1, 2023
Revised Selected Papers, Part II

 Springer

Editors

Demetris Zeinalipour Ⓘ
University of Cyprus
Nicosia, Cyprus

Dora Blanco Heras Ⓘ
University of Santiago de Compostela
Santiago de Compostela, Spain

George Pallis Ⓘ
University of Cyprus
Nicosia, Cyprus

Herodotos Herodotou Ⓘ
Cyprus University of Technology
Limassol, Cyprus

Demetris Trihinas Ⓘ
University of Nicosia
Nicosia, Cyprus

Daniel Balouek Ⓘ
Inria
Nantes, France

Patrick Diehl Ⓘ
Louisiana State University
Baton Rouge, LA, USA

Terry Cojean Ⓘ
Karlsruhe Institute of Technology
Karlsruhe, Germany

Karl Fürlinger Ⓘ
Ludwig-Maximilians-Universität
Munich, Germany

Maja Hanne Kirkeby Ⓘ
Roskilde University
Roskilde, Denmark

Matteo Nardelli Ⓘ
Bank of Italy
Rome, Italy

Pierangelo Di Sanzo Ⓘ
Roma Tre University
Rome, Italy

ISSN 0302-9743 ISSN 1611-3349 (electronic)
Lecture Notes in Computer Science
ISBN 978-3-031-48802-3 ISBN 978-3-031-48803-0 (eBook)
https://doi.org/10.1007/978-3-031-48803-0

Preface

Euro-Par is the prime European conference covering all aspects of parallel and distributed processing, ranging from theory to practice, from small to the largest parallel and distributed systems and infrastructures, from fundamental computational problems to applications, from architecture, compiler, language and interface design and implementation, to tools, support infrastructures, and application performance aspects.

To provide a meeting point for researchers to discuss and exchange new ideas on more specialized themes, cross-cutting issues, and upcoming trends and paradigms, Euro-Par 2023 co-located Workshops, a Demos/Posters track, a PhD Symposium track and, for the first time, a minisymposia track (i.e., scientific sessions that bring together experts to discuss specific topics in a particular field but without publications in the proceedings.) These events complementary to the main conference were held in Limassol, Cyprus between August 28 and September 1, 2023, following the well-established format of their predecessors. The conference was organized by the University of Cyprus at the St. Raphael Resort, Limassol, Cyprus with local arrangements by Easyconferences Ltd.

LNCS volumes 14351 and 14352 contain the papers and extended abstracts presented at the Euro-Par 2023 Workshops, divided into 9 track sections (one per Workshop, one for the Demos/Posters track and one for the PhD Symposium track). Overall, the following seven Workshop proposals were submitted and all of them met the criteria set out in the guidelines and were accepted:

1. The 1st International Workshop on Scalable Compute Continuum (WSCC 2023)
2. The 1st International Workshop on Tools for Data Locality, Power and Performance (TDLPP 2023)
3. The 1st International Workshop on Urgent Analytics for Distributed Computing (QuickPar 2023)
4. The 21st International Workshop on Algorithms, Models and Tools for Parallel Computing on Heterogeneous Platforms (HeteroPar 2023)
5. The 2nd International Workshop on Resource AWareness of Systems and Society (RAW 2023)
6. The 3rd International Workshop on Asynchronous Many-Task systems for Exascale (AMTE 2023)
7. The 3rd International Workshop on Performance and Energy-efficiency in Concurrent and Distributed Systems (PECS 2023)

The following two minisymposia proposals were submitted and both of them met the criteria set out in the guidelines and were accepted:

1. The 1st Minisymposium on Applications and Benefits of UPMEM commercial Massively Parallel Processing-In-Memory Platform (ABUMPIMP 2023)
2. The 1st Minsymposium on Adaptive High Performance Input/Output Systems (ADAPIO 2023)

Each Euro-Par Workshop had an independent program committee, which was in charge of selecting the papers. The Euro-Par Workshops received 55 submitted Workshop papers, with each submission being single-blind reviewed by at least three technical program committee members of the respective Euro-Par Workshops program committee. After the thorough peer-reviewing process, 42 submissions were accepted for presentation at the Euro-Par 2023 Workshops, resulting in an acceptance rate of 76%. LNCS volumes 14351 and 14352 contain the following number of contributions from co-located Workshops, with each paper being 12 pages: 7 papers from WSCC 2023, 5 papers from TDLPP 2023, 3 papers from QuickPar 2023, 12 papers from HeteroPar 2023, 7 papers from RAW 2023, 4 papers from AMTE 2023 and 4 papers from PECS 2023.

The Euro-Par Demos/Posters track received 16 submissions, with each submission being reviewed by at least two technical program committee members. After a thorough single-blind peer-reviewing process, 14 submissions were accepted and included as 4-page papers in these proceedings. The Euro-Par PhD Symposium track received 12 submissions, with each submission being single-blind reviewed by at least three technical program committee members. After a thorough peer-reviewing process, 10 submissions were accepted and included as 6-page papers in these proceedings.

The success of the Euro-Par Workshops/Minisymposia, Demos/Posters track and PhD Symposium track depended on the work of many individuals and organizations. We therefore thank all the organizers and reviewers for the time and effort that they invested. We would also like to express our gratitude to the members of the Euro-Par 2023 Organizing Committee, the General Chair George A. Papadopoulos (University of Cyprus, Cyprus), the Program Co-Chairs Marios D. Dikaiakos (University of Cyprus, Cyprus) and Rizos Sakellariou (University of Manchester, UK), as well as the local staff of Easyconferences Ltd. (Petros Stratis, Nicolas Stratis and Boyana Slavova). Lastly, we thank all participants, panelists, and keynote speakers of the Euro-Par Workshops for their contribution to bring forward a number of productive events that have enriched the diversity and scope of the main conference in significant ways. It was a pleasure to organize and host the Euro-Par 2023 Workshops/Minisymposia, Demos/Posters track and PhD Symposium track in Limassol, Cyprus.

August 2023

Demetris Zeinalipour
Dora Blanco Heras
George Pallis
Herodotos Herodotou
Demetris Trihinas

Organization

Steering Committee

Fernando Silva (Steering Committee Chair)	University of Porto, Portugal
Dora Blanco Heras (Workshops Chair)	University of Santiago de Compostela, Spain
Maciej Malawski (Virtualization Chair)	AGH Univ. of Science and Technology, Poland
Henk Sips (Finance Chair)	Delft Univ. of Technology, The Netherlands
Massimo Torquati (Artifacts Chair)	University of Pisa, Italy
Marco Aldinucci	University of Turin, Italy
Luc Bougé	ENS Rennes, France
Jesus Carretero	Carlos III University of Madrid, Spain
Christos Kaklamanis	Computer Technology Institute and University of Patras, Greece
Paul Kelly	Imperial College London, UK
Thomas Ludwig	University of Hamburg, Germany
Tomś Margalef	Autonomous University of Barcelona, Spain
Wolfgang Nagel	Dresden University of Technology, Germany
George Papadopoulos	University of Cyprus, Cyprus
Francisco Fernández Rivera	University of Santiago de Compostela, Spain
Krzysztof Rządca	University of Warsaw, Poland
Rizos Sakellariou	University of Manchester, UK
Leonel Sousa	University of Lisbon, Portugal
Phil Trinder	University of Glasgow, UK
Felix Wolf	Technical University of Darmstadt, Germany
Ramin Yahyapour	GWDG and University of Göttingen, Germany

Honorary Members

Christian Lengauer	University of Passau, Germany
Ron Perrott	Oxford e-Research Centre, UK
Karl Dieter Reinartz	University of Erlangen-Nürnberg, Germany

General Chair

George A. Papadopoulos   University of Cyprus, Cyprus

Program Chairs

Marios D. Dikaiakos   University of Cyprus, Cyprus
Rizos Sakellariou   University of Manchester, UK

Workshop Chairs

Dora Blanco Heras   University of Santiago de Compostela, Spain
Demetris Zeinalipour   University of Cyprus, Cyprus

Publication Chairs

José Cano   University of Glasgow, UK
Miquel Pericàs   Chalmers University of Technology, Sweden

Local Chairs

Chryssis Georgiou   University of Cyprus, Cyprus
George Pallis   University of Cyprus, Cyprus

Contents – Part II

PhD Symposium

Contents – Part I

The Second International Workshop on Resource AWareness of Systems and Society (RAW 2023)

The Second International Workshop on Resource AWareness of Systems and Society (RAW 2023)

Workshop Description

The Second Workshop on Resource Awareness of Systems and Society (RAW 2023) was co-located with Euro-Par 2023 (https://2023.euro-par.org) and aimed to bring together educators, researchers, and engineers from academia and industry to discuss solutions and open problems in the area of resource-aware computing. RAW 2023 aimed to form a community around resource-aware computing, encompassing classical resource trade-offs, such as energy vs. performance, as well as incorporating novel concepts, such as development time and effort, resilience, or sustainability over product or process life cycles.

RAW 2023 received eight research submissions, of which seven were accepted. The RAW Workshop consisted of four technical sessions with 7 regular presentations and 2 invited talks on the state of the art, early ideas, work in progress, preliminary results, case studies, industrial cases, open problems, and mature results in the form of research results, reports, or demonstrations. Presentation topics were related to different kinds of resources (time, energy, space, data, effort, etc.) and their usage in the development and usage of systems in our environment. Presentations referred to techniques involved in resource measurement, monitoring, controlling, and trade-offs, including the full scope of techniques from background theory to the application of innovative solutions in different domains. Finally, presentations tackled different aspects of the mentioned techniques such as education, training, research, and practice. Authors of the presented work submitted papers on the presented contributions. Submissions were reviewed by an international program committee, where all submitted papers were reviewed by three reviewers in the first cycle, and by the workshop chairs in the second round, checking the completeness of changes and improvements according to the reviewers' comments. Finally, 7 full papers were accepted for publishing in LNCS Workshop Proceedings of Euro-Par 2023.

We are grateful to all PC members and sub-reviewers (see the Section *Organization* that follows) for providing careful and timely opinions on the papers. We are also grateful to CERCIRAS CA19135 and the COST Association (see the following section, too), as well as the local organizing team at Euro-Par 2023 for technical, logistic, and organizational support. We are thankful to all contributors and authors for sharing their ideas and findings with the workshop participants, contributing directly to the success of the second edition of the RAW Workshop. Especially, we would like to express our heartfelt thanks to the invited speakers, Reza Farahani and Aitor Arrieta Marcos, whose enlightening talks added tremendous value to RAW 2023. Their insights and expertise enriched the workshop discussions and contributed to its overall success. We would also like to extend our gratitude to Demetris Zeinalipour and Dora Blanco Heras, the workshop chairs of Euro-Par 2023, for their invaluable support and collaboration in co-locating RAW 2023 with Euro-Par.

Organization

The RAW workshops are organized under the scope of COST Action CA19135 CER-CIRAS: Connecting Education and Research Communities for an Innovative Resource Aware Society, funded by European Cooperation in Science and Technology (COST) Association3 . COST is a funding agency for research and innovation networks. COST Actions help connect research initiatives across Europe and enable scientists to grow their ideas by sharing them with their peers.This boosts their research, career and innovation. CERCIRAS COST Action involves more than 250 participants representing more than 35 countries.CERCIRAS initiated the RAW Workshop series, as a COST Action workshop, but open to all interested participants and presenters with an intention to continue the RAW tradition in the future. Consequently, this chapter is based upon work from CERCIRAS COST Action, involving direct CERCIRAS results and external related ones.

Program Chairs

Maja H. Kirkeby — Roskilde University, Denmark
Gordana Rakić — University of Novi Sad, Serbia

Program Committee

Yasmina Abdeddaïm — Université Gustave Eiffel, LIGM, CNRS, France
Zoran Budimac — University of Novi Sad, Serbia
Marcus Denker — Inria Lille, France
Martin Frieb — Augsburg University, Germany
Padma Iyenghar — University of Osnabrück, Germany
Elinda Kajo Mece — Polytechnic University of Tirana, Albania
Attila Kertesz — University of Szeged, Hungary
Ana Oprescu — University of Amsterdam, The Netherlands
Zoran Pandilov — Ss. Cyril and Methodius University in Skopje, North Macedonia
Radu Prodan — University of Klagenfurt, Austria
Christine Rochange — IRIT – Université de Toulouse, France
Oleksandr Zaitsev — CIRAD, UMR SENS, MUSE, Université de Montpellier, France

List of Subreviewers

Kurt Horvath	University of Klagenfurt, Austria
Christian Piatka	Augsburg University, Germany
Alexander Stegmeier	Augsburg University, Germany

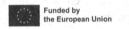

Performance and Energy Aware Training of a Deep Neural Network in a Multi-GPU Environment with Power Capping

Grzegorz Koszczał, Jan Dobrosolski⬤, Mariusz Matuszek⬤,
and Paweł Czarnul(✉)⬤

Faculty of Electronics, Telecommunications and Informatics, Gdansk University of
Technology, Narutowicza 11/12, 80-233 Gdansk, Poland
pczarnul@eti.pg.edu.pl

Abstract. In this paper we demonstrate that it is possible to obtain considerable improvement of performance and energy aware metrics for training of deep neural networks using a modern parallel multi-GPU system, by enforcing selected, non-default power caps on the GPUs. We measure the power and energy consumption of the whole node using a professional, certified hardware power meter. For a high performance workstation with 8 GPUs, we were able to find non-default GPU power cap settings within the range of 160–200 W to improve the difference between percentage energy gain and performance loss by over 15.0%, EDP (Abbreviations and terms used are described in main text.) by over 17.3%, EDS with k = 1.5 by over 2.2%, EDS with k = 2.0 by over 7.5% and pure energy by over 25%, compared to the default power cap setting of 260 W per GPU. These findings demonstrate the potential of today's CPU+GPU systems for configuration improvement in the context of performance-energy consumption metrics.

Keywords: deep neural network training · power capping · multi GPU · performance-energy optimization

1 Introduction and Motivation

Training of deep neural networks is a time consuming and a computationally demanding process. In recent years one could have observed a rapid development in the machine learning field, leading to a constant stream of innovation resulting in the emergence of new neural network topologies of growing complexity (e.g. GPT-3: 175 billion parameters, DLRM-2020: 100 billion parameters). Both models of such record breaking complexity, as well as other frequently used models (e.g. BERT: 340M parameters), require an immense amount of computing power in order to train on enormously large datasets (e.g. GPT-3: 45 TB of data). This trend of creating more and more power hungry models and creating

The original version of this chapter was previously published without open access. A correction to this chapter is available at
https://doi.org/10.1007/978-3-031-48803-0_41

D. Zeinalipour et al. (Eds.): Euro-Par 2023 Workshops, LNCS 14352, pp. 5–16, 2024.
https://doi.org/10.1007/978-3-031-48803-0_1

more extensive data corpse leads to time and energy consuming training processes (e.g. OpenAI Five training took 180 days), resulting in concerns regarding
the monetary cost and carbon footprint, correlated with growing significance of
deep learning related research. One of the proposed solutions, that would not
limit the progression of modern day artificial intelligence (AI), is to utilize the
mechanism of power capping,[1] which has already been proven to be able to provide with the desired energy consumption – execution time trade-off in other
applications [9].

The main goal of this study is to expand knowledge gained during research
regarding power capping during deep neural network (DNN) training on a single
GPU [10] by acquiring meaningful data for multi-GPU configurations. In this
paper we investigate the degree of potential gains when optimizing performance-
energy metrics by application of power caps when performing a deep neural network training in a *multi*-GPU hardware environment. Consideration of multiple
GPUs is important as it is a straightforward and commonly applied technique
to increase system performance, especially for AI workloads. Additionally, the
novelty of our research lies in precise measurements using a professional certified hardware power meter and consideration of whole node's power and -
consequently - energy consumption, contrary to power and energy of computing
devices, as typically measured using Intel RAPL or NVIDIA NVML. We consider
this approach much more practical in situations involving power-performance
optimisation of whole clusters running AI workloads.

Additional motivation comes from the current state in the machine learning
field. In case of natural language processing, the point where increasing the model
size stops positively impacting its performance has not been, and it does not look
like it will be reached anytime soon. With a growing network size and constant
efforts being made to expand quality data corpse that fits the needs of NLP
models, many concerns have been raised in regard to ecological consequences, as
well as total cost of conducting work in the AI field (training of GPT-3 model
from the ground up is estimated to cost 4.6 million USD, with energy usage as
high as 936 MWh) [12]. When taking into consideration that the development
process of a new model, or even fine tuning an existing model to a specific task
using transfer learning takes multiple training cycles in an unavoidable process
of hyper-parameter tuning, the estimated cost and carbon footprint of machine
learning is a considerable problem [23] that needs to be tackled with, both for
AI application feasibility as well as for environmental reasons. Those issues can
be expected to only grow, when considering that models as big as 1.6 trillion
parameters (Google's Switch-C model) have been announced.

The remaining part of the paper is structured as follows. Section "Related
work" discusses similar research in this field, focusing on energy aware

---

[1] Power capping is a mechanism allowing limiting the power draw of a computing
device such as a CPU or a GPU, available through Intel RAPL for Intel CPUs
and NVIDIA NVML for NVIDIA GPUs, resulting in potentially lower performance
but potential for optimization of energy consumption, even throughout extended
application execution time [9–11].

optimizations in AI. The "Methodology" section contains a description of the tested model, data, metrics and conditions necessary to obtain meaningful results. Next comes the "Experiments" section, containing detailed descriptions of the testbed environment and experiments themselves. This description should help interested parties to reproduce our measurements. Finally, we conclude with a summary and an outline of future work.

2 Related Work

Research regarding energy consumption – execution time trade-off is not a novelty, as the topic is constantly being explored, for example in context of multi- and many-core processors [6], or regarding AI workloads using specific frameworks on different platforms [14]. Optimization concerning energy consumption of AI workloads requires methods of estimation of energy and time (such as training or inference). While general frameworks and tools for optimization of energy efficiency of high performance computing (HPC) applications exist (e.g. [17]), a specific energy estimation method and tool has been proposed[2] for a deep neural network model based on its architecture, bitwidth and sparsity [22]. The authors concluded that the number of weights and multiplication-and-accumulation operations are not good metrics for energy consumption estimates and that data movement is more expensive than computation. Energy efficiency of using deep neural networks is considered in the context of using GPUs [24], FPGAs [18], hybrid GPU-FPGA [5] and severely energy and power constrained devices such as unmanned aerial vehicles (UAVs), smartphones [21], Internet of Things (IoT) [16] etc. For example, in [15] authors emphasize the need for energy reduction of machine learning and natural language processing (NLP), citing interesting trade-offs between decrease of energy usage and performance loss while training a transformer-based language model, thanks to power capping. Using NVIDIA V100 it was possible to save approx. 12.3% of energy at the cost of 8.5% performance loss for BERT, and to save approx. 15% energy at the cost of approx. 10% performance loss for DistilBERT. Energy efficiency of neural networks training is studied in paper [20], in particular stating correlation between CO_2 emissions and energy consumed and network architectures. Testing VGG16, VGG19 and ResNet50 architectures and CIFAR10, MNIST datasets in various locations, optimizing accuracy/energy led to either improvement of both energy efficiency and accuracy (MNIST) or improvement of energy efficiency with a loss of accuracy (CIFAR10). The authors also compared energy measurements from software-based CodeCarbon (based on hardware performance counters and I/O models), to those from a hardware meter, showing ratio of values from the former to the latter between 42% and 46% (generally software methods measure power of compute devices and memory only). This results in strong correlation but slightly different offsets for various configurations.

Multiple ways of searching for optimal configurations were proposed, one of them being GPOEO [19], an online energy optimization framework for machine

---

[2] https://energyestimation.mit.edu/.

learning applications run on GPUs. The framework's course of action can be divided into two phases. Firstly, during the offline phase, the framework collects performance and energy logs for various frequency of streaming multiprocessors and memory, which is later used during the online phase, where the frequencies that exhibited best characteristics are applied during the training to optimize a function of energy and time.

Similar goals were achieved by using the widely recognised GPU DVFS technique [25], where a defined power limit was used to limit energy consumption while maintaining the optimal resource utilization leading to limiting the performance loss. It is worth mentioning that this technique is well grounded in energy preserving research regarding GPU computing, with a history of great results (14.4% energy savings with 3% performance loss) in non machine learning RODINIA and ISPASS benchmarks [13].

Visible results achieved in reduction of energy consumption by two exploration algorithms (56% energy consumption decrease, 12% execution time increase) showcase the possibilities of power capping (authors used DEPO, an automatic power capping software tool) when it comes to achieving considerable savings of energy while maintaining an acceptable performance loss, that hopefully can be transferred for other computationally complex tasks.

Another interesting mention is that not all approaches to limit the energy consumption during deep learning workloads revolve around power capping. A great example would be the effort made to minimize the energy expenditure of a computing cluster by shutting down unused nodes using a job allocation method using a MINLP formulation [7]. In paper [23] authors proposed a solution for reduction of a carbon footprint of DNN training. The method realized periodical adjustment of the GPU power limit in order to do so and utilizes a regression model for carbon intensity, taking into account historical data. They formulate a cost minimization problem that takes into account power, carbon intensity, throughput (inversely proportional to time-to-accuracy) and a parameter for definition of importance of carbon efficiency and performance of the training. For evaluation training ResNet50 on the ImageNet dataset, run on an NVIDIA A40 GPU was used, demonstrating reduction of carbon emission by 13.6% at the cost of 2.5% increase of training time compared to the default power configuration.

Even though our study revolves around optimizing the training process of a machine learning model, it is worth noting that it is not the only targeted part of AI by the energy consumption lowering efforts. In paper [1] authors managed to achieve high inference accuracy while keeping the process in the range of desired latency and obtaining gains in terms of energy saving. The proposed solution utilized multi-input-multi-output control framework OptimML, that flexibly adjusts the model size, effectively decreasing the required resources for inference depending on the server's set power cap.

In summary, while there exist works optimizing performance-energy metrics, in particular for AI oriented workloads, there is lack of research if and to what degree power capping can be beneficial in multi-GPU setups when optimizing performance-energy metrics.

3   Methodology

In order to create a way to compare different configurations, a convolutional neural network (CNN) using transfer learning technique utilizing the XCeption [2] model and a custom network top was implemented to solve a classification problem, which was based on a reduced version of well grounded dataset for 450 bird species from kaggle.com. The number of classes was reduced to 69 in order to shorten the test duration, while maintaining a considerable amount of time required to reach the assumed model quality metric (98%) accuracy over the test subset containing five entries for each of the classes kept. In order to keep the workload as stable as possible, a constant dataset was sub-sampled from the original dataset into a reduced version that contained 10000 training images, 345 validation images and 345 test images. The training length was established during several pilot training sessions using the early stopping technique, and was set for a constant five epochs for every configuration, as it was proved to converge for every configuration taking into account slight quality drops connected to multi-GPU training when compared to a single GPU approach. It shall be noted that for our purposes, we actually needed to generate a stable training workload for assessment of power capping impact. The reason behind this approach, compared to one using pretrained models without interfering into their top (e.g. Inception-V3, MobileNet, DenseNet [4]), is to be able to mimic a frequent situation, where a developer is using the transfer learning technique to solve a specific problem.

For the presented measurements we used a certified hardware meter Yokogawa WT310E (0.1% basic measurement accuracy according to the manufacturer), with the sampling frequency set to 10 Hz. Hardware under test was located in a temperature-controlled server room, with ambient temperature set at 18 °C. The ultimate goal was to establish best power capping settings, that provide the user with improved (versus the default power cap configuration) performance-energy conserving trade-offs, in 1/2/4/8 GPUs configurations, measured using the following metrics:

– percentage of energy gain,
– difference between percentage of energy gain and percentage of execution time loss,
– Energy Delay Product (EDP),
– Energy Delay Sum (EDS) – in this case we consider a weighted sum of energy and time $\alpha E + \beta t$, reference point of (t_{ref}, E_{ref}) as well as coefficient k which determines a potential performance loss ratio. This leads to determination of $\alpha = \frac{k-1}{k \cdot E_{ref}}$ and $\beta = \frac{1}{k \cdot t_{ref}}$ [11].

The first metric may be of interest if energy consumption shall be preferred over execution time (such as when the latter is not critical e.g. we are waiting for input data for subsequent computations that are taking much time). The second metric weighs percentage energy gain and percentage performance loss compared to the energy consumption and execution time of the default power cap configuration. In this case positive values of the metric indicates optimized configurations. EDP and EDS are other frequently used single metrics finding trade-offs between energy consumption and execution time [11].

4   Experiments

4.1   Testbed Environment

The tests were performed on an HPC server installed at Gdańsk University of Technology. The system is equipped with the following compute devices: 2x Intel(R) Xeon(R) Silver 4210 @ 2.20 GHZ CPUs (10 physical cores, HT; for a total of 40 logical processors), 8x NVIDIA Quadro RTX 6000 GPUs, each with 24 GB global memory, and 384 GB RAM. For these GPUs, the settable power cap values are in the range of 100 to 260 W. The node is powered by four 1 kW gold standard power supply units, for which we used custom adapter that would allow the Yokogawa meter to measure the power intake of the whole system.

4.2   Application

Due to the vast number of required tests to achieve assumed experiment coverage, an automated way of changing configurations and collecting data from tests has been developed. The application can be divided into four parts, depicted in Fig. 1:

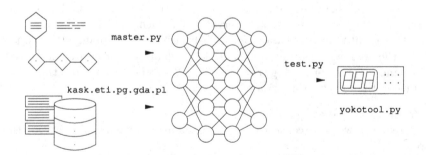

Fig. 1. Test application architecture

- master.py - application entry point containing the scheduler responsible for changing the test parameters (power cap values, the number of GPUs used),

- test.py - main part of the application containing code related to model compilation and the training process. Data is fetched from the user home directory for the needs of the training task. The code manages calling and terminating processes responsible for logging energy consumption data,
- yokotool.py - a Python script responsible for handling the yokotool daemon.

4.3   Efficient Parallelization

In order to guarantee a high level of scalability and efficient parallelization of the training process, several steps have been taken in order to avoid performance drops related to loading data into multiple GPUs, and to ensure an optimized all-reduce step bound to distributed training.

A common problem in non-optimized training scripts is losing performance due to the lack or sub-optimal usage of caches present in GPU execution units. It was solved by utilizing prefetching with an autotuned buffer size provided by the tensorflow.data API. Such a solution makes for an efficient data pipeline, that provides training data batches, as well as optimizes data accesses of threads by moving future batches into L1/L2 caches, allowing for much faster data access.

Optimized distributed training has been achieved by using Horovod, a framework designed and built for highly efficient distributed training of artificial neural networks. Horovod has many advantages over Tensorflow, when it comes to implementation of multi-GPU training scripts, with the most relevant to the goal of this paper being highly efficient communication that utilizes MPI [3] with multithreading and an efficient ring-all-reduce implementation that guarantees good scalability of this step.

4.4   Testing Process and Results

The assumption necessary for sufficient coverage of the power range is to traverse the search-space using a step of 10 W, for each considered hardware configuration (1/2/4/8 GPUs). Regardless of the number of GPUs used in a particular configuration, the same power cap setting was applied to each GPU. The range of tested power cap settings per GPU is shown on the X axes of following charts. After conducting all of the required tests we obtained training results for all considered configurations.[3] For each configuration, i.e. the number of GPUs used for training and a given power cap, 10 runs were executed and results averaged. We measured average execution times, corresponding (low) time standard deviation values, average energy measured over training time (integrated power readings from the hardware power meter over time), corresponding (low) energy standard deviation values, as well as computed metrics for each configuration including: EDP, EDS for $k = 1.5$ and $k = 2.0$ (following [11]).

---

[3] Due to space constraints this data is available at https://cdn.files.pg.edu.pl/eti/ KASK/RAW2023-paper-supplementary-data/Supplementary_data_Performance_ and_power_analysis_of_training_and_performance_quality.pdf.

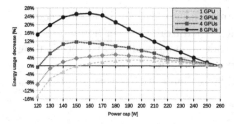

Fig. 2. Percentage energy decrease vs power cap – configurations with 1, 2, 4 and 8 GPUs, compared to default power cap

Fig. 3. Execution time increase vs power cap – 8 GPUs, compared to default power cap

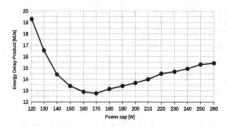

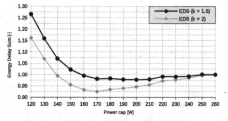

Fig. 4. EDP vs power cap – 8 GPUs

Fig. 5. EDS (k = 1.5 and k = 2.0) vs power cap – 8 GPUs

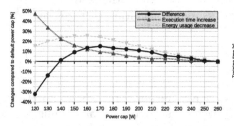

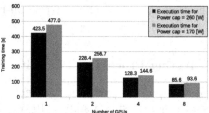

Fig. 6. Difference between percentage energy decrease and percentage time increase vs power cap – 8 GPUs, compared to default power cap

Fig. 7. Training times [s] versus the number of GPUs – for 260 W and 170 W power caps

For 1, 2 and 4 GPUs, interesting results, in the context of optimization of the aforementioned metrics, can be seen in terms of energy gains, as shown in Fig. 2. In those cases, where we are using only 1, 2 and 4 out of the total of 8 GPUs the unused GPUs are left idle. Idle GPUs still contribute to the total power consumption of the node. This does not allow to obtain interesting (notably improved) EDP, EDS nor percentage difference in energy gain and performance loss, compared to the default power cap. It is different, though, for the largest tested configuration, which is the one with 8 GPUs when we use the system to its full potential. In this case we definitely see other than the default power cap configurations, for which energy (Fig. 2), EDP (Fig. 4), EDS (Fig. 5) and percentage difference between energy gain and performance loss (Fig. 6) are significantly improved over those for the default power cap, at the cost of slightly increased running time (Fig. 3). This is summarized in Table 1. While for EDS and k = 1.5 there is a 2.2% improvement, for EDS k = 2.0 we see the improvement of 7.5%, for EDP a notable 17.3%, for the difference of percentage energy gain and percentage performance loss over 15% and for pure energy the maximum gain is over 25%. Our conclusion is that, depending on the chosen goal, power capping can offer a significant improvement in DNN training using a high performance system with multiple (8 in this case) GPUs.

Table 1. Best power cap values and gains for particular metrics – 8 GPUs

Metric	Gain for metric over default power cap configuration [%]	Obtained for power cap setting [W]
Energy	25.39	160
Difference between energy gain [%] and performance loss [%]	15.03	170
EDP	17.32	170
EDS (k = 1.5)	2.26	200
EDS (k = 2.0)	7.52	170

Finally, we can observe scalability of the training process in the multi-GPU setup. In Fig. 7 we present execution times for 1, 2, 4 and 8 GPUs for the two most important power caps: default 260 W per GPU as well as 170 W per GPU being best for optimization of the difference between percentage energy gain and performance loss compared to the default power cap configuration, EDP, EDS with k = 2.0 and close to best for k = 1.5. We can see that increasing the number of GPUs results in good scaling of the training. Specifically, for 4 GPUs we can observe a time speed-up of approx. 3.3 in both cases. For 8 GPUs and the power cap of 260 W a speed-up of 4.95 can be seen while for 170 W a speed-up of 5.1 can be observed.

5   Summary

In the paper we performed performance-energy analysis of training a deep neural network under various power caps in a multi-GPU environment, using 1, 2, 4 and 8 NVIDIA Quadro RTX 6000 GPUs, within a high performance server with 2 Intel Xeon Silver 4210 CPUs. Power measurements were taken and considered for the whole system using a professional hardware power meter Yokogawa WT310E. We show that, depending on the number of GPUs used, enforcing an appropriate power cap allows to obtain percentage energy savings of approx. 3% when using 1 GPU out of 8 GPUs, 5.5% when using 2 GPUs, 11.5% for 4 GPUs and over 25% for 8 GPUs. These growing savings result from the fact that the total power of a smaller number of GPUs constitutes a smaller percentage of the whole machine power (the other GPUs remain idle). The main contribution of our paper is that for the most powerful configuration with 8 GPUs, we were able to determine that enforcing selected power caps, different from the default one (260 W per GPU in our case), allows to obtain significantly optimized values of various performance-energy metrics. In particular, we can improve the difference between percentage energy gain and performance loss by over 15.0% using the power cap of 170 W, EDP by over 17.3% using the power cap of 170 W, EDS with k = 1.5 by over 2.2% using the power cap of 200 W (similar gains within the range of 170–210 W) and EDS with k = 2.0 by over 7.5% using the power cap of 170 W.

Future work will include, given a particular domain problem, optimization that involves, apart from execution time and energy, the neural network model and compute device models, taking into account the monetary cost of compute devices and the system. At a higher level of abstraction, such simulations will be used within a workload stream for which scheduling algorithms enhanced with power capping will be adopted in a supercomputing center, as identified in [8].

Acknowledgment. We would like to thank the administrator of the HPC server at Department of Computer Architecture at the GUT, dr Tomasz Boiński, for support regarding setting up the testbed environment. This work is supported by CERCIRAS COST Action CA19135 funded by the COST Association as well as statutory funds of Dept. of Computer Architecture, Faculty of Electronics, Telecommunications and Informatics, Gdańsk Tech.

References

1. Chen, G., Wang, X.: Performance optimization of machine learning inference under latency and server power constraints. In: 2022 IEEE 42nd International Conference on Distributed Computing Systems (ICDCS), pp. 325–335 (2022). https://doi.org/10.1109/ICDCS54860.2022.00039
2. Chollet, F.: Xception: deep learning with depthwise separable convolutions. In: 2017 IEEE Conference on Computer Vision and Pattern Recognition (CVPR), pp. 1800–1807, July 2017. https://doi.org/10.1109/CVPR.2017.195
3. Czarnul, P., Proficz, J., Drypczewski, K.: Survey of methodologies, approaches, and challenges in parallel programming using high-performance computing systems. Sci. Program. **2020**, 4176794:1–4176794:19 (2020). https://doi.org/10.1155/2020/4176794
4. García-Martín, E., Rodrigues, C.F., Riley, G., Grahn, H.: Estimation of energy consumption in machine learning. J. Parallel Distrib. Comput. **134**, 75–88 (2019). https://doi.org/10.1016/j.jpdc.2019.07.007, https://www.sciencedirect.com/science/article/pii/S0743731518308773

5. He, X., et al.: Enabling energy-efficient DNN training on hybrid GPU-FPGA accelerators. In: Proceedings of the ACM International Conference on Supercomputing, ICS 2021, pp. 227–241. Association for Computing Machinery, New York, NY, USA (2021). https://doi.org/10.1145/3447818.3460371

6. Jabłońska, K., Czarnul, P.: Benchmarking deep neural network training using multi- and many-core processors. In: Saeed, K., Dvorský, J. (eds.) CISIM 2020. LNCS, vol. 12133, pp. 230–242. Springer, Cham (2020). https://doi.org/10.1007/978-3-030-47679-3_20

7. Kang, D.K., Lee, K.B., Kim, Y.C.: Cost efficient GPU cluster management for training and inference of deep learning. Energies 15(2), 474 (2022). https://doi.org/10.3390/en15020474, https://www.mdpi.com/1996-1073/15/2/474

8. Kocot, B., Czarnul, P., Proficz, J.: Energy-aware scheduling for high-performance computing systems: a survey. Energies 16(2), 890 (2023). https://doi.org/10.3390/en16020890, https://www.mdpi.com/1996-1073/16/2/890

9. Krzywaniak, A., Czarnul, P.: Performance/Energy aware optimization of parallel applications on GPUs under power capping. In: Wyrzykowski, R., Deelman, E., Dongarra, J., Karczewski, K. (eds.) PPAM 2019. LNCS, vol. 12044, pp. 123–133. Springer, Cham (2020). https://doi.org/10.1007/978-3-030-43222-5_11

10. Krzywaniak, A., Czarnul, P., Proficz, J.: GPU power capping for energy-performance trade-offs in training of deep convolutional neural networks for image recognition. In: Groen, D., de Mulatier, C., Paszynski, M., Krzhizhanovskaya, V.V., Dongarra, J.J., Sloot, P.M.A. (eds.) Computational Science - ICCS 2022, pp. 667–681. Springer, Cham (2022). https://doi.org/10.1007/978-3-031-08751-6_48

11. Krzywaniak, A., Czarnul, P., Proficz, J.: DEPO: a dynamic energy-performance optimizer tool for automatic power capping for energy efficient high-performance computing. Softw. Pract. Exp. 52(12), 2598–2634 (2022). https://doi.org/10.1002/spe.3139, https://onlinelibrary.wiley.com/doi/abs/10.1002/spe.3139

12. Lai, C., Ahmad, S., Dubinsky, D., Maver, C.: AI is harming our planet: addressing AI's staggering energy cost, May 2022. https://www.numenta.com/blog/2022/05/24/ai-is-harming-our-planet/

13. Leng, J., et al.: GPUWattch: enabling energy optimizations in GPGPUs. SIGARCH Comput. Archit. News 41(3), 487–498 (2013). https://doi.org/10.1145/2508148.2485964

14. Mazuecos Pérez, M.D., Seiler, N.G., Bederián, C.S., Wolovick, N., Vega, A.J.: Power efficiency analysis of a deep learning workload on an IBM "Minsky" Platform. In: Meneses, E., Castro, H., Barrios Hernández, C.J., Ramos-Pollan, R. (eds.) CARLA 2018. CCIS, vol. 979, pp. 255–262. Springer, Cham (2019). https://doi.org/10.1007/978-3-030-16205-4_19

15. McDonald, J., Li, B., Frey, N., Tiwari, D., Gadepally, V., Samsi, S.: Great power, great responsibility: recommendations for reducing energy for training language models. In: Findings of the Association for Computational Linguistics: NAACL 2022. Association for Computational Linguistics (2022). https://doi.org/10.18653/v1/2022.findings-naacl.151

16. Rouhani, B.D., Mirhoseini, A., Koushanfar, F.: Delight: adding energy dimension to deep neural networks. In: Proceedings of the 2016 International Symposium on Low Power Electronics and Design, ISLPED 2016, pp. 112–117. Association for Computing Machinery, New York, NY, USA (2016). https://doi.org/10.1145/2934583.2934599

17. Schuchart, J., et al.: The READEX formalism for automatic tuning for energy efficiency. Computing 99(8), 727–745 (2017)

18. Tao, Y., Ma, R., Shyu, M.L., Chen, S.C.: Challenges in energy-efficient deep neural network training with FPGA. In: 2020 IEEE/CVF Conference on Computer Vision and Pattern Recognition Workshops (CVPRW), pp. 1602–1611 (2020). https://doi.org/10.1109/CVPRW50498.2020.00208
19. Wang, F., Zhang, W., Lai, S., Hao, M., Wang, Z.: Dynamic GPU energy optimization for machine learning training workloads. IEEE Trans. Parallel Distrib. Syst. **33**(11), 2943–2954 (2022). https://doi.org/10.1109/TPDS.2021.3137867
20. Xu, Y., Martínez-Fernández, S., Martinez, M., Franch, X.: Energy efficiency of training neural network architectures: an empirical study (2023)
21. Yang, H., Zhu, Y., Liu, J.: ECC: platform-independent energy-constrained deep neural network compression via a bilinear regression model. In: 2019 IEEE/CVF Conference on Computer Vision and Pattern Recognition (CVPR), pp. 11198–11207. IEEE Computer Society, Los Alamitos, CA, USA, June 2019. https://doi.org/10.1109/CVPR.2019.01146, https://doi.ieeecomputersociety.org/10.1109/CVPR.2019.01146
22. Yang, T.J., Chen, Y.H., Emer, J., Sze, V.: A method to estimate the energy consumption of deep neural networks. In: 2017 51st Asilomar Conference on Signals, Systems, and Computers, pp. 1916–1920 (2017). https://doi.org/10.1109/ACSSC.2017.8335698
23. Yang, Z., Meng, L., Chung, J.W., Chowdhury, M.: Chasing low-carbon electricity for practical and sustainable DNN training (2023)
24. You, J., Chung, J.W., Chowdhury, M.: Zeus: understanding and optimizing GPU energy consumption of DNN training. In: 20th USENIX Symposium on Networked Systems Design and Implementation (NSDI 2023), pp. 119–139. USENIX Association, Boston, MA, April 2023. https://www.usenix.org/conference/nsdi23/presentation/you
25. Zou, P., Li, A., Barker, K., Ge, R.: Indicator-directed dynamic power management for iterative workloads on GPU-accelerated systems. In: 2020 20th IEEE/ACM International Symposium on Cluster, Cloud and Internet Computing (CCGRID), pp. 559–568 (2020). https://doi.org/10.1109/CCGrid49817.2020.00-37

GPPRMon: GPU Runtime Memory Performance and Power Monitoring Tool

Burak Topçu and Işıl Öz(✉)

Izmir Institute of Technology, Izmir, Turkey
{buraktopcu,isiloz}@iyte.edu.tr

Abstract. Graphics Processing Units (GPUs) perform highly efficient parallel execution for high-performance computation and embedded system domains. While performance concerns drive the main optimization efforts, power issues become important for energy-efficient GPU executions. While performance profilers and architectural simulators offer statistics about the target execution, they either present only performance metrics in a coarse kernel function level or lack visualization support that enables performance bottleneck analysis or performance-power consumption comparison. Evaluating both performance and power consumption dynamically at runtime and across GPU memory components enables a comprehensive tradeoff analysis for GPU architects and software developers. This paper presents a novel memory performance and power monitoring tool for GPU programs, GPPRMon, which performs a systematic metric collection and offers useful visualization views to track power and performance optimizations. Our simulation-based framework dynamically collects microarchitectural metrics by monitoring individual instructions and reports achieved performance and power consumption information at runtime. Our visualization interface presents spatial and temporal views of the execution. While the first demonstrates the performance and power metrics across GPU memory components, the latter shows the corresponding information at the instruction granularity in a timeline. Our case study reveals the potential usages of our tool in bottleneck identification and power consumption for a memory-intensive graph workload.

Keywords: GPGPUs · Performance monitoring · Power consumption

1 Introduction

Current data processing tasks require high-performance and energy-efficient computer systems with heterogeneous components. Massively parallel GPU architectures play a crucial role in accelerating parallel workloads such as streaming- and ML-based applications. Since the recent technological developments in GPUs result in more complex systems, it requires more detailed research

The original version of this chapter was previously published without open access. A correction to this chapter is available at
https://doi.org/10.1007/978-3-031-48803-0_41

D. Zeinalipour et al. (Eds.): Euro-Par 2023 Workshops, LNCS 14352, pp. 17–29, 2024.
https://doi.org/10.1007/978-3-031-48803-0_2

effort to increase the execution performance and throughput. Widespread usage of GPUs has raised energy consumption in GPU-based systems and caused power issues to be addressed.

Although GPUs have large computational power, both performance and energy efficiency may decrease for memory-intensive workloads [2,3]. Based on performance improvement and energy-efficiency concerns [4,7,10,11,14], reasoning a GPU application's performance bottlenecks and interpreting power consumption during the execution requires more analytical measurements and rigorous evaluations. While both performance and energy improvements contribute efficient execution of GPU programs, they usually compete with each other, and the design decisions become critical and get complicated requiring the evaluation of the tradeoffs between both factors [1,8,12]. However, evaluating a kernel performance and relating power consumption at kernel basis hides most of the clear evidence for conducting a baseline analysis from many perspectives. Each instruction belonging to a warp, the smallest execution element in the GPU execution context, should be explicitly investigated throughout the execution on cores, as mostly done in multi-core architecture research. Despite that, NVIDIA's GPU profiler (i.e., Nsight Compute Tool), which presents occupancy, IPC, and memory utilization, and the state-of-the-art GPU simulation tools [6,13] report the performance and hardware metrics at the kernel level. None of the tools directly reports GPU programs' dynamic performance, memory access behavior, and power consumption at runtime. Collecting a microarchitectural metric set requires additional effort, and several in-house target-specific works exist for monitoring the runtime performance and power consumption. Nevertheless, repetitive studies to inspect GPU execution dynamically cause redundant effort for the research studies. While a set of profiling tools reports performance and power consumption information about GPU execution, microarchitecture simulators are quite significant in terms of accurately modeling hardware and monitoring the execution behaviors of applications both on micro and macro scales by addressing energy consumption.

In this work, we design and build **GPPRMon**, a runtime performance and power monitoring tool for GPU programs. We target program developers and system architects, who aim to optimize the GPU programs or the hardware considering both performance improvement and energy efficiency based on the dynamic behavior of memory accesses and thread blocks. Our simulation-based framework dynamically collects microarchitectural metrics by monitoring individual instructions and reports performance and power consumption at runtime. Our visualization interface presents both spatial and temporal views of the execution, where the first demonstrates the performance and power metrics for each hardware component including global memory and caches, and the latter shows the corresponding information at the instruction granularity in a timeline. Our tool enables the user to perform a fine-granularity evaluation of the target execution by observing instruction-level microarchitectural features. To the best of our knowledge, this is the first work monitoring a GPU kernel's performance by visualizing the execution of instructions for multiple user-configurable scenarios, relating memory hierarchy utilization with performance, and tracking power dissipation at runtime. Our main contributions are as follows:

– We propose a systematic metric collection that keeps track of instruction-per-cycle (IPC) per streaming multiprocessor (SM) for performance, instruction execution records for each warp to clearly observe issues/completions, memory usage statistics per each sub-unit to interpret its effect on performance and power dissipation statistics per each GPU component at runtime with a configurable sampling cycle by extending the GPGPU-Sim framework.

– By processing metrics, we design and build a visualization framework that concurrently runs with the simulator and displays a kernel's execution status with the following three perspectives: *1) General View* displays the IPC, access statistics of L1D and L2 caches, row buffer utilization of DRAM partitions, and dissipated power by the main components for an execution interval. *2) Temporal View* shows the instruction details with issue and completion cycles for each thread block at warp level. In addition to power consumption statistics for the sub-components in an SM, we place L1D cache access statistics to relate the thread block's performance in the same execution interval. *3) Spatial View* demonstrates the access information and power consumption for each on-chip L1D cache, L2 cache in each sub-partition, and row buffers of DRAM banks in each memory partition.

– We demonstrate the potential usages of our framework by performing experiments for a memory-intensive graph workload. Our tool enables the users to perform detailed performance and power analysis for the target GPU executions.

2 Background

Modern GPU architectures employ a single-instruction-multiple-thread (SIMT) execution in their Streaming Multiprocessors (SM). Each SM includes multiple warp schedulers, an instruction dispatcher, a register file, single and double precision ALUs, tensor cores, special function units (SFU), and load/store units with on-chip memory. An interconnection network connects SMs to off-chip memory partitions on which DRAM and Last-Level caches (LLC) are placed. Apart from the load/stores, all instructions utilize on-chip execution units. However, load/store may require access from the off-chip whenever requested data cannot be found in L1D cache, and data access gets slower for memory instructions moving down the hierarchy.

GPU researchers mostly exploit GPGPU-Sim [6] (hereafter referred to as the simulator) to conduct experimental studies targeting NVIDIA GPUs among the other simulators as it has evolved by tracking developments on the real hardware, such as covering tensor cores in the previous two decades. The simulator provides functional and performance-driven modes such that functional mode enables developers to check the kernel's functional correctness, whereas the performance model simulates the kernel for the configured GPU in a cycle-accurate manner. It officially supports many architectures including Volta GV100. Accel-Wattch power model [5], as part of the simulator, supporting Dynamic Voltage-Frequency Scaling (DVFS), measures energy dissipation for GV100 above 90% accuracy.

3   Methodology

We design and build the GPPRMon tool, which is available as open-source[1], to monitor and visualize kernel performance and power consumption at runtime. Figure 1 displays GPPRMon workflow consisting of two main stages: ① Metric Collection, ② Visualization. GPPRMon systematically calculates IPC rates per SM, records warp instructions with issue/completions cycles per thread block within each SM and dissipated power among the components, and collects memory access statistics for each partition of L1D/L2 caches and DRAM row buffers during the given execution interval based on a configuration provided by the user. Parts 1-a and 1-b in Fig. 1 demonstrate examples of the power and performance metrics, respectively. Part ② reveals GPPRMon's visualizer with three views to show performance overview, memory access statistics, and instruction execution timeline. We build our framework on top of the simulator, and both the metric collector and visualizer are compatible with official GPU configurations given as part of the simulator.

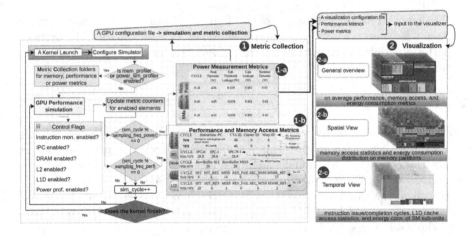

Fig. 1. A general workflow overview of **GPPRMon** framework.

3.1   Metric Collection

GPPRMon systematically records microarchitectural performance and power metrics during the execution as depicted in Part ① in Fig. 1.

3.1.1 Performance Metrics

L1D and L2 Caches: GPPRMon cumulatively counts the accesses on caches and exports the results at the end of the observation interval. A memory request's access status on caches may be one of the following states: i) <u>Hit</u>: Data resides on the cache line; ii) <u>Hit Reserved</u>: The cache line is allocated for the requested data, but the data is still invalid; iii) <u>Miss</u>: The corresponding cache line causes several sector misses, resulting in a bigger dirty counter than the threshold for line eviction, evicting the corresponding cache line; iv) <u>Reservation Failure</u>: The situations in which a line allocation, MSHR entry allocation, or merging an entry with an existing in MSHR fail, or the miss queue is full to hold new requests result in reservation failure; v) <u>Sector Miss</u>: A memory request cannot find the data in the sector of a cache line (i.e., a sector is 32B, whereas a cache line is 128B); vi) <u>MSHR hit</u>: When the upcoming request's sector miss has already been recorded, and request can merge with the existing entry, MSHR hit occurs.

Row Buffers of DRAM Banks: GPPRMon covers row buffer utilization metric collection at runtime within each memory partition for L2 cache misses as row buffer hits save from the additional activation latencies of accessing DRAM cells among the global memory accesses.

IPC: GPPRMon calculates IPC rates for each SM by counting instruction issues through active warp masks and within each configurable sampling execution interval. IPC rates on SMs oscillate during the execution depending on the workload behavior and memory traffic, and one can conduct IPC comparisons to figure out the relation between performance and behavior.

Instruction Monitor: GPPRMon records the issue and completion cycles of instructions with opcode, operand, and PC at warp level within each thread block separately.

3.1.2 Power Metrics

We develop GPPRMon to systematically collect the power distribution on SMs, memory partitions, and the interconnection network. We implement power metrics on top of the AccelWattch [5], which includes modeling for dynamic-voltage frequency scaling (DVFS). GPPRMon maintains the following measurements during runtime for each component apart from idle SM: *Peak Dynamic*(W), the maximum momentary power within the interval, *Sub-threshold Leakage (W)* and *Gate Leakage (W)*, the leaked power (due to current leakage), and *Runtime Dynamic (W)*, the total consumed power. Moreover, GPPRMon supports collecting power metrics either cumulatively or distinctly for each sample, starting from a kernel's execution.

3.2 Visualization

By processing the collected metrics in Part [1], GPPRMon depicts performance and power dissipation with three perspectives at runtime, as represented in Part

2 in Fig. 1, and enables pointing out detailed interaction of an application with hardware.

i **General View**, Part 2-a, presents the average memory access statistics, the overall IPC of GPU, and dissipated power among the major components with application- and architecture-specific information;

ii **Spatial View**, Part 2-b, displays the access statistics of all the memory units on the GPU device memory hierarchy and dissipated overall power among the memory partitions by enabling the monitoring of the entire GPU memory space;

iii **Temporal View**, Part 2-c, demonstrates instruction execution statistics with activation intervals at warp-level for user-specified thread blocks, L1D cache access characteristics and power distribution among the sub-components of SMs by activating the execution monitoring feature.

On Average Memory Access Statistics					
L1D Cache Stats (Av)		**L2 Cache Stats (Av)**		**DRAM Row Util. (Av)**	
Hit Rate	0.003	Hit Rate	0.312	Row Buffer H	0.383
Hit Reserved R	0.001	Hit Reserved R	0.000	Row Buffer M	0.617
Miss Rate	0.038	Miss Rate	0.464		
Reserv. Failure R	0.944	Reserv. Failure R	0.000	Kernel ID: 0	
Sector Miss R	0.013	Sector Miss R	0.223	Cycle Interval: [55000, 56000]	
MSHR Hit R	0.008	MSHR Hit R	0.005	Grid:(1784,1,1) Block:(256,1,1)	
Average IPC on SMs : 1.08				# of active SMs: 80	

Dissipated Power	InterCon. Net	L2	Mem Part.	SMs	GPU
Peak Power (W)					185.63
Total Leakage (W)					17.346
Peak Dynamic (W)	0.338	4.687	137.55	25.704	168.264
Sub-Threshold Leak (W)	0.067	0.138	1.316	13.474	14.995
Gate Leakage (W)	0.011	0.013	0.016	2.168	2.352
Runtime Dynamic (W)	64.618	2.537	823.184	205.174	1095.513

Fig. 2. *General View* visual displaying average cache, DRAM row buffer, power statistics, and kernel-specific information in a specific cycle interval.

Figure 2, an example of our *General View*, presents the overview execution performance of *Kernel 0* for SpMV [15] on GV100 GPU device. It displays average memory access statistics among the active L1D caches, L2 caches, and DRAM banks; average IPC value among the active SMs; dissipated power on major sub-GPU components within the interval of [55000, 56000]. The view includes grid (i.e., 1784 thread blocks) and block dimensions (i.e., 256 threads per block) with the number of actively used SMs so that the users can realize issue mappings of thread blocks to the SMs. For instance, *Kernel 0* executes with an IPC rate of 1.08 and uses the memory hierarchy inefficiently due to high L1 miss and reservation failure rates in the corresponding interval. Moreover, memory partitions consume 75% of the total power dissipation, which validates that SMs mostly stay idle for the target execution.

Figure 3, an example of our *Spatial View*, shows the memory access statistics across the GPU memory hierarchy. On caches, the green emphasizes hit and hit reserved accesses concentration, while the red indicates miss and sector miss intensity, and the blue states reservation failures through miss queues or MSHR.

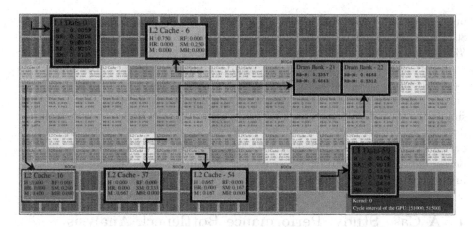

Fig. 3. *Spatial View* explicitly displays memory access statistics for each component belonging to the hierarchy within cycles at runtime. (Color figure online)

Similarly, DRAM bank pixels are colored with a mixture of red and blue to specify the row buffer misses and hits, respectively. *Spatial View* provides a detailed analysis of the memory hierarchy utilization and dissipated power on memory partitions. We zoom in on some memory units in Fig. 3, which presents statistics for the *Kernel 0* in the cycles of [51000, 51500]. In that interval, distinct L1D caches behave similarly, such that almost all L1D caches turn blue due to reservation failure concentration.

PC	OPCODE	OPERAND	ISSUE / COMPLETION
352	fma.rn.f32	%f21 %f20 %f19 %f18	1-8044 / 1-8053
360	st.global.f32	[%rd1] %f21	1-8053 / 1-8107
368	ld.global.f32	%f22 [%rd16 + 24]	1-8071 / 1-8179
376	ld.global.f32	%f23 [%rd14 + 24]	1-8072 / 1-8178
448	add.s32.f32	%r15 %r15 8	2-8072 1-8326 / 2-8082 1-8337
456	setp.ne.s32%p2	%r15 0	2-8082 1-8337 / 2-8088 1-8343
464	@ %p2	bra BBO_2	2-8088 1-8343 / 2-8093 1-8348
168	add.s64	%rd14 %rd15 %rd2	2-8090 1-8345 / 2-8099 1-8354

Dissipated Power	Execution U.	Func. U.	LD/ST U.	IDLE	TOTAL
Peak Dynamic (W)	18.158	1.000	6.546		25.704
Sub-Threshold Leak (W)	10.808	0.587	1.465		13.474
Gate Leakage (W)	0.038	0.074	1.983		2.168
Runtime Dynamic (W)	75.928	1.645	437.529	0.000	515.102

IPC Rate on SM : 3.776

SM ID : 2

Thread Block ID: 2

Kernel ID: 0

Cycle Interval: [8000, 8500]

L1D Cache Stats (Av)	
Hit Rate	0.429
Hit Reserved R	0.000
Miss Rate	0.437
Reserv. Failure R	0.000
Sector Miss R	0.134
MSHR Hit R	0.000

Fig. 4. *Temporal View* monitors the instruction execution timeline together with on-chip cache performance and power consumption of the corresponding SM.

Figure 4, an example of our *Temporal View*, displays a thread block's execution statistics at warp-level, L1D cache statistics, and dissipated power of core components in configurable execution intervals. It presents each warp's PTX instruction sequence. The Issue/Completion column indicates the execution start and writeback times of warp instruction segments within any thread block. For instance, Fig. 4 reveals the execution monitoring of the *Thread Block 2* on *SM 2* for the *Kernel 0* in the cycle range of [8000, 8500]. The instruction dispatcher unit issues two SP global loads pointed by PC = 368 and PC = 376 at cycles 8071 and 8072, and they are completed at cycles 8179 and 8178, respectively. *Temporal View* allows tracking execution duration per instruction.

GPPRMon execution overhead varies depending on the monitoring interval; as it increases, the number of I/O operations in terms of exporting results to output files reduces, decreasing the impact on the simulation time. To illustrate, simulating the SPMV benchmark [15] takes 98 min for the Higgs Twitter Mention data by recording both power and performance metrics per 5000 simulation cycles, while the baseline simulation (i.e., not collecting runtime performance and power metrics) completes the execution at 88 min on RTX 2060S configuration in our local infrastructure.

4   A Case Study: Performance Bottleneck Analysis and Its Power Impacts for a Memory-Intensive Workload

We run *Page Ranking* (PR) CUDA implementation to analyze a memory-bound GPU program and irregular memory access statistics with GPPRMon on Volta architecture-based GV100. The implementation iterates with the *Contribution Step* (K0), *Pull Step* (K1), and *Linear Normalization* (K2) kernels, and the number of iterations varies depending on the data size. Since totally elapsed cycles by application indicate that *K1* dominates the execution at 99.7%, we focus on that kernel execution by monitoring the runtime observation intervals as 100, 500, 1000, 2500, 5000, 10000, 25000, 50000, and 100000 cycles.

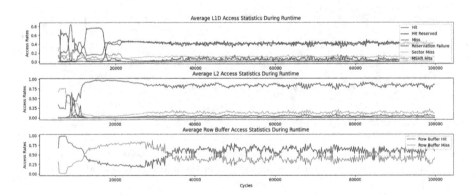

Fig. 5. Detailed average memory access statistics for L1D caches, L2 caches, and DRAM row buffers in the cycle range of [5000, 100000].

Figure 5, which is part of *General Overview*, shows average access statistics on memory units in [5000, 100000] cycles. After caches warming up (i.e., 10000 GPU cycles), while the average miss rate on L1D caches oscillates in [0.14, 0.82], sector misses, which the simulator does not provide separately, vary in $[0.05, 0.31]$ with the metrics sampled for each consecutive 20 cycles without accumulation. We can state that data pollution exists on L1D caches, which breaks exploiting cache locality. For example, $K1$ does not utilize locality on L1D cache since the MSHR hits among L1D misses oscillate slightly in $[0.03, 0.08]$ during the execution. Moreover, Web-Stanford [9] graph size is five times larger compared to the L2 cache size; thus, the overall hit rate on L2 caches is quite high even if we can realize the data sparseness with L1D cache utilization. While the performance metrics hide the statistics of L2 as it counts misses before warming up at kernel launch, the actual L2 hit rate oscillates in $[0.82, 0.95]$ with sampling per 500 cycles. The row buffer locality varies in $[0.2, 0.85]$ in an unstable manner, which verifies data sparsity throughout the execution.

| PC -> 296 | opcode -> ld.global.u64 | operand-> %rd1 [%rd11] |
| PC -> 312 | opcode -> ld.global.u32 | operand-> %rd3 [%rd11+8] |

Interval : 5000-30000
SM ID : 0
Kernel ID : 1

CTA_ID=24	2-5455 0-5455 1-5455 3-5456 4-5469 5-5469 6-5469 7-5470
	2-5826 0-5864 1-6045 3-6075 4-6065 5-6026 6-6087 7-6074
	2-5867 0-5868 5-6027 1-6046 4-6066 7-6076 3-6077 6-6088
	2-5946 0-5948 5-6053 1-6072 4-6092 7-7696 3-6105 6-6114

CTA_ID=104	9-5470 10-5470 8-5470 11-5471 13-5884 14-5891 15-5885 12-5887
	9-6140 10-6141 8-6143 11-6163 13-8076 14-8063 15-8074 12-8122
	9-6141 10-6143 8-6144 11-6164 14-8064 15-8075 13-8077 12-8123
	9-6167 10-6170 8-6173 11-8055 14-8090 15-8867 13-8104 12-8149

CTA_ID=184	16-5472 17-5472 18-5472 19-5473 20-5474 21-5475 22-5474 23-5475
	16-6286 17-6251 18-6969 19-6639 20-6551 21-6492 22-6469 23-6449
	16-6287 17-6252 23-6446 22-6470 21-6493 20-6552 19-6640 18-6971
	16-6313 17-6618 23-7799 22-6496 21-6519 20-6578 19-6666 18-6997

CTA_ID=264	24-5476 26-5476 25-5482 27-5482 28-5484 29-5484 30-5484 31-5486
	24-6619 26-6607 25-6826 27-6579 28-6300 29-6556 30-6635 31-6627
	28-6301 29-6558 27-6580 26-6608 24-6621 31-6629 30-6636 25-6827
	28-6339 29-6584 27-6606 26-6634 24-6647 31-7968 30-6662 25-6853

CTA_ID=344	32-5565 33-5565 34-5565 35-5565 37-5560 36-5560 30-5560 39-5641
	32-6595 33-6719 34-6692 35-6567 37-7711 38-6877 36-7168 39-7214
	35-6568 32-6569 34-6695 33-6720 38-6878 36-7169 39-7215 37-7714
	35-6897 32-6622 34-6721 33-6746 38-6935 36-7379 39-8263 37-7740

CTA_ID=424	41-5570 40-5640 45-5640 44-5642 42-5643 43-5644 47-5704 46-5704
	41-7081 40-6976 45-7244 44-7272 42-7068 43-7039 47-7827 46-7499
	40-6977 43-7040 42-7069 41-7082 45-7245 44-7273 46-7500 47-7830
	40-7003 43-7066 42-7096 41-7108 45-7271 44-7299 46-7659 47-8802

CTA_ID=504	49-5642 48-5704 53-5704 52-5705 51-5705 50-5708 55-5710 54-5714
	49-7281 48-7878 53-7510 52-7468 51-7602 50-7848 55-7538 54-7543
	49-7282 52-7469 53-7511 55-7539 54-7544 51-7603 50-7849 48-7879
	49-7673 52-7495 53-7537 55-8402 54-7570 51-7629 50-7875 48-7905

CTA_ID=584	56-5708 57-5708 61-5714 60-5714 59-5718 58-5720 62-5786 63-5786
	56-7590 57-7630 61-7718 60-7951 59-7779 58-7832 62-7863 63-7919
	56-7591 57-7631 61-7719 59-7780 58-7833 62-7864 63-7917 60-7952
	56-7617 57-7657 61-7745 59-7806 58-7859 62-7890 63-8715 60-7978

Fig. 6. Instruction execution timeline for two load instructions on $SM0$ in the cycle range of $[5000, 30000]$.

Figure 6 displays the instruction issue/completion timeline of 8 TBs (CTAs) running on $SM0$, and the first and second lines point to the load instructions whose $PC = 296$ (loads DP) and $PC = 312$ (loads SP), respectively. We merge multiple snapshots of *Temporal View* in Fig. 6 executing on the $SM0$ to evaluate the performance of load instructions at the same time. Figure 7, a snapshot of *Spatial View*, shows the memory access statistics of representative components within the same interval. We follow the access statistics on the memory hierarchy with Fig. 7 and relate the observations with the issue/completion duration of loads in Fig. 6.

After the kernel launch, each thread collects thread-specific information from parameter memory, which takes 250–450 cycles to process target data addressed with the thread's private registers. The warp schedulers dispatch the load instructions pointed to by the $PC = 296$ (*ld.global.u64*), and all eight warps of TB24 (presented as $CTA\_ID = 24$ in the figure) execute the instruction after Cycle 5455. Furthermore, Fig. 6 reveals that $SM0$ dispatches load instructions from the remaining TBs in the interval of [5470, 5786] after issuing the load instructions of TB24. Figure 7 verifies that no access occurs on some of L1D caches, while none of the L2 caches and DRAM banks are accessed during the preparation time in [5000, 5500] in Part [1]. According to the execution time-line in Fig. 6, none of the data brought to L1D cache of $SM0$ by the warps of TB24 after Cycle 6087 (Warp 6) provides an early completion of the instruction pointed with PC = 296, belonging to the remaining thread blocks. We bold some of the long latencies within each TB for each instruction separately. Additionally, a high reservation failure and no MSHR hit rates on L1D cache of $SM0$ in Part [2] confirms that the locality utilization among TBs on the $SM0$ is significantly low for the first load. If there was locality utilization on L1D cache, we would observe either larger MSHR hit rates or small latencies for the accesses for the completion of the same instructions just after Cycle 6087. Furthermore, Parts [2,3,4,5] reveal that reservation failed requests pointed by PC = 296 cause misses on L2 caches without MSHR merging. Thus, memory requests of the same instruction from different SMs cannot benefit locality on the L2 cache partitions and cause traffic in the lower levels of the memory hierarchy.

Parts [3,4,5,6] in Fig. 7 reveal that the access status of L1D mostly turns to the hit after Cycle 6000. Unlike the load instructions at PC = 296, the loads at PC = 312 (*ld.global.u32*) usually hit. The second line for each TB in Fig. 6 shows that the completion takes much fewer cycles for the loads at PC = 312. To illustrate, while TB504 completes the first load instructions within 2133 cycles, it takes 26 cycles for the second instructions, apart from Warp 63, whose requests result in a miss on both L1D and L2 caches. As a result, the loads at PC = 296 complete the execution in the range of [350, 2250] cycles, whereas the loads at PC = 312 take less than 50 cycles for most of the warps due to the increasing hits on L1D cache. Still, loads at PC = 296 delay the issue of second load instructions due to excessive latency. As a result, the data locality utilization for different memory instructions executing on the same SM may change for the sparse data processing. Additionally, one may follow such runtime behavior change by evaluating cache behaviors with *Spatial View* and memory operation execution statistics with *Temporal View* at the same time.

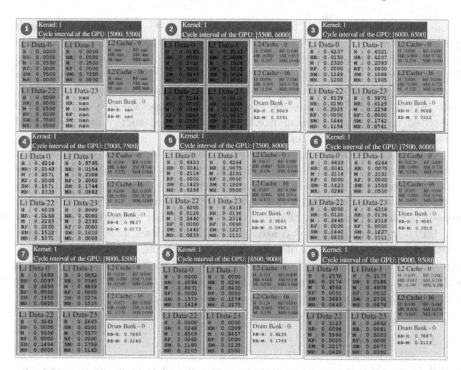

Fig. 7. Sequential memory access statistic snapshots for some of L1D caches, L2 caches, and a DRAM row buffer in the cycle range of [5000, 9500].

Table 1. Dissipated average power in milliWatt during K1's execution on GV100 in the cycle range of [5000,10000].

Cycles	Streaming Multiprocessors					Memory Partitions						NoC	TOTAL
	Exec. Units	Func. Units	LD/ST Unit	Idle	Total	MC FEE	PHY	MC TE	Dram	L2	Total		
5k, 5.5k	2637.5	54.3	35.6	23.7	2751.3	3.7	8.2	4.6	0	0	16.5	0.7	2768.5
5.5k, 6k	597	6.3	860	0	1463.7	177.2	17.8	9.4	557.2	3.4	764.9	26.9	2501.6
6k, 6.5k	614.4	12.4	399.9	0	1026.7	56.1	31.3	16.1	1346.4	3.0	1452.9	92.6	2577.3
6.5k, 7k	708.6	14.4	464.3	0	1187.3	65.5	31.4	16.2	1354.3	3.1	1470.5	94.2	2755.1
7k, 7.5k	686.8	13.9	463.9	0	1164.6	65.6	31.8	16.2	1354.9	3.1	1471.2	94.4	2733.2
7.5k, 8k	795.8	16.3	487.4	0	1299.4	69.9	29.7	15.3	1264.3	3.7	1383.1	96.7	2782.9
8k, 8.5k	543	10.2	335	0	888.2	60.4	30.5	15.7	1341.4	4.4	1452.0	124.7	2469.3
8.5k, 9k	354.5	5.6	249.3	0	609.3	52	31.1	16.1	1362.6	19	1480.7	148	2257.2
9k, 9.5k	474.9	5.3	455.4	0	935.7	80.2	27.8	14.4	1096.9	66.1	1284.4	216.8	2503
9.5k, 10k	446.8	4.8	475.5	0	927	78.2	23.8	12.4	843.2	41	968.7	153.8	2090.4

The dissipated power in Table 1 obtained with the GPPRMon tool matches with observations related to the performance. Registers load thread-specific data (from the parameter memory) during the 5000–5500 cycles, causing higher power consumption on SMs. In the following 4500 cycles, the memory partition's power dissipation gets more than the SMs. In addition, the consumed power by the LD/ST unit is high due to the intense memory operations and pressure on L1D cache, and other units apart from the register file portion of the execution unit get lower after Cycle 5500. The results in Table 1 display that DRAM contains most of the dissipated power in the memory partitions with intense usage of high-bandwidth. As a result, when irregular memory accesses increase, which causes idle SMs and stalled memory pipelines, consumed power gets lower along with performance. However, some load instructions operate at a quarter speed compared to the ideal performance. Hence, addressed energy may be wasted because of the inefficient access behavior on memory.

As a result, we describe how a memory-bound application occupies GPU hardware with architectural visualizations, which include detailed microarchitectural metrics, and instruction execution timeline of the application to explicitly point out long latencies in this case study. In addition, we relate the power consumption patterns with the corresponding runtime execution behavior of the GPU application. In this context, GPPRMon allows us to investigate the runtime execution behaviors of GPU applications at the instruction level. During the execution, users can certainly evaluate how each memory component is exploited spatially. While tracking both GPU occupancy and workload behavior in runtime, users can also track dissipated power at runtime via GPPRMon.

5   Conclusion

GPPRMon proposes a systematic runtime metric collection of instruction monitoring, performance, memory access, and power consumption metrics and it provides the multi-perspective visualizer framework that displays performance, execution statistics of the workload, occupancy of the memory hierarchy, and dissipated power results to conduct baseline analysis on GPUs at runtime. GPPRMon will help to conduct baseline analysis for the literature concerning GPU performance and power dissipation and eliminate the need for additional in-house efforts that involve real-time monitoring and profiling support.

Acknowledgement. This work was supported by the Scientific and Technological Research Council of Turkey (TÜBİTAK), Grant No: 122E395. This work is partially supported by CERCIRAS COST Action CA19135 funded by COST Association.

References

1. Guerreiro, J., Ilic, A., Roma, N., Tomás, P.: DVFS-aware application classification to improve GPGPUs energy efficiency. Parallel Comput. **83**, 93–117 (2019)
2. Hong, J., Cho, S., Kim, G.: Overcoming memory capacity wall of GPUs with heterogeneous memory stack. IEEE Comput. Archit. Lett. **21**(2), 61–64 (2022)
3. Jain, P., et al.: Checkmate: breaking the memory wall with optimal tensor rematerialization. CoRR abs/1910.02653 (2019). http://arxiv.org/abs/1910.02653
4. Jog, A., et al.: OWL: cooperative thread array aware scheduling techniques for improving GPGPU performance. In: Architectural Support for Programming Languages and Operating Systems (ASPLOS), pp. 395–406 (2013)

5. Kandiah, V., et al.: AccelWattch: a power modeling framework for modern GPUs. In: International Symposium on Microarchitecture (MICRO), pp. 738–753 (2021)
6. Khairy, M., Shen, Z., Aamodt, T.M., Rogers, T.G.: Accel-Sim: an extensible simulation framework for validated GPU modeling. In: International Symposium on Computer Architecture (ISCA), pp. 473–486 (2020)
7. Koo, G., Oh, Y., Ro, W.W., Annavaram, M.: Access pattern-aware cache management for improving data utilization in GPU. In: 2017 ACM/IEEE 44th Annual International Symposium on Computer Architecture (ISCA), pp. 307–319 (2017)
8. Krzywaniak, A., Czarnul, P., Proficz, J.: GPU power capping for energy-performance trade-offs in training of deep convolutional neural networks for image recognition. In: Computational Science - ICCS 2022, pp. 667–681 (2022)
9. Leskovec, J., Lang, K., Dasgupta, A., Mahoney, M.: Community structure in large networks: natural cluster sizes and the absence of large well-defined clusters. Internet Math. **6** (2008)
10. Lew, J., et al.: Analyzing machine learning workloads using a detailed GPU simulator. In: 2019 IEEE International Symposium on Performance Analysis of Systems and Software (ISPASS), pp. 151–152 (2019)
11. O'Neil, M.A., Burtscher, M.: Microarchitectural performance characterization of irregular GPU kernels. In: IEEE International Symposium on Workload Characterization (IISWC), pp. 130–139 (2014)
12. Sun, Y., et al.: Evaluating performance tradeoffs on the Radeon open compute platform. In: IEEE International Symposium on Performance Analysis of Systems and Software (ISPASS), pp. 209–218 (2018)
13. Ubal, R., Jang, B., Mistry, P., Schaa, D., Kaeli, D.: Multi2Sim: a simulation framework for CPU-GPU computing. In: International Conference on Parallel Architectures and Compilation Techniques (PACT), pp. 335–344 (2012)
14. Vijaykumar, N., Ebrahimi, E., Hsieh, K., Gibbons, P.B., Mutlu, O.: The locality descriptor: a holistic cross-layer abstraction to express data locality in GPUs. In: International Symposium on Computer Architecture (ISCA), pp. 829–842 (2018)
15. Xu, Z., Chen, X., Shen, J., Zhang, Y., Chen, C., Yang, C.: GARDENIA: a graph processing benchmark suite for next-generation accelerators. ACM J. Emerg. Technol. Comput. Syst. **15**(1), 1–13 (2019)

Towards Resource-Efficient DNN Deployment for Traffic Object Recognition: From Edge to Fog

Dragan Stojanovic[(✉)] [ID], Stefan Sentic, and Natalija Stojanovic [ID]

Faculty of Electronic Engineering, University of Nis, Aleksandra Medvedeva 14, Nis, Serbia
{dragan.stojanovic,stefan.sentic,
natalija.stojanovic}@elfak.ni.ac.rs

Abstract. The paper focuses on the challenges associated with deploying deep neural networks (DNNs) for the recognition of traffic objects using the camera of Android smartphones. The main objective of this research is to achieve resource-awareness, enabling efficient utilization of computational resources while maintaining high recognition accuracy. To achieve this, a methodology is proposed that leverages the Edge-to-Fog paradigm to distribute the inference workload across multiple tiers of the distributed system architecture. The evaluation was conducted using a dataset comprising real-world traffic scenarios and diverse traffic objects. The main findings of this research highlight the feasibility of deploying DNNs for traffic object recognition on resource-constrained Android smartphones. The proposed Edge-to-Fog methodology demonstrated improvements in terms of both recognition accuracy and resource utilization, and viability of both edge-only and edge-fog based approaches. Moreover, the experimental results showcased the adaptability of the system to dynamic traffic scenarios, thus ensuring real-time recognition performance even in challenging environments.

Keywords: Traffic Object Recognition · Edge · Fog · DNN · TensorFlow

1 Introduction

The increasing availability of smartphones with built-in cameras and their widespread adoption among users has opened up new possibilities for intelligent applications in various domains, including traffic object recognition. The ability to accurately identify and classify traffic objects such as cars, trucks, motorcycles, bicycles, and pedestrians is crucial for applications related to traffic management, surveillance, and driver assistance systems. Deep neural networks (DNNs) have shown remarkable performance in image recognition tasks, making them a promising approach for traffic object recognition on Android smartphones.

In this paper, we address the challenges associated with training and deploying DNNs for traffic object recognition on Android smartphones, focusing on the distribution of computational resources from the edge to the fog. We explore different strategies

The original version of this chapter was previously published without open access. A correction to this chapter is available at
https://doi.org/10.1007/978-3-031-48803-0_41

D. Zeinalipour et al. (Eds.): Euro-Par 2023 Workshops, LNCS 14352, pp. 30–39, 2024.
https://doi.org/10.1007/978-3-031-48803-0_3

for deployment, considering the trade-offs between model size, inference speed, and accuracy. Specifically, we evaluate two approaches: (1) quantizing and minimizing the DNN model as TensorFlow Lite and deploying it directly on the Android smartphone, and (2) deploying the original DNN model on a fog server.

Also, we consider distribution of car type detection task between edge for car object detection, and fog for recognizing of type of already detected cars. To enable comprehensive traffic object recognition, we develop a method that operates in two stages. In the first stage, the smartphone processes the video stream captured by its camera to detect the presence of cars. This initial detection is then transmitted to the fog server, where the second stage takes place. The fog server, with more computational resources, performs the recognition of the car type and its corresponding mark, providing detailed information about the identified vehicles.

To evaluate the performance and resource consumption of these traffic object recognition solutions, we implement a demo Android application on the smartphone and a Python/Flask-based server on the fog computer. The communication between the smartphone and the server is established via web sockets, enabling real-time interaction. Through systematic experiments, we examine the performance, accuracy, and resource consumption at both the smartphone and the server for various video data parameters and configurations.

The outcomes of this research provide insights into the effectiveness and feasibility of distributing DNNs for traffic object recognition from the edge to the fog. The findings will contribute to resource-awareness in systems and society by optimizing computational resource utilization while maintaining high recognition accuracy. Moreover, this work lays the foundation for developing intelligent transportation systems that leverage the capabilities of Android smartphones and fog computing infrastructure to enhance traffic safety and management.

2 Related Work

The research on the distribution of deep neural networks (DNNs) for resource-aware systems has gained significant attention in recent years. Several studies have explored different approaches and strategies for optimizing the training and deployment of DNNs in various domains. In the context of object detection and recognition from edge to cloud, several relevant research papers provide valuable insights and inspiration.

Bittencourt et al. [1] discuss the integration and challenges of the Internet of Things (IoT), fog, and cloud continuum, highlighting the need for efficient resource utilization. Lockhart et al. [2] propose Scission, a performance-driven and context-aware cloud-edge distribution approach for DNNs, emphasizing the importance of considering context and performance in distribution decisions. Cho et al. [3] present a study on DNN model deployment on distributed edges, focusing on distributed inference across edge devices.

Lin et al. [4] propose a distributed DNN deployment approach from the edge to the cloud for smart devices, addressing the challenges of efficient utilization of resources in different computing tiers. McNamee et al. [5] advocate for adaptive DNNs in edge computing, emphasizing the need for dynamic adaptation to optimize resource usage. Ren et al. [6] provide a survey on collaborative DNN inference for edge intelligence, exploring the collaborative aspects of inference across edge devices.

Hanhirova et al. [7] characterize the latency and throughput of convolutional neural networks for mobile computer vision, providing insights into the performance aspects of DNNs on resource-constrained devices. Lee et al. [8] propose Transprecise Object Detection (TOD) for maximizing real-time accuracy on the edge, highlighting the importance of accurate object detection for edge scenarios. Parthasarathy et al. [9] introduce DEFER, a distributed edge inference approach for DNNs, focusing on resource-efficient inference in distributed edge environments.

Teerapittayanon et al. [10] investigate distributed DNNs over the cloud, edge, and end devices, highlighting the trade-offs between resource utilization and computational capabilities across different components of the system architecture.

The aforementioned papers contribute to the understanding of resource aware DNN deployment and optimization techniques in various contexts. Our research aims to provide insights into the efficient training and deployment of DNNs for traffic object recognition, considering the resource utilization from edge to fog in the context of Android smartphones.

3   Distributed DNN Deployment from Edge to Fog

Deep Neural Networks (DNNs) have shown promising results in various computer vision tasks, including traffic object detection recognition. In this section we present the solution of two problems related to distribution of DNN in the context of traffic object recognition.

3.1   Traffic Object Recognition

For recognizing traffic objects from the camera on Android smartphones we implement two methods. The training of the DNN model is based on the TensorFlow Object Detection API and specifically utilizes the SSD MobileNet V2 320x320 coco17 tpu-8 pretrained model. To enhance the training process, we have utilized video data captured from an Android phone camera, as well as publicly available traffic video datasets such as the Udacity Self Driving Car Dataset[1], Graz-02 (IG02)[2], and the Bike-rider Detector dataset[3]. Manual labeling was applied to these datasets when necessary to ensure accurate annotation of traffic objects, including cars, trucks, motorcycles, bicycles, and pedestrians.

The first method we propose utilizes the computing power and resources available solely on the smartphone, making it an offline approach. This method does not require a network connection for traffic object recognition within the Android application. To accommodate the limited resources available on the smartphone, the TensorFlow model used for recognition is quantized and converted to TensorFlow Lite form. By optimizing the model, we ensure that it can efficiently operate on the smartphone without compromising its performance. The trained model is integrated into the Android application, enabling real-time traffic object recognition without the need for an internet connection (Fig. 1). This offline method allows for rapid and efficient identification of traffic objects directly on the smartphone.

---

[1] https://public.roboflow.com/object-detection/self-driving-car.
[2] https://lear.inrialpes.fr/people/marszalek/data/ig02/
[3] https://github.com/yonghah/bikerider-detector.

Fig. 1. Android application for traffic object recognition

The second method leverages the capabilities of fog computing by offloading part of the processing to a fog server. In this approach, the video captured by the smartphone's camera is preprocessed within the Android application. Preprocessing steps may include scaling, rotation, and filtering of the captured images to improve the quality and clarity of the input data. The preprocessed images are then encoded in Base64 format and transmitted to the fog server via a Web socket using the SocketIO library. The fog server (implemented using Flask/Python) hosts the original TensorFlow model, which performs the object recognition on the received images. The results of the recognition process are returned to the Android application in JSON format, enabling real-time feedback and visualization of the recognized traffic objects.

By distributing the computational workload between the smartphone and the fog server, the second method offloads resource-intensive tasks to a more powerful computing infrastructure. This approach allows for more accurate and robust recognition of traffic objects, especially in scenarios where the smartphone's resources may be limited. Furthermore, the utilization of fog computing reduces the burden on the smartphone's battery and processing capabilities, leading to improved performance and user experience.

In summary, we have implemented two methods for traffic object recognition using Deep Neural Networks on Android smartphones. Both methods offer distinct advantages in terms of resource utilization, real-time performance, and accuracy, catering to different requirements and constraints which are experimentally evaluated and presented in the next section.

3.2 Car Model Detection

To address the specific problem of car model detection, we propose a two-stage approach that utilizes both edge and fog computing resources. The foundation of our approach is the pretrained convolutional neural network MobileNet V2, which has shown remarkable performance in various computer vision tasks. To train the model for car model detection, we utilize the Stanford Cars Dataset, which consists of over 16,000 images and covers more than 190 different classes of cars.

In the first stage of our approach, the Android application takes advantage of edge computing capabilities to detect cars and determine their positions within the video images. We employ a TensorFlow Lite model, like the one used in the previous implementation, to perform this initial car detection task on the smartphone. Once the cars are identified, the corresponding regions of interest (ROIs) are extracted from the video frames and preprocessed to enhance their quality and suitability for subsequent recognition.

These preprocessed and cropped car images are then transmitted from the Android application to the fog server. The fog server application is responsible for the second stage of the car model recognition process. It utilizes the trained TensorFlow model, which has been specifically trained on the Stanford Cars Dataset, to recognize the model of each car in the received images and returns results back to the Android application (Fig. 2). The fog server's higher computational resources and processing power enable more computationally demanding tasks, such as fine-grained car type classification.

Fig. 2. Car model detection in the Android application

To facilitate communication between the Android application and the fog server, we employ Web sockets. This allows for real-time and bidirectional communication, enabling efficient transmission of preprocessed car images from the smartphone to the server and the subsequent return of the recognition results back to the mobile application. The utilization of Web sockets ensures a seamless and responsive user experience during the car type detection process.

By utilizing both edge and fog computing resources, our two-stage approach optimizes the allocation of computational tasks. The edge computing performed on the smartphone efficiently detects cars and extracts relevant ROIs, reducing the amount of data transmitted to the fog server. This minimizes bandwidth consumption and latency. The more resource-intensive car model recognition is offloaded to the fog server, leveraging its higher computational capabilities and trained model.

In summary, our two-stage approach for car model detection combines edge computing on the Android smartphone with fog computing on the server. The Android application performs car detection and preprocessing on the edge, while the fog server handles the car model recognition task. This approach maximizes the utilization of computing resources and improves the overall performance and accuracy of car model detection in our system.

4 Experimental Evaluation with Resource Awareness

In this section, we present an experimental evaluation of the previously described methods for the distribution of Deep Neural Networks (DNNs) in traffic object recognition. Specifically, we evaluate two implemented solutions: one performed solely within the Android application using a TensorFlow Lite model, and the other executed at the fog server. The experiments have been performed as a case study within the project FAAI - The Future is in Applied AI, Erasmus+KA220-HED - Cooperation partnerships in higher education. The case studies have been implemented and evaluated within WP4 which aims to define and establish applied AI framework for training the future AI experts.

To assess the performance and accuracy of the solutions, as well as their resource consumption (CPU, memory, and energy), we conduct experiments using various video data parameters and configurations. The goal is to gain insights into the trade-offs between the two approaches and understand their behavior under different conditions.

For the evaluation, we employ representative datasets that encompass different traffic scenarios and object types. We ensure that the datasets cover a wide range of traffic scenarios, including diverse lighting conditions, weather conditions, and traffic densities.

To evaluate the Android application solution, we measure its performance and accuracy on the smartphone itself. We analyze the computational requirements, including CPU usage, memory consumption, and energy consumption using Android Profiler tool. Additionally, we assess the accuracy of traffic object recognition by comparing the results against ground truth annotations in the datasets.

Similarly, for the fog server solution, we measure its performance, accuracy, and resource consumption. The server's computational requirements, including CPU usage, memory utilization, and energy consumption, are analyzed. Additionally, we compare the recognition results obtained from the fog server with the ground truth annotations to evaluate the accuracy of the solution. The timely diagram of CPU and memory consumption, as well as energy usage for traffic object recognition performed at Android smartphone and at the fog server is shown in Fig. 3. The maximum CPU utilization during local detection was 33%, while during server detection, it was 14%. The maximum amount of used RAM during local detection was 316 MB, whereas for server detection, it amounted to 240 MB. The size of the TensorFlow model is 11.2 MB. In case of model quantization, it is possible to reduce the model size to 3.2 MB.

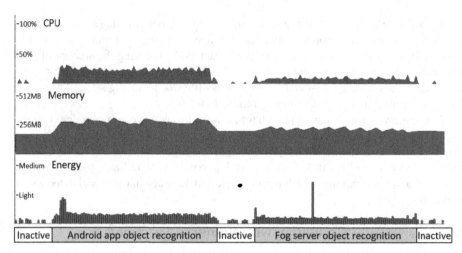

Fig. 3. CPU, memory, and energy usage for edge (smartphone) and fog server solutions

Throughout the experimental evaluation, we vary the video data parameters and configurations to examine the behavior of both solutions under different conditions. This includes varying factors such as video resolution, frame rate, lighting conditions, and traffic densities. By conducting experiments with diverse scenarios, we aim to provide a comprehensive assessment of the performance and resource utilization of each solution.

The experimental evaluation is conducted using appropriate benchmarking tools and metrics to ensure reliable and meaningful results. We measure the execution time, resource utilization, and accuracy of both solutions across different datasets and configurations. The obtained data is analyzed and compared to identify the strengths and limitations of each approach. For all experiments, the Google Pixel 4 phone has been used. The server application runs on a Lenovo Legion laptop computer (CPU: i5-9300H, RAM: 16.0 GB, GPU: nVidia GeForce GTX 1650). The server is set up on a local network so that the mobile application can access it.

The first experiment aimed to measure the accuracy of recognition with varying image resolution and object size. The camera of the phone was directed towards a computer monitor displaying a consistently shrinking image of a car. The testing was conducted for both modes of operation at each of the 4 available resolutions in the application settings. The image quality was set to the maximum (100%, no compression).

Table 1 presents the reliability of detection expressed in percentages. This experiment revealed that the reliability values of detection (and therefore the detection quality) are quite similar for both edge detection and server-based detection. A slight advantage is observed for edge detection at lower image resolutions, which is likely due to additional image processing that occurs when sending the image to the server (encoding and decoding in Base64 format). One potential solution is to utilize a more sophisticated image transport method, such as implementing one of the transfer protocols specifically designed for working with images.

We also measure dependency of performance (speed of execution) on image resolution and image quality. Values are expressed in milliseconds (ms). This experiment

Table 1. Dependency of detection accuracy on image resolution and object size

Object size	Resolution							
	640 × 640		512 × 512		300 × 300		160 × 160	
	Edge	Fog	Edge	Fog	Edge	Fog	Edge	Fog
100%	98.9	97.8	98.7	98.7	98.9	98.3	90.0	84.3
80%	95.4	95.0	95.1	95.4	94.7	93.1	82.4	82.1
50%	89.2	90.0	87.4	88.7	89.9	87.9	83.4	80.5
30%	47.1	42.3	40.1	32.8	31.7	19.7	23.1	17.4
15%	12.3	12.7	10.7	12.1	10.2	2.1	7.4	1.8

aimed to test the impact of image compression on detection speed and image size. The phone camera was directed towards a computer monitor displaying a consistent image of a car. The testing was conducted for both operating modes at each of the 4 available resolutions and image quality settings of 100%, 70%, 50%, 30%, and 20% achieved through JPEG image compression.

Table 2 illustrates the change in detection speed when altering the image characteristics. The quality of the image decreases across the rows, while the resolution decreases across the columns. The values are expressed in milliseconds. It is immediately noticeable that the local detection exhibits significantly higher speed.

Table 2. Dependency of performance (speed of execution) on image resolution and image quality (in ms).

Quality	Resolution							
	640 × 640		512 × 512		300 × 300		160 × 160	
	Edge	Fog	Edge	Fog	Edge	Fog	Edge	Fog
100%	61.4	153.2	58.0	137.0	55.9	103.2	45.8	83.9
70%	56.5	112.2	50.4	99.8	43.9	87.7	43.0	76.9
50%	55.5	108.2	49.8	98.9	43.6	86.7	42.9	76.4
30%	55.3	103.8	49.1	93.1	43.4	84.7	43.4	75.0
20%	54.4	101.8	48.9	90.2	43.9	84.1	42.8	74.9

Regarding local detection, the difference in detection speed between settings A (640 × 640 resolution and 100% quality) and settings B (160 × 160 resolution and 20% quality) amounts to 18.6 ms per frame. Although the difference is difficult to measure precisely, it is evident that the detection quality for smaller objects is noticeably lower with settings B.

When it comes to server-based detection, internet connection speed becomes a significant factor. Since a GPU was utilized, the model execution itself was short (~45 ms), with most of the time being spent on image transportation. During the testing, an internet speed of 55.8 Mbps for download and 7.7 Mbps for upload was used. In the case of edge detection, the byte size of the image does not have as much influence as it does for server-based detection, as each image is transported to the server, and any reduction in image size contributes to increased detection speed. The difference in detection speed between settings A (640×640 resolution and 100% quality) and settings B (160×160 resolution and 20% quality) amounts to 78.3 ms per frame. A significant degradation in detection quality on the server compared to edge detection was observed when decreasing the image resolution.

By evaluating the performance, accuracy, and resource consumption of the Android application solution and the fog server solution, we aim to provide insights into the trade-offs associated with each approach. The experimental evaluation will contribute to a better understanding of the behavior and capabilities of these distribution methods in traffic object recognition tasks. Ultimately, this analysis will assist in selecting the most appropriate solution based on specific requirements, such as available resources, real-time performance, and accuracy.

5 Conclusion

In this paper, we have explored the training and deployment of Deep Neural Networks (DNNs) for traffic object recognition from the camera on Android smartphones, with a focus on the distribution of models across the edge-to-fog computing continuum. We considered several strategies for training and deployment, including the quantization and minimization of models using TensorFlow Lite for deployment on Android smartphones, as well as the deployment of the original TensorFlow model on a fog server.

Our approach to traffic object recognition involved a two-stage process, where the smartphone was used for car detection in the video stream, and the fog server was utilized for car type and mark recognition. We implemented a demo Android application and a fog server, which communicate via web sockets, to evaluate the performance, accuracy, and resource consumption of the traffic object recognition solutions under various video data parameters and configurations.

Through our evaluation, we observed the effectiveness of the different deployment strategies in achieving accurate traffic object recognition. We found that the quantized and minimized model deployed on Android smartphones achieved reasonable performance with efficient resource usage, while the deployment of the original TensorFlow model on the fog server allowed for more complex recognition tasks.

In conclusion, our research contributes to the understanding of DNN distribution for traffic object recognition from edge to fog on Android smartphones. However, there are still several avenues for future research in this area. Some potential directions include:

- Exploration of additional training and deployment strategies, such as federated learning or model partitioning, to further optimize resource utilization across the edge-fog-cloud continuum.
- Investigation of dynamic resource allocation and adaptation techniques to adapt the distribution of DNN models based on changing resource availability and workload demands.

- Development of energy-efficient algorithms and techniques for DNN inference at the edge and fog nodes, considering the limited power resources of mobile devices and resource-constrained edge environments.

By further exploring these research directions, we can continue to advance the field of DNN model slicing across the edge-fog-cloud computing continuum, enabling resource-aware and efficient traffic object recognition systems for various real-world applications.

Acknowledgements. Research presented in this paper is supported by:

• COST Action CERCIRAS - Connecting Education and Research Communities for an Innovative Resource Aware Society - CA19135.

• Erasmus+ Project FAAI: The Future is in Applied AI (WP4 - Artificial Intelligence framework for training in HE) – 2022-1-PL01-KA220-HED-000088359.

• Ministry of Science and Technological Development, Republic of Serbia, 451-03-68/2022-14/200102.

References

1. Bittencourt, L., et al.: The Internet of Things, fog and cloud continuum: integration and challenges. In: Internet of Things, vol. 3–4, pp. 134–155 (2018)
2. Lockhart, L., Harvey, P., Imai, P., Willis, P., Varghese, B.: Scission: performance-driven and context-aware cloud-edge distribution of deep neural networks. In: Proceedings of the IEEE/ACM 13th International Conference on Utility and Cloud Computing (UCC), Leicester, United Kingdom, pp. 257–268 (2020)
3. Cho, E., Yoon, J., Baek, D., Lee, D., Bae, DH.: DNN model deployment on distributed edges. In: Bakaev, M., Ko, I.Y., Mrissa, M., Pautasso, C., Srivastava, A. (eds.) ICWE 2021 Workshops. Communications in Computer and Information Science, vol. 1508, pp. 15–26. Springer, Cham (2021). https://doi.org/10.1007/978-3-030-92231-3_2
4. Chang-You, L., Tzu-Chen, W., Kuan-Chih, C., Bor-Yan, L., Jian-Jhih Kuo, K.: Distributed deep neural network deployment for smart devices from the edge to the cloud. In: Proceedings of the ACM MobiHoc Workshop on Pervasive Systems in the IoT Era (PERSIST-IoT 2019), New York, NY, USA, pp. 43–48 (2019)
5. McNamee, F., Dustdar, S., Kilpatrick, P., Shi, W., Spence, I., Varghese, B.: The case for adaptive deep neural networks in edge computing. In: Proceedings of the IEEE 14th International Conference on Cloud Computing (CLOUD), pp. 43–52 (2021)
6. Ren, W., et al.: A survey on collaborative DNN inference for edge intelligence. Mach. Intell. Res. **20**, 370–395 (2023)
7. Hanhirova, J., Kämäräinen, T., Seppälä, S., Siekkinen, M., Hirvisalo, V., Ylä-Jääski, A.: Latency and throughput characterization of convolutional neural networks for mobile computer vision. In: Proceedings of the 9th ACM Multimedia Systems Conference (MMSys 2018), New York, NY, USA, pp. 204–215 (2018)
8. Lee, J.K., Varghese, B., Woods, R., Vandierendonck, H.: TOD: transprecise object detection to maximize real-time accuracy on the edge. In: Proceeding of the 5th EEE 5th International Conference on Fog and Edge Computing, pp. 53–60 (2021)
9. Parthasarathy, A., Krishnamachari, B.: DEFER: distributed edge inference for deep neural networks. In: Proceedings of the 14th International Conference on COMmunication Systems & NETworkS (COMSNETS), pp. 749–753 (2022)
10. Teerapittayanon, S., McDanel, B., Kung, H.T.: Distributed deep neural networks over the cloud, the edge and end devices. In: Proceedings of the IEEE 37th International Conference on Distributed Computing Systems (ICDCS), Atlanta, GA, USA, pp. 328–339 (2017)

10. Teerapittayanon, S., McDanel, B., Kung, H.T.: Distributed deep neural networks over the cloud, the edge and end devices. In: Proceedings of the IEEE 37th International Conference on Distributed Computing Systems (ICDCS), Atlanta, GA, USA, pp. 328–339 (2017)

The Implementation of Battery Charging Strategy for IoT Nodes

Petar Rajković[1]([✉]) [iD], Dejan Aleksić[2] [iD], and Dragan Janković[1] [iD]

[1] Faculty of Electronic Engineering, University of Niš, Aleksandra Medvedeva 14, Niš, Serbia
{petar.rajkovic,dragan.jankovic}@elfak.ni.ac.rs
[2] Department of Physics, Faculty of Sciences and Mathematics, University of Niš, Niš, Serbia
alexa@pmf.ni.ac.rs

Abstract. The Internet of Things (IoT) nodes dedicated to off-grid usage must fully rely on their battery power for continuous operation. In that sense battery charging process design is one of the focal points for the complete system design. Nowadays, battery charging, for such devices, usually relies on solar power which is not, unfortunately, the source of constant energy. Both environmental and constructive elements could easily make a negative impact on the charging process and reduce the amount of collected energy. Furthermore, if the IoT nodes are in hazardous areas, they are less accessible, and the value of effective battery management is even higher. The requirements for the battery charging process implementation are considered as opposite – on one hand, the requirement is to run charging with the lowest possible frequency and not up to 100%, and on the other hand, the battery should always have enough energy to maintain regular operation. In this research, we present the structure of the custom-developed IoT node based on the ECS32 system-on-a-chip dedicated to operating in remote industrial areas, and with an accent of its battery charging routine. The current routine is based on a standard thresholds approach and improved by including consumption estimates for the predefined periods. This paper presents the first results and should pave the ground for further upgrades. In addition, the comparison with state-of-the-art charging approaches is presented, as the guidelines for future work.

Keywords: Internet of things · resource awareness · industry 4.0 · hardware-software codesign

1 Introduction

The Internet of Things (IoT) nodes are the devices that are nowadays widely installed in industrial facilities [1]. They have different roles, but one common usage is to control sensor networks, acquire data, and forward the results of measurement to the Edge computers. Compared to the standard controlling and computing units, they are smaller, equipped with fewer connectivity options, lower processing power, and perfectly suited for the intended use [2]. The IoT nodes with connected sensors are an integrative part of the ISA-95 [3] software model and belong to levels 0 and 1. Together with Edge and Cloud levels, the IoT nodes make a complete execution model and enable the operation

---

The original version of this chapter was previously published without open access. A correction to this chapter is available at
https://doi.org/10.1007/978-3-031-48803-0_41

© The Author(s) 2024, corrected publication 2024
D. Zeinalipour et al. (Eds.): Euro-Par 2023 Workshops, LNCS 14352, pp. 40–51, 2024.
https://doi.org/10.1007/978-3-031-48803-0_4

of an industrial facility. The enabled interlevel communication could also be configured and controlled remotely [4].

From the hardware realization point of view, the IoT nodes are mostly based on system-on-a-chip components or other compact devices such as ESP32 [11], which was used to develop the device that will be discussed in this research. Yet small, the IoT nodes have enough processing power and connectivity options that could be effectively used as data collection and processing units [5].

In addition, they could be combined with other electronic components, solar panels, and battery sets, and placed into an insulated sealing. In this way, they will become independent IoT nodes that can operate for a long time without any manual intervention. The complete process is strictly defined, and the node must conform to certain industrial standards before deployment to a realistic environment [6, 7].

Due to their compact size, a design that makes them independent from the frequent operator's intervention, and low energy consumption, they are a perfect choice for use in hazardous and remote areas, and, in general, in any off-grid setup where wireless data exchange is the only option. Besides the internal functionality, which should be designed as resource-aware software and hardware, the IoT nodes must utilize a battery charging routine that will allow them continuous independent work.

The simple definition of the requirement, from the previous paragraph, leads to a very complex implementation. The main problem that must be addressed is ensuring a stable battery state when the charging process relies on an unstable source of energy – solar power. Solar power is available, on average, 50% of the time – in some periods of the year more, and some periods of the year less. Next, many environmental factors could further reduce the amount of power that could be collected – clouds, shades from the trees and plants, dust, etc. Also, small errors in device construction and solar panel location could further reduce the possibility of charging the batteries in the best way.

Battery usage is the most stable element of the entire IoT node life cycle. Most of the time, the node is running an optimized low-energy routine. Occasionally, the node must switch to modes where battery usage is increased, and if the moment when these routines start is not synchronized with charging, the node could easily go to the alert state or even drain the battery.

On the other hand, the requirement is to charge the battery in a way to extend its life as much as possible. It means that batteries cannot be charged whenever it is possible and up to 100%. The minimal and maximal energy thresholds are defined depending on the battery type. Keeping the battery above the maximal threshold could significantly reduce its lifespan.

The solution that we started with, was a part of the IoT node implementation, which was dedicated to the work in hazardous areas. This solution was the standard threshold-based charging routine – if the battery is under a minimal threshold the charging will start, and if it is above the maximal threshold the charging will stop.

This basic threshold-related approach is not always suitable, having in mind previously described requirements and environmental and operational impacts. For this reason, we started the research to find the more appropriate charging mechanisms and eventually combine them most effectively. This paper presents the current state of the development of dedicated IoT nodes for use in remote and hazardous areas, focusing on evaluating and analyzing possible battery charging routines.

2 ESP32 Structure and Power Level – The Starting Point in Design

When designing IoT nodes, the common approach is to start with the standard components used in the dedicated industry. The main reason for such rationale is the existing support channels, documentation, and the variety of available solutions which could be a good starting point. Next, when it comes to the standardization of developed devices, it would be much faster since some steps could be skipped. To use the mentioned advantage, we decided to go with the system-on-a-chip. We later extended the system with new components and disable some of the basic features if proved undervalued.

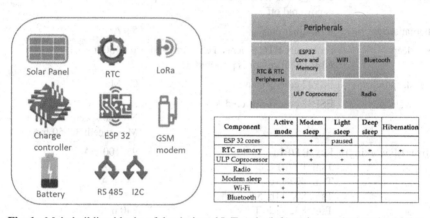

Component	Active mode	Modem sleep	Light sleep	Deep sleep	Hibernation
ESP 32 cores	+	+	paused		
RTC memory	+	+	+	+	+
ULP Coprocessor	+	+	+	+	
Radio	+				
Modem sleep	+				
Wi-Fi	+				
Bluetooth	+				

Fig. 1. Main building blocks of the designed IoT node (left) and operation modes (right)

The proposed IoT node is designed around the ESP32 controller (Fig. 1, left). It is one of the standard industrial components, proven in real exploitation and the laboratory. It runs its operating system called FreeRTOS [15] and it is designed to collect data from sensors, process them and emit them further using its default communication channels – Wi-Fi and Bluetooth [10]. It could support communication to the sensor networks and other devices using RS485 and I2C interfaces.

It is worth mentioning that the ESP32 has a powerful processing design for its category of devices. It does not only emulate parallel processing, but it enables it through its architecture. ESP32 consists of three execution cores – two cores are dedicated to performing computational operations in active mode and one core (ULP Coprocessor) is used when it switches to some of the sleep modes only (Fig. 1, right). Other important parts of ESP32 are connectivity elements – for communication with sensors and actuators (green elements in Fig. 1, right) and wireless data exchange with other devices (red blocks in Fig. 1, right).

The node itself supports one active and four different sleep modes. The transition between modes is supported natively. The highest energy consumption is in the active mode when transmission of 802.11.b is active. It could reach the level of 240 mA (Table 1). Modem sleep is the mode where only the processing part of the ESP32 is active and where both communications to peripherals and radio transmitting parts are disabled. At full processing speed, the execution core could use up to 50 mA, which is slightly above 20% of the maximal power. This means that the node is safe to perform complex calculations most of the time at, not so high energy cost. In light sleep mode, the processing part is paused. It keeps the data in the internal memory but executes no active data processing. The consumption is close to 1 mA.

Table 1. Expected values for energy consumption in ESP32-based nodes (as in [11, 12])

Power Mode	Description	Typical Power Consumption
Power off	CHIP_PU is set to a low level; the chip is powered off	0.1 μA
Hibernation	RTC timer only	5 μA
Deep sleep	From only RTC timer+RTC memory to ULP co-processor is powered on	10–150 μA
Light sleep	ESP32 core is paused	0.8 Ma
Modem sleep	ESP32 core is powered	Slow speed: 2–4 mA Normal speed: 20–25 mA Max speed: 30–50 mA
Active (RF working)	Rcv. BT/BLE Tsm. BT/BLE Tsm. 802.11g Tsm. 802.11b, 54 Tsm. 802.11.b, 1	95–100 mA 130 mA 180 mA 190 mA 240 mA

The characteristic of deep sleep and hibernation modes is that processing cores are fully disabled. The third core, the ULP coprocessor, is active and maintains all necessary signals and flags that make the transition back to active mode fast and efficient.

The hibernation mode keeps only RTC peripherals active and power consumption is at the level of a few μA. The device can stay in this mode for an exceptionally long time but transitioning from hibernate to active mode requires a complex procedure of node start and initialization.

The values shown in Table 1 are measured in laboratory conditions, and it is expected that they could vary up to some percentage compared to the values from the producer data sheet. Furthermore, some additional differences could be introduced as the result of the influence of connected sensors. In the examined case, the node was connected to different RS485-based sensors.

3   Updates in Node Design and Effect on Power Levels

For use in the off-grid environment, a few updates had to be implemented. First, the existing communication part had to be disabled. Bluetooth and Wi-Fi consume a lot of energy, and their range is too limited for use in remote and off-grid areas. Also, placing the node in the casing dedicated to a hazardous environment influences Wi-Fi and Bluetooth connectivity badly (Fig. 2). The battery of type 18650 with a capacity of 3500 mAh, which works on a 3.6 V is used. The chosen battery is of Lithium-Ion technology which is considered a standard for such usage.

Fig. 2. Finalized node before placing in Ex e sealing (left), and sealed with RS485 sensor connected (right)

For this reason, they are replaced with external communication components that use LoRaWAN [13] and GPRS [14] technologies for data exchange. The main idea is to use LoRaWAN all the time [8, 9], and then to switch to GPRS only when it is necessary – when the LoRaWAN module is out of operation or when some specific data transmission must be done only using GPRS.

With the updated design, the energy consumption was measured against the standard design. In both cases, two sensor arrays connected to RS485 were employed. For the updated design LoRaWAN was defined as the preferred communication channel (Comm 1 in Table 2), while for the base design, this was a Wi-Fi connection. The backup communication channel (Comm 2 in Table 2) was the GSM module for the updated and Bluetooth radio for the base design.

The Most visible gain is in active mode with sensors and with Comm 1 channel enabled. Compared to the base design the level of used energy is reduced between 30 and 70% which guarantees longer periods before the battery is recharged.

Not only separate operations, but also working cycles could affect energy consumption. Since it is obvious that data transmission uses the highest percentage of energy, the battery will last longer if the number of data transmissions can be reduced, especially when the backup channel (Comm 2) is active.

Table 2. Comparison of energy consumption in updated and base design in different working modes

Power Mode	Updated Design	Base Design
Active mode	36 mA	>100 mA <50 mA
Active mode+2 RS485	69 mA	149–200 mA
Light sleep	7.5–8.4 mA	0.8 mA
Active mode+Comm 1	98 mA	130 mA
Active mode+Comm2	Active: 412 mA Idle: 21 mA	>200 mA

4 Charging Strategy

From the point of view of battery usage, the most convenient scenario is to have a standardized set of functionalities that could ensure a stable level of energy consumption. It means that, if possible, to have, over a longer period, an estimate that could differ within a few percentages, will be an ideal working mode. However, this is not always achievable. As has been presented before, different data transmission devices use significantly different amounts of energy. Then, when the node must be updated, or when lost connection to the sensor devices, and constantly trying to reconnect, it will use more energy than usual.

Next, different active and different sleep modes use various levels of energy. Also, the transition from a mode to a mode could initiate peaks in consumption if some initiation procedure must be run. As has been presented in the previous section, energy usage during the node operation depends on its working mode and the required frequency of actions.

When evaluating data usage between the three most important parts of the nodes' cycles, data processing could use different levels of power depending on its activity, but it is usually in line with data collection. Data collection from the sensors requires significantly lower consumption of energy compared to data transmission to the Edge level. Regardless of the communication means, data transmission is the most energy-consuming part of the process.

Data transmission modules are very different in their range, speed, and data package volume. By default, ESP32 offers Wi-Fi and Bluetooth. Unfortunately, these two integrated communication parts use too much power and have a very limited range for the need of the IoT node that should run in battery-only mode. Even, when the integrated communication components of ESP32 are disabled, and replaced with more efficient external devices, data transmission still requires more energy.

4.1 Standard Energy Levels

To ensure a proper node operation state, the energy level in the battery should always be adequate. For this reason, the separate task is developed and integrated into the IoT node's software model. It is intended to drive the charge controller and execute chosen charging strategies. To control the charging process, the following basic signals and threshold values are defined:

– Standard low battery level (SL in further text) – the energy level after which the charging process starts automatically
– Standard high battery level (SH in further text) – the energy level when the charging process stops automatically
– Alarm low battery level (AL in further text) – the energy level when the node sends the alarm of the highest priority to the Edge level and stops all activities
– Operation Mode (OM in further text) – the charging process could be executed in the automatic mode, the controlled mode, or charging could be disabled.

4.2 Automatic Charging

The default operation mode for the charging controller is automatic. In this mode, the charging process checks periodically the energy level of the battery, and if it reaches SL, the charging process starts. The node continues its operation normally while the battery is charging, and when it reaches SH, the charging process stops. Depending on the charging power source, this approach could be efficient. In the case when the node's charging routine depends on solar power, this approach could be a bit problematic. As has been mentioned, sunlight is available in certain areas at most 50% of the time. These periods of active sunlight are not constant and even the duration of day and night differs daily. Furthermore, the effect of the other natural elements and construction properties of the device could reduce the period when sunlight is available.

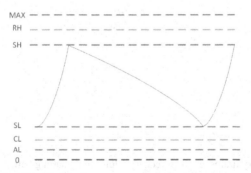

Fig. 3. Ideal energy consumption/charging

From the implementational point of view, this approach is the easiest and usually is the first choice in implementation. Whenever the charging controller starts or stops the charging process it sends this piece of information to the Edge level with the appropriate timestamp. Now these data are collected at the Edge level and forwarded to the cloud store. Currently, these data are continuously stored at the cloud level. They are used to analyze node functionality and to early identify malfunctions.

The default charging process is defined in this way to ensure longer battery life. For most of the available battery types, the best use case is if their power level varies between

SL and SH thresholds. If they are often filled or drained, it could reduce their operational life. In the ideal case, the battery level will stay between the two mentioned thresholds, and the device will run without interruption, having an energy line as presented in Fig. 3.

4.3 Extension on Automatic Charging – Introducing Alarms

Unfortunately, this scenario is not always possible. First, when automatic charging gets triggered, it could happen during the night or during the period when the sunlight is not bright enough. Then, the solar panel will not generate enough power to raise the energy level in the battery.

The case when the charging gets started, but the energy level is still going down will trigger the alarm signal from the IoT node. The signal will be received at the Edge level and registered. Since the charging controller frequently reads the energy level in the battery it could continue to trigger alarms that indicate that the energy level is still reducing despite the charging process having been initiated.

If the energy level gets further reduced, it will reach CL (Charging required Level) after some time. At that moment, the IoT node will send the alarm of a higher priority to the Edge computer and reconfigure its operation strategy by reducing the number of data transmission operations.

If the battery level continues to degrade, after some time it will reach the AL threshold (Fig. 4, left). This is considered the alarm of the highest level, and the node will stop all the operations it could and switch to hibernation sleep mode. Up to that time, based on the data received in the Edge and then forwarded to the cloud level, the operation engineers could decide what to do with the affected IoT node.

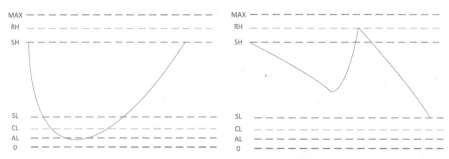

Fig. 4. Intensive battery drains and then recharge (left) and charging battery in controlled mode (right)

One of the simplest ways to prevent this situation is to enable the calculation of the energy use depending on the time of the day and with the introduction of one additional check level. It would be SL increased by some percentage (like 10 or 20%). In this case, the charging routine will check the remaining time until sunset, and the increased SL. If the energy level fell to SL+10% and the remaining period of the day is i.e., 10% of sunlight, the charging process will start immediately.

This is a simple and effective approach, making the possibility to have additional charging periods with the lowest possible effect on battery life. The problem with such an approach is that node must have info about sunrise and sunset daily, and that node must run more complex checks.

4.4 Controlled Charging Mode

As explained, the default automatic mode is the easiest to implement and the entire logic could be incorporated into the IoT node's programmatic structure. The next operation mode for the charging controller is the controlled mode. The controlled mode is initiated from the Edge level, and it is intended to instantly trigger the charging process. Regardless of the current battery level, when the switch to the controlled mode signal gets received, the charging process will start immediately.

If the start signal is followed by the requested high level (RH in the further text), the battery will be charged until the requested level is reached, regardless of the value set for SH (Fig. 4, right). With this process, the SH level itself will not be changed, but it will be omitted during a single charging run. When the battery level reaches RH, the charging process will stop, and the node will go back to automatic mode.

When in the controlled charging mode, the battery could lose power as in automation charging mode. In this case, the same alarm procedure was explained before.

In the end, the charging controller could be disabled. Regularly this happens when the IoT node is connected to the power grid, but this situation is out of the scope of our paper.

4.5 Charging Mode Comparison

Besides the automatic mode, driven by SL and SH thresholds is easy to implement, in some cases, it will not provide sufficient energy for the IoT node. Depending on the type of operation, it could be considered extremely harmful for the entire industrial system if the data from remote sensors are not received regularly.

For this reason, it is important to make the charging process more adaptive and efficient. Having in mind that the transition to controlled charging mode with the predefined RH could be triggered from the Edge or Cloud level at any time brings a dose of safety, but the process should be somehow automated to ensure less frequent (ideally never happening) situations when the IoT node goes to the alarm states.

The default strategy uses only the current energy level as the considered parameter. Luckily, the charging controller regularly reads the battery status and could upload (or store locally) these data for further analysis. Based on this, the average energy consumption per hour could (ACH in further text) be calculated. Since the node reads data from the sensors in the standard periods, and since the energy consumption during these operations is in tight boundaries, this value could be an additional input for the decision of when to start charging.

The initial improvement would be to calculate the sum of SL and the value that is the result of the multiplication of ACH with the number of hours until sunrise. If this sum is higher than the current amount of energy in the battery, the charging process could start immediately. It is important to mention that there is no point if the charging process run during the night, since the solar panel cannot generate energy, and the system will only generate unnecessary alarms. In this way, the number of required charging processes would be slightly higher, but the risk of the transition to the alarm state will be significantly reduced. The next improvement would be to include the weather report and check if the potential period with a lower amount of sunlight is ahead. In this way, the charging process could run up to a higher threshold than SH, and in this way bring the higher operational period to the battery.

It is important to say, that the frequency of charging depends on the battery capacity and the effectiveness of the solar panel and the charging component. With the standardized working mode, with two RS485 sensors attached and a LoRa module used for data transmission, our node will need one charge weekly or bi-weekly. This period is long, and the weather could change several times. Also, if the need to use more expensive, in terms of energy, GPRS communication channel energy will be drained much faster, and thus the possibility to react fast and run charging is a necessity.

5 Related Work and Actual Solutions

Since the segment of our research related to the battery charging process is in an early stage and this paper present only the first result and basic analysis, checking on the actual solution in this area is of the highest significance for us.

In [16], the authors discussed traditional charging control methods as well as battery management systems. While the charging control methods, such are constant current (CC), constant voltage (CV), or pulse charging (PC) are encapsulated in the charge controller, and closer to the hardware design, our focus was on battery management systems. One approach that we plan to implement in the future is fuzzy logic control of energy storage. This could be overlooked as the update over standard charging based on the threshold. The idea is to let the battery charge fast up to SH level, and then to maintain this level until it is possible. In this way, the battery will stay at high power for a longer period. On the other hand, this could require the usage of more complex charging controller logic which could require a bigger component which would require then bigger casing. The next approach presented in [16] that we found interesting is the model of predictive control of energy storage systems. Using the suggested multi-step ahead predictions based on accumulated parameters value would help in the process of determining the right moment when to start charging. This would be a step forward compared to our updated scenario since we currently rely only on time until the next sunrise and estimated consumption per hour.

The study presented in [17] explains 26 different battery charging strategies. To us, this was important since it explicitly focused on the charging characteristics of Li-ion batteries. Comprehensively, controlled parameters, cut-off conditions, and observed parameters are explained. Furthermore, the limitations together with the suggested modifications for fast charging are elaborated. In the end, the framework for the fast battery process is presented. The main idea in the proposed framework is to use artificial intelligence and machine learning to make the charging process more effective. On our end, we are preparing to make the move in this direction by collecting the necessary parameters and uploading them to the cloud.

556565656565656565556565656565656565656565656565656

The article [18] brings a review of the latest approaches in battery management systems. The study relies on the analysis of numerous actual works and ends up with recommendations for prominent system design. With the anticipated growth of battery management systems by more than 50% annually until 2030 [19], this research area is considered highly important and with the expected high-level improvements. This research also indicates the importance of machine learning and building an adaptive battery management system that should consider multiple parameters for their operations.

The additional benefit of the study [18] is that it does not analyze only battery charging techniques, but also considers other supporting technologies that should further improve the complete area. The creation of digital twins, as we started with, will make efficient control and system performance prediction. Blockchain technologies could be used to enable higher security levels for data transfer in battery management systems. And, in the end, machine learning and deep learning are pointed out as the most important techniques to fine-tune charging processes.

6 Conclusion and Future Work

While developing the IoT node for use in off-grid, remote, and hazardous areas, the initial focus was on the hardware and software implementation to achieve the lowest possible energy consumption. Due to the exploitation phase, it was noticed that simple battery management, as described in this paper, is not good enough, and in some cases, the node could go into the alarm state due to the low battery level.

To overcome this problem, we started with the implementation of an improved charging management system. As the first step, we introduced externally controlled charging, which could be triggered from the Cloud or Edge level and force the IoT node to start to charge the battery. Next, we replaced simple threshold-based charging with an improved process that considers not only the current battery level but the estimated energy consumption and the time until the next sunrise. The focus is currently on the definition of the process based on the improved techniques and machine learning to define autonomous models which will ensure if possible IoT node operation in the off-grid environment. This paper describes our first step in the research and makes the ground for further projects.

Acknowledgments. The Ministry of Education, Science, and Technological Development of the Republic of Serbia have funded this work, grant number 451-03-68/2022-14/ 200102. This work has been supported by the cost action CA 19135 CERCIRAS (Connecting Education and Research Communities for an Innovative Resource Aware Society).

References

1. Kumar, S., Tiwari, P., Zymbler, M.: Internet of Things is a revolutionary approach for future technology enhancement: a review. J. Big Data **6**(1), 1–21 (2019)
2. Paiola, M., Gebauer, H.: Internet of Things technologies, digital servitization and business model innovation in BtoB manufacturing firms. Ind. Mark. Manage. **89**, 245–264 (2020)

3. ISA-95 standard page, available online. https://www.isa.org/standards-and-publications/isa-standards/isa-standards-committees/isa95. Accessed 26 Feb 2023
4. Callebaut, G., Leenders, G., Van Mulders, J., Ottoy, G., De Strycker, L., Van der Perre, L.: The art of designing remote IoT devices—technologies and strategies for a long battery life. Sensors 21(3), 913 (2021)
5. Seferagić, A., Famaey, J., De Poorter, E., Hoebeke, J.: Survey on wireless technology trade-offs for the industrial Internet of things. Sensors 20(2), 488 (2020)
6. Guidelines for integrated risk assessment and management in large industrial areas. https://www-pub.iaea.org/MTCD/publications/PDF/te_994_prn.pdf. Accessed 22 Apr 2023
7. Increase safety Ex e standards, available online. https://www.nsw.gov.au/testsafe/electrical/explosive-atmosphere/increased-safety. Accessed 26 Feb 2023
8. Bouguera, T., Diouris, J.-F., Chaillout, J.-J., Jaouadi, R., Andrieux, G.: Energy consumption model for sensor nodes based on LoRa and LoRaWAN. Sensors 18, 2104 (2018)
9. Rajab, H., Cinkler, T., Bouguera, T.: Evaluation of Energy Consumption of LPWAN Technologies, available at Research Square (2021). https://doi.org/10.21203/rs.3.rs-343897/v1
10. Ensworth, J.F., Reynolds, M.S.: BLE-backscatter: ultralow-power IoT nodes compatible with Bluetooth 4.0 low energy (BLE) smartphones and tablets. IEEE Trans. Microwave Theory Tech. 65(9), 3360–3368 (2017)
11. ESP32-WROOM-32 Datasheet. https://cdn-shop.adafruit.com/product-files/3320/3320_module_datasheet.pdf. Accessed 25 Feb 2023
12. ESP32 Series Datasheet. https://www.espressif.com/sites/default/files/documentation/esp32_datasheet_en.pdf. Accessed 25 Feb 2023
13. LoRaWAN module SimTech SX1268 Factsheet. https://www.semtech.com/products/wireless-rf/lora-connect/sx1268. Accessed 25 Feb 2023
14. SimCom SIM800H module resource page. https://datasheetspdf.com/pdf/823439/SIMCom/SIM800H/1
15. FreeRTOS resource page. https://www.freertos.org/. Accessed 26 Feb 2023
16. Banguero, E., Correcher, A., Pérez-Navarro, Á., Morant, F., Aristizabal, A.: A review on battery charging and discharging control strategies: application to renewable energy systems. Energies 11(4), 1021 (2018)
17. Bose, B., Garg, A., Panigrahi, B.K., Kim, J.: Study on Li-ion battery fast charging strategies: review, challenges and proposed charging framework. J. Energy Storage 55, 105507 (2022)
18. Krishna, G., Singh, R., Gehlot, A., Akram, S.V., Priyadarshi, N., Twala, B.: Digital technology implementation in battery-management systems for sustainable energy storage: review, challenges, and recommendations. Electronics 11(17), 2695 (2022)
19. Battery Management System Market Research Report: By Battery Type, Connectivity, Topology, Vertical—Global Industry Analysis and Forecast to 2030—Global Industry Analysis and Demand Forecast to 2030

subMFL: Compatible subModel Generation for Federated Learning in Device Heterogeneous Environment

Zeyneddin Oz[1]([✉]) [iD], Ceylan Soygul Oz[3] [iD], Abdollah Malekjafarian[2] [iD],
Nima Afraz[1] [iD], and Fatemeh Golpayegani[1] [iD]

[1] School of Computer Science, University College Dublin, Belfield, Dublin, Ireland
`zeyneddin.oz@ucdconnect.ie`
[2] School of Civil Engineering, University College Dublin, Belfield, Dublin, Ireland
[3] DOCOsoft, NexusUCD, Belfield Office Park, Dublin, Ireland

Abstract. Federated Learning (FL) is commonly used in systems with distributed and heterogeneous devices with access to varying amounts of data and diverse computing and storage capacities. FL training process enables such devices to update the weights of a shared model locally using their local data and then a trusted central server combines all of those models to generate a global model. In this way, a global model is generated while the data remains local to devices to preserve privacy. However, training large models such as Deep Neural Networks (DNNs) on resource-constrained devices can take a prohibitively long time and consume a large amount of energy. In the current process, the low-capacity devices are excluded from the training process, although they might have access to unseen data. To overcome this challenge, we propose a model compression approach that enables heterogeneous devices with varying computing capacities to participate in the FL process. In our approach, the server shares a dense model with all devices to train it: Afterwards, the trained model is gradually compressed to obtain submodels with varying levels of sparsity to be used as suitable initial global models for resource-constrained devices that were not capable of train the first dense model. This results in an increased participation rate of resource-constrained devices while the transferred weights from the previous round of training are preserved. Our validation experiments show that despite reaching about 50% global sparsity, generated submodels maintain their accuracy while can be shared to increase participation by around 50%.

Keywords: Resource-constrained heterogeneous edge devices ·
Federated learning · Model pruning · Mobile edge devices

1 Introduction

1.1 Background

The widespread use of smart devices like smartphones, tablets, and Internet of Things (IoT) devices of various sizes and purposes, is driving the progress of

The original version of this chapter was previously published without open access. A correction to this chapter is available at
https://doi.org/10.1007/978-3-031-48803-0_41

D. Zeinalipour et al. (Eds.): Euro-Par 2023 Workshops, LNCS 14352, pp. 52–64, 2024.
https://doi.org/10.1007/978-3-031-48803-0_5

services in smart environments, including smart cities, intelligent transport systems and infrastructure [1–3]. Furthermore, the massive quantity of edge devices is expected to generate extensive data requiring processing and analysis through automated methods. Machine learning can fuel the emergence of novel applications in smart environments by using those data [4]. Smart cities and their associated services such as intelligent traffic management, waste management, surveillance, and infrastructure monitoring are examples of such environments.

The exponential growth of generated data by IoT and mobile devices, along with demands for low latency computation, privacy, and scalability, drives the shift to edge computing. This approach enhances model training by placing computation nearer the data source hence reducing the data transmission latency. However, edge devices (i.e., edge nodes) often have limited computation power, storage, and energy capacity, making it challenging to run computationally intensive applications, mainly when a large amount of data must be processed [5].

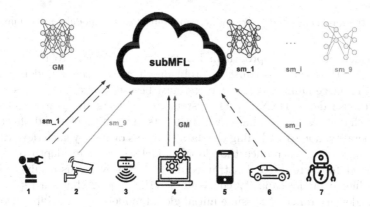

Fig. 1. A representation of subMFL working with a dense global model (GM) and generated submodels ($SM = [sm_1, sm_2, ..., sm_9]$).

Distributed machine learning refers to multi-node machine learning algorithms and systems that are designed to improve performance, increase accuracy, and scale to larger input data sizes [6]. Powerful parallel and distributed computing systems have recently become widely accessible in multi-core processors and cloud computing platforms that are applicable to problems traditionally addressed by centralised and sequential approaches [7]. Standard distributed learning involves training Deep Neural Networks (DNNs) on cloud servers and deploying them to edge nodes. However, this will not perform well for applications needing low latency, privacy, and scalability. Centralized model training demands data sharing, however, this may discourage data owners from granting access to their data for the purpose of model training.

In such a setting, machine learning models must be trained either at the same nodes that generate them (also can be defined as an agent, client, worker or device) or at a set of intermediate nodes, each collecting a subset of the data. Federated Learning (FL) [8] enables distributed machine learning across a large number of devices without requiring them to share their data with a central server. Once the devices train their local model using the devices' local model parameters it is returned to the central servers to be aggregated with other submodels and get distributed to all devices. A key challenge in deploying FL is the vast heterogeneity of devices [9], ranging from low-end IoT e.g., humidity sensors to mobile devices, as shown in Fig. 1, each having access to various types and amounts of data and hardware.

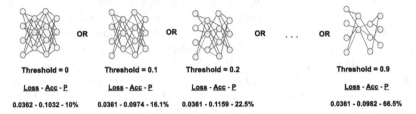

Fig. 2. Standard Federated Learning system's initial global models' performance.

The widely accepted approach in FL requires all devices to use the same global model. However, this causes a problem when large-scale models such as DNNs with a large number of parameters must be used by resource-constrained devices. To use dense DNNs in FL systems, developers frequently choose to exclude such devices from training, which results in training bias and affects the model generality, due to excluding the data that was owned by such devices [10]. Another approach is to reduce the global model's size by its depth or width, to accommodate the resource-constrained devices. However, this results in lower accuracy due to model capacity constraints [11]. Figure 2 shows a representation of the density range of possible initial global models by the width (dropped neurons or links) that own randomly generated weights in the Standard Federated Learning (S-FL). Picking one of the models arbitrarily as a global model to share with all devices to train leads to a tradeoff between participation rate and model learning constraints, due to the size of the selected model. While randomised model selection leads to this issue, DNNs pruning has the potential to generate sparse and suitable models. For instance, to utilise in FL, this compression technique is proposed to generate purposefully sparse models to address challenges such as communication overhead [12], data heterogeneity [13], and inclusion of heterogenous devices [14].

1.2 Related Works

Looking at the literature in more detail, FedSCR [12] reduces upstream communication by clustering parameter update patterns and using sparsity through structure-based pruning. Hermes [15] uses structured pruning to find small subnetworks on each device, and only updates from these subnetworks are communicated, improving communication and inference efficiency. AdaptCL [16] sends different stage pruned models to each device to synchronize the FL process in a heterogeneous environment and converge device update response times.

To address data heterogeneity, some methods cluster devices based on parameters and aggregate each cluster's parameters separately [13]. In [17] a custom pruning was introduced that maximizes the coverage index via utilising a local pruning mask, considering both pruning-induced errors and the minimum coverage index, instead of solely preserving the largest parameters.

Considering the pruning in terms of device heterogeneity, in PruneFL [18], first an initial device is selected to prune the initial global model, and then further pruning involves both the server and devices during the FL process. Thus, a good starting point can be found for the FL process involving all devices. In [19], before the FL process, it is suggested to run local dataset-aware pruning, in order to achieve device-related models. In [20], it is proposed that during FL training, the server determines a pruning ratio and allocates wireless resources adaptively. Then, a threshold-based device selection strategy is used to further improve the learning performance. The approach of FedPrune [21] is to send randomly different sub-models to devices from the server side to find the optimum sub-model. FedMP [22] enables each device to avoid training the entire global model by determining specific pruning ratios. In FjORD [14], system diversity is considered and the same model size is not shared to all devices, instead, the model size is tailored to the devices.

1.3 Motivations and Contributions

There have been works investigating the implementation of DNNs pruning in FL. However, there is a need for determining a specific pruning ratio or the computation cost of the pruning process is left to the device side in existing studies that address device heterogeneity. This results in extra energy costs until finding the optimum trainable model architecture due to over pruning process on such resource-constrained devices.

In this paper, we focus on developing a novel model that enables heterogeneous devices to participate in the FL process by proposing a Compatible subModel Generation in FL (subMFL). subMFL aims to produce suitable submodels considering their initial accuracy despite their smaller size, instead of randomly generated smaller models in S-FL. In this model, an initial dense Global Model (GM) with low learning constraints is shared with all devices and it is trained by devices with enough resources. When training is completed, the model is pruned dataless to generate compatible submodels to be used by resource-constrained devices, without a need for prior knowledge of their computation and communication capabilities or determining a specific pruning ratio. For evaluation purposes, different threshold values are used to generate submodels with different sparsity levels. The accuracy of models and the level of participation of devices for each set are then reported. Our main contributions in this paper are as follows:

- **Server-side model pruning:** The over-pruning process on the device side leads to extra energy loss. In our work, the pruning stage is completely carried to the server without the need for any data sample.

– **Compatible subModels generation:** By assuring that the trained dense model's weights are transferred to generated submodels, resource-constrained devices benefit from the data used to train GM by beginning to train a model with satisfactory accuracy.
– **Increased heterogeneous devices participation rate:** subMFL tailors the FL paradigm, for environments that include heterogeneous devices with various levels of computational resources by assigning suitable pre-trained and compressed initial global models that fit their resources (Fig. 1).

2   Compatible SubModel Generation in Federated Learning

In this paper, we propose a Compatible subModel Generation model to enhance Federated Learning (subMFL) in environments with heterogeneous resource constraint devices with varying computational capacities. subMFL uses pruning to generate a set of compatible sparsed submodels using a trained dense Global Model (GM). Those will be initial global model architectures with suitable size that allows resource-constrained devices to join in the upcoming training cycles.

Algorithm 1. subMFL: Compatible subModel Generation in Federated Learning

---

1: Server generates GM architecture
2: $W_{GM} = $ TRAINMODELONDEVICES(W_{GM}, D, T)
3: $SM = $ GENERATESUBMODELS(W_{GM})
4: **for** each W_{sm_i} in SM **do**
5:    $D = $ DROPDEVICES(W_{sm_i}, D)
6:    $W_{sm_i} = $ TRAINMODELONDEVICES(W_{sm_i}, D, T)
7: **end for**

---

subMFL Flow: Algorithm 1 shows the overall flow of subMFL. The stages are: A dense global model is generated in the server and distributed to all devices to be trained (T represents the global training round and we set it as 100 in our simulation. $W = [w_0, w_1, \ldots, w_n]$, $0 \leq w_i \leq 1$ for $0 \leq i \leq n$ represents weights and W_{GM} are weights of GM). GM is trained with capable devices and then a set of sparsed submodels ($SM = [sm_1, sm_2, \ldots, sm_9]$) is generated by pruning this GM using different threshold values. Afterwards, SM will be sent to all devices starting from the densest to the sparsest submodel, and each device chooses to train the densest compatible submodel based on its computational resources. At each step, the devices themself make a decision to join the next round based on their local model accuracy. Devices that reach their preferred accuracy exit the training process, and the next submodel is not shared with them. We represent devices with $D = [d_1, d_2, \ldots, d_{1000}]$ and in line 5, we update this device set based on their preference. Thus, such devices do not consume further energy when the target accuracy is reached. Each component of subMFL is as follows:

Training: Algorithm 2 shows the training procedure we used, which is the process in standard federated learning (S-FL). Weights of the current global model are shared with D to train with T global round. At each round, local models (W_{LMs}^t) are collected and aggregated, to update the global model with new weights. Then, this updated W_{GM} are shared with D to be updated again with their local datasets. In device heterogeneous environments, each device needs a different amount of time to complete its local training which causes synchronisation issues. On the other hand, in subMFL, devices that are slow to train the current model already cannot send local updates, however, the model is trained with higher capacity devices. Including GM, there is SM that will be trained and at each step of distributing a sparser submodel, devices that have near resource capacity train the distributed model, which leads the server to receive local models synchronously. In this way, we do not need pre-information about the devices' computation capacity or determine a specific pruning ratio.

Algorithm 2. Training Process:

1: **function** TRAINMODELONDEVICES(W_M, D, T)
2:     **for** each round $t = 1, 2, \ldots, T$ **do**
3:         Server shares W_M^t with devices D
4:         Server receives W_{LMs}^t from devices D
5:         W_M^t = ModelAggregate(W_{LMs}^t) with FedAvg
6:     **end for**
7:     **return** W_M^t
8: **end function**

For the aggregation process, we use the FedAvg algorithm [23], which is an advanced aggregation strategy that has the benefits of convergence guarantees. This algorithm will be updated according to the current SM architecture.

Algorithm 3. Generating SubModels:

1: **function** GENERATESUBMODELS(W_{GM})
2:     $Threshold = 0$
3:     $SM = []$
4:     **while** $Threshold < 1$ **do**
5:         $Threshold = Threshold + 0.1$
6:         **for** each w_i in W_{GM} **do**
7:             **if** $w_i < Threshold$ **then**
8:                 $w_i = 0$
9:             **end if**
10:        **end for**
11:        Add W_{GM} to SM
12:    **end while**
13:    **return** SM
14: **end function**

Generating SubModels: DNNs pruning is used to generate the SM from the GM to be distributed to the resource-constrained devices. This will increase the participation of the heterogeneous devices that could not take part in the training process due to having a more limited resource capacity. In FL, due to security and privacy concerns, the server is unable to see any data sample which makes it unsuitable to prune DNNs on the server side with the majority of pruning methods. For this reason, we utilised a dataless pruning method on the server side, which is critical for real-world applications. In this way, all pruning processes are carried out at the server to decrease energy usage in resource-constrained devices. Also, we used an unstructured pruning strategy based on the L1-norm, due to its independence from network configuration [24].

Algorithm 3 shows submodels generation, where a *Threshold* variable that ranges from 0 to 0.9, increasing 0.1 each time is defined for pruning the GM. In this process, the weights of the GM are below the selected threshold will be set to 0. The remaining weights will be transferred from the current global model to the newly pruned submodel. Since the threshold is incremented by 0.1, GM produces 9 different submodels ($sm_i \in SM$) with various sparsification ratios. As shown in Fig. 3, GM (see the red model) is the dense model and SM (see the blue models) is generated using the pruned version of the trained GM.

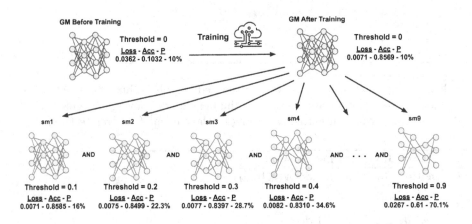

Fig. 3. Loss, Accuracy and Participation performance of SM using MNIST.

Dropping Devices: When devices reach their target accuracy they don't train the next SM (Fig. 1 represents the scenario, device-5 trains one of sm_i, but doesn't attend to train sm_9). For this reason, the server shares the next densest model only with devices that join the training. Algorithm 4 shows how the server updates D, which includes the devices that join the training. In line 3, $d_{jTargetMinAcc}$ shows minimum target accuracy for the device d. Following this approach, we reduce energy usage by omitting devices that reached the target.

Algorithm 4. Dropping Devices:

1: **function** DropDevices(W_{sm_i}, D)
2:     **for** each device d_j in D **do**
3:         **if** $d_{jTargetMinAcc} \leq sm_{iAcc}$ **then**
4:             Remove d_j from D
5:         **end if**
6:     **end for**
7:     **return** D
8: **end function**

As a result, instead of picking a random global model architecture generated with random weights as shown in Fig. 2, trained GM can produce SM, and then those SM can be shared to train with resource-constrained devices as sparser global models. In our approach, even though the next global models become smaller and have learning constraints due to compression, unlike S-FL, it keeps transferred weights from devices trained GM and benefits from their unseen data. Thus, GM is tuned to the available resource of devices, and devices can pick a sm_i. This way, resource-constrained devices aren't excluded from training.

3   Experiment

We used 1000 devices and shared data randomly with an equal sample size. 10% of devices can train the dense global model (GM) and the remaining devices that have lower computational capacity train one of sm_i.

Datasets: Following the literature in this area, we used LeNet-5 [25] architecture with MNIST [26] and FMNIST [27] datasets which are used for image recognition tasks. While MNIST is a dataset of handwritten digits, FMNIST is a dataset of images depicting various clothing items.

Settings: We have performed the simulation using Pytorch [28] and Flower [29] framework. The global round is set to 100 and the local epoch is 3. The validation data percentage is 10 and the batch size is 64. We used Adam [30] optimiser with a 0.001 learning rate. The remaining parameters are as follow: betas = (0.9, 0.999), eps = 1e−08, weight decay = 0, amsgrad = False, foreach = None, maximize = False, capturable = False, "min fit clients" and "min eval clients" = 3.

Availability: In real-life scenarios, it is unlikely to receive parameters from all devices in every round due to factors such as mobility, low energy, and connection issues. Therefore, we assumed that only 30% of devices are available. If this number is decreased, the convergence time of GM increases.

Baseline: We used standard Federated Learning (S-FL) as our baseline.

Evaluation Metrics: Our evaluation metrics include accuracy (Acc), loss (Loss), participation number (P), and global sparsity (GS) of S-FL and subMFL. Server-side threshold-based model pruning is used to generate SM. For instance, when the threshold is set as 0.1, parameters of GM under 0.1 are reduced to 0, to generate the first submodel. To generate sparser submodels, the threshold increases until 0.9. By increasing the threshold, submodels become sparser, reducing computational cost and increasing the number of participating devices. We analyse metrics based on different threshold values and compare the results of subMFL generated SM with sparse models in S-FL using the same thresholds. The code of this work is publicly available at: https://github.com/zeyneddinoz/subMFL.

3.1   Results

Table 1. Metrics values based on thresholds for MNIST dataset.

	T	S-FL Acc	subMFL Acc	S-FL Loss	subMFL Loss	S-FL P	subMFL P	S-FL GS	subMFL GS
GM	0.0	0.1032	0.1032	0.0362	0.0362	100	100	0.0	0.0
$sm1$	0.1	0.0974	0.8585	0.0361	0.0071	161	160	6.19	6.05
$sm2$	0.2	0.1159	0.8499	0.0361	0.0075	225	223	12.57	12.38
$sm3$	0.3	0.0935	0.8397	0.0361	0.0077	284	287	18.48	18.70
$sm4$	0.4	0.1133	0.8310	0.0361	0.0082	353	346	25.39	24.66
$sm5$	0.5	0.1135	0.8301	0.0361	0.0084	423	410	32.34	31.09
$sm6$	0.6	0.0986	0.8422	0.0361	0.0081	478	475	37.83	37.56
$sm7$	0.7	0.0823	0.8472	0.0361	0.0084	551	536	45.18	43.61
$sm8$	0.8	0.0892	0.8380	0.0362	0.0110	614	607	51.40	50.78
$sm9$	0.9	0.0982	0.6169	0.0361	0.0267	665	701	56.56	60.13

Table 1 reports the results we obtained from different thresholds (T, e.g. 0.1 to 0.9) to generate 9 different submodels ($sm_i \in SM$, see Fig. 3) which includes accuracy, loss, number of participating devices (P) and global sparsity (GS) on generated models. To compare with S-FL, we picked models with different sparsification levels based on the same threshold values as shown in Fig. 2. In our experiments, the pruning method increases the sparsification of trained GM significantly, while maintaining good accuracy in subMFL. Parallel to the increased model sparsity, the number of participating devices increases.

Accuracy vs Global Sparsity: As shown in Fig. 4-a and Fig. 4-c, the results show that when the threshold value is incremented global sparsity increases. However, independent from the sparsification of models, S-FL accuracy remains around 10%, due to picked models always starting with randomly generated weights. On the other hand, in the beginning, the dense global model (GM) accuracy is the same as in S-FL, however, after training GM, generated submodels (SM) accuracy values are high. Thus, although the global model was sparsed, the transferred weights from previous training allowed the model to maintain a good level of accuracy. For instance, even though when global sparsity increases by around 50%, the accuracy decreases by only about 2% for the MNIST dataset. For the same condition, the accuracy percentage decreases approximately by 10, for the FMNIST dataset.

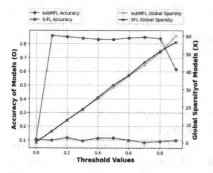
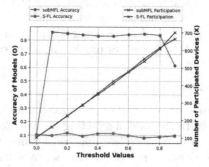

(a) Accuracy vs Global Sparsity Percentage with MNIST benchmark.

(b) Accuracy vs Number of Participating Devices with MNIST benchmark.

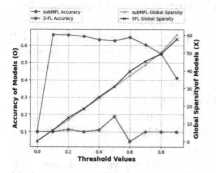
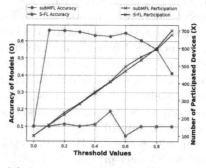

(c) Accuracy vs Global Sparsity Percentage with FMNIST benchmark.

(d) Accuracy vs Number of Participating Devices with FMNIST benchmark.

Fig. 4. Accuracy vs Global Sparsity and Accuracy vs Participation.

Accuracy vs Participation: As a result of compression, resource-constrained devices can train compressed submodels, and the participation number increases (see Fig. 4-b and Fig. 4-d). The percentage of models' global sparsity increases the participation rate in parallel and both S-FL and subMFL have similar results. However, newly attended devices start to train a more accurate global model. For instance, the number of devices participating in the FL system increases by nearly 60% for both S-FL and subMFL. However, due to transferred weights from GM, SM shows good accuracy performance even before training. For the MNIST dataset, accuracy remains around 83%, until the $Threshold$ value reaches 0.8. For the FMNIST dataset, the accuracy maintains higher than 60%, until the $Threshold$ value reaches 0.7.

Comparing participation performance, assume that a middle-level sparse model is selected as a global model in S-FL. All devices will start to train a model with Threshold = 0.5 and random weights. Based on Fig. 4-b and Fig. 4-d, participation of devices will be under 45% and higher computation capacity devices will train a model with higher learning constraints, in order to accommodate resource-constrained devices. On the other hand, subMFL provides each device to train and own optimal models by sharing sparse models in descending order. Those shared models are SM generated by a pre-trained GM which results in good accuracy, despite being compressed models. Figure 4-b and Fig. 4-d show that subMFL increases participation up to 70%.

3.2   Discussion

Resource-constrained devices need smaller models to train and share their local models. In the case of selecting a small global model to share on the server side, due to the model's learning constraints, the model cannot generalise patterns in datasets. In the other case when a large global model is shared, resource-constrained devices are unable to train the model, due to computational capacity. This leads to bias in trained models and affects performance negatively.

To provide dense DNNs to edge devices in heterogeneous environments, a flexible method should be utilised. State-of-the-art practice involves model pruning to compress these models for resource-limited devices. However, when the model pruning process is left to the device side, it results in extra energy consumption while they need to train their own local models. For this reason, it is necessary to generate methods to increase the heterogeneous device participation rate while pruning models on the server side. In this paper, we addressed this issue by serving compatible submodels to resource-constrained devices.

To sum up, only 10% of data is utilised to train GM due to 10% of devices being capable to train it. However, results show that it is possible to generate compatible SM via pruning GM with different threshold values. Those SM can be shared with resource-constrained devices as new global models to train. Thus, the number of participating devices increases, and since SM owns tuned parameters from trained GM, those SM start with good accuracy.

The core idea of our work is to show that instead of selecting a random global model with a performance of around 10% accuracy and distributing it to train (the S-FL approach), starting to train a dense global model and then pruning it to generate submodels is a useful approach, due to transferred pre-trained weights result in compressed submodels with a good accuracy performance. Even though new training rounds begin, those submodels can be served to resource-constrained devices that need to participate with a reasonable starting accuracy. Thus, at the end of the process, each device owns the optimal trainable model.

4   Conclusion and Future Works

In this paper, we proposed subMFL which is a submodel generation technique using model pruning to increase the participation of heterogeneous devices for federated learning. This is done without a need for prior information on devices' hardware/computing capabilities or determining a specific pruning ratio. In our approach, a dense model is distributed to all devices in the system for training. Then, the trained model is pruned gradually in the server without the need for a data sample, so as to generate a set of submodels. Those submodels are shared with resource-constrained devices to train as compatible sparsed models to raise participation numbers. Also, since sparsed submodels hold tuned weights from the trained dense model, they have satisfactory accuracy even before training, despite being compressed.

Future work could address more in-depth theoretical research regarding improving submodels used as global models that are trained with different device groups by combining their parameters to increase models' generality. Additionally, advanced compression methods can be used to reduce communication overhead in addition to tackling device heterogeneity.

Acknowledgment. This project has received funding from RE-ROUTE Project, the European Union's Horizon Europe research and innovation programme under the Marie Skłodowska-Curie grant agreement No 101086343.

References

1. Golpayegani, F., Ghanadbashi, S., Riad, M.: Urban emergency management using intelligent traffic systems: challenges and future directions. In: 2021 IEEE International Smart Cities Conference (ISC2), pp. 1–4. IEEE (2021)
2. Ghanadbashi, S., Golpayegani, F.: An ontology-based intelligent traffic signal control model. In: 2021 IEEE International Intelligent Transportation Systems Conference (ITSC), pp. 2554–2561. IEEE (2021)
3. Malekjafarian, A., Golpayegani, F., Moloney, C., Clarke, S.: A machine learning approach to bridge-damage detection using responses measured on a passing vehicle. Sensors **19**(18), 4035 (2019)
4. Lv, Z., Chen, D., Lou, R., Wang, Q.: Intelligent edge computing based on machine learning for smart city. Futur. Gener. Comput. Syst. **115**, 90–99 (2021)
5. Safavifar, Z., Ghanadbashi, S., Golpayegani, F.: Adaptive workload orchestration in pure edge computing: a reinforcement-learning model. In: 2021 IEEE 33rd International Conference on Tools with Artificial Intelligence (ICTAI), pp. 856–860. IEEE (2021)
6. Galakatos, A., Crotty, A., Kraska, T.: Distributed machine learning (2018)
7. Peteiro-Barral, D., Guijarro-Berdiñas, B.: A survey of methods for distributed machine learning. Prog. Artif. Intell. **2**, 1–11 (2013)
8. McMahan, H.B., Moore, E., Ramage, D., y Arcas, B.A.: Federated learning of deep networks using model averaging. arXiv preprint arXiv:1602.05629 2, 2 (2016)
9. Li, T., Sahu, A.K., Talwalkar, A., Smith, V.: Federated learning: challenges, methods, and future directions. IEEE Signal Process. Mag. **37**(3), 50–60 (2020)
10. Kairouz, P., et al.: Advances and open problems in federated learning. Foundations and Trends in Machine Learning (2021)
11. Caldas, S., Konečny, J., McMahan, H.B., Talwalkar, A.: Expanding the reach of federated learning by reducing client resource requirements. arXiv:1812.07210 (2018)

12. Wu, X., Yao, X., Wang, C.L.: FedSCR: structure-based communication reduction for federated learning. IEEE Trans. Parallel Distrib. Syst. **32**(7), 1565–1577 (2020)
13. Vahidian, S., Morafah, M., Lin, B.: Personalized federated learning by structured and unstructured pruning under data heterogeneity. In: 2021 IEEE 41st International Conference on Distributed Computing Systems Workshops (ICDCSW) (2021)
14. Horvath, S., Laskaridis, S., Almeida, M., Leontiadis, I., Venieris, S., Lane, N.: FjORD: fair and accurate federated learning under heterogeneous targets with ordered dropout. In: Advances in Neural Information Processing Systems, vol. 34 (2021)
15. Li, A., Sun, J., Li, P., Pu, Y., Li, H., Chen, Y.: Hermes: an efficient federated learning framework for heterogeneous mobile clients. In: Proceedings of the 27th Annual International Conference on Mobile Computing and Networking, pp. 420–437 (2021)
16. Zhou, G., Xu, K., Li, Q., Liu, Y., Zhao, Y.: AdaptCL: efficient collaborative learning with dynamic and adaptive pruning. arXiv preprint arXiv:2106.14126 (2021)
17. Zhou, H., Lan, T., Venkataramani, G., Ding, W.: On the convergence of heterogeneous federated learning with arbitrary adaptive online model pruning. arXiv preprint arXiv:2201.11803 (2022)
18. Jiang, Y., et al.: Model pruning enables efficient federated learning on edge devices. IEEE Trans. Neural Networks Learn. Syst. **34**(12), 10374–10386 (2022)
19. Yu, S., Nguyen, P., Anwar, A., Jannesari, A.: Adaptive dynamic pruning for Non-IID federated learning. arXiv preprint arXiv:2106.06921 (2021)
20. Liu, S., Yu, G., Yin, R., Yuan, J., Shen, L., Liu, C.: Joint model pruning and device selection for communication-efficient federated edge learning. IEEE Trans. Commun. **70**(1), 231–244 (2021)
21. Munir, M.T., Saeed, M.M., Ali, M., Qazi, Z.A., Qazi, I.A.: FedPrune: towards inclusive federated learning. arXiv preprint arXiv:2110.14205 (2021)
22. Jiang, Z., Xu, Y., Xu, H., Wang, Z., Qiao, C., Zhao, Y.: FedMP: federated learning through adaptive model pruning in heterogeneous edge computing. In: 2022 IEEE 38th International Conference on Data Engineering (ICDE), pp. 767–779 (2022)
23. McMahan, B., Moore, E., Ramage, D., Hampson, S., y Arcas, B.A.: Communication-efficient learning of deep networks from decentralized data. In: Artificial Intelligence and Statistics, pp. 1273–1282. PMLR (2017)
24. Anwar, S., Hwang, K., Sung, W.: Structured pruning of deep convolutional neural networks. ACM J. Emerg. Technol. Comput. Syst. (JETC) **13**(3), 1–18 (2017)
25. LeCun, Y., Bottou, L., Bengio, Y., Haffner, P.: Gradient-based learning applied to document recognition. Proc. IEEE **86**(11), 2278–2324 (1998)
26. LeCun, Y.: The MNIST database of handwritten digits (1998). http://yann.lecun.com/exdb/mnist/
27. Xiao, H., Rasul, K., Vollgraf, R.: Fashion-MNIST: a novel image dataset for benchmarking machine learning algorithms. arXiv preprint arXiv:1708.07747 (2017)
28. Paszke, A., et al.: PyTorch: an imperative style, high-performance deep learning library. In: Advances in Neural Information Processing Systems, vol. 32 (2019)
29. Beutel, D.J., et al.: Flower: a friendly federated learning research framework. arXiv preprint arXiv:2007.14390 (2020)
30. Kingma, D.P., Ba, J.: Adam: a method for stochastic optimization. arXiv preprint arXiv:1412.6980 (2014)

Towards a Simulation as a Service Platform for the Cloud-to-Things Continuum

Wilson Valdez[1]([⊠]) , Hamza Baniata[1,2] , Andras Markus[1] ,
and Attila Kertesz[1,2]

[1] University of Szeged, Dugonics ter 13, Szeged 6720, Hungary
{wilson,baniatah,markusa,keratt}@inf.u-szeged.hu
[2] FrontEndArt Software Limited, Somogyi u. 13, Szeged 6720, Hungary

Abstract. In the past years, we have seen an unprecedented pace of technological development in smart applications. Smart Systems incorporate securely connected sensors, actuators, and data processing resources to provide digital services. They provide a wide range of smart applications using emerging technologies that address governmental or industrial processes or citizen life in smart cities, and many of them have been affected by the COVID-19 pandemic which involved a general lack of trust. Integrating Blockchain-based data management into smart systems can enhance the performance, trust, and privacy of their applications, which are getting more and more crucial. In this paper, we propose a vision for a unified Simulation as a Service platform, which will be able to model and investigate Blockchain-based smart systems exploiting IoT, Fog, and Cloud Computing infrastructures.

Keywords: Simulation · Blockchain · Internet of Things · Fog Computing · Cloud Computing

1 Introduction

The Cloud Computing (CC) paradigm provides on-demand access to computing resources such as processing power, storage, and applications over the Internet. It has revolutionized the way organizations manage their Information Technology (IT) infrastructure by offering several advantages, including scalability, flexibility, cost savings, and reduced IT complexity. The adoption of CC is expected to continue to grow, driven by the increasing demand for digital services, the need for agility and cost savings, as well as the rise and current development of paradigms such as the Internet of Things and Artificial Intelligence [1]. The

This work is partially supported by CERCIRAS COST Action CA19135 funded by the COST Association, and by the national project TKP2021-NVA-09 implemented with the support provided by the Ministry of Innovation and Technology of Hungary from the National Research, Development and Innovation Fund.

D. Zeinalipour et al. (Eds.): Euro-Par 2023 Workshops, LNCS 14352, pp. 65–75, 2024.
https://doi.org/10.1007/978-3-031-48803-0_6

Internet of Things (IoT) is a global IT infrastructure where physical and virtual objects, devices, and sensors collect and exchange data interconnected through the Internet by using standard communication protocols. Currently, the number of connected IoT devices has reached 21.8 billion in 2021 (projected to be 31 billion in 2025) [2]. Hence, the vast data volume produced by these devices can overwhelm and strain cloud resources, impacting IoT application performance. To tackle this issue, the Fog Computing (FC) paradigm has emerged as a solution that enhances IoT applications by bringing cloud resources closer to devices, reducing network latency, and enhancing response time [3].

There is still an unprecedented pace of technological developments in smart systems. A Smart System (SS) incorporates the processes and functions of sensing, actuation, and control to describe and analyze a situation, and to make decisions based on the available data in a predictive or adaptive manner, thereby performing smart actions [4]. Smart devices or things are fundamental components of a SS generally connected to other devices or networks via different wireless protocols. They can operate to some extent interactively and autonomously, which has been standardized to some extent by the IoT paradigm. SSs address environmental, societal, and economic challenges like limited resources, climate change, population aging, and globalization. As a result, they are increasingly used in a large number of sectors, such as transportation, healthcare, energy, security, logistics, ICT, and manufacturing. SSs can also be categorized via regions by referring to smart homes for smaller, and smart cities for larger areas.

Artificial Intelligence (AI) is the ability of machines to learn from data and perform tasks that would typically require human intelligence [5]. AI plays a crucial role in automating tasks, optimizing performance, improving user experiences, and driving innovation and growth in industries, particularly in the context of CC and IoT. CC provides the necessary infrastructure for storing and processing large datasets, essential for training AI models. IoT devices generate vast amounts of data that can be leveraged to enhance AI models and enable intelligent decision-making. Machine Learning (ML) is a key component of AI, allowing machines to learn from data and improve performance over time. ML encompasses different types, including supervised, unsupervised, and reinforcement learning, which find applications in various domains [6]. Nevertheless, solutions applying ML in Smart Systems (SS) exploiting IoT, CC, and FC, might suffer from its centralized data management scheme for model training, which can be problematic due to the network saturation generated by the huge amount of data, as well as data sources heterogeneity, and data criticism, which lead to problems such as data sharing [7].

Federated Learning (FL) paradigm emerges to enable ML on distributed data by moving the training process to the data instead of moving the data to the training location. FL enables the global model generation that can be distributed to nodes, which then train their data with the same model [8]. This approach circumvents the necessity of transferring extensive data to a centralized location, mitigating privacy concerns and data breach risks. FL facilitates ML model training on distributed data across numerous devices or networks, making it highly advantageous for IoT, FC, and Edge Computing (EC). Using

FL, organizations can improve their ML model's accuracy, and minimize the associated with centralized data storage, security, privacy, and processing [9].

Blockchain (BC) is the base technology of currently available cryptocurrency systems, which was first introduced by S. Nakamoto [10], as an underlying technology that guarantees a trusted, fully distributed, digital money system. A BC system is basically a distributed computing system that is able to store and process a Distributed Ledger (DL) in a Peer-to-Peer (P2P) network model. The reliable distributed decision-making mechanisms of the proposed BC network motivated their deployment on the distributed cloud servers and at the edge of the network. Different BC models were expected to strongly support CC during the life cycle of information processing and management in complex scenarios [11]. Specifically, computational power and immutable storage abilities were the two main properties that BC-CC integrated systems provide.

The integration of CC, IoT, FC, AI/FL, and BC technologies is widely argued to be the SS applications enabling factor. Such integration was proposed and realized in many novel research articles, e.g. [12], and industry-oriented projects provided by ICT leaders, e.g. IBM[1]. In these contributions, the development teams showcased how each integration indeed enhanced the SS application performance (e.g., latency, throughput, security, distributed consistency, decision accuracy, energy efficiency, and privacy) [13]. Indeed, without these technologies, SS application would have remained an unattainable theory.

However, those SS applications had to be tested and evaluated extensively in order to prove their reliability and out-performance compared to classical systems. In most cases, SS applications under construction were individually simulated using tools that were either specifically implemented for their specific targeted applications, or using tools that do not include all factors and elements of realized SS application. For example, simulation tools specifically developed for evaluating BCs were used on a side to individually evaluate the BC part of the implemented SS application. Meanwhile, different CC-IoT-FC tools were used to evaluate the Cloud-Edge part of the system.

In this position paper, we tackle this issue by introducing a SIMulation-as-a-Service (SIMaaS) framework that deploys CC, IoT, FC, AI, and BC technologies for reliable simulation of comprehensive SS applications. We have already developed two comprehensive simulation tools, namely FoBSim [14] and DISSICT-CF-Fog [15], which simulate many scenarios that are typically realized in BC and CC-IoT-Fog applications, respectively. In SIMaaS, our goal is to integrate these tools into a unified comprehensive framework for simulating BC-assisted Cloud-Edge SS applications. We aim to use AI technology to optimize the harmonization process and predict optimal configurations based on user-defined parameters. Also, we explore the integration of AI methods into deployed tools to enhance the generation of realistic emulation results.

The paper is structured as follows: Sect. 2 reviews the use and need of emerging technologies for Smart Systems, and Sect. 3 presents related simulation approaches. Section 4 introduces our main proposal for a simulation as a service approach, and finally Sect. 5 concludes the paper.

---

[1] https://www.ibm.com/topics/blockchain-ai.

2   State-of-the-Art in Using Emerging Technologies for Smart Systems

The vast amount of data generated by devices poses challenges for both centralized and decentralized computing systems within CC. While decentralization has helped to mitigate some of these challenges, technologies such as IoT, FC, ML, FL, and BC have addressed them significantly. The integration of these technologies has the potential to enhance the functioning of various application fields within Smart Systems, which leverage technology to improve efficiency, sustainability, and quality of life for residents. This section presents a discussion of some literature reviews and survey papers related to the integration of these technologies to enhance IoT solutions, with a special focus on FC, BC, and FL, and their capabilities and features.

Table 1. Literature reviews integrating IoT-BC-FC-FL technologies

Survey	Year	Aim	Weaknesses
Alzoubi et al. [16]	2022	Analyses the integration of BC and FC; establish seven areas for integrating them, and state some challenges.	Misses AI and FL in the analysis, as well as a discussion about simulation tools in the domain and smart systems applications, are not considered
Li et al. [17]	2022	Analyses and discuss privacy and security in the field of BC-based FL methodologies. Besides, technical taxonomy and classification of existing approaches and algorithms	Misses FC in the analysis. Besides, although discusses smart environments, the survey does not discuss the need for simulation tools for smart systems
Nguyen et al. [18]	2021	Analyses Mobile EC, FL, and BC. Introduces the term FLChain as the combination of BC and FL, and presents a complete taxonomy of FLCHain design and use cases.	While the survey analyses Mobile-EC, it misses FC. Moreover, the simulation needs are not stated
Nguyen et al. [19]	2021	Analyses IoT-FL integration with an emphasis on the roles of FL in IoT. It presents a standardization of FL-IoT Architecture. Analyses the application of FL in some IoT fields (i.e., smart cities, UAVs)	Misses BC as well as FC as part of the analysis. Besides, the simulation tools' needs are not stated beyond of analyze some application fields
Ali [20]	2021	Analyzes the integration of BC and FL. It describes privacy issues and techniques to solve them. The survey shows a taxonomy of architectures for FL-BC for IoT.	Misses FC as part of the analysis. Although discuss some usages, It also does not analyze smart systems applications as well as simulation tools

Table 1 summarizes six literature review studies in the last three years on the integration of the aforementioned technologies. In general, most of the solutions integrate these technologies in pairs, such as BC-FC, BC-FL, and FC-FL. These studies provide valuable taxonomies and insights into how to integrate these technologies in terms of architecture, applications, mechanisms, and algorithms, among others. However, studies also reveal that there are still open issues related to security, interoperability, scalability, heterogeneity, and distributed data management, as well as new potential applications and integration of IoT-BC-FC-FL. In general, these findings highlight the need for further research and development in integrating these paradigms. In addition, two important aspects must be considered. First, integrating these technologies (BC-FC-FL) is a promising research direction that requires further investigation. Second, the creation of simulation tools is necessary to test and customize SS applications, as well as to evaluate the performance of the integrated system in different scenarios.

3   Related Simulation Approaches

3.1   Blockchain Simulation

Generally, BC-based systems are designed and tested with reference to different layers, including Infrastructure (i.e., devices and equipment used to perform the BC computations, communications, and/or storage services), Data Layer (e.g., structures of shared data, encryption methods/mechanisms, storage frameworks/approaches, etc.). The Network Layer defines the connections among elements of the first layer, including technical aspects of the P2P communication protocols. The Consensus Layer represents the rules that network members must follow to maintain the security of the system. Additionally, this layer defines different conceptual types of system elements such as miners, users, servers, full nodes, light nodes, etc. The concrete definition of protocols and mechanisms of those layers should produce robust, application-oriented, and security-oriented BC-based systems. That is, a careful and accurate design process of those layers enables BC-based solutions that adhere to the initial applications' requirements. Accordingly, the Application layer defines the developed system interfaces, business and economic models, system monitoring tools, etc. Examples of applications where BC technology was found beneficial include IoT, SS, FC, Cryptocurrency applications, decentralized credential governance, NFTs, and many more.

As discussed by Smetanin et al. [21], BC-based systems can be evaluated, benchmarked, and validated either formally (e.g. Markov Chains, Queuing Theory), by emulation (e.g. Cloud-based, real testbeds), or by simulation (e.g. Block-Sim [22], FoBSim [14]). During the first design and implementation stages of these BC-based solutions, simulations play a pivotal role in the parameterization and configuration recommendations. This is because most BC simulation frameworks are open-source and freely available. However, most available simulators require sufficient programming skills, computing resources, runtime environments, and continuous reconfiguration to find the appropriate parameterization for a scenario. Furthermore, most of these simulators target a specific mechanism or a small portion of the BC network workflow. For example, all of these tools allow the simulation of one consensus algorithm, one application, or fixed/limited data structure templates.

To address those limitations, earlier we proposed FoBSim [14], an extensible and open-source simulation framework that allows to reliably mimic integrated BC-FC applications using five different consensus algorithms, four possible application templates, including cryptocurrency and smart contracts, and further allows to deploy the BC network in the fog or end-user layer without affecting any other parameters.

3.2   IoT-Fog-Cloud Simulation

Using simulation tools in order to validate and evaluate various algorithms and methodologies for Distributed Computing infrastructures is a common research practice, since they realistically mimic real computing systems, yet are affordable. With the emergence of IoT and FC, simulator requirements were expanded not just to model aspects of CC, but to simulate IoT-Fog-Cloud ecosystems in order to investigate the cooperation of the Cloud-to-Things Continuum. To accommodate this, certain simulators started their path as standalone cloud simulators, but later they were further developed towards IoT and/or fog modeling.

The requirements of a well-usable simulator include (but are not limited to) the following properties and capabilities [23]: (i) granularity of basic infrastructure modeling, including physical and virtual machines, containers, and IoT entities such as sensors and actuators; (ii) granularity of higher-level components such as network, energy, mobility, and cost modeling; (iii) support for processing types (i.e., batch and stream processing); (iv) methods for resource management (i.e., scheduling, offloading, and migration algorithms); (v) a graphical user interface for configuration and result analysis (occasionally with XML, JSON descriptions); and finally, (vi) availability of source code and appropriate code quality (including comments and code complexity) to facilitate the learning curve of the simulator.

IoT-Fog-Cloud simulators are typically (discrete) event-based, meaning that the simulation time and real-time are separated. Thus, events occur only at discrete (simulated) moments, where the inner state of the concrete simulation can change until it reaches the stopping condition. General-purpose simulators improve scalability by simplifying less relevant parts of the system and reducing granularity. These solutions focus on high-level components, supporting expandability, and the degradation of reliability is negligible. On the other hand, network simulators consider modeling detailed connections among the network components, including communication protocols, which may restrict extensibility and scalability.

With the emergence of FC, cloud-based research is still present and active, due to constantly emerging new technologies. OpenDC [24] provides simulation options for data centers with virtual machines and containers equipped with energy and cost meters, and it also addresses the latest trends in serverless computing, and supports modeling of ML-based TensorFlow workloads.

CloudSim is the most decisive simulator in the field of CC so far, therefore, numerous extensions are built upon it to broaden its capabilities for analyzing complex systems. For instance, the latest version of iFogSim, which follows expands the sense-process-actuate model and investigates application scheduling and dynamic resource provisioning in an IoT-Fog-Cloud environment, it expands its functionality with service migration and mobility, cluster formation involving the multi-layered topology, and microservice deployment, as well.

Besides, it is worth mentioning PureEdgeSim [25], which is not a direct extension of CloudSim, but CloudSim Plus, which is already an improved version of the original cloud simulator. This phenomenon also strengthens the lack of interoperability among the different code bases, since these versions are typically developed by different research groups. However, PureEdgeSim supports the integration of IoT with cloud and edge resources, resource management with task offloading decisions, and IoT devices with mobility functions.

To deal with the challenges of complex IoT-Fog-Cloud systems, we proposed the DISSECT-CF-Fog [15] by extending the DISSECT-CF cloud simulator. This simulation solution is independent of any CloudSim-base simulators, and its modular structure and own discrete event system make it competitive in research. It is able to utilize multi-layered Fog-Cloud architecture, and IoT sensors and actuators. Its application model is based on virtual machines, but it supports both batch- and stream-processing-based simulations. It also supports pricing schemes for real providers, energy measurements, and device mobility. Offloading algorithms ensure optimal resource management. However, support of blockchain-based evaluation is missing; DISSECT-CF-Fog's abilities make it a perfect choice for our proposed Simulation as a Service platform.

4   The Proposed Simulation as a Service Platform

Building on our previously proposed simulator solutions, we aim to create a comprehensive simulation environment that is capable of evaluating integrated SSs. Figure 1 depicts our envisioned SIMaaS framework, which will be able to simulate and analyze blockchain-based smart systems. The current version of DISSECT-CF-Fog can model application executions at three main layers, namely cloud, fog, and end-user layers, while FoBSim handles the end-user and fog layers. Users of SIMaaS can provide requirements of the smart applications with various parameters they plan to develop. Once the application requirements are given through the GUI of SIMaaS, they are converted to a unified description format, and the Parameter Classifier is triggered to extend and fine-tune the given parameters. It will also use machine learning algorithms with possible pre-analysis executions of the simulators for fine-tuning. First, FoBSim will be used to determine infrastructure needs for blockchain operation for the given application, the results of which will be added to the application description and forwarded to DISSECT-CF-Fog to perform the simulation of the whole application in the second step. The raw analysis results meeting the expected QoS (e.g., latency, energy efficiency, throughput, budget) are passed to the Compact Analyzer, whose main

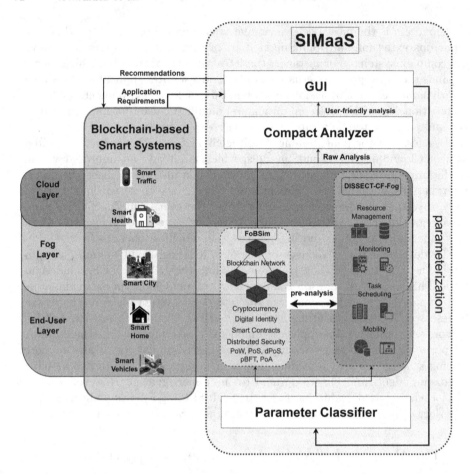

Fig. 1. Components of the proposed SIMaaS framework

objective is to prepare and unify the results in an understandable form for proper representation at the GUI. We may also configure DISSECT-CF-Fog to request FoBSim for a modified initial analysis and a more fitting application description. Finally, the developers can view the final parameterization recommendations and expected behavior metrics of the system.

The adoption and mass acceptance of smart applications is greatly hindered by the general lack of trust associated with the nature of monitoring and tracing apps, and the reluctance of people to share their personal data. Integrating Blockchain-based data management and AI methods (e.g., FL) into SSs can enhance the performance, trust, and privacy of their applications, which are getting more and more crucial. To enhance trust prior to solution deployment, reliable simulations can be performed to predict the behavior of such solutions. Our SIMaaS proposal is expected to mainly address the limitations [21] of current integrated SS simulation tools as follows:

– Abstraction vs. Accuracy: We aim to optimize the balance between the needed accuracy of system configuration, and the parameter and run-time abstraction methods usually deployed in simulation frameworks. Focusing the framework on abstract evaluation of different system elements is beneficial for achieving bug-free tools, but it harms the correctness and accuracy of the final results when highly complex systems are being simulated. The balance between these two factors is a determinant for valid simulations and evaluations. We aim to address this issue by deploying hierarchical algorithms with Pareto optimizations to obtain simulation results closest to real testbeds.
– Access to historical data: We will use available real-world data for two main reasons – as a reference objective for our optimization algorithms and as a benchmark comparison point for users of the SIMaaS tool. Additionally, we will allow users to save their previously run simulation scenarios (including configurations and results) so that they will save time and cost for future simulation attempts.
– Benchmarks for comparisons: We also plan to provide comprehensive reference configuration parameters that are dynamically changing in real-time while users are inputting their parameter configurations. In this way, users can easily define their initial application requirements using templates based on real cases that have been previously deployed, tested, or simulated.
– Relation of characteristics: We will use our knowledge, experience, and continuously published state-of-the-art analysis related to the configuration of BC and CC-based SSs, for example [26]. Accordingly, pre-analysis shared between the two simulators shall be the most accurate and efficient (in terms of computational and time cost).
– Resource constraints: This is related to the previous knowledge of the SIMaaS users, related to all the technologies deployed within. It is rare to have developers who are individually knowledgeable about accurate and realistic parameterization of all these technologies integrated into one solution. For this reason, our team aims to collectively define those constraints, as we do have members who are individually knowledgeable of the constraints of two or more integrated technologies. In this way, developers would be required to provide ranges of (instead of crisp) numerical configuration values.
– Machine learning: We will use recent advances and reliable AI methods (e.g., FL) to mainly address two issues, namely continuous learning on system initial configuration recommendations, and AI-integrated Pareto optimization of pre and raw analysis. We will also provide modifiable ML templates that simulate several AI-BC integrated solutions. This service is planned to be provided as checkboxes in the GUI so that developers can assess AI integration with BC-based SSs.
– User-friendliness: We also plan to fine-tune a GUI that allows for easy configuration and characterization of SS scenarios to be simulated. After the simulation, the GUI is planned to provide readable and visualized analysis that facilitates making fast final design decisions.

Concerning the use cases we aim to cover and support with our comprehensive simulation environment, we plan to support the investigation of smart systems exploiting all novel ICT technologies we addressed in this paper: IoT, cloud, fog, and edge infrastructures, as well as Blockchain networks, and AI-based services. The use cases we covered so far with DISSECT-CF-Fog include sensor-based and drone-supported weather prediction and IoT-assisted logistics scenarios, while with FoBSim we analysed blockchain-based healthcare and certification management scenarios. In the future, we aim to address unified scenarios, where the complementary capabilities of the two simulators can be exploited.

5 Conclusion

The use of emerging technologies has an undeniable effect on the evolution of Smart Systems, providing various smart applications addressing governmental and industrial processes, and the citizen life of smart cities. In this position paper, we proposed a SIMulation-as-a-Service (SIMaaS) framework for designing and analyzing the behavior of smart systems exploiting Cloud and Fog Computing, the Internet of Things, Blockchain, and Artificial Intelligence methods. In this vision, we build on our previously developed FoBSim and DISSICT-CF-Fog simulators and integrate their use to support the modeling of BC-assisted Cloud-Edge smart system applications. We plan to use AI technology to optimize this harmonization and predict optimal configurations for the simulated smart applications. We also plan to provide a reusable template-based environment to assist future realization as a public service.

References

1. Gill, S.S., et al.: AI for next generation computing: emerging trends and future directions. Internet of Things **19**, 100514 (2022)
2. Vailshery, L.S.: Number of Internet of Things (IoT) connected devices worldwide from 2019 to 2021, with forecasts from 2022 to 2030 (2022). https://www.statista.com/statistics/1183457/iot-connected-devices-worldwide/
3. Iorga, M., Feldman, L., Barton, R., Martin, M., Goren, N., Mahmoudi, C.: The NIST definition of fog computing. National Institute of Standards and Technology, Technical report (2017)
4. Akhras, G.: Smart materials and smart systems for the future. Can. Mil. J. **1**(3), 25–31 (2000)
5. Helm, J.M., et al.: Machine learning and artificial intelligence: definitions, applications, and future directions. Curr. Rev. Musculoskelet. Med. **13**, 69–76 (2020)
6. Alpaydin, E.: Machine Learning: The New AI. MIT Press, Cambridge (2016)
7. Liu, B., Ding, M., Shaham, S., Rahayu, W., Farokhi, F., Lin, Z.: When machine learning meets privacy: a survey and outlook. ACM Comput. Surv. (CSUR) **54**(2), 1–36 (2021)
8. McMahan, B., Moore, E., Ramage, D., Hampson, S., y Arcas, B.A.: Communication-efficient learning of deep networks from decentralized data. In: Artificial Intelligence and Statistics, pp. 1273–1282. PMLR (2017)
9. Beutel, D.J., et al.: Flower: a friendly federated learning research framework. arXiv preprint arXiv:2007.14390 (2020)

10. Nakamoto, S.: Bitcoin: a peer-to-peer electronic cash system. Manubot, Technical report (2019)
11. Garcia-Font, V.: SocialBlock: an architecture for decentralized user-centric data management applications for communications in smart cities. J. Parallel Distrib. Comput. **145**, 13–23 (2020)
12. Singh, S., Sharma, P.K., Yoon, B., Shojafar, M., Cho, G.H., Ra, I.-H.: Convergence of blockchain and artificial intelligence in IoT network for the sustainable smart city. Sustain. Urban Areas **63**, 102364 (2020)
13. Singh, S., Rathore, S., Alfarraj, O., Tolba, A., Yoon, B.: A framework for privacy-preservation of IoT healthcare data using federated learning and blockchain technology. Futur. Gener. Comput. Syst. **129**, 380–388 (2022)
14. Baniata, H., Kertesz, A.: FoBSim: an extensible open-source simulation tool for integrated fog-blockchain systems. PeerJ Comput. Sci. **7**, e431 (2021)
15. Markus, A., Al-Haboobi, A., Kecskemeti, G., Kertesz, A.: Simulating IoT workflows in DISSECT-CF-Fog. Sensors **23**(3), 1294 (2023)
16. Alzoubi, Y.I., Gill, A., Mishra, A.: A systematic review of the purposes of blockchain and fog computing integration: classification and open issues. J. Cloud Comput. **11**(1), 1–36 (2022)
17. Li, D., Luo, Z., Cao, B.: Blockchain-based federated learning methodologies in smart environments. Clust. Comput. **25**(4), 2585–2599 (2022)
18. Nguyen, D.C., et al.: Federated learning meets blockchain in edge computing: opportunities and challenges. IEEE Internet Things J. **8**(16), 12 806–12 825 (2021)
19. Nguyen, D.C., Ding, M., Pathirana, P.N., Seneviratne, A., Li, J., Poor, H.V.: Federated learning for Internet of Things: a comprehensive survey. IEEE Commun. Surv. Tutorials **23**(3), 1622–1658 (2021)
20. Ali, M., Karimipour, H., Tariq, M.: Integration of blockchain and federated learning for Internet of Things: recent advances and future challenges. Comput. Secur. **108**, 102355 (2021)
21. Smetanin, S., Ometov, A., Komarov, M., Masek, P., Koucheryavy, Y.: Blockchain evaluation approaches: state-of-the-art and future perspective. Sensors **20**(12), 3358 (2020). https://www.mdpi.com/1424-8220/20/12/3358
22. Faria, C., Correia, M.: BlockSim: blockchain simulator. In: 2019 IEEE International Conference on Blockchain (Blockchain), pp. 439–446. IEEE (2019)
23. Kunde, C., Mann, Z.A.: Comparison of simulators for fog computing. In: Proceedings of the 35th Annual ACM Symposium on Applied Computing, pp. 1792–1795 (2020)
24. Mastenbroek, F., et al.: OpenDC 2.0: convenient modeling and simulation of emerging technologies in cloud datacenters. In: 2021 IEEE/ACM 21st International Symposium on Cluster, Cloud and Internet Computing (CCGrid), pp. 455–464 (2021)
25. Mechalikh, C., Taktak, H., Moussa, F.: PureEdgeSim: a simulation framework for performance evaluation of cloud, edge and mist computing environments. Comput. Sci. Inf. Syst. **18**(1), 43–66 (2021)
26. Pflanzner, T., Baniata, H., Kertesz, A.: Latency analysis of blockchain-based SSI applications. Future Internet **14**(10), 282 (2022)

Cormas: The Software for Participatory Modelling and Its Application for Managing Natural Resources in Senegal

Oleksandr Zaitsev[1]([✉])(iD), François Vendel[1,2], and Etienne Delay[1,3]

[1] CIRAD, UMR SENS, MUSE, Université de Montpellier, Montpellier, France
{oleksandr.zaitsev,francois.vendel,etienne.delay}@cirad.fr
[2] Institut Sénégalais de Recherches Agricoles (ISRA), CNRF, Dakar, Senegal
[3] Ecole Supérieur Polytechnique (ESP), UMMISCO, Dakar, Senegal

Abstract. Cormas is an agent-based simulation platform developed in the late 90s by the Green research at CIRAD unit to support the management of natural resources and understand the interactions between natural and social dynamics. This platform is well-suited for a participatory simulation approach that empowers local stakeholders by including them in all modelling and knowledge-sharing steps. In this short paper, we present the Cormas platform and discuss its unique features and their importance for the participatory simulation approach. We then present the early results of our ongoing study on managing pastoral resources in the Sahel region, identify the problems faced by local stakeholders, and discuss the potential use of Cormas at the next stage of our study to collectively model and understand the effective ways of managing the shared agro-sylvo-pastoral resources.

Keywords: resource management · agent-based modelling · participatory simulation · software

1 Introduction

In recent years, there has been an increased interest in decentralization and multi-agent systems, particularly in the participatory approaches that involve stakeholders in the process of designing the model and interacting with its simulations [4,5]. Such techniques have been formalized in the companion modelling (ComMod) approach [3,9] that suggests to update the always-imperfect model iteratively by collecting feedback from stakeholders. Based on the years of field expertise, the Green research unit has created the platform for multi-agent simulation Cormas (common pool resources and multi-agent simulations) which

This work was sponsored by the CASSECS project: https://www.cassecs.org/.

The original version of this chapter was previously published without open access. A correction to this chapter is available at
https://doi.org/10.1007/978-3-031-48803-0_41

D. Zeinalipour et al. (Eds.): Euro-Par 2023 Workshops, LNCS 14352, pp. 76–84, 2024.
https://doi.org/10.1007/978-3-031-48803-0_7

implements the commod approach and provides a unique interactive experience that is well adapted for participatory simulations.

In this short paper, we explain the ComMod approach and participatory simulations. We briefly overview the Cormas platform and discuss its original functionalities. We then present the early research results of our ongoing study on managing pastoral resources in Senegal and discuss the potential application of Cormas and participatory modelling at the next stage of our study.

The rest of this paper is structured as follows. In Sect. 2, we introduce participatory modelling and the ComMod approach. In Sect. 3, we present the Cormas platform for agent-based simulations. In Sect. 4, we present the first results of our ongoing study on managing pastoral resources in Senegal and discuss the application of Cormas. In Sect. 5, we discuss the related work and Sect. 6 concludes the paper.

2   ComMod Approach and Participatory Simulation

Companion Modelling (ComMod) [3,9] is a formalized approach that is based on a continuous feedback loop between researchers and various stakeholders. The model should be iteratively updated based on the field situation in an endless loop *"modelling" -> "field work" -> "modelling" -> "field work" -> ...*, thus creating a process which produces an imperfect model but iteratively makes it "less imperfect". At each iteration, the model is discussed together with stakeholders. Their feedback and hypotheses are then used to update the model. ComMod approach has two main objectives:

1. *Understanding complex environments* by making researchers interact with stakeholders and seek a mutual recognition of everyones representation of the research problems.
2. *Supporting the collective decision-making process* by incorporating different points of view and allowing stakeholders to learn and share knowledge with researchers but also among themselves.

While being particularly well adapted for role-playing games, the ComMod approach has also been successfully applied with *multi-agent simulations* in the form of a *participatory simulation* [4,7,14]. In conventional participatory modelling process, local stakeholders (the objects of study) are only contacted for data collection. They are not involved in the other stages of the study. ComMod is a more inclusive approach which involves stakeholders also in the process of model design, simulation analysis, and even decision making.

Collectively designing simulation models together with stakeholders is a process that could benefit from dedicated tools. In the following section, we describe one of those tools — a multi-agent simulation platform that was designed to implement the ComMod approach and provides several unique features to support interactive simulation.

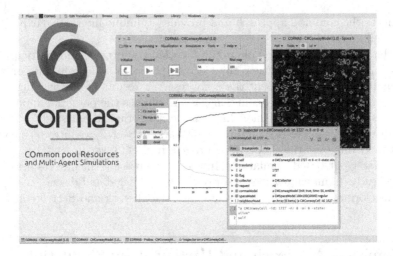

Fig. 1. A screenshot of Cormas platform running the simulation of Conway's Game of Life. It contains a simulation control interface, a visualization of the space, displaying a grid cells that can be dead (black) or alive (green), a chart of two measurements (probes) - the numbers of dead and alive cells at each iteration, and the inspector window which allows user to see the properties of an individual cell and interact with it. (Color figure online)

3   Cormas Platform

Cormas[1] (**CO**mmon pool **R**esources and **M**ulti-**A**gent **S**imulations) is a platform for multi-agent modelling implemented in 1997 by the Green[2] research unit of CIRAD[3] based on the object-oriented programming language Smalltalk [8]. The original version of Cormas was implemented in VisualWorks Smalltalk, which is now a proprietary software system owned by Cincom[4]. There is an ongoing effort[5] to migrate Cormas to Pharo[6] — a modern purely object-oriented programming language designed in the tradition of Smalltalk and distributed under the open-source MIT license.

---

[1] http://cormas.cirad.fr/.

[2] In 2021, the Green research unit (Gestion des ressources renouvelables et environnement) became part of the mixed research unit SENS (Savoirs, Environnement, et Sociétés): https://umr-sens.fr/.

[3] CIRAD (Centre de coopération internationale en recherche agronomique pour le développement) is a French agricultural research and international cooperation organization working for the sustainable development of tropical and Mediterranean regions: https://www.cirad.fr/.

[4] https://www.cincomsmalltalk.com/main/products/visualworks/.

[5] https://github.com/cormas/cormas.

[6] https://pharo.org/.

Cormas was originally designed to simplify the simulation of resource management and modelling the interactions between natural and social dynamics. A model in Cormas can be defined either by programming it in Smalltalk (the platform provides all the building blocks that can be composed and extended) or through a graphical user interface that helps users to implement the model but the full implementation still requires them to write code. The model can be composed of agents, which can be located in space and communicate to one another, and patches that define the space for agents. The platform provides various tools for analysing the model and interacting with it. As can be seen in Fig. 1, users can visualize the space chart the progression of observed parameters, inspect specific agents or patches, and even interact with them while the simulation is running. Cormas also allows users to work with geographical data by importing actual maps with multiple layers of information from GIS files (geographic information systems).

3.1   What Makes Cormas Unique?

Compared to other existing modelling platforms, Cormas stands out by being interactive and well adapted for the participatory modelling. This is highlighted by its three unique features:

- *Different "points of view"*. Cormas allows modellers to define multiple visual representation for each entity thus letting its users observe the simulation from different "points of view" at the same time (see Fig. 2).
- *Inspecting entities*. Through the dynamic and interactive nature of Smalltalk environment, every entity (agent, patch, etc.) in a Cormas model can be inspected and controlled directly at every step of the simulation.
- *Stepping back in time*. Cormas allows modellers to return to any past moment in the simulation runtime change the parameters or manipulate entities, and resume the simulation.

Over the years, those three features proved to be useful in the sessions of participatory simulation, allowing multiple people to observe the model from different perspectives and interact with it during the simulation runtime, thus engaging stakeholders, encouraging communication and knowledge sharing.

4   Using Cormas to Manage Pastoral Resources in Senegal

To demonstrate the application of Cormas and the companion modelling approach, in this section, we present the first insights from our ongoing study on the managemnet of pastoral resources in two pastoral units: Velingara-Ferlo and Younoufere. Both are located in the Ranerou-Ferlo department of Senegal where new reforestation initiatives are being implemented. According to Faye *et al*, [13], the *pastoral unit* is the space and the set of resources polarised by a pastoral borehole — a hydraulic infrastructure installed to secure pastoralism

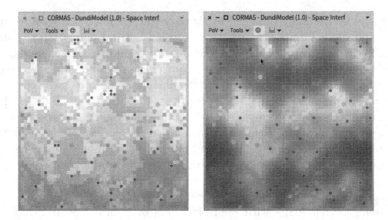

Fig. 2. Different "points of view" (PoV) of the same model can be displayed simultaneously. The left PoV shows the amount of grass that grows on a patch of land (intensity of green and yellow indicates the amount of fresh or dry grass) while the right PoV shows the humidity of each patch of land (intensity of blue indicates the amount of ground water). Red circles represent cows that eat grass and pink circles represent trees that consume water. (Color figure online)

and allow permanent access to water [15]. Both units in our study are mostly populated by the Fulani people, for whom pastoralism or agro-pastoralism and mobility are characteristic of their way of life until now. The region contains sylvo-pastoral reserves — large protected areas intended to limit the exploitation natural resources, as well as the reforestation plots that were installed as part of the Great Green Wall Initiative[7] in order to fight against desertification in Sahel [11].

Both were initially under the authority of Water and Forest services. Soon after, the GGW faced to certain limits, which include replantation low rate success and social conflicts [11]. To solve these problems, GGW accelerator was initiated in 2021 in furtherance of improving consideration to local realities and participation.

Now, there is a lot of hydraulic constructions in pastoral unit and an overlaying of power instances in natural resources management which questions relevance of actual structuration of agro-sylvo-pastoral governance.

4.1 First Field Mission

As part of this ongoing study, we have conducted a first field mission between mid-December 2022 and late April 2023. We stayed 40 days in the field, engaging in participatory observation and conducting 45 semi-directed interviews by

---

[7] The Great Green Wall project was launched in 2007 by several African countries, aiming to create a strip of forest from Senegal to Djibouti, crossing areas mostly devoted to pastoralism: https://www.unccd.int/our-work/ggwi.

a directive sampling of local stakeholders (farmers, herders, and farmer-herders) as well as local decision makers (prefecture, Water and Forestry Services, municipality, drill community management, and the pastoral unit management). The aim of this mission was to establish first contact with local people, learn about local practices, the transition of those practices, the management of natural resources, and local preoccupations. The first insights of our study helped us identify the key natural resources and main problems that are faced by local communities with respect to managing those resources. We also formulated the research questions that will guide the first iteration of companion modelling intended to better understand the identified problems and collectively find the solutions.

4.2 First Insights

Key Natural Resources. Inside the Ferlo region, most local practices and especially pastoralism are driven by the availability of water [2,12], which is the most important natural resource in our study. It affects two secondary resources: grass and trees, which are essential to support the lives of local communities. Grass is used as food for animals, trees are used for construction, firewood, fodder, food, and medicine [11].

Problems Faced by Stakeholders. By discussing with people in the local communities, we have identified the following problems that they face in both pastoral units in our study:

P1: Decline in solidarity between villages. People have reported that the relationship, trust, and communication with neighbouring villages is declining over years.

P2: Conflict between locals and transhumants (pastoral nomads) for sharing limited resources; transhumans do not respect local rules and village chiefs are losing their legitimacy.

P3: Poor collective management of shared agro-silvopastoral resources. People claim that pastoral unit is ineffective due to the lack of communication and bad management.

Research Questions. With respect to the problems listed above, we ask the following research questions that can guide the first iteration of the companion modelling process:

RQ1: What is the best scale to manage resources in the pastoral units? Should the management be delegated to the autonomous reforestation plots or is it more effective to manage it at the the level of a whole pastoral unit?

RQ2: How to goup villages to achieve effective collaboration and resource management among them while avoiding conflicts?

We hypothesize that the informal groupments of villages, which need to be adaptive to face uncertainties (demographic, social), can be an effective form of managing agro-sylvo-pastoral resources. Such groupment would empower local stakeholders to protect the resources that support their livelihoods, exchange knowledge, and transmit information to the higher levels of authority. It would facilitate communication and relegitimize local and customary power.

4.3   Next Steps with Cormas

As part of implementing the companion modelling approach in this study, we envision two applications of Cormas for participatory simulation.

The first application is based on creating a model at the scale of a pastoral unit, where spatial patches represent different types of landscapes and are characterized by the amount and accessibility of pastoral resources. In such a model, the agents can be individual animals or entire herds. The interactive session based on multiple "points of view", the possibility to explore multiple scenarios would allow to collectively explore social relationships inside the pastoral unit and understand how they can be improved. By exploring different ways to group people, we can experiment with different scales of managing resources in the pastoral unit.

The second application is based on communicating agents that represent different institutions responsible for managing the pastoral unit. Cormas allows to represent the interactions between those agents and the sharing of information in the form of exchanging messages through the communication channels. By collectively exploring those interactions with different groups of stakeholders, we hope to better understand the problem of poor communication and propose a feasible solution.

5   Related Work

Both the companion modelling (ComMod) [3,9] and the Cormas platform for participatory simulations [8] were introduced by the Green research unit of CIRAD. Over the years, they found many applications in the field of natural and social sciences [5,6]. LePage *et al,* [14] analysed the usage of Cormas by the research community over the period of 12 years. They reported that the user community of Cormas was mainly interested in context-specific participatory agent-based simulation, with more than 50 training sessions organized over 6 continents.

There were multiple applications of the participatory funtionalities of Cormas in the Sahel region. D'aquino *et al,* [10] combined Cormas simulation together with role-playing games to empower stakeholders in the land use planning process in the Senegal River valley. Bah et al. [1] used Cormas for collective mapping of land and resource usage in Thieul village, Senegal. Their study relied on the geographical information that could be loaded into Cormas as a spatial model. Although this study focused on different problems, it was performed in an environment similar to ours and adopted the same methodology. The simulation of Bah et al. was implemented using the VisualWorks version of Cormas from 13 years ago. We intend to replicate it using the Pharo version of Cormas.

6 Conclusion

The participatory simulation approach includes stakeholders not only at stage of data collection, but also for model design, analysis, and discussion. This encourages the sharing of knowledge between stakeholders and contributes to the collective decision making. The Cormas platform for multi-agent simulations was designed to implement the companion modelling approach and provides some unique features for participatory simulations: multiple "points of view", ability to inspect and manipulate agents, and step back in time. In our ongoing study in two pastoral units in Senegal, we adopt the companion modelling approach to improve the management of pastoral resources. Through interaction with the local population, we have identified three problems faced by stakeholders with respect to the resource management in those pastoral units. We have also formulated two research questions that will guide the first iteration of the future participatory simulation session designed with Cormas. We present the vision for the two Cormas models that we plan to use at the next stage of our study and explain how the features of Cormas will contribute to the collective understanding and management of natural resources.

Acknowledgments. We are grateful to the CASSECS project for sponsoring this work and the mission of Oleksandr Zaitsev to Senegal. We would also like to thank Dundi Ferlo project for financing the PhD of François Vendel and ISRA CNRF for hosting him in their office in Dakar, Senegal.

References

1. Bah, A., Touré, I., Le Page, C., Ickowicz, A., Diop, A.T.: An agent-based model to understand the multiple uses of land and resources around drillings in Sahel. Math. Comput. Model. **44**(5–6), 513–534 (2006)
2. Barral, H., et al.: Systèmes de production d'élevage au sénégal dans la région du ferlo: synthèse de fin d'études d'une équipe de recherches pluridisciplinaire. France, Orstom, Paris (1983)
3. Barreteau, O., et al.: Our companion modelling approach. J. Artif. Soc. Soc. Simul. **6**(1) (2003)
4. Becu, N., Neef, A., Schreinemachers, P., Sangkapitux, C.: Participatory computer simulation to support collective decision-making: potential and limits of stakeholder involvement. Land Use Policy **25**(4), 498–509 (2008)
5. Bommel, P.: Participatory modelling and interactive simulation to support the management of the commons. Université Montpellier II, Habilitation à diriger des recherches (2020)

6. Bommel, P., Becu, N., Le Page, C., Bousquet, F.: Cormas: an agent-based simulation platform for coupling human decisions with computerized dynamics. In: Kaneda, T., Kanegae, H., Toyoda, Y., Rizzi, P. (eds.) Simulation and Gaming in the Network Society, vol. 9, pp. 387–410. Springer, Singapore (2016). https://doi.org/10.1007/978-981-10-0575-6_27

7. Bommel, P., et al.: A further step towards participatory modelling. fostering stakeholder involvement in designing models by using executable UML. J. Artif. Soc. Soc. Simul. **17**(1) (2014)

8. Bousquet, F., Bakam, I., Proton, H., Le Page, C.: Cormas: common-pool resources and multi-agent systems. In: Pasqual del Pobil, A., Mira, J., Ali, M. (eds.) Tasks and Methods in Applied Artificial Intelligence. IEA/AIE 1998. LNCS, vol. 1416, pp. 826–837. Springer, Heildelberg (1998). https://doi.org/10.1007/3-540-64574-8_469

9. Bousquet, F., Barreteau, O., Le Page, C., Mullon, C., Weber, J.: An environmental modelling approach: the use of multi-agent simulations. Adv. Environ. Ecol. Model. **113**(122) (1999)

10. D'aquino, P., Le Page, C., Bousquet, F., Bah, A.: Using self-designed role-playing games and a multi-agent system to empower a local decision-making process for land use management: the selfcormas experiment in Senegal. J. Artif. Soc. Soc. Simul. **6**(3) (2003)

11. Delay, E., Ka, A., Niang, K., Touré, I., Goffner, D.: Coming back to a commons approach to construct the great green wall in Senegal. Land Use Policy **115**, 106000 (2022)

12. Diop, A.T., Sy, O., Ickowicz, A., Touré, I.: Politique d'hydraulique et gestion de l'espace et des ressources dans la région sylvopastorale du sénégal (ferlo). CNEARC-SAGERT (2003)

13. Faye, M.: La gestion communautaire des ressources pastorales du ferlo sénégalais: l'expérience du projet d'appui à l'élevage. Élevage et gestion des parcours au Sahel, implications pour le développement, pp. 165–172 (2001)

14. Le Page, C., Becu, N., Bommel, P., Bousquet, F.: Participatory agent-based simulation for renewable resource management: the role of the cormas simulation platform to nurture a community of practice. J. Artif. Soc. Soc. Simul. **15**(1) (2012)

15. Wane, A., Ancey, V., Grosdidier, B.: Les unités pastorales du sahel sénégalais, outils de gestion de l'élevage et des espaces pastoraux. projet durable ou projet de développement durable? Développement durable et territoires. Économie, géographie, politique, droit, sociologie (Dossier 8) (2006)

The 3rd International Asynchronous Many-Task systems for Exascale (AMTE 2023)

Asynchronous Many-Task systems for Exascale (AMTE)

Workshop Description

The workshop, Asynchronous Many-Task Systems for Exascale (AMTE) 2023, was held on August 23rd in conjunction with the 29th International European Conference on Parallel and Distributed Computing (Euro-Par) as an in-person event in Limassol, Cyprus. The workshop explored the advantages of task-based programming on modern and future high-performance systems. It gathered developers, users, and proponents of these models and systems to share experiences, discuss how they meet the challenges posed by Exascale system architectures, and explore opportunities for increased performance, robustness, and full-system utilization.

The workshop was organized by Patrick Diehl, Steven R. Brandt, Zahra Khatami, and Parsa Amini. The keynote was given by Brad Richardson (Berkeley Lab), and the invited talk was given by Jeff Hammond (NVIDIA).

This volume of LNCS comprises selected contributions of attendees from this event. The contributed papers range from optimization of asynchronous many-task runtime systems to applications. This workshop has shown that AMTs are widely used in academia, industry, and national laboratories, and researchers are working to address some challenges posed by Excascale system architectures.

Organization

Steering Committee

Parsa Amini   Halpern-Wight Inc., USA
Steven R. Brandt   Louisiana State University, USA
Patrick Diehl   Louisiana State University, USA
Zahra Khatami   NVIDIA, USA

Program Committee

Weile Wei   Lawrence Berkeley National Laboratory, USA

Jan Ciesko   Sandia National Laboratories, USA
Peter Thoman   University of Innsbruck, Austria
Hartmut Kaiser   Louisiana State University, USA
Dirk Pleiter   KTH Royal Institute of Technology in Stockholm, Sweden

Brad Richardson   Sourcery Institute, USA
Tianyi Zhang   Amazon Web Services, USA
Nikunj Gupta   Amazon, USA
Sumathi Lakshmiranganatha   Los Alamos National Laboratory, USA

Malleable APGAS Programs and Their Support in Batch Job Schedulers

Patrick Finnerty[1]([⊠])(iD), Leo Takaoka[1], Takuma Kanzaki[1], and Jonas Posner[2](iD)

[1] Kobe University, Kobe, Japan
{finnerty.patrick,takaoka,kanzaki}@fine.cs.kobe-u.ac.jp
[2] University of Kassel, Kassel, Germany
jonas.posner@uni-kassel.de

Abstract. Malleability—the ability for applications to dynamically adjust their resource allocations at runtime—presents great potential to enhance the efficiency and resource utilization of modern supercomputers. However, applications are rarely capable of *growing* and *shrinking* their number of nodes at runtime, and batch job schedulers provide only rudimentary support for these features. While numerous approaches have been proposed for enabling application malleability, these typically focus on iterative computations and require complex code modifications. This amplifies the challenges for programmers, who already wrestle with the complexity of traditional MPI inter-node programming.

Asynchronous Many-Task (AMT) programming presents a promising alternative. Computations are split into many fine-grained *task*s, which are processed by *worker*s. This way, AMT enables transparent task relocation via the runtime system, thus offering great potential for efficient malleability. In this paper, we propose an extension to an existing AMT system, namely *APGAS for Java*, that provides easy-to-use malleability. More specifically, programmers enable application malleability with only minimal code additions, thanks to the simple abstractions we provide. Runtime adjustments, such as process initialization and termination, are automatically managed. We demonstrate the ease of integration between our extension and future batch job schedulers through the implementation of a simplistic malleable batch job scheduler. Additionally, we validate our extension through the adaption of a load balancing library handling multiple benchmarks. Finally, we show that even a simplistic scheduling strategy for malleable applications improves resource utilization, job throughput, and overall job response time.

Keywords: Malleable Runtime System · Job Scheduling · APGAS

1 Introduction

In the realm of modern supercomputing, the prevalence of dynamic and irregular workloads—which embodies varying computational demands and unpredictable computational patterns—is steadily rising. Compounded with the traditional

© The Author(s), under exclusive license to Springer Nature Switzerland AG 2024
D. Zeinalipour et al. (Eds.): Euro-Par 2023 Workshops, LNCS 14352, pp. 89–101, 2024.
https://doi.org/10.1007/978-3-031-48803-0_8

static resource allocations on supercomputers, this leads to inefficient resource utilization and diminished overall performance.

On today's supercomputers, users submit their applications to the *batch job scheduler* in the form of *jobs*, specifying the number of nodes and the required time. The batch job scheduler then decides which jobs are executed in which order and on which nodes. Typically, nodes are used by jobs exclusively, meaning a node is never utilized by two jobs simultaneously. Thus, the scheduler's role of allocating nodes to jobs amounts to solving a 2-dimensional knapsack problem.

This leads to resource under-utilization, as the job shapes (*required time × number of nodes*) submitted by users may not perfectly fit within the total available node capacity. An approach to alleviate this issue involves introducing *elasticity* for jobs, allowing them to dynamically change their number of nodes at runtime. As shown in Table 1, jobs can therefore be categorized into four classes based on who determines the number of nodes a job runs with and when this determination is made [7]. In this article, we focus on *malleable jobs*. These are capable of dynamically changing the number of nodes they use following the batch job scheduler's instructions.

Table 1. Job classification by *Feitelson and Rudolph* [7]

Decision	by job	by batch job scheduler
at job start	*rigid*	*moldable*
at runtime	*evolving*	*malleable*

Malleable jobs offer a number of opportunities for batch job schedulers. For instance, they make it possible to shrink their current allotment to allow other jobs to be started earlier. Conversely, batch job schedulers can also increase the allotments of running jobs, accelerating their completion. Thus, elasticity promises to enhance resource utilization, improve job throughput, and optimize overall performance.

However, programming malleable applications remains more difficult than regular rigid ones. Moreover, batch job schedulers and traditional inter-node programming models such as MPI provide rudimentary support for malleability. While numerous approaches for this purpose have been proposed, they often require complex modifications to application codes. They also typically focus on iterative computations, which provide "natural" synchronization points for resource adjustment [11].

Asynchronous Many-Task (AMT) programming is a promising approach to facilitate programmer productivity, handle dynamic and irregular workloads, and enable malleability with minor changes to application codes. In AMT, programmers split large computations into many fine-grained *tasks*, which are then dynamically mapped to processing units, called *workers*, by the AMT runtime system. Due to this transparent resource management, AMT offers great potential to provide flexible and efficient solutions for malleability. Such AMT applications could adapt to resource changes by relocating tasks and data to added resources and away from released resources. While this potential for malleability has been recognized [4,15], a lack of AMT systems that support malleability in an efficient and simple way still remains.

This article aims to bridge this gap by proposing a malleability extension to an AMT library, namely the open-source *APGAS for Java* [19] (*APGAS* in short). *APGAS* extends the well-known *Partitioned Global Address Space (PGAS)* programming model by adding *asynchronous* task capabilities. Although the original *APGAS* supported changes in the number of processes, it did so in a very rudimentary manner [19]. This was recently improved in the context of the *lifeline-based Global Load Balancing (GLB)* library [15], but the proposed malleability technique was tightly intertwined with *GLB*. This work disentangles *APGAS* and *GLB* and makes the following main contributions:

- We propose an innovative malleability technique and implement it as an extension to *APGAS* [19]. Our extension empowers programmers to enable application malleability, requiring only small code additions thanks to our clear abstractions. Runtime adjustments, including process initiation and termination, are automatically managed by our extension.
- We substantiate the usability of our malleable *APGAS* through the adaptation of *GLB* including a collection of its benchmarks.
- We propose a generic communication interface that enables running *APGAS* applications to react to *shrink* and *grow* orders from a batch job scheduler. We also develop a rudimentary malleable batch job scheduler capable of communicating with malleable *APGAS* applications.
- We perform an evaluation by processing a job batch comprising both malleable and rigid *APGAS* jobs managed by our job scheduler. Our results show that even a simplistic scheduling strategy improves resource utilization, job throughput, and overall job response time.

The remainder of this article is structured as follows. We first cover some background on *APGAS* in Sect. 2. We then introduce our malleability extension to *APGAS* in Sect. 3 before evaluating it in Sect. 4. We then discuss related work in Sect. 5 before concluding in Sect. 6. All the software discussed in this article is publicly available.[1]

2 Background on the APGAS Programming Model

The *Partitioned Global Address Space (PGAS)* [6] programming model facilitates programmer productivity for inter-node parallel programs. It allows programmers to see memory as a single, logically partitioned global address space where each node maintains its local memory. PGAS offers direct access to remote memory locations, alleviating the need for explicit message-passing operations

---

[1] https://github.com/ProjectWagomu.

as for, e.g., MPI. Within PGAS, programmers can dictate data locality through the global address space, optimizing data locality and boosting performance.

Several programming languages and runtime libraries implement PGAS in different ways, e.g., X10 [20], Chapel [5], UPC++ [2] and many more. In this work, we extend the open-source *APGAS for Java library* [19] (*APGAS* for short), which is derived from IBM's X10 project [20]. In *APGAS*, *places* correspond to a portion of the global address space and are typically mapped to a physical node or processor in a distributed system. The added *Asynchrony* allows applications to create a large number of asynchronous *tasks* which are processed by processing units, called *workers*.

Places are sequentially numbered from 0 to $n-1$ for an n-process execution. The `asyncAt` construct allows asynchronous task spawn at a remote place. Task termination is managed with the `finish` construct, which only completes once all transitively spawned asynchronous tasks have been processed. This is illustrated in Listing 1, where the `Bye` message in line 6 is printed only after each place has completed printing its `Hello` message in line 3.

Listing 1. Distributed Hello World in *APGAS*

```
1  finish (()->{
2    for (Place p : places()) {
3      asyncAt(p, ()->{ System.out.println("Hello_from_" + here()); });
4    }
5  });
6  System.out.println("Bye");
```

3   Malleable Programs in APGAS

At its most fundamental level, a malleable program needs to react to *shrink* and *grow* orders initialized by the batch job scheduler. In the programming model implemented by *APGAS*, this finds an intuitive translation consisting of removing and adding places to the global address space as illustrated in Fig. 1.

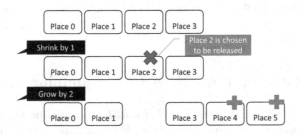

Fig. 1. Malleable *APGAS* program reacting to shrink/grow orders

This requires *APGAS* to be able to communicate with the batch job scheduler following a certain protocol. Additionally, *APGAS* must be capable of adding and removing processes at runtime. Finally, some level of preparation in response to changes in resources must be performed by the running program.

To enable malleability in *APGAS*, we designed a generic framework composed of several components. First, the `MalleableCommunicator` is responsible for communicating with the batch job scheduler. Secondly, the `Malleable-Handler` defines the actions that need to be performed upon receiving a *shrink* or *grow* order from the batch job scheduler. As this is application-dependant, programmers are expected to implement this `MalleableHandler` to specify these actions.

In the following, we introduce our new programming abstractions in Sect. 3.1. We then explain how *APGAS* interacts with the batch job scheduler in Sect. 3.2, followed by the consequences on the programming model in Sect. 3.3.

3.1   Programmer Abstractions

We provide an interface for the programmers to implement the `Malleable-Handler`. A single instance of this handler will be prepared on `place(0)` and its methods automatically called by *APGAS* when the corresponding orders are received. This interface presents the following four methods for programmers to implement:

- `List<Place> preShrink(int nbPlaces)`
- `void postShrink(int nbPlaces, List<Place> removedPlaces)`
- `void preGrow(int nbPlaces)`
- `void postGrow(int nbPlaces, List<Place> continuedPlaces,`
            `List<Place> newPlaces)`

Shrinking. In `preShrink`, programmers choose the places to be released and perform any preparatory steps prior to their effective termination. Typically, data and tasks are relocated from the places to be released to the remaining ones.

APGAS only terminates the corresponding processes once the `preShrink` method returns. This allows programmers to use the *APGAS* constructs in a stable runtime, thereby guaranteeing that all necessary preparations have completed. Upon successful process termination, `postShrink` is called to signal the end of the transition period.

Growing. Similar to shrinking, `preGrow` and `postGrow` are called before and after an increase in the number of places. In `preGrow`, the number of places to be added is specified. For convenience, the places that were continued/added are indicated in two distinct lists as parameters to method `postGrow`.

Handler Registration. To enable malleability, programmers implement the `MalleableHandler` and register it. Until the registration, the program ignores any orders sent by the batch job scheduler and is effectively considered rigid.

We justify this design by the fact that no arbitrary program can be malleable until some level of initialization has been performed. This is true of the MalleableHandler in particular, as it may need specific data structures pertaining to the running program to be initialized before it can be created. Hence, we consider that an *APGAS* program is malleable from the moment the Malleable-Handler is registered.

Example: GLB Library. The *lifeline-based Global Load Balancing (GLB)* is a fully distributed work-stealing scheme that was first implemented as a library in X10 [17,22,23] and later ported to Java [8,14]. It introduces fixed stealing channels (the *lifelines*) through which places that run out of work signal lifeline buddys and passively wait until work is received. We build on an existing malleable GLB implementation [15], but adapt it to our new malleable *APGAS*, thus significantly reducing its complexity as detailed below:

- preShrink: disconnects the places to be removed from the lifeline network and relocates those places' work and intermediary result to continued places.
- postShrink: no operation to be performed.
- preGrow: no operation to be performed.
- postGrow: new places are initialized and join the lifeline work-stealing network.

The MalleableHandler is registered when the computation begins and the application remains malleable until its completion. While other approaches often need synchronisation points—most commonly provided by iterative computations [11]—our combination of *GLB* and *APGAS* does not require any interruption of the computation to react to malleability orders.

3.2 Scheduler Interactions

The MalleableCommunicator communicates with the batch job scheduler. While the abstract class we provide implements the general procedures for *shrink* and *grow* orders, child classes have to implement the communication protocol of the batch job scheduler.

We provide the implementation SocketMalleableCommunicator inspired by *Prabhakaran et al.* [16]. True to its name, it uses a socket to receive malleable orders from a batch job scheduler. The socket is opened to receive connections upon the programmer registering the MalleableHandler. At this stage, the application is capable of receiving *shrink* and *grow* orders. The socket remains open until the main method completes, at which point it is shut down.

Shrink Orders. When the batch job scheduler sends a *shrink* order, the socket expects to receive the string shrink followed by the number of nodes to release. The order is then transmitted to preShrink. When the place to be released are identified, the corresponding nodes to release are identified with an internal mapping of *APGAS*. After *APGAS* is called to shut down the corresponding places, the nodes on which they were running are returned to the scheduler through the socket connection. The shrinking procedure is then completed by calling method `postShrink`.

Grow Orders. Similar to *shrink* orders, for *grow* orders the batch job scheduler sends the strings `grow` followed by the number of nodes to increase, and the nodes to spawn new places on. The order is transmitted to `preGrow`. When `preGrow` returns, new places are started on the designated nodes by the *APGAS* runtime. When all new places have successfully started, `postGrow` is called. The expansion is completed with an acknowledgment sent to the batch job scheduler.

3.3   Consequences on the Programming Model

As discussed above, malleable *APGAS* programs can add/remove places at runtime. This straightforward concept has significant consequences on the programming model, challenging several seemingly intuitive assumptions.

In a regular *APGAS* program, places are sequentially numbered from 0 to $n-1$ for an n-process execution. For a *shrink* order, programmers decide which places to remove. The ids of these removed places are not reused when new places are added, potentially leading to gaps in place numbering (see Fig. 1).

Another consequence of changing the number of places is a potential disruption to ongoing `for loops` on participating places. Consider the `for loop` in line 2 of Listing 1. If a change in allotment is ongoing, such a loop may try to spawn asynchronous tasks using `asyncAt` on a place that is currently leaving the computation, resulting in an error; or places that recently joined the runtime may be left out of the for loop.

This is why we introduce four methods for programmers to specify the actions to perform before and after any malleability order. This way, programmers can prevent any ongoing `for loop` from spawning a task that would fail immediately or, more likely, ensure that any such ongoing `for loop` is allowed to complete before `preShrink` or `preGrow` returns and the actual malleable change occurs. In the case of *GLB*, this involves temporarily pausing inter-place stealing to ensure that places to be removed are no longer considered.

The existing *APGAS* implementation has certain limitations, notably the inability to remove `place(0)`. This is due to its unique role in runtime setup and its responsibility for executing the `main` method. This justifies our decision to assign the `MalleableCommunicator` and `MalleableHandler` roles to `place(0)`, given that this place is an immutable component of the runtime.

Another limitation is the inability for the `finish` construct to be relocated to another place. As this construct controls task termination, it is not possible to immediately release a place containing a `finish` with pending tasks. These pending tasks need to complete for the `finish`'s continuation to in turn complete. Only then will the place be shut down.

Table 2. Batch composition and number of nodes required for each job type

rigid jobs			malleable jobs				
type	nb	nodes	type	nb	min	max	fixed
r1	3	2	m1	2	2	8	6
r2	7	4	m2	2	2	12	6
r3	3	6	m3	4	4	8	6
r4	3	8	m4	1	4	10	8
			m5	1	4	12	9
			m6	2	6	10	7
			m7	2	6	12	8

4   Evaluation

In this section, we evaluate our malleable *APGAS* implementation. We start by introducing our rudimentary batch job scheduler, followed by the evaluation of malleability's benefits by executing jobs on a small Beowulf cluster in Sect. 4.1. Then, we discuss interoperability and future expansions in Sect. 4.2.

4.1   Batch Submission

We developed a rudimentary batch job scheduler employing the *First-Come First Served (FCFS)* strategy to schedule jobs. All submitted jobs are kept in a single queue. Malleable jobs are considered to be moldable as well and are submitted with a *minimum* and *maximum* number of nodes. In turn, the batch job scheduler chooses the number of nodes with which they are started.

The scheduler may change the allotment of a running malleable jobs under the following conditions: running malleable jobs are shrunk if that would free enough nodes to start the next job in the queue; otherwise, currently running malleable jobs are grown up to their respective maximum number of nodes.

We prepared a batch consisting of 30 jobs that are all submitted to our 12-node Beowulf cluster. Among these 30 jobs, 14 of them are malleable *GLB* jobs (Unbalanced Tree Search adapted from [15]). We compare the obtained schedule when only rigid jobs and a mix of rigid and malleable jobs are considered. For the rigid batch, the same jobs as in the malleable batch are submitted; the malleable jobs are converted to rigid jobs requiring a number of nodes between the minimum and maximum number of nodes. The details of the jobs used are shown in Table 2. The first 5 min of the schedule (showing the first 10 jobs) are shown in the Gantt charts of Fig. 2, with overall scheduling metrics presented in Table 3.

As expected, the presence of malleable jobs allows the scheduler to reduce allotments to allow jobs to be scheduled earlier. This can be seen in the average waiting time which is reduced by about 15%, and in Fig. 2 where job #5 and #9

Table 3. Scheduling performance metrics

Workload	rigid	rigid and malleable	
total execution time (m)	21.4	18.2	(−15%)
avg cluster utilization	72.3%	83.4%	(+15%)
avg job waiting time (s)	563.8	476.7	(−15%)
avg job execution time (s)	57.6	83.7	(+45%)
avg job response time (s)	621.4	560.4	(−10%)

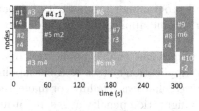

(a) with rigid jobs only

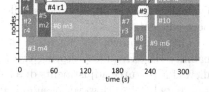

(b) with malleable and rigid jobs

Fig. 2. Gantt chart of the first 5 min of the job schedule

are shrunk to allow the next job to start earlier. Of course, as their allotment is reduced, this tends to increase job execution times (on average 45% longer), but this is overall beneficial, with the average turnaround time of jobs reduced by about 10%, and the total time needed to process the entire batch reduced by about 15%. The average cluster utilization (percentage of the computational resources used) is increased from 72.3% to 83.4% by introducing malleable jobs.

Of course, there are a number of factors that are particularly favorable to malleable workloads in our small-scale experiment. First, the size of the cluster (12 nodes) makes it likely for rigid jobs to not fit properly and introduce large gaps of unused resources. Secondly, the scheduling algorithm we used is simplistic. Slightly more advanced techniques such as *backfilling* [21] could further improve performance for both the rigid and malleable workloads.

Nevertheless, these results confirm our expectation that introducing malleable workloads is beneficial for the performance of individual jobs and the entire cluster. They also demonstrate our malleable *APGAS* implementation was able to adequately respond to allotment changes ordered by the scheduler.

4.2 Interoperability and Future Expansion

As discussed above, we took care to make the architecture of the malleable runtime as modular as possible. `MalleableHandler` needs to be implemented by programmers as how to handle malleability is application-specific. `Malleable-Communicator` provides a generic framework for communications with the batch job system.

As discussed in Sect. 3.2, our current implementation relies on sockets. To allow compatibility with future batch job schedulers supporting malleability, only the `MalleableCommunicator` would need to be adapted to allow existing applications to be ported to this new scheduler.

5   Related Work

While malleability has not yet been established in everyday supercomputing, several approaches have been proposed [1,9]. Each technique has distinct characteristics and may vary in effectiveness and programmer productivity impact. Typically, malleability solutions tailored to specific applications or fields prove more efficient.

The well-known *checkpoint/restart* technique can enable application malleability [10]. Regularly storing the running application's state as a checkpoint allows for resource adjustments due to unforeseen hardware failures or malleability orders [10,18]. However, a significant reconfiguration penalty arises, requiring checkpoint writing as well as application termination and restart. In-memory checkpoint writing can mitigate this penalty [24]. While checkpoint/restart can be semi-transparently implemented at the user level, it still requires adaptations of user codes [12,13]. In contrast, our proposed malleable *APGAS* does not require any checkpointing/restarting and facilitates programmer productivity through clear and easy-to-use abstractions.

Programming systems supporting user-level malleability are rare, with a few exceptions such as ULFM [3] and X10 [20]. While *APGAS* initially supported place changes, it did so in a rudimentary manner [19] before it was improved [15]. Our work further refines the concept and improve usability significantly.

DMRlib [11] establishes a common interface for all MPI implementations to support malleability by automating data redistribution and hide the reconfiguration internals. Another approach rather close to ours is that of Charm++ [16]. Contrary to the PGAS programming model which exposes the distributed nature of the computation to the programmer, the programming model adopted by Charm++ hides this nature to the programmer. As a result, converting existing programs so that they become malleable can be done without significant code modifications, simply by activating the internal load balancing strategy. Both of these works are combined with a customized version of a batch job scheduler, Slurm and Torque/Maui respectively, whereas we resorted to implementing an ad-hoc scheduler for the purpose of the evaluation presented here.

Malleable algorithm research has mainly focused on iterative computations offering natural synchronization points for application adaptation [11]. While our malleable *APGAS* requires few user code additions, it is not limited to iterative computations but is nicely suitable for dynamic and irregular workloads.

AMT's malleability potential remains largely untapped. Prior research has explored worker addition in a resilient *GLB* variant in X10 [4], but lacked a shrinking protocol. A multi-worker *GLB* variant in *APGAS* enabled both shrinking and expansion [8,15]. We adapted this *GLB* variant and several benchmarks to our new malleable *APGAS* to demonstrate its ease of use. However, while we used *GLB* as an application, our malleability is not limited to *GLB* but extends to a more generic parallel programming system, *APGAS*. To the best of our knowledge, no research has proposed such a easy-to-use malleable AMT.

6 Conclusion

In this work, we proposed an extension to an existing AMT system, namely *APGAS*, that allows applications to effortlessly adapt resource allocation via minimal user code additions. Runtime adjustments, such as process initiation and termination, are automatically managed by our malleable *APGAS*.

We showed the seamless integration potential of our malleable *APGAS* with future batch job schedulers, demonstrated through the implementation of a rudimentary batch job scheduler. The usability of our approach was validated via the adaptation of the *GLB* library. Furthermore, we showed that even a simplistic scheduling strategy for malleable applications improves resource utilization, job throughput, and overall job response time.

Future research could explore the development of *evolving* applications that autonomously initiate shrink/grow requests, rather than relying on the orders initiated by the batch job scheduler. However, determining the optimal timing and conditions for such requests, as well as how batch job schedulers should respond to respond to these requests (given that not all grow requests can be satisfied) remains an open question.

References

1. Aliaga, J.I., Castillo, M., Iserte, S., Martín-Álvarez, I., Mayo, R.: A survey on malleability solutions for high-performance distributed computing. Appl. Sci. **12**(10), 5231 (2022). https://doi.org/10.3390/app12105231
2. Bachan, J., et al.: UPC++: a high-performance communication framework for asynchronous computation. In: International Parallel and Distributed Processing Symposium, pp. 963–973. IEEE (2019). https://doi.org/10.1109/IPDPS.2019.00104
3. Bland, W., Bouteiller, A., Herault, T., Bosilca, G., Dongarra, J.: Post-failure recovery of MPI communication capability. Int. J. High Performance Comput. Appl. **27**(3), 244–254 (2013). https://doi.org/10.1177/1094342013488238
4. Bungart, M., Fohry, C.: A malleable and fault-tolerant task pool framework for X10. In: Proceedings of International Conference on Cluster Computing. IEEE (2017). https://doi.org/10.1109/cluster.2017.27
5. Chamberlain, B.L.: Programming models for parallel computing. In: Chapel, pp. 129–159. MIT (2015). https://doi.org/10.7551/mitpress/9486.003.0008

6. De Wael, M., Marr, S., De Fraine, B., Van Cutsem, T., De Meuter, W.: Partitioned global address space languages. Comput. Surv. **47**(4), 1–27 (2015). https://doi.org/10.1145/2716320
7. Feitelson, D.G., Rudolph, L.: Toward convergence in job schedulers for parallel supercomputers. In: Feitelson, D.G., Rudolph, L. (eds.) JSSPP 1996. LNCS, vol. 1162, pp. 1–26. Springer, Heidelberg (1996). https://doi.org/10.1007/bfb0022284
8. Finnerty, P., Kamada, T., Ohta, C.: A self-adjusting task granularity mechanism for the Java lifeline-based global load balancer library on many-core clusters. Concurrency Comput. Pract. Experience **34**(2) (2021). https://doi.org/10.1002/cpe.6224
9. Galante, G., da Rosa Righi, R.: Adaptive parallel applications: from shared memory architectures to fog computing. Clust. Comput. **25**(6), 4439–4461 (2022). https://doi.org/10.1007/s10586-022-03692-2
10. Herault, T., Robert, Y.: Fault-Tolerance Techniques for High-Performance Computing. Springer, Cham (2015). https://doi.org/10.1007/978-3-319-20943-2
11. Iserte, S., Mayo, R., Quintana-Ortí, E.S., Peña, A.J.: DMRlib: easy-coding and efficient resource management for job malleability. Trans. Comput. **70**(9), 1443–1457 (2021). https://doi.org/10.1109/tc.2020.3022933
12. Maghraoui, K.E., Desell, T.J., Szymanski, B.K., Varela, C.A.: Dynamic malleability in iterative MPI applications. In: International Symposium on Cluster Computing and the Grid. IEEE (2007). https://doi.org/10.1109/ccgrid.2007.45
13. Moody, A., Bronevetsky, G., Mohror, K., de Supinski, B.R.: Design, modeling, and evaluation of a scalable multi-level checkpointing system. In: International Conference for High Performance Computing, Networking, Storage and Analysis. IEEE (2010). https://doi.org/10.1109/sc.2010.18
14. Posner, J., Fohry, C.: Cooperation vs. coordination for lifeline-based global load balancing in APGAS. In: Proceedings of Workshop on X10, pp. 13–17. ACM (2016). https://doi.org/10.1145/2931028.2931029
15. Posner, J., Fohry, C.: Transparent resource elasticity for task-based cluster environments with work stealing. In: International Conference on Parallel Processing Workshop, pp. 1–10. ACM (2021). https://doi.org/10.1145/3458744.3473361
16. Prabhakaran, S., Neumann, M., Rinke, S., Wolf, F., Gupta, A., Kale, L.V.: A batch system with efficient adaptive scheduling for malleable and evolving applications. In: Proceedings Int. Parallel and Distributed Processing Symposium, pp. 429–438 (2015). https://doi.org/10.1109/IPDPS.2015.34
17. Saraswat, V.A., Kambadur, P., Kodali, S., Grove, D., Krishnamoorthy, S.: Lifeline-based global load balancing. In: Proceedings on Principles and Practice of Parallel Programming, pp. 201–212. ACM (2011). https://doi.org/10.1145/1941553.1941582
18. Shahzad, F., Wittmann, M., Kreutzer, M., Zeiser, T., Hager, G., Wellein, G.: A survey of checkpoint/restart techniques on distributed memory systems. Parallel Process. Lett. **23**, 1340011 (2013). https://doi.org/10.1142/s0129626413400112
19. Tardieu, O.: The APGAS library: resilient parallel and distributed programming in Java 8. In: Proceedings of the ACM SIGPLAN Workshop on X10, pp. 25–26. ACM (2015). https://doi.org/10.1145/2771774.2771780
20. Tardieu, O., et al.: X10 and APGAS at petascale. In: Proceedings of Principles and Practice of Parallel Programming, pp. 53–66. ACM (2014). https://doi.org/10.1145/2555243.2555245
21. Wong, A.K., Goscinski, A.M.: Evaluating the EASY-backfill job scheduling of static workloads on clusters. In: International Conference on Cluster Computing. IEEE (2007). https://doi.org/10.1109/clustr.2007.4629218

22. Yamashita, K., Kamada, T.: Introducing a multithread and multistage mechanism for the global load balancing library of X10. J. Inf. Process. **24**(2), 416–424 (2016). https://doi.org/10.2197/ipsjjip.24.416
23. Zhang, W., et al.: GLB: lifeline-based global load balancing library in X10. In: Proceedings Workshop on Parallel Programming for Analytics Applications, pp. 31–40. ACM (2014). https://doi.org/10.1145/2567634.2567639
24. Zheng, G., Ni, X., Kale, L.V.: A scalable double in-memory checkpoint and restart scheme towards exascale. In: Proceedings of International Conference on Dependable Systems and Networks Workshops. IEEE (2012). https://doi.org/10.1109/dsnw.2012.6264677

Task-Level Checkpointing for Nested Fork-Join Programs Using Work Stealing

Lukas Reitz[✉] and Claudia Fohry

University of Kassel, Germany, Research Group Programming Language, Kassel, Germany
{lukas.reitz,fohry}@uni-kassel.de

Abstract. Recent Exascale supercomputers consist of millions of processing units, and this number is still growing. Therefore, hardware failures, such as permanent node failures, become increasingly apparent. They can be tolerated with techniques such as Checkpoint/Restart (C/R), which saves the whole application state transparently, and, in case of failure, restarts the application from the saved state; or application-level checkpointing, which saves only relevant data via explicit calls in the program. C/R has the advantage of requiring no additional programming expense, whereas application-level checkpointing is more efficient and allows to continue running the application on the intact resources (localized shrinking recovery).

An increasingly popular approach to code parallel applications is Asynchronous Many-Task (AMT) programming. Here, programmers identify parallel subcomputations, called tasks, and a runtime system assigns the tasks to worker threads. Since tasks have clearly defined interfaces, the runtime can automatically extract and save their interface data. This approach, called task-level checkpointing (TC), combines the respective strengths of C/R and application-level checkpointing.

AMTs come in many variants, and so far TC has only been applied to a few, rather simple variants. This paper considers TC for a different AMT variant: nested fork-join programs (NFJ) that run on clusters of multicore nodes under work stealing. We present the first TC implementation for this setting and evaluate it with three benchmarks and up to 1280 workers. We observe an execution time overhead of around 28% and neglectable recovery costs. (A preliminary version of this work has been presented in reference [1]. The present paper extends the algorithm therein, and for the first time implements and experimentally evaluates it.)

Keywords: Asynchronous Many-Task Programming · Fault Tolerance · Task-Level Checkpointing · Work Stealing

1 Introduction

Modern supercomputers have reached Exascale and consist of millions of processing units. For instance, the Frontier machine has over eight million cores [2].

© The Author(s), under exclusive license to Springer Nature Switzerland AG 2024
D. Zeinalipour et al. (Eds.): Euro-Par 2023 Workshops, LNCS 14352, pp. 102–114, 2024.
https://doi.org/10.1007/978-3-031-48803-0_9

With an increasing component count, hardware failures become more apparent [3]. Recent studies estimate permanent node failures in supercomputers with a million cores to happen between every 5.2 min [4] and 53 min [5].

A popular approach to tolerate hardware failures is *Checkpoint/Restart* (C/R). It saves the whole application state periodically at global synchronization points and, when a hardware failure is detected, restarts the application from the last saved checkpoint [6]. C/R incurs a significant running time overhead due to the synchronization and I/O to the cluster file system. Another well-known approach is *application-level checkpointing*. Here, the programmer inserts function calls to save only relevant data. Application-level checkpointing is more efficient, but requires additional programming effort. Several variants of it permit to continue running the application after failure on the intact resources, which is called *shrinking recovery*, and/or confine the failure handling to directly affected resources, which is called *localized recovery* (e.g., [7,8]).

While C/R and application-level checkpointing have different pros and cons, an intermediate approach, called *task-level checkpointing* (TC), promises to achieve transparency, efficiency, and localized shrinking recovery together. Unlike the above general-purpose approaches, TC is specialized to Asynchronous Many-Task (AMT) programs, an increasingly popular programming paradigm with examples such as HPX [9], OpenMP tasks [10], Chapel [11], and Cilk [12]. AMT programs partition the computation into units, called *tasks*, and a runtime system maps the tasks to lower-level resources. TC operates in the runtime system. It exploits the clearly defined interfaces of tasks to automatically save task descriptors and interface data.

AMT environments differ widely in their *task models*, i.e., in the mechanisms for task generation and cooperation. Examples include side effect-based task cooperation (such as in Chapel), Sequential Task Flow, Dynamic Independent Tasks, and Nested Fork-Join [13]. Moreover, the AMTs differ in their target architectures and in the runtime algorithms for task assignment. Thus far, TC has only been studied for a few, rather simple settings (e.g., [7,14]).

This paper proposes a TC scheme for a new setting, namely Nested Fork-Join programs running on clusters with multi-worker processes under work stealing. *Nested Fork-Join (NFJ)* programs begin the computation with a single task, which eventually returns the final result. Then each task may spawn child tasks that return their respective results to the parent. The term *work stealing* refers to the term *workers* for the compute resources that process the tasks. In our setting, workers are threads of multiple processes on different cluster nodes. Each worker maintains a task *queue*, from which it takes tasks for processing and into which it inserts newly generated tasks. If the queue is empty, the worker becomes a *thief* and tries to steal tasks from another worker, called *victim*. We consider a recent and efficient variant of work stealing, called *lifeline-pure* [15].

Our new TC scheme has to keep the checkpoints consistent despite stealing-related task migration. For that, we build on a previous TC scheme for Dynamic Independent Tasks (DIT), called AllFT [8]. Major changes of AllFT were required because: 1) NFJ differs from DIT insofar as NFJ returns task results to the parent, whereas DIT uses them directly in the computation of the final result. 2) Lifeline-pure uses a work-first policy, in which child tasks are processed before parent tasks, whereas AllFT assumes that parent tasks are processed first. 3) We consider multi-worker processes, whereas AllFT is restricted to single-worker processes.

Like AllFT, our scheme can handle any number of permanent worker failures, including simultaneous failures and failures during recovery. Failures never compromise a returned result, and program abort occurs in only a few rare cases. To the best of our knowledge, our scheme is the first TC scheme for NFJ, as well as the first TC scheme for multi-worker processes under work stealing.

We implemented the scheme and evaluated it. In experiments with up to 1280 workers, we observed a fault-tolerance overhead of up to 28.3% and neglectable costs for recovery.

Section 2 describes NFJ, the lifeline-pure scheme, and AllFT. Then, Sect. 3 presents our new TC scheme, and Sect. 4 sketches the implementation. Experimental results are provided and discussed in Sect. 5. The paper ends with related work and conclusions in Sects. 6 and 7, respectively.

2 Background

2.1 Nested Fork-Join Programs (NFJ)

Listing 1 depicts pseudocode of a naive recursive Fibonacci program in NFJ. The computation begins with root task f(n) for a given n. Then each task spawns two child tasks whose results are assigned to variables a and b. At the sync statement, the parent task waits until all previous assignments have been performed. Beyond the example, NFJ programs contain an implicit sync at the end of each task. Furthermore, we assume the tasks to be free of side effects.

Listing 1. NFJ example: naive recursive Fibonacci implementation

```
f(n) {                      // 0
    if (n < 2) return 1;
    a = spawn f(n−1);       // 1
    b = spawn f(n−2);       // 2
    sync;                   // 3
    return a + b;
}
```

The execution of NFJ programs gives rise to a tree, such as the one for the Fibonacci example in Fig. 1. In the figure, rounded rectangles denote functions spawned as tasks. Numbers 0 to 3 correspond to the sequential code sections marked in Listing 1. For instance, section 0 runs from the beginning of the function until the spawn of the first child. Downward edges (solid) mark spawns, and upward edges (dotted) mark result returns at explicit or implicit sync's.

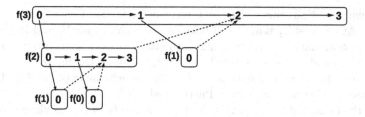

Fig. 1. Execution of nested fork-join programs

2.2 Lifeline-pure Scheme

As noted in Sect. 1, the tasks are executed by a set of worker threads from multiple processes. Each worker owns a *task queue*, and the workers balance their load via work stealing.

The lifeline-pure scheme [15] is an efficient work-stealing variant that adapts lifeline-based global load balancing [16] to multi-worker processes and NFJ. The scheme uses *cooperative* work stealing, in which a thief sends a steal request to the victim, and the victim actively responds with either *loot* or a reject message. In our case, the loot is always the oldest task from the victim pool. In lifeline-pure, a thief first attempts to steal from up to w random victims, and then, if not successful, from up to z *lifeline buddies* [15]. These are preselected victims, which remember any unsuccessful *lifeline steal requests*, and, if they obtain tasks later, share these tasks with the thief. After z unsuccessful lifeline steal requests, a thief becomes inactive. It is reactivated when a lifeline buddy sends tasks. The program ends when the root task has finished.

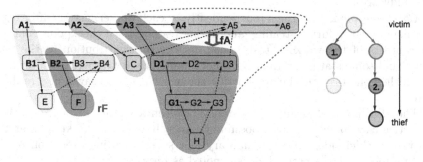

Fig. 2. Work stealing under the work-first policy

The lifeline-pure scheme deploys a *work-first* policy, in which a worker encountering a **spawn** branches into the child task and puts the continuation of the parent task into its queue. Thereby, *continuation* denotes the remaining computation of the parent task together with variable values. Continuations are represented by *frames*. Figure 2 illustrates work-first work stealing. The notation is the same as in Fig. 1, but the task structure differs to facilitate further discussion. Each color marks the work performed by a particular worker.

The computation starts with the green worker (called Green) processing the A frame. At the first spawn, Green branches into child task B, and Brown later steals the continuation of A. In general, thieves process parent frames, and victims process children, as illustrated on the right side of the figure.

Only few cluster implementations of the above scheme exist [17,18]. The one in [18] uses active messages in a Partitioned Global Address Space (PGAS). When a thief encounters a sync, it sends the frame back to the victim (or transitively to all victims) for result matching. Note that the parent frame is sent back to the child (and not vice versa), even though the arrows in Fig. 2 indicate that logically the result is incorporated into the parent. When a victim finishes a task whose parent is away, it locally saves the result and steals a new task.

For an example, consider Red in Fig. 2. It stole frame B from Green at B2, and was stolen from by Yellow at B3. Red finished F before Yellow returned. So Red kept the result (called rF) and stole the A frame from Brown at A3. Later, Blue stole the A frame at A4 and already returned it (called fA) at the sync opening A5. So fA resides at Red again, as the dotted red line indicates. Now consider the time when A has finished all sections printed in bold and is going to branch into H. At this time, Red holds rF, fA, a local pool with D2 and G2, and a descriptor of H. Furthermore, Red knows the identities of all victims and thieves with still unmatched results: Green and Yellow for the B2 frame, and Brown for the A3 frame. In its entirety, this information forms Red's *state*.

2.3   Original Task-Level Checkpointing Scheme for DIT

We refer to the AllFT scheme from Posner et al. [8], which encompasses a checkpointing procedure, a steal protocol, a restore protocol, and a selection scheme for buddy workers:

Checkpointing is performed independently by each worker, mainly after regular time intervals, during stealing, and during restore. Each checkpoint contains the contents of the worker's task queue, its current contribution to the final result, and some status information. Checkpoints are always written after having finished one task and before starting the next. They are saved in a resilient store.

The *steal protocol* ensures consistency between a victim, a thief, and their respective checkpoints, despite possible failures. It involves checkpoints at the victim and thief sides, and a temporary loot saving. During execution of the steal protocol, the respective loot is denoted as *open*.

The *restore protocol* presupposes that all workers are informed about failures, although possibly at different times. One designated other worker, called *buddy*, adopts the tasks from the failed worker's checkpoint and makes sure that open loot sent *from* the failed worker is taken over by either the thief or the buddy. Open loot sent *to* the failed worker is taken care of by the victim. Altogether the protocol guarantees that each task is executed exactly once.

The *selection scheme for buddy workers* is based on a consecutive numbering of the workers with wraparound. The *buddy* of a failed worker is defined as the next worker alive in this *ring*. Buddy selection is still nontrivial, since AllFT allows simultaneous failures and failures during recovery. Thus the role of buddy can move during an ongoing recovery. Details and a case-by-case analysis of correctness are given in reference [19].

3   Task-Level Checkpointing for NFJ

We applied the following major changes, which are further explained below:

1. We modified the contents of checkpoints so that they include the state of an NFJ worker. Also we clarified the times of checkpoint writing.
2. We newly added a frame return protocol and extended the restore protocol by the adoption of results and frames.
3. We adapted the buddy worker selection scheme to multi-worker processes.

As illustrated in Fig. 2, the *state* of a worker W consists of:

- the current contents of W's local pool,
- locally saved task results of W that are yet to be incorporated into their parent frame (e.g., rF),
- frames returned to W from their thieves that are awaiting result incorporation (e.g., fA),
- the identities of victims of W to which W has yet to return the respective stolen frame,
- the identities of thieves of W that have yet to return their frame to W, and
- a task descriptor of the next task (if relevant, see below).

Like in AllFT, checkpoints are only written when the worker is outside task processing. Thus, there are two possible occasions for checkpoint writing:

A. At a spawn: After having stored the parent frame and before branching into the child (e.g., before branching into H).
B. At the end of a function: After having finished the function and *either* after incorporating the result into the parent frame (e.g., after finishing H and incorporating its result into the G frame); *or* after storing the result locally (e.g., after finishing F and storing rF).

The last item from the definition of worker state is relevant in occasion A, but not in occasion B. In occasion B, the next task will either be taken from the local queue, and is then part of the state anyway, or be stolen anew, and is then contained in the checkpoint that is written during the steal protocol.

Checkpoints contain the worker state plus the same status information as in AllFT. The steal protocol is almost identical to that in AllFT, since the handshaking to reach consistency is independent from the contents of checkpoints. We merely added bookkeeping for the identities of victims and thieves.

NFJ differs from DIT in result handling. Since DIT computations keep the task results at each worker, AllFT just includes them in checkpoints and need not deal with consistency. NFJ computations, in contrast, unify task results with their frames by sending back the frames to the victims, and thus we need to deal with consistency. The consistency problem in frame return resembles the one in stealing insofar as data (a frame or loot, respectively) are moved from one worker to another. We solve it with a *frame return protocol*, which closely resembles the steal protocol from AllFT, except that it is initiated by the sender (there is no preceding steal request).

The *restore protocol* extends that of AllFT. Let X denote the failed worker, and B the buddy of X, respectively. Then, like in AllFT, B adopts X's tasks and any loot sent *from* X. Additionally, now, B adopts all task results and frames from X's checkpoint, as well as all open frames sent *from* X. B just stores the results and frames from the checkpoint alongside its own ones: The results will eventually be located by their associated thieves (see below); and the frames are awaiting results from X's tasks, which have been adopted by B as well. For each open frame sent from X, buddy B resends it (duplicates can be detected [8]). The identities of the recipients are known to B from X's checkpoint. Frames sent *to* X are handled by the sender, as is open loot sent to X in AllFT. Unlike the loot, however, the frames can not be taken back by the sender. Instead, the sender delivers them to the owner of the associated results, which is B. The sender locates B as being the next worker alive in the ring of workers. Frames to X that are finished later are handled the same way.

AllFT assumes all workers are equal when defining the ring. For our multi-worker processes, we number the workers in the ring blockwise: workers of process 0 get numbers $0 \ldots d - 1$, workers of process 1 get numbers $d \ldots 2d - 1$, etc. While individual worker failures can still be handled, usually it is processes that fail. A process failure is handled like a simultaneous failure of multiple workers. By definition, the buddy of all of these workers is the first worker of the next process. As usual, it is responsible for the restore of all failed workers. We chose the above numbering scheme although it may create some temporary load imbalances, since it enables most workers to continue task processing despite the failure. Senders of loot/frames to X recognize that a whole process has failed and avoid trying every single worker in the search for the buddy.

4   Implementation

Our implementation is based on the APGAS for Java library [20] for programming distributed parallel applications, and on a resilient store, called IMap, from Hazelcast [21]. We realize communication with active messages, which are processed by threads of the Java fork-join pool [22].

Part of the IMap accesses must be synchronized, and we protect them with the same lock object as used for the local queue (as in reference [8]). Internally, the IMap saves the checkpoints as key-value pairs, groups the pairs into partitions, and evenly distributes the partitions over nodes. We configured the IMap so that the checkpoints of all workers from the same process are mapped to the same partition, to reduce network communication during restore.

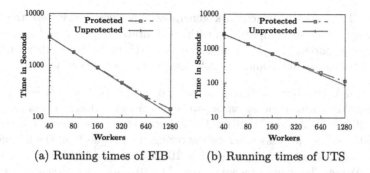

(a) Running times of FIB   (b) Running times of UTS

Fig. 3. Running times with and without protection in failure-free execution

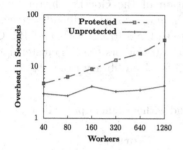

Fig. 4. Overhead of SYN with and without protection in failure-free execution

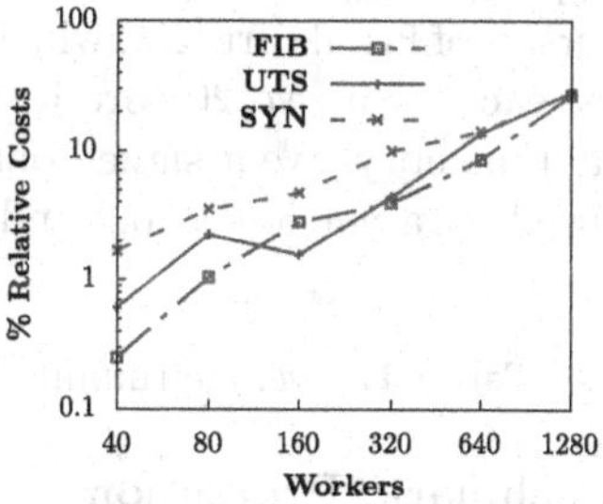

Fig. 5. Protection costs for FIB, UTS, and SYN in failure-free execution

The IMap works with at most six replicas of each partition. If more than six cluster nodes fail simultaneously or in close succession, a checkpoint may be irrecoverably lost and the program aborts. This is the only occasion in which our TC scheme aborts. AllFT, in contrast, also aborts after failure of worker 0, due to differences in termination detection between DIT and NFJ.

5 Experiments

5.1 Experimental Setting

We used three benchmarks:

- FIB: The Fibonacci benchmark resembles that from Sect. 2 for $n = 67$, except that we spawn a task for only one of the two recursive function calls.
- UTS: The Unbalanced Tree Search benchmark generates an irregular tree, using some statistical method that allows to control the number of child nodes. The tree is not stored, but its number of nodes is counted on-the-fly. We used a geometric distribution with expected value $b = 4$ for the distribution of child nodes, initial seed $s = 19$ for a pseudorandom number generator, and tree height $d = 19$.

- SYN: The synthetic benchmark generates a perfect w-ary task tree. Each task runs a dummy computation with configurable duration and then reports back to its parent [14]. We configured $m = 10^6$ tasks per worker with total duration $T_{calc} = 100$ s, and $v = 20\%$ load variance between workers.

FIB and UTS allow setting a sequential cut-off (C), which is a problem size threshold at which the spawn keyword is ignored. Like in reference [15], we set $C = 30$ for FIB and $C = 6$ for UTS. Parameter k denotes the number of tasks that a worker processes before answering steal requests in the lifeline-pure scheme. Like in reference [15], we set $k = 10$ for FIB, $k = 16$ for UTS, and $k = 1$ for SYN. We set the regular backup interval to 10 s, like in reference [8]. Finally, we used six replicas of each partition in the IMap.

Experiments were conducted on a partition of the Goethe cluster of the University of Frankfurt [23], which consists of homogeneous Infiniband-connected nodes, each with two 20-core Intel Xeon Skylake Gold 6148 CPUs and 192 GB of main memory. We assigned one process with 40 workers to each cluster node, and used Java version 19.0.2 and the APGAS for Java library from [24].

Table 1. Average running times with and without failure protection

Benchmark	Protection	Workers					
		40	80	160	320	640	1280
FIB	protected	3532.39	1798.49	907.52	464.96	244.30	144.31
	unprotected	3523.55	1780.05	882.657	447.40	225.07	113.65
UTS	protected	2628.18	1372.52	707.35	370.94	200.20	114.25
	unprotected	2612.21	1342.14	696.51	355.36	176.22	89.06
SYN	protected	104.70	106.32	109.05	113.55	118.11	132.93
	unprotected	102.97	102.71	104.13	103.32	103.54	104.27

5.2 Failure-free Runs

Figures 3a, 3b, and 4 depict the performance of failure-free FIB, UTS, and SYN executions with and without protection. Corresponding raw data are given in Table 1. All values are averages over 10 runs.

Figures 3a and 3b depict running times. They employ strong-scaling to give an impression of magnitudes. In both figures, the costs for protection increase with the number of workers. At 1280 workers, the difference in running times is 144.3 s vs 113.7 s (FIB) and 114.3 s vs 89.1 s (UTS).

Figure 4 depicts overhead instead of running time, which here includes both the costs of load balancing and the costs of protection. One can see that the overhead increases with the number of workers up to 32.9%.

The results from Figs. 3 and 4 are summarized in Fig. 5, which shows the relative costs of protected runs over unprotected runs as percentage. As the figure illustrates, the relative costs are similar for the three benchmarks, with a maximum of 28.3% for UTS at 1280 workers.

5.3   Estimation of Restore Overhead

In a second group of experiments, we estimated the restore overhead after worker failures. This overhead includes the times for: failure detection, execution of the restore protocol, and reprocessing of the lost tasks.

We estimated the overhead with the help of a methodology from reference [8]. For that, we measured the running times of three program executions: (A) with 640 workers, (B) with 600 workers, and (C) with 640 workers, of which 80 workers (2 processes) were stopped after half of the expected running time by calling System.exit(). The expected running time for execution (C) was determined with the help of execution (A).

Because executions (B) and (C) use the same average number of processing workers, we roughly estimated the restore overhead as the difference between the running times of executions (C) (291.28 s) and (B) (277.38 s). Thereby the numbers are averages over 50 runs of each execution.

As can be seen from the numbers above, the restore overhead is about 5% of the running time. Since this number refers to a failure of 80 workers, the overhead of a single worker failure is negligible.

6   Related Work

While this paper focuses on permanent node failures, other resilience techniques consider silent data corruptions (SDC), such as bit flips. A prominent technique to protect against SDC is replication. It can be realized on the task level [25–27] and may selectively determine tasks to replicate [28].

Existing tools to achieve fault-tolerance for permanent node failures include BLCR for transparent C/R, and SCR for application-level checkpointing [6]. In addition to application-level checkpointing, other application-level techniques are Algorithm-Based Fault Tolerance (ABFT) and naturally fault-tolerant algorithms [29].

Besides checkpointing, task-level fault tolerance can be achieved by leveraging the natural task duplication during work stealing, which is called supervision [18]. Supervision was compared to TC for DIT [14]. In this reference, supervision was observed to have less overhead than TC in failure-free runs, and TC to have lower recovery costs [14]. The fault tolerance overheads were about 1% for both methods, including a reasonable number of failures.

The lifeline-pure scheme arose as a simplification of a preceding hybrid scheme, in which workers balance their load via shared queues within each process, and via lifeline-based global work stealing between the processes [30]. The lifeline-pure scheme is usually more efficient than the hybrid scheme [15]. Its efficiency can be further improved through locality- and load-aware victim selection [15]. For the hybrid scheme, a fault tolerance approach has been sketched in reference [31].

In addition to AllFT, other TC schemes for DIT have been studied in the literature (e.g., [8,14]). Previous work on TC also referred to the STF task model on clusters with centralized task assignment [7].

7   Conclusions

In this paper, we have shown that TC can protect NFJ programs against permanent hardware failures. We presented the first TC implementation for NFJ, which is also the first TC implementation for multi-worker processes under work stealing.

We evaluated our scheme in experiments with three benchmarks and up to 1280 workers, and observed running time overheads of up to 28.3% and negligible recovery costs. The overheads are higher than those of TC for DIT, but lower than typical C/R overheads. The higher costs than in DIT are partly due to the need for an additional frame return protocol. Nevertheless, we expect that future work may be able to reduce the costs with low-level optimizations.

Finally, our success in transferring TC from DIT to NFJ suggests that TC may be generalized to further task models.

References

1. Fohry, C.: Checkpointing and localized recovery for nested fork-join programs. In: International Symposium on Checkpointing for Supercomputing (SuperCheck) (2021). https://arxiv.org/abs/2102.12941
2. Laboratory, O.R.N.: Frontier. https://www.olcf.ornl.gov/frontier
3. Herault, T., Robert, Y.: Fault-Tolerance Techniques for High-Performance Computing. Springer, Cham (2015). https://doi.org/10.1007/978-3-319-20943-2
4. Benoit, A., Herault, T., Fèvre, V.L., Robert, Y.: Replication is more efficient than you think. In: Proceedings of International Conference for High Performance Computing, Networking, Storage and Analysis (SC), pp. 1–14. ACM (2019)
5. Losada, N., González, P., Martín, M.J., Bosilca, G., Bouteiller, A., Teranishi, K.: Fault tolerance of MPI applications in exascale systems: the ULFM solution. Future Generation Comput. Syst. (FGCS) **106**, 467–481 (2020)
6. Shahzad, F., Wittmann, M., Kreutzer, M., Zeise, T., Hager, G., Wellein, G.: A survey of checkpoint/restart techniques on distributed memory systems. Parallel Process. Lett. (PPL) **23**(4), 1340011–1340030 (2013)
7. Lion, R., Thibault, S.: From tasks graphs to asynchronous distributed checkpointing with local restart. In: Proceedings of International Conference on High Performance Computing, Networking, Storage and Analysis (SC) Workshops (FTXS), pp. 31–40. ACM (2020)
8. Posner, J., Reitz, L., Fohry, C.: A comparison of application-level fault tolerance schemes for task pools. Future Generation Comput. Syst. (FGCS) **105**, 119–134 (2019)

9. Kaiser, H., Heller, T., Adelstein-Lelbach, B., Serio, A., Fey, D.: HPX: a task based programming model in a global address space. In: Proceedings of International Conference on Partitioned Global Address Space Programming Models (PGAS), pp. 1–11. ACM (2014)
10. OpenMP Architecture Review Board: OpenMP application programming interface (version 5.2). openmp.org (2021)
11. Chamberlain, B.L., Callahan, D., Zima, H.P.: Parallel programmability and the Chapel language. Int. J. High Perform. Comput. Appl. (IJHPCA) **21**(3), 91–312 (2007)
12. Blumofe, R.D., Leiserson, C.E.: Scheduling multithreaded computations by work stealing. J. ACM **46**(5), 720–748 (1999)
13. Fohry, C.: An overview of task-based parallel programming models. In: Tutorial at European Network on High-performance Embedded Architecture and Compilation Conference (HiPEAC) (2019)
14. Posner, J., Reitz, L., Fohry, C.: Task-level resilience: checkpointing vs. supervision. Special Issue Int. J. Netw. Comput. (IJNC) **12**(1), 47–72 (2022)
15. Reitz, L., Fohry, C.: Lifeline-based load balancing schemes for asynchronous many-task runtimes in clusters. Special Issue J. Parallel Comput. (PARCO) **116**, 103020 (2023)
16. Saraswat, V.A., Kambadur, P., Kodali, S., Grove, D., Krishnamoorthy, S.: Lifeline-based global load balancing. In: Proceedings of SIGPLAN Symposium on Principles and Practice of Parallel Programming (PPoPP), pp. 201–212. ACM (2011)
17. Blumofe, R.D., Lisiecki, P.A.: Adaptive and reliable parallel computing on networks of workstations. In: Proceedings of Annual Conference on USENIX, pp. 1–10 (1997)
18. Kestor, G., Krishnamoorthy, S., Ma, W.: Localized fault recovery for nested fork-join programs. In: Proceedings of Internetional Symposium on Parallel and Distributed Processing (IPDPS), pp. 397–408. IEEE (2017)
19. Fohry, C., Bungart, M., Plock, P.: Fault tolerance for lifeline-based global load balancing. J. Softw. Eng. Appl. (JSEA) **10**(13), 925–958 (2017)
20. Tardieu, O.: The APGAS library: resilient parallel and distributed programming in Java 8. In: Proceedings of SIGPLAN Workshop on X10, pp. 25–26. ACM (2015)
21. Hazelcast: The leading open source in-memory data grid. http://hazelcast.org
22. Lea, D.: A Java fork/join framework. In: Proceedings of the Conference on Java Grande, pp. 36–43. ACM (2000)
23. TOP500.org: Goethe-HLR. https://www.top500.org/system/179588
24. IBM: The APGAS library for fault-tolerant distributed programming in Java 8 (version from Oct 10, 2016). https://github.com/x10-lang/apgas
25. Paul, S.R., et al.: Enabling resilience in asynchronous many-task programming models. In: Yahyapour, R. (ed.) Euro-Par 2019. LNCS, vol. 11725, pp. 346–360. Springer, Cham (2019). https://doi.org/10.1007/978-3-030-29400-7_25
26. Gupta, N., Mayo, J.R., Lemoine, A.S., Kaiser, H.: Towards distributed software resilience in asynchronous many- task programming models. In: Workshop on Fault Tolerance for HPC at eXtreme Scale (FTXS), pp. 11–20 (2020)
27. Kurt, M.C., Krishnamoorthy, S., Agrawal, K., Agrawal, G.: Fault-tolerant dynamic task graph scheduling. In: Proceedings of International Conference for High Performance Computing, Networking, Storage and Analysis (SC), pp. 719–730. ACM (2014)
28. Subasi, O., Yalcin, G., Zyulkyarov, F., Unsal, O., Labarta, J.: Designing and modelling selective replication for fault-tolerant HPC applications. In: International Symposium on Cluster, Cloud and Grid Computing (CCGRID), pp. 452–457 (2017)

29. Semmoud, A., Hakem, M., Benmammar, B.: A survey of load balancing in distributed systems. Int. J. High Perform. Comput. Netw. **15**, 233 (2019)
30. Finnerty, P., Kamada, T., Ohta, C.: Self-adjusting task granularity for global load balancer library on clusters of many-core processors. In: Proceedings of International Workshop on Programming Models and Applications for Multicores and Manycores (PMAM). ACM (2020)
31. Reitz, L.: Task-level checkpointing for nested fork-join programs. In: Proceedings of International Parallel and Distributed Processing Symposium (IPDPS), Ph.D. Forum, Extended Abstract. IEEE (2021)

Making Uintah Performance Portable for Department of Energy Exascale Testbeds

John K. Holmen[1]([✉])(iD), Marta García[2](iD), Abhishek Bagusetty[2](iD),
Allen Sanderson[3], and Martin Berzins[3](iD)

[1] Oak Ridge National Laboratory, Oak Ridge, TN, USA
holmenjk@ornl.gov
[2] Argonne National Laboratory, Lemont, IL, USA
{mgarcia,abagusetty}@anl.gov
[3] University of Utah, Salt Lake City, UT, USA
{allen,mb}@sci.utah.edu

Abstract. To help ease ports to forthcoming Department of Energy (DOE) exascale systems, testbeds have been made available to select users. These testbeds are helpful for preparing codes to run on the same hardware and similar software as in their respective exascale systems. This paper describes how the Uintah Computational Framework, an open-source asynchronous many-task (AMT) runtime system, has been modified to be performance portable across the DOE Crusher, DOE Polaris, and DOE Sunspot testbeds in preparation for portable simulations across the exascale DOE Frontier and DOE Aurora systems. The Crusher, Polaris, and Sunspot testbeds feature the AMD MI250X, NVIDIA A100, and Intel PVC GPUs, respectively. This performance portability has been made possible by extending Uintah's intermediate portability layer [18] to additionally support the Kokkos::HIP, Kokkos::OpenMPTarget, and Kokkos::SYCL back-ends. This paper also describes notable updates to Uintah's support for Kokkos, which were required to make this extension possible. Results are shown for a challenging radiative heat transfer calculation, central to the University of Utah's predictive boiler simulations. These results demonstrate single-source portability across AMD-, NVIDIA-, and Intel-based GPUs using various Kokkos back-ends.

© The Author(s), under exclusive license to Springer Nature Switzerland AG 2024
D. Zeinalipour et al. (Eds.): Euro-Par 2023 Workshops, LNCS 14352, pp. 115–126, 2024.
https://doi.org/10.1007/978-3-031-48803-0_10

Keywords: Asynchronous Many-Task Runtime System · Performance Portability · Parallelism and Concurrency · Portability · Software Engineering

1   Introduction

Forthcoming Department of Energy (DOE) exascale systems pose new challenges for large-scale simulation codes. These challenges include understanding how to manage the increased concurrency, deep memory hierarchies, heterogeneity, and diversity of such systems. Most notable among challenges are the new hardware and software featured among systems such as the exascale DOE Frontier [12] and DOE Aurora [11], which include AMD- and Intel–based GPUs, respectively. This is a challenge as it is a significant departure from prior heterogeneous high performance computing (HPC) systems featuring NVIDIA-based GPUs.

Development for exascale systems is enabled and simplified by testbeds that have been made available to select users through early access programs such as the Aurora Early Science Program and the Frontier Center for Accelerated Application Readiness Program. These testbeds feature the same hardware and similar software as in their respective exascale system. This availability eases the preparation of user codes for forthcoming exascale systems by allowing developers to port their codes to the target architectures while waiting for exascale systems to enter production and open to users.

This paper describes how the Uintah Computational Framework, an open-source asynchronous many-task runtime system, has been extended to run in a performance portable manner across the DOE Crusher, DOE Polaris, and DOE Sunspot testbeds in preparation for portable simulations across the exascale DOE Frontier and DOE Aurora systems. The Crusher, Polaris, and Sunspot testbeds feature the AMD MI250X, NVIDIA A100, and Intel PVC GPUs, respectively. These runs have been made possible by extending Uintah's intermediate portability layer [18] to also support the Kokkos::HIP, Kokkos::OpenMPTarget, and Kokkos::SYCL back-ends. This paper also describes notable updates to Uintah's support for Kokkos, which were required to make this extension possible. These updates include rewriting device-specific portions of Uintah's runtime to make use of portable Kokkos abstractions rather than raw CUDA.

To demonstrate Kokkos capabilities, a case study using Uintah's newly extended intermediate portability layer and runtime system are examined for a challenging radiative heat transfer calculation, central to the University of Utah's predictive boiler simulations. This case study shows single-source portability across AMD-, NVIDIA-, and Intel-based GPUs with various Kokkos back-ends. For AMD-based GPUs, single-source portability is shown using the Kokkos::HIP and Kokkos::OpenMPTarget back-ends. For NVIDIA-based GPUs, single-source portability is shown using the Kokkos::CUDA, Kokkos::OpenMPTarget, and Kokkos::SYCL back-ends. For Intel-based GPUs, single-source portability is shown using the Kokkos::OpenMPTarget and Kokkos::SYCL back-ends. Note, an experimental Kokkos::OpenACC [43] back-end providing cross-vendor support is also available. However, functionality of this back-end was not tested as a part of this work.

The remainder of this paper is structured as follows. Section 2 provides an overview of the Uintah Computational Framework. Section 3 describes the extension of Uintah's intermediate portability layer to support the Kokkos::HIP, Kokkos::OpenMPTarget, and Kokkos::SYCL back-ends and updates to Uintah's support for Kokkos. Section 4 describes the benchmark used for experiments. Section 5 describes the systems used for experiments and presents results gathered on the DOE Crusher, DOE Polaris, and DOE Sunspot testbeds. Section 6 describes related work and Sect. 7 concludes this paper.

2 The Uintah Computational Framework

The Uintah Computational Framework is an open-source asynchronous many-task (AMT) runtime system and block-structured adaptive mesh refinement (SAMR) framework specializing in large-scale simulation of fluid-structure interaction problems. These problems are modeled by solving partial differential equations on structured adaptive mesh refinement grids. Uintah is based upon novel techniques for understanding a broad set of fluid-structure interaction problems [4].

Through its lifetime, Uintah has been ported to a diverse set of major HPC systems. Examples using Uintah's MPI+Kokkos capabilities include the NSF Frontera [20], DOE Lassen [19], DOE Summit [20], NSF Stampede 2 [17,18], DOE Theta [35], and DOE Titan [35] systems. Other examples include the National Research Center of Parallel Computer Engineering and Technology (NRCPC) Sunway TaihuLight [44], DOE Titan [23,25,33], NSF Stampede [17,33], DOE Mira [4,33], and NSF Blue Waters [4] systems.

The work presented here extends past efforts by demonstrating Uintah's first successful ports to heterogeneous HPC systems featuring AMD- and Intel-based GPUs. This work makes use of Uintah's MPI+Kokkos capabilities through the runtime's heterogeneous MPI+Kokkos task scheduler [19]. This scheduler supports use of 1 GPU and a subset of CPU cores per MPI process on heterogeneous CPU+GPU nodes and executes tasks simultaneously across the host and device based upon user-specified tags indicating where a task can run. For this work, the majority of tasks were run on the GPU. Note, Uintah does not yet support GPU-aware MPI. More details on Uintah's heterogeneous MPI+Kokkos task scheduler can be found in a recent paper [19].

3 Extending Uintah's Intermediate Portability Layer

Introduced in 2019 [18], Uintah's intermediate portability layer consists of 3 components: (1) loop-level support providing application developers with framework-specific abstractions (e.g., generic parallel loop statements) that map to interface-specific abstractions (e.g., PPL-specific parallel loop statements), (2) application-level support that includes a tagging system to identify which interfaces are supported by a given loop, and (3) build-level support that includes selective compilation of loops to allow for incremental refactoring and simultaneous use of multiple underlying programming models for heterogeneous HPC systems. More details on Uintah's intermediate portability layer can be found in a recent paper [18].

The goal of this intermediate layer is for application developers to, hopefully, need only adopt the layer once to support current and future interfaces to underlying programming models. For application developers, this layer allows for easy adoption of underlying programming models without requiring knowledge of low-level implementation details. For infrastructure developers, this layer allows for easy addition, removal, and tuning of interfaces behind-the-scenes in a single location, reducing the need for far-reaching changes across application code.

As a part of this work, Uintah's intermediate portability layer has been extended to support the Kokkos::HIP, Kokkos::OpenMPTarget, and Kokkos::SYCL back-ends. Prior to this extension, however, notable updates to Uintah's use of Kokkos were necessary to make use of the latest Kokkos releases. Section 3.1 describes these updates and the state of Uintah's support for Kokkos. Note, these updates and extensions were made without any required changes to user-facing abstractions.

3.1 State of Uintah's Support for Kokkos

Prior to this work, Uintah's support for Kokkos was limited to use of the Kokkos::OpenMP and Kokkos::CUDA back-ends. This support had two key limitations: (1) use of the Kokkos::CUDA back-end required use of a patched version of Kokkos release 2.7.00 from May 2018 with custom modifications from Uintah developers to add support for asynchronous execution [35], and (2) Uintah's heterogeneous MPI+Kokkos task scheduler [19] used raw CUDA behind-the-scenes for task scheduling, which is described further in [20]. Though they eased rapid research development, these limitations posed challenges when working to additionally support the Kokkos::HIP, Kokkos::OpenMPTarget, and Kokkos::SYCL back-ends, which required use of Kokkos releases newer than 2.7.00.

Prior to adding support for new back-ends, limitation (1) was addressed first to deprecate Uintah's Kokkos 2.7.00 patch and modernize Uintah's use of Kokkos. This patch pre-dated Kokkos execution space instance functionality and implemented instance-like functionality to achieve asynchronous execution of parallel patterns when using the Kokkos::CUDA back-end. Deprecation was a critical first step as Kokkos development has been advancing rapidly with regular releases adding new functionality and back-end support. To deprecate this patch, the only changes required in Uintah were minor interface changes. Deprecation of this patch has been key for allowing Uintah's use of Kokkos to be updated more quickly as new Kokkos versions are released. Additionally, this allows us to stay up to date with third party libraries used by Uintah that also make use of the latest Kokkos releases (e.g., Hypre [13]).

Next, limitation (2) was addressed to remove the remaining raw CUDA used in Uintah's heterogeneous MPI+Kokkos task scheduler. This task scheduler used cudaMemcpyAsync for asynchronous host-to-device (H2D) and device-to-host (D2H) transfers and cudaStreamQuery to check the status of transfers. CUDA streams, CUDA memory allocations, and CUDA kernels were also used behind-the-scenes. Raw CUDA was replaced with portable alternatives by (1) replacing use of CUDA streams with Kokkos execution space instances, (2) replacing use of CUDA memory allocations with Kokkos::kokkos_malloc, (3) replacing use of CUDA kernels with Kokkos::parallel_for, (4) replacing use of cudaMemcpyAsync with Kokkos::deep_copy, and (5) replacing use of cudaStreamQuery with Kokkos::fence.

With limitation (1) and (2) addressed as a part of this work, Uintah's use of Kokkos was then updated from the May 2018 release to 2023 releases. Specifically, March 2023 release 4.0.0 was used for this work. This update allowed Uintah to make use of newly supported Kokkos back-ends including Kokkos::HIP, Kokkos::OpenMPTarget, and Kokkos::SYCL. To support these back-ends, Uintah's Kokkos::CUDA-specific device support was broadened to offer general device support through multiple back-ends. To ease parameter tuning, command-line options were also added to allow the user to specify the execution policy type (e.g., TeamPolicy, RangePolicy, and MDRangePolicy) and low-level parameters (e.g., chunk size and tile size) at run-time. Note, Uintah's use of Kokkos::OpenMP::partition_master was also deprecated as a part of this update due to the functionality being deprecated in Kokkos. A replacement was implemented using Kokkos::partition_space.

4 Radiation Modeling

Parallel reverse Monte-Carlo ray tracing (RMCRT) methods [23,25] are one of several methods available within Uintah for solving the radiative transport equation. RMCRT models radiative heat transfer using random walks across rays cast throughout the computational domain. These rays are traced in reverse, towards their origin, to eliminate the need to trace rays that may never reach an origin. During ray traversal, the amount of incoming intensity absorbed by the origin is computed. This incoming intensity is then used to aid in solving the radiative transport equation. The work presented here uses Uintah's 2-Level RMCRT-based radiation model to solve the Burns and Christon benchmark problem described in [6]. More detailed information on RMCRT can be found in a recent dissertation [22].

5 Experiments

Experiments made use of the DOE Crusher, DOE Polaris, and DOE Sunspot testbeds at the Oak Ridge Leadership Computing Facility and Argonne Leadership Computing Facility, respectively. Crusher, Polaris, and Sunspot feature AMD-, NVIDIA-, and Intel-based GPUs, respectively. For this reason, performance portability is important.

5.1 Crusher

Crusher is a testbed featuring the same hardware and similar software as the exascale Frontier system. Crusher and Frontier are maintained at the Oak Ridge Leadership Computing Facility. Frontier and Crusher (also known as Frontier TDS) are currently Number 1 and Number 32 on June 2023's Top500 list [38].

The Crusher testbed is comprised of 192 HPE Cray EX235a nodes, each with one 64-core AMD EPYC 7A53 "Optimized 3rd Gen EPYC" CPU and four AMD MI250X GPUs, each with 2 Graphics Compute Dies (GCDs). Each compute node has 512 GB of DDR4 memory and 512 GB of high-bandwidth memory (HBM2E), 64 GB per GCD. The CPU is connected to the GPUs via AMD's Infinity Fabric which delivers a bandwidth of 36+36 GB/s. All GCDs on a Crusher node are interconnected via Infinity Fabric delivering up to 50+50 GB/s for GCDs across GPUs, and up to 200+200 GB/s for GCDs on the same GPU. Compute nodes on Crusher are interconnected via HPE's Slingshot 11 interconnect.

5.2 Polaris

Polaris is a testbed featuring a similar heterogeneous CPU+GPU node configuration and similar software as the forthcoming exascale Aurora system. Polaris and Aurora are maintained at the Argonne Leadership Computing Facility. Polaris is currently Number 19 on June 2023's Top500 list [38].

The Polaris testbed is comprised of 560 HPE Apollo Gen10+ nodes, each with one 32-core AMD EPYC Milan 7543P CPU and four NVIDIA A100 GPUs connected via NVLink. Each compute node has 512 GB of DDR4 memory and 160 GB of high-bandwidth memory (HBM2), 40 GB per GPU. Compute nodes on Polaris are currently interconnected via HPE's Slingshot 10 interconnect and are scheduled to be upgraded to Slingshot 11 in 2023.

5.3 Sunspot

Sunspot is a testbed featuring the same hardware and similar software as the forthcoming Aurora system. Sunspot and Aurora are maintained at the Argonne Leadership Computing Facility.

The Sunspot testbed is comprised of 128 HPE Cray EX nodes, each with two Intel Xeon CPU Max Series(Sapphire Rapids) processors and six Intel Data Center GPU Max Series (Ponte Vecchio/PVC), each with 2 Stacks. Each compute node has 512 GB of DDR5 memory, 512 GB of high-bandwidth memory (HBM) on each CPU, and 128 GB of high-bandwidth memory (HBM) on each GPU. Compute nodes on Sunspot are interconnected via HPE's Slingshot 11 interconnect.

5.4 Testbed Comparisons

For testbed comparisons, experiments explored performance of various GPU architectures (i.e., AMD MI250X, NVIDIA A100, and Intel PVC) using problems

Table 1. Single-node timings across AMD MI250X, NVIDIA A100, and Intel PVC GPUs. For Crusher, 1 MPI process is used per AMD MI250X GCD. For Polaris, 1 MPI process is used per NVIDIA A100 GPU. For Sunspot, 1 MPI process is used per Intel PVC Stack.

Testbed Used	Devices Used	Back-End Used	Execution Policy	Mean Time per Timestep (s)
Crusher	1x MI250X (2 GCDs)	Kokkos::HIP	MDRange	51.7
	1x MI250X (2 GCDs)	Kokkos::OpenMPTarget	MDRange	53.3
Polaris	1x A100	Kokkos::CUDA	Range	28.9
	1x A100	Kokkos::OpenMPTarget	Team	48.7
	1x A100	Kokkos::SYCL	Range	37.1
Sunspot	1x PVC (2 Stacks)	Kokkos::OpenMPTarget	Team	55.6
	1x PVC (2 Stacks)	Kokkos::SYCL	MDRange	48.6
Crusher	4x MI250X (8 GCDs)*	Kokkos::HIP	MDRange	64.1
	4x MI250X (8 GCDs)*	Kokkos::OpenMPTarget	MDRange	75.2
Polaris	4x A100*	Kokkos::CUDA	Range	39.2
	4x A100*	Kokkos::OpenMPTarget	Team	60.3
	4x A100*	Kokkos::SYCL	Range	47.4
Sunspot	6x PVC (12 Stacks)*	Kokkos::OpenMPTarget	Team	82.0
	6x PVC (12 Stacks)*	Kokkos::SYCL	MDRange	65.9

*This configuration corresponds to use of a full node.

sized to provide each GCD/GPU/Stack with eight 128^3 fine mesh patches. Note, additional demonstration of Uintah's portable capabilities can be found among MPI+Kokkos results gathered on the NSF Frontera [20], DOE Lassen [19], DOE Summit [20], NSF Stampede 2 [17,18], DOE Theta [35], and DOE Titan [35] systems.

Simulations were launched using 1 MPI process per GCD/GPU/Stack. Experiments were performed to identify optimal run configurations using each Kokkos back-end that worked on the target architecture with various Kokkos execution policy types and parameters. Optimal run configurations were used for the results to follow.

The simulation domain is decomposed into a collection of patches, which are distributed across MPI processes. Here, a patch refers to the collection of cells executed by a loop. The radiation modeling problem also uses adaptive mesh refinement to coarsen/refine patches [24]. Domain decomposition and, thus, patch size is user-specified at run-time and remains fixed throughout the simulation.

Problems were sized to provide each MPI process with eight 128^3 fine mesh patches. The problem is weak-scaled when moving from one device to a full node. The problem was configured to cast 50 rays per cell and used a mesh refinement ratio of 4. Results have been averaged over 7 consecutive timesteps. Note, this problem does not weak scale as configured due to communication requirements. However, excellent weak-scaling is possible through the use of aggressive mesh refinement to reduce communication requirements [22].

Table 1 shows single-node timings across MI250X, A100, and PVC for the Burns and Christon benchmark problem on a 2-level structured adaptive mesh refinement grid. For each testbed, results were gathered using problems sized to provide each MPI process with $256 \times 256 \times 256$ cells on the fine mesh and $64 \times 64 \times 64$ cells on the coarse mesh, respectively, for one fine mesh patch size (128^3 cells per fine mesh patch). These results are encouraging as they demonstrate the portability of Kokkos across DOE exascale testbeds. In addition to being able to run across multiple architectures with Kokkos, we were also able to run across multiple Kokkos back-ends on a given architecture. Note, Kokkos back-ends are supported to varying degrees on individual architectures. For example, use of Kokkos::SYCL is not tested or officially supported on AMD-based GPUs as of this writing.

6   Related Work

Uintah is one of many asynchronous many-task runtime systems and block-structured adaptive mesh refinement frameworks. Examples of similar AMT runtime systems include Charm++ [28], HPX [27], IRIS [29,34], Legion [2], PaRSEC [5], and StarPU [1]. Other examples of AMT-based approaches include the combination of OpenMP tasking and target offloading [42]. Examples of similar SAMR frameworks include BoxLib [46] (superseded by AMReX [45]), Cactus [14], and Parthenon [15]. An analysis of performance portability for representative AMT runtime systems, including Uintah, can be found in a recent technical report [3]. A review of representative SAMR frameworks, including Uintah, can be found in a recent survey [9].

Kokkos is one of many performance portability layers offering a single interface to multiple underlying programming models (e.g., CUDA, HIP, OpenACC, OpenCL, OpenMP, etc.). Examples of similar performance portability layers are OCCA [32], RAJA [21], and SYCL [37]/DPC++ [36]. Examples of Exascale Computing Project codes using Kokkos can be found in a recent survey [10]. Examples of "real-world" applications using Kokkos include ArborX [30], BabelStream [8], K-Athena [16] (superseded by AthenaPK [15]), kEDM [39], LAMMPS [40], and Octo-Tiger [7,31] with a more extensive collection of applications using Kokkos documented on their GitHub [41]. A review of exascale challenges and performance portable programming models can be found in a recent survey [26].

7   Conclusions and Future Work

This study has helped demonstrate Uintah's preparedness for forthcoming DOE exascale systems. Specifically, this work documents Uintah's first portable use of AMD- and Intel-based GPUs, whereas prior work was limited to NVIDIA-based GPUs. This preparedness has been made possible by the extension of Uintah's intermediate portability layer [18] to additionally support the Kokkos::HIP, Kokkos::OpenMPTarget, and Kokkos::SYCL back-ends. This extension has been made possible by notable updates to Uintah's support for Kokkos.

Kokkos capabilities have been shown across the DOE Crusher, DOE Polaris, and DOE Sunspot testbeds when using Uintah's intermediate portability layer to make portable use of AMD-, NVIDIA-, and Intel-based GPUs, respectively, for the benchmark examined. At the device- and node-level, single-source portability is shown across AMD-, NVIDIA-, and Intel-based GPUs using various Kokkos back-ends. This portability offers encouragement as we prepare to make portable use of the DOE Aurora and DOE Frontier systems. Next steps include portable simulations across the DOE Aurora and DOE Frontier systems to help better understand how Uintah scales across exascale systems.

Acknowledgments. This material is based upon work originally supported by the Department of Energy, National Nuclear Security Administration, under Award Number(s) DE-NA0002375. This research used resources of the Argonne Leadership Computing Facility, which is a DOE Office of Science User Facility supported under Contract DE-AC02-06CH11357. This research used resources of the Oak Ridge Leadership Computing Facility, which is a DOE Office of Science User Facility supported under Contract DE-AC05-00OR22725. This work was supported by the Office of Science, U.S. Department of Energy, under Contract DE-AC02-06CH11357. Support for Allen Sanderson comes from the University of Texas at Austin under Award Number(s) UTA19-001215 and a gift from the Intel One API Centers Program. The authors would like to thank the ALCF and OLCF for early access to exascale testbeds, including those operated by the Joint Laboratory for System Evaluation (JLSE) at Argonne National Laboratory. The authors would also like to thank the Aurora Early Science Program and Kokkos developer communities for their continued support with special thanks to Daniel Arndt, Rahulkumar Gayatri, Varsha Madananth, and Patrick Steinbrecher.

References

1. Augonnet, C., Thibault, S., Namyst, R., Wacrenier, P.A.: StarPU: a unified platform for task scheduling on heterogeneous multicore architectures. Concurrency Comput. Pract. Experience **23**(2), 187–198 (2011)
2. Bauer, M., Treichler, S., Slaughter, E., Aiken, A.: Legion: expressing locality and independence with logical regions. In: Proceedings of the International Conference on High Performance Computing, Networking, Storage and Analysis, p. 66. IEEE Computer Society Press (2012)
3. Bennett, J., et al.: ASC ATDM level 2 milestone #5325: Asynchronous many-task runtime system analysis and assessment for next generation platforms. Technical report, Sandia National Laboratories (2015)
4. Berzins, M., et al.: Extending the uintah framework through the petascale modeling of detonation in arrays of high explosive devices. SIAM J. Sci. Comput. **38**(5), 101–122 (2016)
5. Bosilca, G., Bouteiller, A., Danalis, A., Faverge, M., Herault, T., Dongarra, J.J.: PaRSEC: exploiting heterogeneity to enhance scalabilityBerzins. Comput. Sci. Eng. **15**(6), 36–45 (2013)
6. Burns, S., Christon, M.: Spatial domain-based parallelism in large-scale, participating-media, radiative transport applications. Numer. Heat Transfer **31**(4), 401–421 (1997)
7. Daiß, G., et al.: Beyond fork-join: integration of performance portable Kokkos kernels with HPX. In: 2021 IEEE International Parallel and Distributed Processing Symposium Workshops (IPDPSW), pp. 377–386. IEEE (2021)

8. Deakin, T., Price, J., Martineau, M., McIntosh-Smith, S.: Evaluating attainable memory bandwidth of parallel programming models via babelstream. Int. J. Comput. Sci. Eng. **17**(3), 247–262 (2018)
9. Dubey, A., et al.: A survey of high level frameworks in block-structured adaptive mesh refinement packages. J. Parallel Distrib. Comput. (2014)
10. Evans, T.M., et al.: A survey of software implementations used by application codes in the exascale computing project. Int. J. High Perform. Comput. Appl. **36**(1), 5–12 (2022)
11. Argonne Leadership Computing Facility: Aurora (2023). https://www.alcf.anl.gov/aurora
12. Oak Ridge Leadership Computing Facility: Frontier (2023). https://www.olcf.ornl.gov/frontier/
13. Falgout, R.D., Li, R., Sjögreen, B., Wang, L., Yang, U.M.: Porting hypre to heterogeneous computer architectures: strategies and experiences. Parallel Comput. **108**, 102840 (2021). https://doi.org/10.1016/j.parco.2021.102840
14. Goodale, T., et al.: The cactus framework and toolkit: design and applications. In: Palma, J.M.L.M., Sousa, A.A., Dongarra, J., Hernández, V. (eds.) VECPAR 2002. LNCS, pp. 197–227. Springer, Heidelberg (2003). https://doi.org/10.1007/3-540-36569-9_13
15. Grete, P., et al.: Parthenon-a performance portable block-structured adaptive mesh refinement framework. Int. J. High Perform. Comput. Appl. 10943420221143775 (2022)
16. Grete, P., Glines, F.W., O'Shea, B.W.: K-Athena: a performance portable structured grid finite volume magnetohydrodynamics code. IEEE Trans. Parallel Distrib. Syst. **32**(1), 85–97 (2020)
17. Holmen, J.K., Humphrey, A., Sunderland, D., Berzins, M.: Improving uintah's scalability through the use of portable kokkos-based data parallel tasks. In: Proceedings of the Practice and Experience in Advanced Research Computing 2017 on Sustainability, Success and Impact, pp. 27:1–27:8. PEARC17, ACM, New York, NY, USA (2017)
18. Holmen, J.K., Peterson, B., Berzins, M.: An approach for indirectly adopting a performance portability layer in large legacy codes. In: 2019 IEEE/ACM International Workshop on Performance, Portability and Productivity in HPC (P3HPC), pp. 36–49 (2019). https://doi.org/10.1109/P3HPC49587.2019.00009
19. Holmen, J.K., Sahasrabudhe, D., Berzins, M.: A heterogeneous MPI+PPL task scheduling approach for asynchronous many-task runtime systems. In: Proceedings of the Practice and Experience in Advanced Research Computing 2021 on Sustainability, Success and Impact (PEARC21). ACM (2021)
20. Holmen, J.K., Sahasrabudhe, D., Berzins, M.: Porting uintah to heterogeneous systems. In: Proceedings of the Platform for Advanced Scientific Computing Conference. PASC 2022, Association for Computing Machinery, New York, NY, USA (2022). https://doi.org/10.1145/3539781.3539794
21. Hornung, R.D., Keasler, J.A.: The raja portability layer: overview and status. Technical report, Lawrence Livermore National Laboratory (LLNL), Livermore, CA (2014)
22. Humphrey, A.: Scalable Asynchronous Many-Task Runtime Solutions to Globally Coupled Problems. Ph.D. thesis, School of Computing, University of Utah (2019)
23. Humphrey, A., Harman, T., Berzins, M., Smith, P.: A scalable algorithm for radiative heat transfer using reverse monte Carlo ray tracing. In: Kunkel, J.M., Ludwig, T. (eds.) High Performance Computing. LNCS, vol. 9137, pp. 212–230. Springer, Cham (2015). https://doi.org/10.1007/978-3-319-20119-1_16

24. Humphrey, A., Meng, Q., Berzins, M., Harman, T.: Radiation modeling using the uintah heterogeneous CPU/GPU runtime system. In: Proceedings of the first conference of the Extreme Science and Engineering Discovery Environment (XSEDE 2012). Association for Computing Machinery (2012)

25. Humphrey, A., Sunderland, D., Harman, T., Berzins, M.: Radiative heat transfer calculation on 16384 GPUs using a reverse monte Carlo ray tracing approach with adaptive mesh refinement. In: 2016 IEEE International Parallel and Distributed Processing Symposium Workshops (IPDPSW), pp. 1222–1231 (2016)

26. Johnson, A.: Area exam: general-purpose performance portable programming models for productive exascale computing (2020)

27. Kaiser, H., et al.: Hpx - the c++ standard library for parallelism and concurrency. J. Open Source Softw. 5(53), 2352 (2020). https://doi.org/10.21105/joss.02352

28. Kale, L.V., Krishnan, S.: Charm++: a portable concurrent object oriented system based on c++. In: Proceedings of the Eighth Annual Conference on Object-oriented Programming Systems, Languages, and Applications, pp. 91–108. OOPSLA 1993, ACM, New York, NY, USA (1993)

29. Kim, J., Lee, S., Johnston, B., Vetter, J.S.: Iris: a portable runtime system exploiting multiple heterogeneous programming systems. In: 2021 IEEE High Performance Extreme Computing Conference (HPEC), pp. 1–8 (2021). https://doi.org/10.1109/HPEC49654.2021.9622873

30. Lebrun-Grandié, D., Prokopenko, A., Turcksin, B., Slattery, S.R.: ArborX: a performance portable geometric search library. ACM Trans. Math. Softw. 47(1) (2020). https://doi.org/10.1145/3412558

31. Marcello, D.C., et al.: Octo-Tiger: a new, 3D hydrodynamic code for stellar mergers that uses Hpx parallelization. Monthly Notices R. Astron. Soc. 504(4), 5345–5382 (04 2021). https://doi.org/10.1093/mnras/stab937

32. Medina, D.S., St-Cyr, A., Warburton, T.: OCCA: a unified approach to multithreading languages. arXiv preprint arXiv:1403.0968 (2014)

33. Meng, Q., Humphrey, A., Schmidt, J., Berzins, M.: Investigating applications portability with the uintah DAG-based runtime system on PetaScale supercomputers. In: Proceedings of SC13: International Conference for High Performance Computing, Networking, Storage and Analysis, pp. 96:1–96:12 (2013)

34. Monil, M.A.H., Miniskar, N.R., Liu, F.Y., Vetter, J.S., Valero-Lara, P.: LaRIS: targeting portability and productivity for lapack codes on extreme heterogeneous systems by using iris. In: 2022 IEEE/ACM Redefining Scalability for Diversely Heterogeneous Architectures Workshop (RSDHA), pp. 12–21 (2022). https://doi.org/10.1109/RSDHA56811.2022.00007

35. Peterson, B., et al.: Demonstrating GPU code portability and scalability for radiative heat transfer computations. J. Comput. Sci. 27, 303–319 (2018)

36. Reinders, J., Ashbaugh, B., Brodman, J., Kinsner, M., Pennycook, J., Tian, X.: Data Parallel C++: Mastering DPC++ for Programming of Heterogeneous Systems using C++ and SYCL. Springer, Cham (2021). https://doi.org/10.1007/978-1-4842-5574-2

37. Rovatsou, M., Howes, L., Keryell, R.: Khronos Group SYCL 2020 Specification (2023). https://www.khronos.org/registry/SYCL/specs/sycl-2020/pdf/sycl-2020.pdf

38. Strohmaier, E., Dongarra, J., Simon, H., Meuer, M.: June 2023 — TOP 500 (2023). https://top500.org/lists/top500/2023/06/

39. Takahashi, K., et al.: kEDM: a performance-portable implementation of empirical dynamic modeling using Kokkos. In: Practice and Experience in Advanced Research Computing. PEARC 2021, Association for Computing Machinery, New York, NY, USA (2021). https://doi.org/10.1145/3437359.3465571

40. Thompson, A.P., et al.: LAMMPS - a flexible simulation tool for particle-based materials modeling at the atomic, meso, and continuum scales. Comput. Phys. Commun. **271**, 108171 (2022). https://doi.org/10.1016/j.cpc.2021.108171

41. Trott, C.: Apps Using Kokkos (2018). https://github.com/kokkos/kokkos/issues/1950

42. Valero-Lara, P., Kim, J., Hernandez, O., Vetter, J.: OpenMP target task: tasking and target offloading on heterogeneous systems. In: Chaves, R., et al. (eds.) Euro-Par 2021. LNCS, vol. 13098, pp. 445–455. Springer, Cham (2022). https://doi.org/10.1007/978-3-031-06156-1_35

43. Valero-Lara, P., Lee, S., Gonzalez-Tallada, M., Denny, J., Vetter, J.S.: KokkACC: enhancing Kokkos with openACC. In: 2022 Workshop on Accelerator Programming Using Directives (WACCPD), pp. 32–42 (2022). https://doi.org/10.1109/WACCPD56842.2022.00009

44. Yang, Z., Sahasrabudhe, D., Humphrey, A., Berzins, M.: A preliminary port and evaluation of the uintah amt runtime on sunway taihulight. In: 9th IEEE International Workshop on Parallel and Distributed Scientific and Engineering Computing (PDSEC 2018). IEEE (2018)

45. Zhang, W., et al.: AMReX: a framework for block-structured adaptive mesh refinement. J. Open Source Softw. **4**(37), 1370 (2019). https://doi.org/10.21105/joss.01370

46. Zhang, W., Almgren, A.S., Day, M., Nguyen, T., Shalf, J., Unat, D.: Boxlib with tiling: an AMR software framework. CoRR abs/1604.03570 (2016)

Benchmarking the Parallel 1D Heat Equation Solver in Chapel, Charm++, C++, HPX, Go, Julia, Python, Rust, Swift, and Java

Patrick Diehl[1,2]($\boxtimes$) , Max Morris[1], Steven R. Brandt[1], Nikunj Gupta[4], and Hartmut Kaiser[1,3]

[1] Center of Computation and Technology, Louisiana State University, Baton Rouge, USA
{pdiehl,mmorris,sbrandt,hkaiser}@cct.lsu.edu
[2] Department of Physics and Astronomy, Louisiana State University, Baton Rouge, USA
[3] Department of Computer Science, Louisiana State University, Baton Rouge, USA
[4] Amazon LLC (Work done before joining Amazon), Seattle , USA
nknikunj@amazon.com

Abstract. Many scientific high performance codes that simulate *e.g.* black holes, coastal waves, climate and weather, etc. rely on block-structured meshes and use finite differencing methods to solve the appropriate systems of differential equations iteratively. This paper investigates implementations of a straightforward simulation of this type using various programming systems and languages. We focus on a shared memory, parallelized algorithm that simulates a 1D heat diffusion using asynchronous queues for the ghost zone exchange. We discuss the advantages of the various platforms and explore the performance of this model code on different computing architectures: Intel, AMD, and ARM64FX. As a result, Python was the slowest of the set we compared. Java, Go, Swift, and Julia were the intermediate performers. The higher performing platforms were C++, Rust, Chapel, Charm++, and HPX.

Keywords: Asynchronous programming · Concurrency · Julia · Chapel · Rust · Go · Charm++ · HPX · Swift · Java · C++

1 Introduction

Several languages and libraries are emerging to provide better support for parallel programming, particularly asynchronous programming. This work explores some of the frameworks available for shared memory parallelism.

Asynchronous execution can be implemented in various ways, *e.g.* via coroutines, senders/receivers, futures, or queues. Table 1 provides an overview of the features for parallelism supported by the frameworks investigated. This work implements a 1D stencil-based heat equation solver as a model problem, using asynchronous queues to exchange ghost zone cells.

D. Zeinalipour et al. (Eds.): Euro-Par 2023 Workshops, LNCS 14352, pp. 127–138, 2024.
https://doi.org/10.1007/978-3-031-48803-0_11

Table 1. Overview of the programming languages: *(1)* the parallelism approaches they provide, *(2)* supported operating systems, *(3)* the license, and *(4)* reference. The C++ 17 standard was used as a base. The symbol $\sim$ indicates that Charm++ uses internal coroutines, but these are not accessible to the user, and Chapel solely provides a parallel for loop.

Approach	Async	Coroutine	Parallel algorithm	Win	Linux	Mac	Licence	Ref
C++ 17	✓	✓	✓	✓	✓	✓	GNU	–
Java	✓	X	X	✓	✓	✓	GNU	[2]
Swift	✓	✓	X	✓	✓	✓	Apache	–
Chapel	✓	X	$\sim$	✓	✓	✓	Apache	[7]
Charm++	✓	$\sim$	X	✓	✓	✓	Own	[12]
HPX	✓	✓	✓	✓	✓	✓	Boost	[11]
Go	X	X	X	✓	✓	✓	BSD	–
Python	✓	✓	X	✓	✓	✓	BSD	[21]
Julia	✓	✓	X	✓	✓	✓	MIT	[5]
Rust	✓	X	✓	✓	✓	✓	MIT	[16]

We implement this model code using several different platforms: *(1)* Chapel [6] by HPE; *(2)* Julia [5] by Julia Inc, Go by Google; *(3)* Swift by Apple; *(4)* Charm++ [12] by Charmworks; *(5)* Standard C++; *(6)* HPX [11] developed primarily at LSU; *(7)* Python developed by open source communities; and *(8)* Rust driven by Mozilla.

Previously, a comparison of Parallel Research Kernels for MPI, MPI+OpenMP, UPC, Charm++, and Grappa was made in 2016 in [22]. A comparison of *programmability, performance, and mutability* of Charm++, Legion, and Unitah was made in 2015 [4]. A comparison of Julia, Python\ Numba, and Kokkos was made in [9].

This paper will compare the benefits and challenges of a much broader set of languages. We faced several challenges in implementing the appropriate solver. How much work did it take to achieve the performance we finally accepted? Next, we compare the performance of the languages on Intel, AMD, and A64FX CPUs. Finally, we discuss the trade-offs of using each of the various platforms.

The paper is structured as follows: Sect. 2 introduces the model problem. Section 3 briefly overview the languages and libraries and emphasizes the challenges and benefits we experienced during the implementation. Section 4 compares programming details. Section 5 compares code metrics, *e.g.* the number of lines of codes needed to implement the benchmark. Section 6 compares the performance of the codes on Intel, AMD, and A64FX CPUs.

2   Model Problem

The one-dimensional heat equation on a 1-D loop (*e.g.* limp noodle) ($0 \leq x < L$) with the length L for all times $t > 0$ is described by

$$\frac{\partial u}{\partial t} = \alpha \frac{\partial^2 u}{\partial x^2}, \quad 0 \leq x < L, t > 0, \tag{1}$$

with α as the material's diffusivity. For the discretization in space, we use the N grid points $x = \{x_i = i \cdot h \in \mathbb{R} \mid i = 0, \ldots, N - 1\}$, with the grid spacing h and we use 2nd order finite differencing. For the discretization in time, we use the Euler method, $i.e.$

$$u(t + \delta t, x_i) = u(t, x_i) + \delta t \cdot \alpha \frac{u(t, x_{i-1}) - 2 \cdot u(t, x_i) + u(t, x_{i+1})}{2h}, \tag{2}$$

with the initial condition $u(0, x_i) = x_i$. To model a loop, we use periodic boundary conditions, $i.e.$ $u(t, x) = u(t, L + x)$.

The parallel algorithm was implemented by having multiple threads of execution each sequentially applying Eq. 2 on a local segment of the grid. We used queues to communicate ghost zones between the segments. We note that for this problem, the queues are single-producer, single-consumer and, therefore, in principle, don't need synchronization (although synchronization to suspend/resume threads seemed to help in some cases).

While this problem is small and extremely simple, it has much in common with many high performance codes that simulate black holes, coastal waves, atmospheres, etc. Block-structured meshes that use finite differences are common and essential for modeling various physical systems.

3   Programming Languages and Libraries

In this section, we comment on the benefits and challenges of each language or framework for the example problem. All code is available on GitHub[1]. Table 1 shows the availability of each approach on various OS, the Licence used, etc.

3.1   Chapel

The Chapel code was one for which we needed to write our own queue. In this case, the full/empty bit synchronization mechanism that the language provides was helpful. The `coforall` loop, which assigns a different thread to each iteration, provided a convenient mechanism for launching the outer loop.

Because Chapel is designed to make writing parallel programming easier, we also tested a synchronous version of the heat code that did not attempt to segment the array. This code did not scale quite as well as the segmented code that exchanged ghost zones, but the simplicity of the code should make this an appealing option. Though not directly part of the heat equation, Chapel also lacked a built-in way to append to a file. However, opening a file, seeking to the end, and writing is possible. We also add that the support we received from questions asked in the Chapel Gitter was exceptional. We found Chapel among the higher performing codes, comparable to Rust or C++.

---

[1] https://github.com/diehlpk/async_heat_equation.

3.2   Charm++

Charm++ derives parallelism through chares that runs on a Processing Element (PE), usually a core of a processor. Multiple chares run asynchronously while communicating using messages. To implement our stencil code, we decomposed the grid into a 1D chare array with neighbors sharing the ghost value every iteration through messages. Send and Receive functions have entry method attribute set as `expedited`. This allows messages to go directly to the converse scheduler reducing latency further. A reduction at the end triggers the completion of the heat exchange to main-chare.

3.3   C++ 17

The C++ 17 code implements a fork and join approach using the `std::thread` library. A small queue class was coded by hand, using `std::mutex` and `std::condition_variable`. Because the queue is single-producer single-consumer, it does not require explicit synchronization. Nevertheless, we synchronize when the queue is empty because that seems slightly faster. C++ does not currently provide guarantees of memory safety or data race safety as Rust does, but we note that the language landscape is constantly changing. We expect that "profiles" will eventually provide these guarantees for C++.

3.4   C++ Standard Library for Concurrency and Parallelism (HPX)

The HPX code was based on the C++ code, except that it uses `hpx::thread` instead of `std::thread`, and uses `chanel_spsc` instead of a hand-written queue. The major difference is that HPX uses lightweight threads on top of the operating system threads to avoid context-switching overheads.

3.5   Go

We use `go func` to launch worker threads (goroutines) and buffered channels using `make()` to facilitate the exchange of ghost zones. For synchronization of the goroutines, we use `sync.WaitGroup` and add threads by calling `waitGroup.Add()`, and synchronize the threads by calling `waitGroup.Wait()`. As this paper was written, Go was not yet heavily used in scientific computing. At the time of this writing, only *biogo*, an HPC bioinformatics toolkit [14], is available.

3.6   Julia

Both Python and Fortran clearly inspire Julia. It is a good choice for Fortran programmers who want to get into scripting, as it will offer some familiarity in using one as the default start for array indexes (instead of zero) and its use of end to mark the end of a block.

In our Julia code, we implemented our own queue. Since Julia does not support classes directly (though it has structs), we found it convenient to use arrays. For parallelism, we used Julia's `Thread.@threads for` loop macro.

3.7   Python

For the grid segments, we use `NumPy` [10], which gives us SIMD out of the box. For concurrency, we use `from` **threading** `import` **Thread** to launch the worker for each data segment, and we use `from` **queue** `import` **Queue** to synchronize the exchange of ghost nodes. The queue is, therefore, synchronized and possibly has lower performance than it could be. We did attempt to create a queue class by hand, as we did with C++, but it did not perform better than the built-in `queue.Queue` object. Unsurprisingly, perhaps, Python is the slowest code of the set we are considering in this paper, despite using NumPy. This is undoubtedly because it is an interpreted language. While Julia is faster than Python, the startup time seems to be a bit longer (especially with option -O3).

3.8   Rust

We use `std::thread::scope` to launch worker threads, and non-blocking channels from `std::sync::mpsc` to facilitate the exchange of ghost zones. We avoided using `unsafe`, working only in the safe subset of Rust. In addition to the regular implementation of the heat code, we have a version with SIMD vectorization using the unstable `portable_simd` feature. This improves performance over the non-vectorized version with a few threads, but the improvement diminishes as the number of threads increases. We considered only the non-SIMD version in our final measurements to remain consistent with the other languages. Rust is not yet widely adopted in scientific computing. However, we found two such scientific codes that are available: *Lumol*[2], a molecular simulation engine; and *Rust-Bio* [15], a bioinformatics library. Because of its guarantees concerning data race conditions and memory access, as well as its high performance, Rust is a potentially good choice for new scientific programming projects. However, Rust has vastly different syntax and semantics than more traditional languages like C++, Java, and Python, all of which may make for a steep learning curve.

3.9   Swift

We had to use `UnsafeMutableBufferPointer<Double>` to avoid unnecessary calls of `await` for accessing the elements of arrays. These buffers allow explicit vectorization on newer x86 and Apple Silicon. See, for example, `addingProduct`. However, we could not measure a significant improvement using these functions. For concurrency, we use `await` with `TaskGroup{ body: { group in}}` to launch chunks of works on each thread and `for` `wait` _ in `group{}`. Swift claims to be safe by design and produces software that runs lightning-fast. Unfortunately, we had to disable the safety feature to get a performant code. It may be that simulating the heat equation is not a good fit for Swift's design. We have not yet found any scientific simulation codes built on Swift. Python and Julia share similar patterns. Chapel is somehow unique due to its compactness.

---

[2] https://lumol.org/.

3.10 Java

The Java code was of intermediate performance. This was somewhat expected since it does not target high performance computing. However, it is not unknown either. Java has several thread-safe queue objects. We used an `ArrayBlockingQueue` for the ghost zone exchange, giving it a size equal to the number of threads (approximately twice as much as it could theoretically use). It also has several threading systems to choose from. In this case, we chose the FixedPoolThread, which matches our consistent and uniform workload.

Overviews of Java in HPC are available here [1,20]. One virtue that Java continues to have is simplicity. It was designed for "average programmers" and does not have a lot of syntax a new programmer needs to learn (though it becomes a little more complex with each version). It's choice to borrow much of C++'s constructs makes it feel familiar from its first use.

4 Remarks on the Implementation Details

This section focuses on the implementation details and showcases similarities and differences. One aspect is the safety, *e.g.* memory, included in the language. Rust and Swift have implemented some sanity checks, for example, for memory access. For Rust, we could avoid using `unsafe` and worked only in the safe subset of Rust. However, for Swift, we had to use `UnsafeMutableBufferPointer` to get the reported performance. Another aspect is the usage of SIMD for scientific computations. Here, some of the approaches, like Python, allowed SIMD as the default for NumPy. Other approaches, like Rust and Swift, provide SIMD as a language feature, while others rely on external libraries, like C++, Charm++, HPX, or Julia. Measuring the elapsed time and parsing command line options was decent in all the languages. Creating files and appending the performance data to the file was more accessible in some than others. For example, Chapel lacks a built-in way to append to a file. Handling files in Swift was rather complex; we just piped it to the console. For the synchronization for the ghost elements, we decided to rely on Queues for our code. Some approaches, like Python, Rust, and Go, provide queues or equivalent mechanisms. For other approaches, we had to implement the queue using features included in the language. Next to these features, we identified similar code patterns. For example, the Swift code (`TaskGroup`)and Go code (`WaitGroup`) uses similar semantics to group the threads and synchronize them. HPX, C++, and Rust use fewer abstraction layers and act on the bare thread libraries.

5 Comparison of the Asynchrony

Figure 1a shows the lines of code (LOC) for each approach. The numbers were determined with the Linux tool `cloc`[3] and exclude comments. Here, Chapel has

---

[3] https://github.com/AlDanial/cloc.

the least amount of lines of code due to its high-level language design. Second, is Python and third is Julia. Next, Swift, HPX, and Go have similar lines of code. Rust and C++ are close. Charm++ and Java have the most lines of code. While we tried to be reasonably uniform in our coding methodology, we note that some codes include a hand-written queue and some do not. Regardless, these numbers might differ if a different person coded the problem.

Even so, lines of code are just one metric and do not tell the whole story about the code's complexity. Inspired by [18], we use a scale to determine how complicated it was to develop the code and relate it to the performance of the code, see Fig. 1b. For the scale from slow to fast, we use the computational time on Intel CPUs in Fig. 2a. We use the average

$$T_{\text{average}}(\text{approach}) := {}^{(T_2(\text{approach}) + T_{20}(\text{approach}) + T_{40}(\text{approach}))}/_3 \qquad (3)$$

of the computational time on two cores T_2, on 20 cores T_{20}, and 40 cores T_{40}. We arrange these averages linearly on the interval $[-1, 1]$ on the y scale. Quantifying the performance based on computational time was quite objective. However, quantifying how easy or hard it was to implement the code in various approaches might be subjective. Therefore, we agreed on using the **Constructive Cost Model** (COCOMO) [3,19]. Note that the COCOMO model is a general model without any specialization in parallel programming. There has been much discussion in the HPC community about the model, however, the HPC community did not invent a specialized model yet. For example, the COCOMO II model was used in [17] to analyze its cost parameters for the investigated parallelization projects with OpenACC on NVIDIA GPUs. Some overview of performance metrics in HPX is given in [13]. Until we get a specialized model for parallel computing or HPC, the COCOMO model is a reasonable candidate. We use the tool *Sloc Cloc and Code* (scc)[4] to get the COCOMO metrics for each approach. We use the Estimated Schedule Effort using the organic option to estimate how long it would take to implement the code in a month. We arranged these values on linearly on the interval $[-1, 1]$ on the x scale. Figure 1b shows the classification using this metric. The first cluster is Python, Julia, and Chapel. These three languages were classified as easier to implement for this specific application.

One possible cause of Python's slowness might be the queue implementation. However, our own queue implementation did not help. The second cluster is Swift, Charm++, and HPX. Where HPX and Charm++ have a slightly better performance. The third cluster is C++ 17, Rust, and go. Here the performance of C++ 17 and Rust were comparable. Interestingly, Java had a decent performance and was classified as the most difficult. Mostly, we assume, due to much boilerplate code produced by Java. Subjectively, we would identify Java as one of the more accessible codes to implement, so the COCOMO classification is not perfect. However, it is a place to start in assessing various programming languages.

---

[4] https://github.com/boyter/scc.

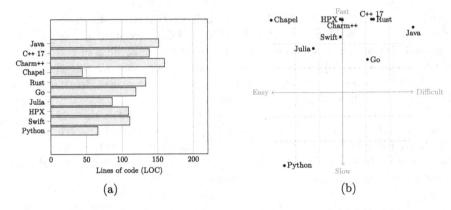

Fig. 1. Software engineering metrics: (a) Lines of codes for all implementations. The numbers were determined with the Linux tool *cloc* and (b) Two-dimensional classification using the computational time and the COCOMO model.

Table 2. Software versions and dependencies. The nightly build from April 23 was used for Rust, since we needed SIMD support. HPX was built using boost 1.78, hwloc 2.8.0, and jemalloc 5.3. If needed, CMake 3.20 was used for building.

Python 3.10	Julia 1.8.5	Chapel 1.30	Go 1.20.3	Charm++ *6f7f105b*
Swift 5.8	HPX 1.8.1	OpenJDK 20	gcc 11.2.1	Rust nightly (April 23)

Table 3. R^2 correlation of the fit of the measured data points for all approaches and architectures, computed using Python NumPy.

Architecture	C++	Charm++	Chapel	Rust	Go	Julia	HPX	Swift	Python	Java
Intel® Xeon® Gold 6148	0.49	0.36	0.45	0.52	0.28	0.41	0.52	0.56	0.43	0.03
AMD™ EPYC™ 7H12	0.48	0.45	0.53	0.49	0.75	0.12	0.42	0.02	0.46	0.12
Arm A64FX	0.49	0.52	0.08	0.40	0.52	0.42	0.73	–	0.90	0.32

6   Performance Measurements

In this section, we compare the performance of the approaches on the following CPUs: ARM A64FX, AMD EPYC™ 7543, and Intel® Xeon® Gold 6140, respectively. Table 2 shows the versions and dependencies of the compilers or interpreters. We report the cells processed per second for all methods. We know that FLOPS would be a better quantity. However, not all the approaches provided a convenient interface to Papi. Figure 2 shows the computation time for all approaches on all three architectures. Table 3 shows the R^2 correlation for all line fits computed using Python NumPy.

6.1 Intel

Figure 2a shows the performance on Intel®Xeon®Gold 6148 Skylake. Here, Python was the slowest approach. Swift and Julia are comparable. For larger than 10 threads Go behaves slightly better than Swift and Julia. For smaller core counts up to eight cores, the remaining approaches behave similarly. However, Chapel gets slower for higher node counts. For Rust, Charm++, and HPX the performance is comparable. HPX is for larger node counts the fastest, but has a high variance, see R^2 in Table 3.

6.2 AMD

Figure 2b shows the performance on AMD EPYC 7H12. Python is the slowest approach. After that, Swift and Julia are comparable for smaller core counts, but after that, Swift gets slower. Go is faster, but had a high variation. Chapel and Rust are comparable. Charm++ and C++ are close. HPX is comparable, but with a high variance, see R^2 in Table 3.

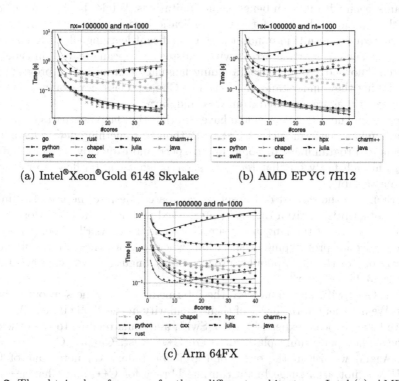

(a) Intel®Xeon®Gold 6148 Skylake   (b) AMD EPYC 7H12

(c) Arm 64FX

Fig. 2. The obtained performance for three different architectures: Intel (a), AMD (b), and A64FX (c). The baseline was 1 000 000 discrete nodes and 1000 time steps. Swift is missing on A64FX, since no package was provided for Rocky Linux. The lines are the curve fits obtained with `curve_fit` from Python SciPy.

6.3 A64FX

Note that Ookami uses *Rocky Linux* and no Swift package was provided for this OS. Rocky Linux was developed to be a binary-compatible with Red Hat Enterprise Linux, however, Red Hat Universal package provided by Swift had some library version mismatches. Figure 2c on A64FX. Here, Python was the slowest, as on all architectures. Chapel behaves differently on A64FX and is the second slowest. Go is in the middle as before. Rust and C++ are comparable up to 16 cores, and C++ outperforms Rust for larger node counts. Charm++ is the second fastest. HPX is the fastest system on A64FX, however with a large variation, see the R^2 in Table 3. We want to emphasize that some of the approaches might not optimize for A64FX yet and just support the architecture, since they might not target it.

7 Conclusion

There are an increasing number of viable platforms for creating high performance programs, each with its own benefits and limitations. While these platforms can make the creation of high performance applications easier, learning to use a new language requires a shift in mindset and a significant learning effort. Even small differences, such as starting arrays with 1 instead of 0, can create confusion.

Often, knowledge of one programming language can mislead a programmer into thinking they understand another. The Chapel "class" for example did not behave exactly as we expected from C++ and Java.

Ideally, any new language should have tutorials that help new users transition from a familiar platform such as C++ or Python to something new. This allows experienced programmers to come up to speed more quickly without having to slog through fairly familiar territory such as what control flow is or how to declare a variable.

Python was the slowest of the set we compared, despite the use of NumPy. This is not surprising given that it is interpreted and not built for performance. However, because of the language's simplicity and short REPL time, it may be a good choice for prototyping or situations where performance is not critical. It is clearly one of the most popular programming languages available, according to the 2023 Tiobe index[5].

Java, Go, Swift, and Julia were the intermediate performers in our experiments. We list them in the order of their popularity in the Tiobe Index. We note that we have the least expertise in Go, Swift, and Julia relative to the others.

The higher performing platforms were C++, Rust, Chapel, Charm++, and HPX. Again, we list in the order of the Tiobe Index. We note that of this set, HPX is not a language but a runtime library for C++, and Charm++ is a declaration language designed to be used in conjunction with C++ rather than a full-blown language.

---

[5] https://doi.org/10.1038/s41586-020-2649-2.

We will not name a winner with respect to speed. The higher performing platforms were mostly similar in what they achieved. The tests in this paper are dependent on the hardware, the version of the interpreters and compilers, the particular problem chosen, the amount of effort applied, and our level of expertise (which varied by platform).

One solution does not fit all. Despite being the slowest, Python will undoubtedly continue to be one of the most popular. C++ will likely remain "everyone's second choice." Rust's innovative ideas will make it ideally suited for many applications. Chapel and Julia make many HPC tasks easier.

Future Work

Since this paper only considers a stencil-based one-dimensional code, other numerical applications would be needed for a more comprehensive comparison. Various collections of high performance codes and parallel algorithms exist, many of which have significant overlap in the kinds of things they do. Can a good representative subset be identified? One significant question would be to investigate distributed programming for some of these languages and platforms. For Python and Rust, MPI bindings are available. However, Chapel, Charm++, Julia, and HPX provide higher abstraction levels for communication. What benefits do these approaches have for the programmer? For high performance programming in general? Another aspect to explore is the GPU support using native languages, like CUDA or RocM; or abstraction layers, like Kokkos or SYCL.

Supplementary materials

The code for all examples is available on GitHub®[6] or Zenodo™ [8], respectively. A Docker image to compile/run all examples is available here[7].

Acknowledgments. The authors would like to thank Stony Brook Research Computing and Cyberinfrastructure, and the Institute for Advanced Computational Science at Stony Brook University for access to the innovative high-performance Ookami computing system, which was made possible by a $5M National Science Foundation grant (#1927880). We thank Steve Canon and Nick Everitt for their remarks on the Swift code and Brad Chamberlain and Jeremiah Corrado for their remarks on the Chapel code.

References

1. Amedro, B., et al.: Current state of Java for HPC. Ph.D. thesis, INRIA (2008)
2. Arnold, K., Gosling, J., Holmes, D.: The Java Programming Language. Addison Wesley Professional, Boston (2005)
3. Barry, B., et al.: Software engineering economics. New York **197**, 140 (1981)

---

[6] https://github.com/diehlpk/async_heat_equation.
[7] https://hub.docker.com/r/diehlpk/monte-carlo-codes.

4. Bennett, J., et al.: ASC ATDM level 2 milestone# 5325: asynchronous many-task runtime system analysis and assessment for next generation platforms. SAND2015-8312 (2015)
5. Bezanson, J., et al.: Julia: a fresh approach to numerical computing. SIAM Rev. **59**(1), 65–98 (2017)
6. Chamberlain, B.L., Deitz, S., Hribar, M.B., Wong, W.: Chapel. Programming Models for Parallel Computing, pp. 129–159 (2015)
7. Chamberlain, B.L., et al.: Parallel programmability and the chapel language. Int. J. High Perform. Comput. Appl. **21**(3), 291–312 (2007)
8. Diehl, P., et al.: Benchmarking the Parallel 1D Heat Equation Solver in Chapel, Charm++, C++, HPX, Go, Julia, Python, Rust, Swift, and Java (2023). https://doi.org/10.5281/zenodo.7942453. https://doi.org/10.5281/zenodo.7942453
9. Godoy, W.F., et al.: Evaluating performance and portability of high-level programming models: Julia, python/numba, and kokkos on exascale nodes (2023)
10. Harris, C.R., et al.: Array programming with NumPy. Nature **585**(7825), 357–362 (2020)
11. Kaiser, H., et al.: HPX-the C++ standard library for parallelism and concurrency. J. Open Source Softw. **5**(53), 2352 (2020)
12. Kale, L.V., Krishnan, S.: Charm++ a portable concurrent object oriented system based on C++. In: Proceedings of the Eighth Annual Conference on Object-oriented Programming Systems, Languages, and Applications, pp. 91–108 (1993)
13. Kepner, J.: High performance computing productivity model synthesis. Int. J. High Perform. Comput. Appl. **18**(4), 505–516 (2004)
14. Kortschak, R.D., et al.: bíogo: a simple high-performance bioinformatics toolkit for the go language. J. Open Source Softw. **2**(10), 167 (2017)
15. Köster, J.: Rust-bio: a fast and safe bioinformatics library. Bioinformatics **32**(3), 444–446 (2016)
16. Matsakis, N.D., Klock II, F.S.: The rust language. In: ACM SIGAda Ada Letters, vol. 34, pp. 103–104. ACM (2014)
17. Miller, J., et al.: Applicability of the software cost model COCOMO II to HPC projects. Int. J. Comput. Sci. Eng. **17**(3), 283–296 (2018)
18. Pennycook, S.J., et al.: Navigating performance, portability, and productivity. Comput. Sci. Eng. **23**(5), 28–38 (2021)
19. Stutzke, R.D., Crosstalk, M.: Software estimating technology: A survey. Los. Alamitos, CA: IEEE Computer Society Press (1997)
20. Taboada, G.L., et al.: Java for high performance computing: assessment of current research and practice. In: Proceedings of the 7th International Conference on Principles and Practice of Programming in Java, pp. 30–39 (2009)
21. Van Rossum, G., Drake, F.L.: Python 3 Reference Manual. CreateSpace, Scotts Valley, CA (2009)
22. Van der Wijngaart, R.F., et al.: Comparing runtime systems with exascale ambitions using the parallel research kernels. In: Kunkel, J., Balaji, P., Dongarra, J. (eds.) ISC High Performance 2016. LNCS, vol. 9697, pp. 321–339. Springer, Cham (2016). https://doi.org/10.1007/978-3-319-41321-1_17

The 3rd International Workshop on Performance and Energy-efficiency in Concurrent and Distributed Systems (PECS 2023)

Workshop on Performance and Energy-efficiency in Concurrent and Distributed Systems (PECS)

Workshop Description

Concurrent and distributed computer architectures, based on multi/many-core or distributed computer units, have become a de facto standard in computer systems. Today, these architectures take a role at any scale, from high-end servers to personal and mobile devices, and they underlie various recent computing paradigms, such as Cloud, Edge and Fog Computing.

The continuously growing level of hardware parallelism and heterogeneity has led concurrent and distributed systems to be even more complex to optimize, in particular in terms of energy efficiency and performance, which are known to be highly interrelated. Nonetheless, these aspects are of paramount importance, especially because of the high demand for electricity by the IT sector. This facet is further exacerbated by the recent energy crisis and the rising energy prices.

Actually, various aspects of concurrent and/or distributed systems that make it complex to deal with them (like the complexity of the underlying architectures, data dependencies, the use of shared resources, the hardware heterogeneity) can also offer new opportunities for designing novel methods and techniques for their energy and performance optimization.

PECS aims to establish a venue for both academia and industry to discuss challenges and perspectives, and to explore methods, techniques and tools for energy efficiency and performance optimization in concurrent and distributed systems.

The third edition of the workshop (PECS 2023) took place on August 28th in Limassol, Cyprus, in conjunction with the Euro-Par conference. The format of the workshop included a keynote speech, followed by a session of technical presentations. The workshop was attended by about 15 people throughout the day.

PECS 2023 received 4 regular papers. These underwent a double-blind review process and 3 papers were accepted. The accepted papers cover performance and energy efficiency topics targeting different computing systems and architectures, such as in-memory computing systems, HPC systems, and supercomputers. One additional paper, related to the keynote speech, was reviewed and accepted for publication. The paper presents a new performance and energy efficiency optimization methodology for parameterizable hardware.

The PECS 2023 organizers would like to thank the members of the Program Committee for contributing to the paper review process and the Euro-Par conference organizers for hosting the workshop, especially the Euro-Par workshop organizers for their continued support.

Organization

General Chair

Pierangelo Di Sanzo   Roma Tre University, Italy

Steering Committee Chair

Alessandro Pellegrini   University of Rome Tor Vergata, Italy

Program Chair

Romolo Marotta   University of Rome Tor Vergata, Italy

Program Committee

Vicenç Beltran	Barcelona Supercomputing Center, Spain
Bruno Ciciani	Sapienza University of Rome, Italy
Marta Garcia Gasulla	Barcelona Supercomputing Center, Spain
Sebastiano Peluso	Facebook, USA
Francesco Quaglia	University of Rome Tor Vergata, Italy
Paolo Romano	INESC-ID, Portugal
Eric Rutten	Inria, France

A Performance Modelling-Driven Approach to Hardware Resource Scaling

Alexandre Rodrigues$^{(\boxtimes)}$ (ID), Leonel Sousa (ID), and Aleksandar Ilic (ID)

INESC-ID, Instituto Superior Tecnico, Universidade de Lisboa, Rua Alves Redol, 9,
1000-029 Lisboa, Portugal
`{alexandre.d.rodrigues,leonel.sousa,aleksandar.ilic}@inesc-id.pt`

Abstract. The continuous demand for higher computational performance and the stagnating developments in the general purpose processor landscape have led to a surge in interest for highly specialized and efficient hardware. Combined with the rising popularity of parameterizable hardware, a new opportunity to optimize these architectures for particular workloads arises, largely driven by the RISC-V Instruction Set Architecture (ISA). This work present an application-specific optimization methodology for general purpose processors, enabling the development of architectures which are faster and more efficient for their designated workloads. Driven by the Cache-Aware Roofline Model (CARM) insights, the methodology guides the configuration of the memory and computational subsystems of the processor. We apply this methodology to two applications, demonstrating up to a $2.67\times$ performance increase and a $1.34\times$ improvement to energy efficiency.

Keywords: Hardware Design · Roofline modelling · RISC-V

1 Introduction

As the slowing-down of Moore's Law and Dennard Scaling is felt more and more in the world of computing, the demand for greater computational power has become synonymous with a search for efficient hardware [16]. With thermal constraints hindering the performance growth of general purpose processors, the High-Performance Computing (HPC) ecosystem has shifted some of its focus towards specialized hardware, with domain-specific accelerators and co-processors growing in popularity in recent years, both in academia and enterprise [3].

The development of domain-specific accelerators enables designers to create highly specialized and efficient architectures. As these focus on a single or few tasks, they do not require the complex control logic or diverse set of functional units common to most CPUs or GPUs, and can dedicate additional computational resources to the target application [3]. These factors often lead to architectures exhibiting remarkable performance and efficiency when compared to general purpose hardware performing the same task [2,3,10]. However,

D. Zeinalipour et al. (Eds.): Euro-Par 2023 Workshops, LNCS 14352, pp. 143–154, 2024.
https://doi.org/10.1007/978-3-031-48803-0_15

these architectures require significant expertise and effort to develop, requiring designers to be familiar with hardware description languages and the associated concepts.

At the same time, there is an increasing availability of open-source, configurable hardware, fueled by the widespread adoption of the RISC-V open standard ISA, with notable examples such as the BOOM processor [18] or the Ara [4] accelerator. These parameterizable architectures are a novel opportunity for the design of domain-specific hardware, scaling their hardware resources to match application requirements. However, this process is not trivial, with the current literature lacking resources and methods to match the capabilities of the hardware to the characteristics of an application. This is a gap this paper intends to address, employing insightful performance modelling techniques to create a clear methodology that guides the architectural parameterization.

To demonstrate the capabilities of proposed architectures, state-of-the-art works often make use of insightful roofline modelling techniques such as the Original [17] or Cache-Aware Roofline Model (CARM) [6]. These performance models provide an intuitive understanding of the hardware performance characteristics, showcasing it through visual means. Furthermore, they help contextualize application performance within the scope of the hardware capabilities, thus they are often used in software optimization to provide insight into what strategies allow to better exploit the available memory and compute resources.

Given this context, in this paper we propose a robust, application-specific optimization methodology for hardware, leveraging the CARM's insights to improve the architecture performance and efficiency for the target workload. This proposal follows of our previous work [14], which focused on architectural optimizations for Sparse Matrix-Vector Multiplication (SpMV). This work presents a significantly more comprehensive hardware optimization methodology, which is not focused on a single kernel and can be applied to a much wider range of applications. Furthermore, the conducted experimental validation is based on a more accurate and configurable processor model, and includes power, energy and area estimates, which more thoroughly validate our proposal.

The methodology proposed herein makes use of the insights provided by the CARM to identify the performance upper-bounds of the architecture and the requirements of the application, using these metrics to provide guidelines for scaling the hardware resources. The resulting architecture exhibits increased performance and energy efficiency when running the target workload, matching its memory and computational resources with the application's profile. Applying the methodology for SpMV resulted in a 2.67× increase in performance and a 1.34× improvement to energy efficiency.

2 Background and Related Work

The state-of-the-art approaches tackling the development of domain-specific hardware typically focus on specialized accelerators, commonly implemented on FPGAs. A hardware accelerator for SpMV is proposed in [10], designed to exploit a proposed compressed format for sparse matrices which promotes data reuse, and implemented in an FPGA. The paper [2] proposes an FPGA-based accelerator for fully homomorphic encryption, demonstrating speedups of up to 456× compared to conventional, general purpose processors. These approaches demonstrate significant performance improvements, but require the development of accelerators from scratch, which is an involved process.

Some works have explored the development of hardware based on one or more applications, using their performance and instruction profile to drive architectural parameterization. The work proposed in [12] presents a set of tools for early co-design of HPC systems, using the insights provided by instruction tracing and emulation tools to drive the design of a RISC-V vector accelerator, as well as an associated compiler. The paper [15] describes the design process of the A64FX processor, part of the Fugaku supercomputer. It employed analytical models and a simulator to evaluate the performance of a set of HPC kernels for a variety of architectural parameters, using the resulting estimates to arrive at the processor's final configuration. While these works use specific applications to aid in hardware development process, they lack a structured approach to the parameterization, relying mostly on simple performance metrics.

The use of Roofline Modelling has become increasingly popular in recent years, mainly for software optimization and performance evaluation of novel hardware [5]. The CARM [6] stands out in this class of models by introducing a distinct approach, modelling multiple levels of the memory hierarchy in a single plot, thereby providing more detailed and accurate performance characterization, while still retaining the intuitive nature of the original roofline plot [17]. It takes into account the performance limits of a processor's Floating-point Units (FPUs) (F_p, FLOP/s) and the realistically attainable bandwidth of each level of the memory subsystem (Byte/s). By correlating an application's Arithmetic Intensity (AI) (its ratio between FLOPs and bytes) with the attainable performance (F_a, FLOP/s), this modeling approach serves as an intuitive and powerful tool for identifying the architectural limits and application performance. Equation 1 describes this relationship, also dependent on the bandwidth of the memory level in question, B:

$$F_a(AI) = \min\{B \cdot AI, F_p\} \qquad (1)$$

The CARM plot has one roofline for each of the architecture's memory levels, each one with two distinct regions: the memory-bound section is enclosed by the sloped section of the roof, while the horizontal roof to the right represents the compute-bound region. These regions intersect at the ridge point, where both the memory subsystem and the FPUs are at full capacity.

The model is well established and integrated in the Intel® Advisor [13] as a tool for software optimization for both Intel® CPU and GPU devices. In a nutshell, this model facilies the identification of performance bottlenecks and provides valuable insights towards the improvements areas a software or hardware engineer should focus on during the optimization process. Although it is widely used for application characterization and optimization on general-purpose computing platforms, the research on the use of roofline principles for performance evaluation and design of novel hardware is in its very early days [5].

This work continues our exploration of the CARM's potential for domain-specific hardware design [14], using its insights to develop a methodology for domain-specific optimization of general purpose processors. While most papers proposing domain-specific hardware focus on accelerators, which require significant expertise to develop, this work explores the use of increasingly common parameterizable processors for specialized tasks. We provide a structured approach to their configuration, using performance modelling insights to devise clear optimization guidelines. The proposed methodology can be a valuable tool for hardware design space exploration, an alternative to the current trends towards specialized hardware accelerators.

3 Performance Modelling-Driven Hardware Optimization Methodology

The proposed hardware optimization methodology has two major goals for any given application: i) increasing the performance of target architecture for that particular task, and ii) improving the energy efficiency. Performance increases are achieved by scaling up the resources limiting the execution, while efficiency improvements stem from the removal of unused resources. Ideally, the methodology seeks to scale the memory and compute resources such that the application fully exercises both or, in the context of the CARM, the relevant roofline's ridge point moves to the application's AI.

In this section, we detail our proposal and the core concepts it is based on. We begin with a description of the methodology and the optimization guidelines it provides, followed by the concept of AI range and how it influences these guidelines. Lastly, the architectural parameters that may be scaled through the methodology are explored, discussing how they are expected to affect the architectural performance roofs.

3.1 Optimization Guidelines

The proposed methodology is composed of three steps: i) the cache size optimization, ii) the performance optimization, and iii) the efficiency optimization. The first step aims at promoting an application's data to a higher cache level (one closer to the core), increasing the bandwidth at which it can be transferred, which can have a positive impact on performance and energy efficiency. This promotion is achieved by scaling up the size of the cache level above the one the application's data is stored in, so that its size can accommodate the dataset. Conversely, memory levels above this can be scaled down or removed outright, helping to free power and area resources which can be applied elsewhere.

In the context of the CARM, promoting data through an increase in cache size does not produce a change in the performance roofs. Instead, the point representing the application's performance moves vertically, to the roofline above

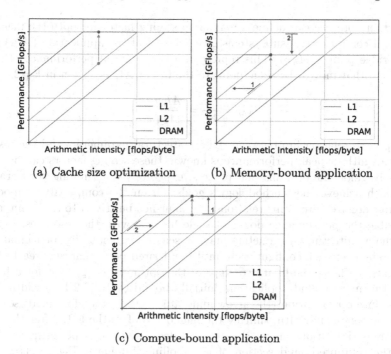

Fig. 1. CARM plots exemplifying the application of the hardware optimization methodology's steps (Cache size (a), Performance (1) and Efficiency (2)) to hypothetical workloads

associated with the upgraded memory level. This is exemplified in Fig. 1a, which shows a hypothetical application transitioning from the L2 to the L1 roof following an increase in size of the L1 cache, becoming compute-bound.

Following a cache size optimization, the second step seeks to scale up the resources imposing a bottleneck on the execution, which must first be identified. Depending on the application's AI and which section of the respective roofline it falls under, it may be classified as memory-bound or compute-bound. As such, this step seeks to increase the memory bandwidth for a memory-bound application, or raise the peak arithmetic performance for a compute-bound application. This process produces visible changes to the architectural roofline, with a memory bandwidth increase shifting the ridge point and memory-bound region to the left, while an increase to the arithmetic performance raises the compute roof.

Finally, the third step has the goal of scaling down the unused resources, which are again identified through the CARM. A memory-bound classification hints at an excess of computational resources, while a compute-bound application has excessive memory bandwidth. The excess resources are scaled down, with a reduction in computational resources lowering the compute roof, while a reduction in memory bandwidth moves the ridge point to the left.

Furthermore, we can define a maximum scaling factor for both the memory (k_M) and compute (k_C) subsystems given the AI of the application (AI_A) and of the ridge point (AI_{RP}). This represents the change in performance of each subsystem that moves the ridge point to the target AI, as shown in Eq. 2:

$$k_M = \frac{1}{k_C} = \frac{AI_{RP}}{AI_A} \tag{2}$$

If the precise relationship between the architectural parameters and the resulting bandwidth or peak performance is known, these scaling factors can be used to closely guide the optimization process, expeditely determining the parameters which achieve the methodology's goals. Given the complexity of modern computer architectures, this relationship might not be trivial to ascertain, as it is possible the performance does not scale linearly with the resources. In this case, the architectural parameters may be scaled incrementally, benchmarking the system after each configuration until the desired performance is reached.

Figure 1b shows the final two steps of the optimization process for a hypothetical memory-bound application, initially bound by the L2 bandwidth. The performance optimization (the arrow annotated with 1) therefore increases this level's memory bandwidth, shifting the memory roof to the left. After this, the efficiency optimization (arrow 2) calls for a decrease in peak performance, lowering the compute-bound section of the roofline. Similarly, Fig. 1c shows the optimization process, but for a compute-bound application bound by the L1 roof. This means the performance optimization corresponds to an increase of the compute performance and raises the corresponding roof (arrow 1), and the efficiency optimization translates to a decrease in the excess memory bandwidth, which shifts the L1 ridge point to the right (arrow 2).

These optimizations can be thought of intuitively as moving the ridge point of the relevant performance roof to the application's AI, which is the final result for the examples in Figs. 1b and 1c. With this, the application is perfectly positioned to fully exploit the available resources, simultaneously exercising the memory and compute subsystems to their limit.

3.2 Arithmetic Intensity Range

While the proposed methodology has assumed applications operate at a single AI, this is not always the case, as the ratio between the memory and arithmetic instructions may vary during the application's runtime, or depend on the data being processed. A more detailed analysis of the attainable performance can be made by introducing the concept of AI range, i.e. the range of values a given application's AI can achieve. This highlights the portion of the roofline that dictates the performance upper-bound of the application, which can encompass different sections of the roofline. By identifying this range, it is possible to guide the optimization while considering all possible AIs the target application can cover, creating hardware which improves the performance of the application, irrespective of the specific datasets processed or the kernels that constitute it.

Using this concept, any point within the AI range may be chosen as the optimization target, depending on the optimization goals. For instance, an efficient approach is targeting the limit of the AI range closest to the original ridge point, which ensures the increased memory or compute resources benefit the entire range. Conversely, targeting the opposite end of the range will scale up the attainable performance further still, but will not affect the entirety of the AI range and thus only improve the performance of certain kernels or datasets.

3.3   Architectural Parameters

With the hardware optimization methodology described, it is important to identify how the optimization guidelines may be implemented in a typical processor. Seeing as how most modern processors feature distinct clock domains for their shared caches, adjusting the cache frequency is a viable option to scale the memory bandwidth. Alternative options can also be considered, such as scaling the number of Miss Status Holding Registers (MSHRs) or the response latency. Scaling the processor's arithmetic performance can be done through its functional units, by changing the number of FPUs. Their latency can also be explored, as increasing it in a non-pipelined context can scale down the compute roof more substantially when a single FPU remains.

While our previous study [14] was limited to evaluating the effect of the cache size and functional unit latency, a more thorough set of parameters are explored here. This allows for the performance of the memory and compute subsystems to be scaled in both directions, more freely manipulating the roofline for improvements to both the performance and efficiency.

It is also important to scale any associated resources in accordance, ensuring any new units or additional bandwidth can be used effectively. For example, the processor's front-end should be sufficient to provide any additional units with work, and the number of load-store units should be adequate for the memory bandwidth. Furthermore, physical constraints such a power and area budget or a frequency limit must be considered when applying the methodology, adapting the guidelines to limit or omit steps which would break these constraints.

4   Experimental Results

The experimental validation performed in this work uses gem5 [11], a computer architecture simulator with a set of parameterizable CPU models. This work makes use of gem5's most detailed processor model, the *O3CPU*. This out-of-order processor, here based on the RISC-V ISA, is initially parameterized with a 32 kB L1 cache, a 128 kB L2 cache clocked at 500 MHz, two pipelined FPUs and a core frequency of 1GHz, which the private cache shares. Additionally, McPAT [9] is used to obtain estimates for the power consumption and die area based on the architectural parameters and execution statistics. In our experiments, we modify this architecture in three ways: The cache size is increased to promote the dataset, the L2 frequency is adjusted to scale the memory bandwidth, and the number of FPUs and their latency is modified to scale the compute roof.

The hardware optimization methodology is applied for two target applications, SpMV, a computational kernel that is typically memory bound and whose AI depends on the input data, and an application comprised of multiple computational kernels, adapted from PolyBench's [1] *gemver* benchmark.

4.1   SpMV

Sparse Matrix-Vector Multiplication is a widely used computational kernel which plays a critical role in a number of fields, ranging from industry to engineering and machine learning. It can be written as $A \cdot x = y$, where x and y are dense vectors, while A represents a sparse matrix, typically with very few non-zero values [8]. The specific implementation discussed here focuses on the Compressed Sparse Rows (CSR) format, which uses three arrays to encode the sparse matrix: *val* contains the non-zero values, *colIdx* their column indexes, and *rowPtr* the index of each row's first non-zero element within the other two arrays. *rowPtr* is used to index the *val* and *colIdx* arrays, the latter of which is used to index the values in the x vector, calculating the matrix-vector product.

A hand-optimized version of the SpMV kernel for the CSR format was developed, written in RISC-V assembly. *rowPtr* and *colIdx* are comprised of 32-bit integers, while the *val* and x arrays use double-precision floating-point numbers. This kernel's optimization focuses on heavily unrolling the inner loop (by a factor of 256), and on dynamically calculating the jump address within the unrolled portion, based on the remaining non-zero values in each row. This leads to a significant reduction in conditional branching, which tends to be particularly detrimental in the case of SpMV due to its unpredictable sparsity patterns, thus improving the application's performance and approximating it to the architecture's performance upper-bounds.

As the characteristics of the sparse matrix heavily influence the application's control flow, its AI also fluctuates, varying with the input data. Through an analysis of the developed algorithm, it is possible to determine its AI as a function of the characteristics of the sparse matrix, in particular its number of rows (m) and number of non-zero values (nnz), as shown in Eq. 3.

$$AI = \frac{FLOPs}{Bytes} = \frac{m + 2 \cdot nnz}{4 + 20 \cdot nnz + 12m} \tag{3}$$

By excluding the possibility of matrices with empty rows (meaning there is at least one non-zero value per row) we can determine the range of AIs from this expression, which is delineated as $\left[\frac{3}{32}, \frac{1}{10}\right]$.

Ten sparse matrices of a similar size (between 152 and 202 kB) and of varying densities and sparsity patterns were sourced from SuiteSparse [7], covering a substantial portion of the AI range of SpMV. The three steps of the optimization methodology were applied for this dataset, with this process depicted in Fig. 2, which shows the application's AI range shaded in red, and the performance for

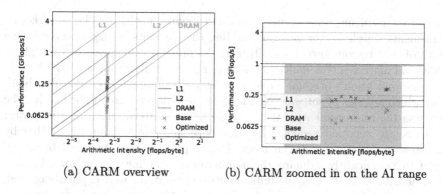

(a) CARM overview   (b) CARM zoomed in on the AI range

Fig. 2. The optimization process applied to SpMV (Color figure online)

each of the matrices, before (gray) and after (red) the optimization. It begins
with an increase in size of the L2 cache to 256 kB, promoting the data to this
roofline, where the application is memory-bound. This moves the application's
performance vertically (each matrix represented by a cross in the plot), from the
DRAM to the L2 roofline. The second step is then applied, increasing the L2
cache's frequency to 1000 MHz, which improves the L2's bandwidth, the cause of
the execution bottleneck. This shifts the L2 and DRAM ridge points to the left,
improving the attainable performance of the AI range. Finally, the efficiency
optimization is implemented, lowering the peak performance by employing a
single non-pipelined FPU with a 2-cycle latency, which lowers the compute roof
without detracting from the attainable performance. With these operations combined, the L2 ridge point moves to the upper limit of the AI range, substantially
improving the SpMV performance compared to the baseline.

McPAT is then used to estimate the power consumption, energy usage and die
area of both implementations. The average performance and power consumption
increase substantially following the application of the methodology, going from
0.1 GFLOP/s to 0.266 GFLOP/s, and from 2.459 W to 4.946 W respectively.
However, the disproportionate increase in performance means the final architecture exhibits higher energy efficiency, with the average energy required to
compute all matrices decreasing from 6.006 mJ to 4.495 mJ. The changes to the
FPUs also offset the area cost of the cache size increase, meaning the optimized
architecture sees its die area decrease from 31.321 mm^2 to 30.219 mm^2.

4.2 Multikernel Application

The Multikernel Application is a workload comprised of four different computational kernels, adapted from PolyBench's [1] *gemver* benchmark. It operates on
two scalar constants, α and β, an $N \cdot N$ matrix A, and eight vectors of length
N, namely x, y, z, w, $u1$, $u2$, $v1$ and $v2$. The first kernel, or kernel 1, calculates
the outer product of the vector pairs $u1$, $v1$ and $u2$, $v2$ and adds the resulting
matrices to A. Kernel 2 consists of a dense matrix-vector multiplication, using

the matrix resulting from kernel 1 and multiplying it with y. The third kernel implements simple vector addition, adding the elements of the z vector to the result of the previous kernel. Finally, kernel 4 produces the w vector through an additional matrix-vector multiplication, using the results from kernels 1 and 3.

The application's original implementation was obtained from PolyBench [1], after which a series of software optimization techniques were applied to it. The first was the improvement of the memory access pattern, ensuring the matrix elements are accessed sequentially (row-wise and not column-wise), thereby maximizing the reuse of cache lines. The loops were then unrolled by a factor of 16, significantly reducing the number of control flow instructions. Finally, array accesses with unchanging indices between iterations were explicitly cached, replacing them with variables updated in the outer loop. This allows the compiler to not generate redundant load instructions, instead keeping those values in registers. These optimizations collectively improve the application's performance, better aligning it with the performance upper-bounds represented in the CARM.

Following the implementation, and considering a dataset where $N = 128$, the application's AI can be determined analytically for each of the kernels and the overall workload by calculating the ratio between floating-point operations performed and bytes loaded/stored. This results in an AI range of $\left[\frac{1}{12}, \frac{1}{2}\right]$, and an overall AI of 0.353. Considering matrix and array elements of 32-bits, the size of the dataset (the size of A and all of the vectors) is determined to be 68 kB, after which the optimization process can begin.

In order to demonstrate the benefits of the concept of AI range, a more naive optimization approach is initially undertaken, targeting the application's overall AI. This process is illustrated in Fig. 3a, which characterizes each of the kernels and the overall application (annotated with App) on the CARM. The cache optimization is omitted, as promoting the data to the L1 cache would require it to be resized to 128 kB due to gem5's constraints, a sharp increase which would make the L2 redundant. As the application appears memory-bound, the L2 cache's frequency is then increased to 550 MHz. Combined with the efficiency optimization, which removes one of the FPUs, this results in the L2 ridge point shifting to the overall AI of the application. Despite this, the application performance decreases, mainly driven by the reduction in performance of kernels 1 and 2. The higher AI of the first kernel means it becomes compute-bound following the efficiency optimization, substantially lowering its attainable performance. Kernel 2's performance surpasses the L2's upper-bounds, which suggests some of the data it accesses is cached in L1. Notably, the implementation makes repeated accesses to the x vector, whose size allows for it to be kept in the L1 cache. The sections of the kernel that can reuse the L1 data receive it at a higher bandwidth, and are therefore capable of achieving a higher performance. By lowering the compute roof, these sections become increasingly compute-bound, limiting the performance of the overall kernel.

The detailed, kernel-level analysis of the performance is then used to guide hardware optimization process, avoiding the previous pitfalls by targeting the

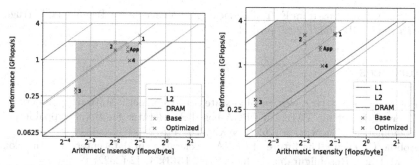

(a) First optimization approach, with the L2 @ 550 MHz and 1 FPUs

(b) Second optimization approach, with the L2 @ 800 MHz and 2 FPUs

Fig. 3. The optimization process applied to the Multikernel Application

upper limit of the application's AI range. This is achieved by increasing the L2 cache's frequency to 850 MHz, aligning the ridge point of the L2 roofline with kernel 1, and improving the attainable performance for all kernels. The efficiency optimization must now be omitted, given the AI target for the ridge point has been reached. The result from this optimization approach is depicted in Fig. 3b, showing an improved performance for each of the kernels, with an 8% improvement to the performance of the overall application.

5   Conclusions and Future Work

We proposed a hardware optimization methodology guided by the Cache-Aware Roofline Model, applied to a RISC-V CPU in order to accelerate and improve the efficiency of target applications. The intuitive nature of the CARM's insights leads to the equally intuitive optimization guidelines proposed herein, providing a high-level approach to the process of architectural configuration. The methodology was shown to be effective at improving performance, energy efficiency and die area, also demonstrating the value of thoroughly analyzing the application's AI range. Demonstrated here for two applications, this methodology can be applied to other computational kernels, potentially laying the groundwork for the efficient design exploration of future domain-specific processors.

In the future, we aim at adapting this methodology for dynamic performance scaling, combining performance profiling and roofline modelling to selectively disable sections of the architecture. By scaling the performance roofs at runtime, we aim to bring the methodology's benefits to fixed architectures, using the CARM's insights to improve energy efficiency without sacrificing performance.

Acknowledgements. This project has received funding from the European High Performance Computing Joint Undertaking (JU) under Framework Partnership Agreement No 800928 and Specific Grant Agreement No 101036168 (EPI SGA2), Grant Agreement No 956213 (SparCity) and Grant Agreement No 101092877 (SYCLOPS).

It also received funding from FCT (Fundação para a Ciência e a Tecnologia, Portugal), through the UIDB/50021/2020 project.

References

1. PolyBench/C. https://web.cse.ohio-state.edu/~pouchet.2/software/polybench/
2. Agrawal, R., et al.: FAB: An FPGA-based Accelerator for Bootstrappable Fully Homomorphic Encryption (2022). arXiv:2207.11872
3. Bobda, C., et al.: The future of FPGA acceleration in datacenters and the cloud. ACM Trans. Reconfigurable Technol. Syst. **15**(3), 1–42 (2022)
4. Cavalcante, M., et al.: Ara: a 1-GHz+ scalable and energy-efficient RISC-V vector processor with multiprecision floating-point support in 22-nm FD-SOI. IEEE Trans. Very Large Scale Integr. Syst. **28**(2), 530–543 (2020)
5. Chen, X., et al.: ReGraph: Scaling Graph Processing on HBM-enabled FPGAs with Heterogeneous Pipelines. Technical report, arXiv:2203.02676, arXiv (2022)
6. Ilic, A., Pratas, F., Sousa, L.: Cache-aware roofline model: upgrading the loft. IEEE Comput. Archit. Lett. **13**(1), 21–24 (2014)
7. Kolodziej, S., et al.: The SuiteSparse matrix collection website interface. J. Open Source Softw. **4**(35), 1244 (2019)
8. Kulkarni, A.V., Barde, C.R.: A Survey on Performance Modelling and Optimization Techniques for SpMV on GPUs, vol. 5 (2014)
9. Li, S., et al.: McPAT: an integrated power, area, and timing modeling framework for multicore and manycore architectures. In: Proceedings of the IEEE/ACM International Symposium on Microarchitecture, pp. 469–480. ACM, New York (2009)
10. Li, S., Liu, D., Liu, W.: Optimized data reuse via reordering for sparse matrix-vector multiplication on FPGAs. In: IEEE/ACM International Conference on Computer Aided Design (ICCAD), Munich, Germany, pp. 1–9. IEEE (2021)
11. Lowe-Power, J., et al.: The gem5 Simulator: V20.0+. arXiv:2007.03152 (2020)
12. Mantovani, F., et al.: Software Development Vehicles to enable extended and early co-design: a RISC-V and HPC case of study (2023). arXiv:2306.01797
13. Marques, D., et al.: Performance analysis with cache-aware roofline model in intel advisor. In: 2017 International Conference on High Performance Computing & Simulation (HPCS), pp. 898–907 (2017)
14. Rodrigues, A., Ilic, A., Sousa, L.: Performance modelling-driven optimization of RISC-V hardware for efficient SpMV. In: Bienz, A., Weiland, M., Baboulin, M., Kruse, C. (eds.) High Performance Computing. ISC High Performance 2023. LNCS, vol. 13999, pp. 486–499. Springer, Cham (2023). https://doi.org/10.1007/978-3-031-40843-4_36
15. Sato, M., et al.: Co-design for A64FX manycore processor and "Fugaku". In: SC20: International Conference for High Performance Computing, Networking, Storage and Analysis, Atlanta, GA, USA, pp. 1–15. IEEE (2020)
16. Shalf, J.: The future of computing beyond Moore's Law. Philos. Trans. Royal Soc. A Math. Phys. Eng. Sci. **378**(2166), 20190061 (2020)
17. Williams, S., Waterman, A., Patterson, D.: Roofline: an insightful visual performance model for floating-point programs and multicore architectures. Technical report, 1407078 (2009)
18. Zhao, J., et al.: SonicBOOM: The 3rd Generation Berkeley Out-of-Order Machine, p. 7 (2020)

Energy Efficiency Impact of Processing in Memory: A Comprehensive Review of Workloads on the UPMEM Architecture

Yann Falevoz$^{(\boxtimes)}$ (ID) and Julien Legriel (ID)

UPMEM, 6 Pl. Robert Schuman, 38000 Grenoble, France
yfalevoz@upmem.com

Abstract. Processing-in-Memory (PIM) architectures have emerged as a promising solution for data-intensive applications, providing significant speedup by processing data directly within the memory. However, the impact of PIM on energy efficiency is not well characterized. In this paper, we provide a comprehensive review of workloads ported to the first PIM product available on the market, namely the UPMEM architecture, and quantify the impact on each workload in terms of energy efficiency. Less than the half of the reviewed papers provide insights on the impact of PIM on energy efficiency, and the evaluation methods differ from one paper to the other. To provide a comprehensive overview, we propose a methodology for estimating energy consumption and efficiency for both the PIM and baseline systems at data center level, enabling a direct comparison of the two systems. Our results show that PIM can provide significant energy savings for data intensive workloads. We also identify key factors that impact the energy efficiency of UPMEM PIM, including the workload characteristics. Overall, this paper provides valuable insights for researchers and practitioners looking to optimize energy efficiency in data-intensive applications using UPMEM PIM architecture.

Keywords: Processing in memory (PIM) · UPMEM architecture · Data-centric architectures · Workload optimization · High-performance computing · Computational efficiency · Energy consumption · Energy efficiency

1 Introduction

With the exponential growth of data-intensive applications, traditional compute-centric architectures have become a bottleneck for efficient and scalable processing. The demand for high-performance computing has pushed the limits of Moore's Law, leading to a growing disparity between the processing power

This paper is supported by European Union's Horizon Europe programme (HORIZON-CL4-2021-HUMAN-01 and HORIZON-EIC-2021-PATHFINDEROPEN-01), under SustainML and BioPIM projects.

© The Author(s) 2024, corrected publication 2024
D. Zeinalipour et al. (Eds.): Euro-Par 2023 Workshops, LNCS 14352, pp. 155–166, 2024.
https://doi.org/10.1007/978-3-031-48803-0_13

of CPUs and the bandwidth of memory. This has resulted in significant performance degradation and energy inefficiencies when dealing with large-scale data-intensive workloads.

1.1 Limitations of Traditional Compute-Centric Architectures for Data-Intensive Workloads

Traditional compute-centric architectures, with separate processing and memory components, face limitations with data-intensive workloads. The "memory wall" or "data movement bottleneck" arises due to the extensive data movement between processor and memory [25]. This poses challenges for applications that demand processing large data volumes, leading to high energy consumption and latencies [14]. As a result, data-intensive applications suffer from performance degradation, and the energy consumption can be unsustainable. Despite solutions like caching and prefetchers, which offer some performance improvements, they still rely on compute-centric architectures and are constrained by data movement limitations.

1.2 From Data Movement to Data Processing

Processing in Memory (PIM) is a promising paradigm that tackles traditional compute-centric architecture limitations [18]. With PIM, processing occurs directly within the memory where data resides, eliminating data movement between processor and memory [18,25,26]. This yields significant energy savings, vital for energy-conscious data centers, and reduced latency, especially for data-intensive workloads. By reducing energy consumption, PIM can facilitates the development of more efficient, sustainable and cost effective computing systems for machine learning, data analytics, and graph processing [18]. Moreover, it unlocks new applications and breakthroughs in scientific research, drug discovery, and other areas where large-scale data analysis is required.

1.3 UPMEM Architecture

UPMEM PIM is the first commercial PIM product available on the market [11]. It offers a radical new approach to data processing by combining DRAM and logic functions in the same chip, allowing for ultra-fast data access and processing, and eliminating the need for frequent data transfers between the memory and the processor. This results in a substantial overall reduction in power consumption and latency, as well as improved scalability and performance.

An UPMEM PIM server is a standard application server where most of the DIMM slots have been populated with PIM DIMMs (Fig. 1a). Standard and UPMEM DIMMs coexist in the server and the firmware is made aware of the specific configuration. A typical configuration totalizes 20 PIM DRAM modules.

A module takes the form of a standard DDR4-2400 DIMM (Fig. 1b). It has a capacity of 8GB, and embeds 16 PIM chips on it, 8 on each side. Inside each chip, 8 processors coexist (Fig. 1b). These processors are called DPU, standing for Data Processing Unit. A typical configuration then totalises 2560 DPUs for 160 GB of PIM DRAM.

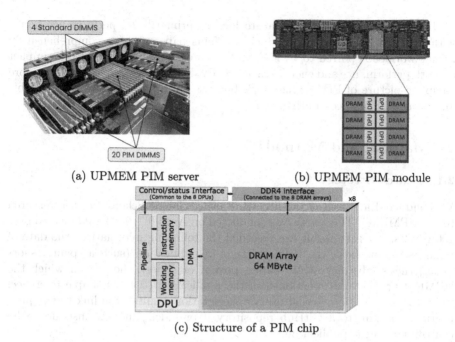

(a) UPMEM PIM server   (b) UPMEM PIM module

(c) Structure of a PIM chip

Fig. 1. UPMEM PIM platform

A DPU is a custom proprietary 32-bit processor, inspired by the RISC philosophy, but adapted to the specific design challenges of DRAM manufacturing processes. It shares the access with the host CPU to a DRAM bank, called Main RAM (Fig. 1c). Instruction and data caches are replaced by an instruction RAM and a Working RAM. DPUs are independent from each others' memory and run asynchronously relative to each other. 24 hardware threads can execute independently of each other in a DPU. All inter DPU communication takes place through the host CPU. This architecture allows every DPU to efficiently work within their own fragment of the dataset and even with their own programming routine if chosen to be different. This technology comes with a set of tools designed to make the porting of applications as smooth as possible.

Each DPU can be programmed with standard tools and skillset. UPMEM provides a complete software stack that enables DPU programs to be written in C and APIs in common languages for host programming. Communication libraries make it easy to configure the DPUs, organise distribution of data, scheduling, and retrieve results. The compiler for the DPU target is based on LLVM and comes with an efficient tool for debugging based on LLDB.

1.4   Objectives

Since the launch of UPMEM's PIM architecture, researchers have shown growing interest in exploring its potential for accelerating data-intensive workloads. Numerous papers report impressive speedups of tens or even hundreds of times compared to traditional architectures in various applications like genomics, analytics, and artificial intelligence.

However, most existing literature focuses primarily on performance gains, with little attention to energy efficiency. This paper aims to comprehensively review workloads ported to UPMEM's PIM product, quantifying PIM's impact on both performance and energy efficiency. By doing so, we aim to present a more complete picture of PIM technology's benefits and its potential for sustainable and energy-efficient computing.

2   Material and Methods

2.1   Search Strategy

We conducted a search of the literature using Google Scholar, with the search term "UPMEM". The search was conducted on April 6th, 2023, and yielded over 100 results. For each result, we recorded the following information: the date of publication, the field, the title, the type of publication (such as paper, short paper, thesis, abstract, white paper, poster, or slides), the way in which the UPMEM product was mentioned in the publication (such as simple reference, technical presentation, actual use, or acceleration results), the link to the publication, the link to a GitHub repository if provided, and the institutes who contributed to the publication.

2.2   Inclusion Criteria

To ensure the relevance of our review, we limited our search to publications that met the following inclusion criteria:

1. The publication must be written in English
2. The publication must be a paper available in full-text format.
3. The publication must provide sufficient details on the experiment setup to evaluate the gain in energy efficiency.
4. The publication must provide acceleration results, not just in terms of speedup, but in terms of throughput or execution times for both PIM and reference implementations, or at least provide data to calculate this information. It will be required to evaluate the gain in energy efficiency.
5. The acceleration results must have been measured on real hardware, and on the latest version of UPMEM PIM DIMMs. This excludes publications prior to 2021, for which this version of UPMEM PIMs were not yet available. This condition is related to the requirement of knowing the power consumption of the PIM modules to evaluate the gain in energy efficiency.
6. The publication must show that efforts to optimise performance have been made, that is, that the work was not just to show that porting is feasible.

We excluded duplicate publications and publications that did not meet these criteria.

2.3 Estimation of Energy Efficiency Gain

Less than half of the resulting papers provide insights on the impact of PIM on energy efficiency. However, these papers differ in their evaluation methods, making it challenging to compare and draw conclusions from the results. To provide a comprehensive overview of the energy efficiency impact of PIM, we have decided to propose data center level approach. To estimate the energy efficiency of the PIM system and compare it with the baseline system:

1. For the reference servers, we gathered power data (TDP) from datasheets and specifications provided by manufacturers for main parts of the systems, that is processors and DIMMs (Table 1). We have added up these figures and, to ensure accuracy, we also added a base consumption of 115W for the chassis, fans, common modules and PSU efficiency loss, to calculate the power consumption of each system. The resulting value has been verified to be relevant with various online power calculators [3,9] for different configurations. For the PIM server, in addition to the server's power consumption calculated using the preceding method, we accounted for the measured power consumption of the PIMM DIMMs, which is 23.22W.
2. We applied a Power Usage Effectiveness (PUE) [20] factor to take into account the power consumed by the whole data center infrastructure including servers, network switches, and cooling facilities. We used a factor of 1.55, which was the average in 2022 [16].
3. To calculate the energy per execution, we multiplied the power consumption of each system by the execution time given in the paper or divided it by the throughput, depending on what is available in the paper.
4. Finally, we compared the energy per execution of the PIM system with that of the baseline system, considering it is dedicated to the specific workload, to evaluate the gain in energy efficiency.

Table 1. Power consumption

Component	TDP (W)
Intel Xeon Silver 4110/4215/E5-2630 v4	85 [5,7,8]
Intel Xeon Gold 5120	105 [4]
Intel Xeon E5-2697 v2	130 [6]
32GB DDR4-2666 RDIMM	5
64GB DDR4-3200 RDIMM	5.5
NVIDIA A100	300 [2]

As an example, a standard UPMEM PIM server with 2 x INTEL Xeon Silver 4215 processors, 4 x 32 GB DDR4-2666 RDIMMs and 20 x UPMEM PIM DIMMs results in a power consumption of 770 W. Taking into account the PUE, this leads to 1193 W. Considering a workload with an execution time of 10 ms on that server, the energy per execution would be of 11,93 J.

While this rudimentary approach offers a good initial trend for evaluating energy efficiency gain, it cannot replace direct measurements on a real PIM system and may introduce some unfavorable bias. For instance, it assumes the CPU power consumption remains the same in the PIM system, even though it is significantly less solicited due to offloading computations to the PIM cores. Additionally, we did not consider the substantial reduction in data transfers between the CPU and DRAM, which can have a notable impact on energy consumption. In particular, read operations in DRAM consume approximately 100 and 1000 times more energy than multiplication and addition, respectively [27]. Neglecting these aspects can impact energy consumption significantly and underestimate the PIM system's true energy efficiency gain.

3 PIM Implementations of Modern Workloads

3.1 Mathematical Functions

Item et al. [23] discusses the problem of the limited instruction sets of PIM architectures and the need for efficient support for **transcendental functions** and other hard-to-calculate operations in PIM systems. The authors present TransPimLib, a library that provides CORDIC-based and Lookup Table-based methods for trigonometric functions, hyperbolic functions, exponentiation, logarithm, square root, etc. They implement TransPimLib for the UPMEM PIM architecture and evaluate its methods in terms of performance and accuracy, using microbenchmarks and three full workloads (Blackscholes, Sigmoid, Softmax).

Blackscholes that use Multiplication-based Fuzzy Lookup Table (M-LUT) and LDEXP-based Fuzzy Lookup Table (L-LUT) versions are, respectively, within 75% and 82% the performance of the 32-thread CPU baseline. The fixed-point L-LUT version is 62% faster than the 32-thread CPU baseline. In this last case, the speedup achieved does not translate into a gain in terms of energy efficiency. In fact, the power consumption of the PIM server is significantly higher compared to the traditional server, which translates into a 58% increase in energy costs, i.e. 69.8 additional Joules per operation. Nonetheless, as the authors point out, TransPimLib's techniques can curtail the need for data transfer from PIM cores to the CPU for applications using neural networks and machine learning algorithms, resulting in a speedup of 6 to 8 times compared to executing them on the host CPU.

3.2 Databases

Baumstark et al. [13] presents an approach to integrating PIM technology into a **query processing engine** of a database management system (DBMS) by leveraging adaptive query compilation. PIM technology moves computation directly to memory, which can improve the performance of DBMSs. The evaluation on UPMEM system was conducted using the Social Network Benchmark (SNB) dataset from the Linked Data Benchmark Council (LDBC). The experiment setup used two Intel Xeon Silver 4215R processors, 512 GB of DRAM, and four UPMEM DIMMs. The evaluation used the first three Interactive Short Read queries from the SNB dataset.

The results of the evaluation showed that the proposed approach speeds up query compilation time up to 30 times compared to the baseline compiler, which has resulted in a reduction of up to 1/3 in the overall query execution time. Given the power consumption of the two configurations, the gain in speed translates into a 17% gain in energy efficiency, that is, the PIM server saves up to 66 J per operation.

Baumstark et al. [12] discusses the benefits of PIM technology for improving the performance of **graph database traversal**. The authors used the Social Network Benchmark (SNB) dataset from the Linked Data Benchmark Council (LDBC) to evaluate the performance of this approach in a graph database management system (DBMS) and used a graph database engine called Poseidon, which supports both a persistent memory storage engine and an in-memory mode. The experiments were performed on a system with two Intel Xeon Silver 4215R, 512 GB of DRAM, and 4 UPMEM DIMMs.

The benchmarks shows that UPMEM PIM technology can outperform the runtime of a comparable CPU execution, especially when high parallelism is used. The inclusion of table transfer time between the host and the DPU results in a 30% reduction of the total table scan execution time. It is worth noting that this performance improvement is achieved despite a limited number of DPUs. The similar power consumption of the two configurations leads to a 11% gain in energy efficiency, that is, 26 J saved per operation.

Kang et al. [24] focuses on designing a **practical ordered index** for PIM, which can achieve low communication cost and high load balance regardless of the degree of skew in data and queries. The authors present PIM-tree, a practical ordered index that leverages the strengths of host CPU and PIM nodes to overcome load imbalance problems. The authors conducted experiments using UPMEM PIM architecture with 16 UPMEM DIMMs and compared the results with those of two traditional indexes performed on a machine that has two Intel Xeon E5-2630 v4 CPUs.

The results show that the PIM-tree outperforms state-of-the-art indexes, with more than 2x speedup compared to state-of-the-art indexes on a machine with similar performance for an INSERT operation. Given the power consumption of the two configurations, this translates into a 20% reduction in energy consumption, i.e. up to 40 J saved per operation.

3.3   Artificial Intelligence (AI)

Gómez-Luna et al. [21] evaluates the potential of PIM architectures in accelerating the **training of machine learning (ML) algorithms**, which is a computationally intensive process frequently memory-bound due to large training datasets. The authors implemented four representative classical ML algorithms, including linear regression, logistic regression, decision tree, and K-Means clustering, on the UPMEM PIM architecture. They rigorously evaluated and characterized the algorithms in terms of accuracy, performance, and scaling, comparing them to their counterparts on CPU and GPU, using the Criteo dataset.

The experimental results show that the PIM implementation of decision tree is 73.4× faster than a state-of-the-art CPU version, and 5.3× faster than a state-of-the-art GPU version. This translates into an energy gain of almost 30x and 4.2x respectively, that is 159 kJ and 17.8 kJ per execution. K-Means clustering on PIM is 2.7× and 2.76× faster than state-of-the-art CPU and GPU versions, respectively. This results into an energy gain of 10% and 2.2x respectively, i.e. 3.7 and 62.8 kJ saved per execution.

Das et al. [15] discusses the implementation of two **Convolutional Neural Networks (CNNs)**, YOLOv3 and eBNN, on the UPMEM PIM system, and compare the performance of their implementation with several other recently proposed PIM architectures.

Results showed that the performance speed-up of eBNN inference performance with respect to traditional CPU-based system scales up linearly as more parallel processing elements (DPU) are incorporated in the UPMEM system, reaching 92x for a complete PIM server whith 2560 DPU. Despite the large difference in power consumption between the PIM server and the reference server, the high acceleration factor results in a significant gain in energy efficiency, with a reduction factor of 36.6x, i.e. 199 μJ per execution.

3.4 Genomics

Diab [17] propose Alignment-in-Memory (AIM), a framework for high-throughput **sequence alignment** using PIM, and compares the performance of UPMEM PIM with 3 conventional CPU systems in accelerating memory-bound sequence alignment workloads.

The authors observe that UPMEM outperforms the CPU systems in the majority of cases, even when data transfer time is included. **Needleman-Wunsch (NW)** speedup is low with speedups achieved of 1.1x, 1.78x and 1.5x over the three reference systems respectively and do not translates into energy gain. **Smith-Waterman-Gotoh (SWG)** and **GenASM** show a moderate acceleration (2.8x–6.2x) that translates in a slight energy gain (1.4x–2.7x). In the case of SWG, however, this moderate gain translates into a significant absolute value per execution (240 kJ–1.9 MJ) due to the long duration of this workload. **Wavefront algorithm (WFA)** and **WFA-adaptive** show strong accelerations compared to system 1 and 2 (30.1x–36.5x), that translate into significant energy gain (13.1x–14.5x) and absolute energy per execution that range from 5 to 5.5 kJ.

4   Discussion

4.1   Moving to a Larger Scale: Implications for Data Center Operations

The present study highlights the significant variation in speedup and energy efficiency gains across different workloads. To facilitate a proper comparison, it is imperative to move to a larger scale for a comprehensive understanding of the implications. Therefore, the energy saved/wasted in GWh by 1000 PIM servers operating as a small data center was determined by running the same number of run executions as the baseline server over a period of three years (Fig. 2), which is the standard depreciation period for a server. This approach provides a valuable perspective on energy efficiency gains and highlights the potential for significant savings in energy consumption by adopting more energy efficient computing techniques.

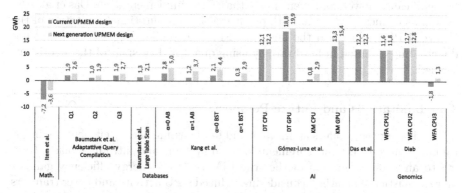

Fig. 2. Comparison of energy savings and wastage in GWh over 3 years for 1000 PIM servers vs. 1000 baseline servers in a small data center, for the current and next generation of UPMEM PIM DIMMs.

On one hand, savings can be significant for workloads with energy efficiency gains, reaching up to 12.7GWh over the typical 3-year depreciation period compared to CPU configurations and up to 18.8GWh compared to GPU configurations. At electricity prices of $0.192/kWh [1], this translates to a cost reduction of up to $2.4M and $3.6M respectively on operating expenses (OPEX) over the same period. On the other hand, for certain workloads, such as transcendental functions, the acceleration does not compensate for the additional power induced by PIM DIMMs. This results in an increased OPEX charge. This highlights the importance of carefully considering workload characteristics when designing and optimising computing systems, as the potential for energy savings can vary significantly depending on the specific workload being performed.

The natural next step would be to assess the impact in terms of Total Cost of Ownership (TCO), but this is beyond the scope of this paper.

4.2   Best Suited Applications to Run on UPMEM PIM

Certain types of applications are particularly well-suited to run on UPMEM PIM processors. These include applications that exhibit: (1) data-intensive workloads, which are memory-bound on compute-centric architectures [22], and for which DPUs compute time is largely dominant over data transfer time; (2) workloads with data-level parallelism (i.e. little or no communication across DPUs) [22], allowing every DPUs to efficiently work within their own fragment of the dataset; (3) applications with irregular data access patterns; and (4) applications with algorithms difficult to vectorise.

It is worth noting that applications that only use the operations supported by the hardware show much greater performance and energy efficiency gains [22]. For example, Giannoula et al. [19] showed that their sparse matrix vector multiplication implementation on UPMEM PIM outperforms CPU implementation for data types for which the multiplication is supported by the hardware, while performance for data types for which the multiplication is software emulated can be significantly lower, and event worse than CPU implementation. Das et al. [15], as well as Gómez-Luna et al. [21], overcame the computational limitation of the UPMEM PIM related to the fact that FPs are emulated by software and not directly implemented in hardware by using quantified versions of the algorithms studied.

4.3   Limitations and Future Perspectives

While this approach offers an initial trend for assessing energy efficiency gains, it cannot replace direct measurements on real systems and introduce biases leading to an underestimation of the true PIM system's energy efficiency gain. A more sophisticated method considering reduced CPU activity and fewer transfers between CPU and DRAM would provide a more accurate estimate. Measuring power consumption on real systems remains the most reliable approach.

While this study presents a comprehensive review of existing literature on the UPMEM PIM architecture and its performance benefits, some publications that did not meet the selection criteria may still present interesting results. In particular Gómez-Luna et al. [22] covers workloads and fields of application that were not included in this review. The paper discusses the performance of UPMEM PIM systems compared to a CPU and a GPU for various benchmarks, but lacks the necessary data for assessing energy impact, as execution times do not include transfer times, and speedups compared to CPU and GPU are given without corresponding execution times. The PIM system outperforms the CPU and GPU for most of the benchmarks, being on average 23.2×, and up to 629.5× faster than the CPU, and on average 2.54×, and up to 57.5× faster than the GPU. Moreover, as the UPMEM PIM system is still a relatively new technology, there may be other studies and applications that have not yet been explored.

As the UPMEM PIM architecture continues to evolve [10], there are several improvements that could enhance its performance and energy efficiency. The next version of the architecture includes improvements to the DPU's performance and programmability, such as a frequency increased to 466 MHz or 30% power reduction at same frequency, and direct access to WRAM from the host while the DPU owns the bank. This enables faster processing and more efficient resource utilization. Figure 2 shows the impact of the reduced power consumption of this new design operating at the same frequency. Future versions may support additional operations, expanding the range of applications that can benefit from the PIM approach.

5 Conclusions

This paper reviews the use of UPMEM PIM in different computing domains and finds that it can enhance the performance and energy efficiency of certain applications. However, the benefits vary depending on the workload. The characteristics of suitable applications and implications for data centers are discussed, providing valuable insights into the potential of UPMEM PIM as a high-performance and energy-efficient computing solution.

References

1. Electricity prices. https://www.globalpetrolprices.com/electricity_prices/. Accessed 15 Apr 2023
2. GPU NVIDIA A100. https://www.nvidia.com/en-us/data-center/a100/
3. Intel power calculator. https://servertools.intel.com/power-calculator/
4. Intel Xeon gold 5120. https://www.intel.com/content/www/us/en/products/sku/120474/intel-xeon-gold-5120-processor-19-25m-cache-2-20-ghz/specifications.html
5. Intel Xeon processor e5-2630 v4. https://www.intel.com/content/www/us/en/products/sku/92981/intel-xeon-processor-e52630-v4-25m-cache-2-20-ghz/specifications.html
6. Intel Xeon processor e5-2697 v2. https://www.intel.com/content/www/us/en/products/sku/75283/intel-xeon-processor-e52697-v2-30m-cache-2-70-ghz/specifications.html
7. Intel Xeon silver 4110. https://www.intel.com/content/www/us/en/products/sku/123547/intel-xeon-silver-4110-processor-11m-cache-2-10-ghz/specifications.html?wapkw=%20Intel%20Xeon%20Silver%204110
8. Intel Xeon silver 4215. https://www.intel.com/content/www/us/en/products/sku/193389/intel-xeon-silver-4215-processor-11m-cache-2-50-ghz/specifications.html?wapkw=Silver%204215
9. Outervision® power supply calculator. https://outervision.com/power-supply-calculator
10. Safari live seminar: Fabrice devaux, 2 Feb 2022. https://safari.ethz.ch/safari-live-seminar-fabrice-devaux-feb-2-2022/. Accessed 27 Apr 2023
11. UPMEM tech paper. https://www.upmem.com/
12. Baumstark, A., Jibril, M.A., Sattler, K.U.: Accelerating large table scan using processing-in-memory technology. In: König-Ries, B., Scherzinger, S., Lehner, W., Vossen, G. (eds.) BTW 2023. Gesellschaft für Informatik e.V. (2023). https://doi.org/10.18420/BTW2023-51

13. Baumstark, A., Jibril, M.A., Sattler, K.U.: Adaptive query compilation with processing-in-memory (2023). https://doi.org/10.1109/ICDEW58674.2023.00035
14. Boroumand, A., et al.: Google workloads for consumer devices: mitigating data movement bottlenecks. SIGPLAN Not. **53**(2), 316–331 (2018). https://doi.org/10.1145/3296957.3173177
15. Das, P., Sutradhar, P.R., Indovina, M., Dinakarrao, S.M.P., Ganguly, A.: Implementation and evaluation of deep neural networks in commercially available processing in memory hardware. In: 2022 IEEE 35th International System-on-Chip Conference (SOCC), pp. 1–6 (2022). https://doi.org/10.1109/SOCC56010.2022.9908126
16. Davis, J., et al.: Uptime institute global data center survey results 2022 (2022). https://uptimeinstitute.com/resources/research-and-reports/uptime-institute-global-data-center-survey-results-2022. Accessed 15 Apr 2023
17. Diab, S., Nassereldine, A., Alser, M., Gómez-Luna, J., Mutlu, O., Hajj, I.E.: A framework for high-throughput sequence alignment using real processing-in-memory systems (2023). https://doi.org/10.48550/arXiv.2208.01243
18. Fujiki, D., Wang, X., Subramaniyan, A., Das, R.: In-/Near-Memory Computing, vol. 16. Morgan & Claypool Publishers (2021). https://doi.org/10.1007/978-3-031-01772-8
19. Giannoula, C., Fernandez, I., Gómez-Luna, J., Koziris, N., Goumas, G., Mutlu, O.: Sparsep: towards efficient sparse matrix vector multiplication on real processing-in-memory systems (2022). https://doi.org/10.48550/arXiv.2201.05072
20. Gyarmati, L., Trinh, T.A.: Energy efficiency of data centers. In: Kim, J.H., Lee, M.J. (eds.) Green IT: Technologies and Applications, pp. 229–244. Springer, Heidelberg (2011). https://doi.org/10.1007/978-3-642-22179-8_12
21. Gómez-Luna, J., et al.: An experimental evaluation of machine learning training on a real processing-in-memory system (2023). https://doi.org/10.48550/arXiv.2207.07886
22. Gómez-Luna, J., Hajj, I.E., Fernandez, I., Giannoula, C., Oliveira, G.F., Mutlu, O.: Benchmarking a new paradigm: experimental analysis and characterization of a real processing-in-memory system. IEEE Access **10**, 52565–52608 (2022). https://doi.org/10.1109/ACCESS.2022.3174101
23. Item, M., Gómez-Luna, J., Guo, Y., Oliveira, G.F., Sadrosadati, M., Mutlu, O.: Transpimlib: a library for efficient transcendental functions on processing-in-memory systems (2023). https://doi.org/10.48550/arXiv.2304.01951
24. Kang, H., Zhao, Y., Blelloch, G.E., Dhulipala, L., Gu, Y., McGuffey, C., Gibbons, P.B.: PIM-tree: a skew-resistant index for processing-in-memory. Proc. VLDB Endow. **16**(4), 946–958 (2022). https://doi.org/10.14778/3574245.3574275
25. Mutlu, O., Ghose, S., Gómez-Luna, J., Ausavarungnirun, R.: A modern primer on processing in memory. In: Aly, M.M.S., Chattopadhyay, A. (eds.) Emerging Computing: From Devices to Systems, pp. 171–243. Springer, Singapore (2023). https://doi.org/10.1007/978-981-16-7487-7_7
26. Mutlu, O., Ghose, S., Gómez-Luna, J., Ausavarungnirun, R.: Processing data where it makes sense: enabling in-memory computation. Microprocess. Microsyst. **67**, 28–41 (2019). https://doi.org/10.1016/j.micpro.2019.01.009
27. Sze, V., Chen, Y.H., Yang, T.J., Emer, J.S.: Key metrics and design objectives. In: Sze, V., Chen, Y.H., Yang, T.J., Emer, J.S. (eds.) Efficient Processing of Deep Neural Networks, pp. 43–58. Springer, Cham (2020). https://doi.org/10.1007/978-3-031-01766-7_3

Online Job Failure Prediction in an HPC System

Francesco Antici[✉][iD], Andrea Borghesi[iD], and Zeynep Kiziltan[iD]

University of Bologna, Bologna, Italy
{francesco.antici,andrea.borghesi3,zeynep.kiziltan}@unibo.it

Abstract. Modern High Performance Computing (HPC) systems are complex machines, with major impacts on economy and society. Along with their computational capability, their energy consumption is also steadily raising, representing a critical issue given the ongoing environmental and energetic crisis. Therefore, developing strategies to optimize HPC system management has paramount importance, both to guarantee top-tier performance and to improve energy efficiency. One strategy is to act at the workload level and highlight the jobs that are most likely to fail, prior to their execution on the system. Jobs failing during their execution unnecessarily occupy resources which could delay other jobs, adversely affecting the system performance and energy consumption. In this paper, we study job failure prediction at submit-time using classical machine learning algorithms. Our novelty lies in (i) the combination of these algorithms with Natural Language Processing (NLP) tools to represent jobs and (ii) the design of the approach to work in an online fashion in a real system. The study is based on a dataset extracted from a production machine hosted at the HPC centre CINECA in Italy. Experimental results show that our approach is promising.

1 Introduction

High Performance Computing (HPC) is a term used in Computer Science to represent the practice of aggregating computing power to solve complex problems. HPC machines are organized in clusters and they consist of several computing units (nodes) networked together to work in parallel and boost processing speed. Nodes are connected through a low-latency internal network bus, which routes traffic to mimic the behaviour of a single computer. The last decades have witnessed a massive increase in the number of components, accelerators and consequently consumption of computational power of HPC centers. This trend has been fuelled by the development of computational- hungry techniques, indeed HPC systems play a fundamental role in the field of data science, and are widely used for computationally intensive tasks in various fields, such as quantum mechanics, weather forecasting, climate research.

Latest HPC systems have reached exascale performance, namely 10^{18} operations per second, and in the future more systems are expected to have similar characteristics [4]. Machines of such scale must comply with certain standard of

© The Author(s), under exclusive license to Springer Nature Switzerland AG 2024
D. Zeinalipour et al. (Eds.): Euro-Par 2023 Workshops, LNCS 14352, pp. 167–179, 2024.
https://doi.org/10.1007/978-3-031-48803-0_35

performance and energy efficiency, hence it is fundamental to develop strategies to optimize their workload management. One strategy is to highlight the jobs that are most likely to fail, prior to their execution on the system. Jobs failing during their execution unnecessarily occupy resources which could delay other jobs, adversely affecting the system performance and energy consumption. We distinguish between failures due to external factors, such as problems with the computing nodes, networking issues, workload manager downtime (*exogenous* failures) [13], and those due to internal reasons, such as wrongly configured submission scripts and software bugs (*endogenous* failures) [7]. We here focus on the latter category. Forecasting failures due to internal factors a priori would allow to adopt ad-hoc workload management strategies. For instance, we could enforce system power saving policies by exploiting job power prediction models, such as the one presented in [1]. Quantifying the power required by a job would allow us to estimate the system power consumption and reduce it by rescheduling jobs which are likely to fail to time spans when the system power consumption is lower.

In this paper, we present a Machine Learning (ML) based classification approach to predict endogenous job failures. Our approach is applicable to data that can be collected from a production machine and leverages only the information available at job submission time (hence does not require any instrumentation of the users' code nor any change to standard workload submission workflow). This information might have different formats, and text is among them. To extract more meaningful job information from such textual data, we employ Natural Language Processing (NLP) tools and improve the classification performance of the ML models. To the best of our knowledge, this is the first work that exploits an NLP method to represent jobs during classification. Contrary to the majority of the past studies which work on random splits of historical data, the proposed methodology can be deployed in an *online* context where jobs are continuously submitted by users to a real production system. We demonstrate the validity of our approach on a dataset collected from a production machine Marconi100 hosted at the HPC centre CINECA[1] in Italy.

2   Related Work

In this paper, we restrict the related work to the study of failures in large-scale systems at job/application level. In [8], the authors analysed workload traces in a grid, showing the correlations between failure characteristics and performance metrics. Works like [5,9] tackled application failure prediction in cloud computing by using recurrent neural networks on resource usage data and performance logs, extracted from Google cluster workload traces. Also in [15] the authors relied on the resource usage data of a job to predict its failure, but in the scope of an HPC center.

These approaches do not take into account the human factors (error in the code, the submission, etc.), which are responsible for many job failures [11].

---

[1] https://www.hpc.cineca.it/hardware/marconi100.

Therefore, the trend is shifting towards the use of data collected from a workload manager to predict failure using job features, as done in [2,10,11]. In [2], the authors use a decision tree algorithm to predict job failure on two HPC workloads. In [10], they survey several ML techniques to perform the same task on a Google cluster workload trace and other two HPC workloads. A similar approach is reported in [11] on another workload; in addition, they use NLP techniques to assign similar names to similar jobs executed by the same user. All this past work, which are most related to ours, evaluate their approach on random splits of data, which is not realistic because testing could be done on data which is chronologically placed in between the training data traces. Our work differs in two ways: (i) we propose to use NLP techniques to represent jobs for classification via all the job information available at job submission time, (ii) our approach can be deployed in a more realistic *online* context and is thus evaluated on a streaming data, by continuously retraining the classification model on recent (past) data, and testing it on (future) data which has not been seen.

3   Background

In this section, we first present our workload dataset and then the ML models we employ for job failure prediction.

3.1   M100 Dataset

The data used in this study is extracted from the M100 workload [3] which is the result of more than two years of monitoring on Marconi100, an HPC system hosted at CINECA[2] in Italy. Marconi100 is a tier-0 supercomputer deployed in production since May 2020 and, at the time of writing, is ranked 24th in the top500 list[3]. The cluster is composed of 980 computing nodes, each equipped with two 16-cores IBM POWER9 AC922 processors at 3.1 GHz, four NVIDIA Volta V100 GPUs, and 256 GB RAM. The resources are accessed through eight login nodes, and all the components are connected by a Mellanox Infiniband EDR DragonFly+ 100 Gb/s network infrastructure. Resources are allocated through job submission to Slurm, the workload manager installed in the system.

M100 contains data ranging from the computing nodes' internal information such as core load, temperature, power consumption, to the system-wide information, including the liquid cooling infrastructure, the air-conditioning system, the power supply units, workload manager statistics, and job-related information. For the purposes of our work, we focus on the data which describes the jobs present in the workload by features related to their submit-time, run-time and end-time. The first category contains the information available when a job is submitted, such as submission time, requested resources, user information and system state. The second category comprises the information about the job

---

[2] https://www.cineca.it.

[3] https://www.top500.org.

Table 1. Job ES labels and their distribution in the M100 dataset.

Name	Description	%
Completed	Job completed execution without errors	79%
Failed	Job terminated for an unknown reason	10%
Cancelled	Job did not start execution due to an error in submission	8%
Timeout	Job terminated due to reaching the time limit	2%
Out of memory	Job terminated due to more memory access than allocated	0.6%
Preempted	A higher-priority job delayed the job execution	0.1%
Node fail	Job terminated due to a failure in an allocated node	0.01%

launch, such as waiting time, execution start time, and the actually allocated resources. At job termination, the end-time features are collected, e.g., ending time, duration and outcome of the execution. The full list of job features is available at the dataset repository[4].

One feature related to the execution outcome is the job Exit State (ES) label, which is assigned to each job by Slurm as an interpretation of the job's Exit Code (EC). This code is formed by a pair of numbers; we consider only the first one, which refers to a system response that reports success, failure, or the reason of an unexpected result from job launch. An EC value of 0 means successful completion, while any $EC \neq 0$ represents an error encountered during execution. Table 1 describes the ES labels assigned to the jobs in our dataset, along with their distribution. As seen in the table, the dataset is highly unbalanced. This is not surprising, because in a real production machine the failures should be minimized to guarantee correct functioning of the system. Nevertheless, the percentage of the jobs not successfully completed is more than 20% (more than 1 out of 6 millions of jobs), representing an important threat to the system performance.

3.2   Classification and NLP Models

We approach the prediction task as a binary classification problem. We exploit supervised and unsupervised techniques for classification, as well as a pre-trained state-of-the-art NLP model to represent jobs during classification.

As for supervised algorithms, we consider the widely adopted Decision Tree, Random Forest and Logistic Regression. Decision Tree (DT) is a non-parametric method used for classification and regression, which predicts the value of a target variable by learning simple decision rules inferred from the data features. Random Forest (RF) is an ensemble method based on creating a diverse set of DT classifiers by introducing randomness in each DT construction. The prediction of the ensemble is given as the averaged prediction of the individual classifiers. Individual DTs typically exhibit high variance and tend to overfit. The aim

---

[4] https://gitlab.com/ecs-lab/exadata/-/blob/main/documentation/plugins/job_tab le.md.

of the ensemble method is to remove the error by taking an average of those predictions. Logistic Regression (LR) instead maps the probability of a label given the features of the data. It is usually faster than the other techniques and because of that is one of the most popular classification algorithms.

As an unsupervised algorithm, we employ k-Nearest Neighbors (KNN) which is a type of instance-based learning that does not construct a general internal model, but rather project data points into a N-dimensional feature space and then consider their distances. Classification is computed from a simple majority vote of the k-nearest neighbors of each data point, where k is a hyperparameter. The k-nearest neighbors are computed based on a distance metric, which could be for instance Cosine Distance (CD) and Minkowski Distance of order p (MWD_p). Given two vectors X and Y, representing the data points in the feature space, the distances are calculated as $CD(X,Y) = 1 - \cos\theta = 1 - \frac{X \cdot Y}{\|X\|\|Y\|}$ and $MWD_p(X,Y) = \sqrt[p]{\sum_{i=1}^{n} |X_i - Y_i|^p}$ where θ is the cosine of the angle between the vectors and MWD_p is a generalization of the Euclidean distance.

Sentence-BERT (SBERT) [12] is a modification of the pre-trained BERT [6] language model. BERT is a well-known family of models based on the transformer architecture [14], used to give a numeric representation of words (or subwords) that takes into account the context in which these words are used. While BERT works well with classification tasks, it does not work equally well with regression tasks, such as sentence similarity. SBERT produces representations of sentences, not individual words, that are particularly apt for regression tasks. The representation of a string of text produced by SBERT is a fixed-size 384-dimensional floating-point array.

4   Methodology

In this section, we describe our methodology to job failure prediction. The workflow can be divided into two phases: (i) data preparation and (ii) job failure prediction.

4.1   Data Preparation

To train and test our classifiers, we consider a part of the dataset[5] and use only the data collected between May 2020 and October 2020. The reason is that this is the only period where the dataset contains information on the requested resources and the job EC, which we need for our prediction task. We collect the job data in a data frame and then prepare it for model training and inference.

Feature Selection. In order to describe the characteristics of a job in a classification task, we need to associate it with certain features. We focus only on job submit-time features, as we want to compute a prediction before job allocation. The features available in the dataset are listed in Table 2 along with their

---

[5] https://doi.org/10.5281/zenodo.7588815.

Table 2. Job features description.

Name	Description	Type
Name	Job name assigned by the user	String
Command	Command executed to submit the job	String
Account	Account to be charged for job execution	String
User id	ID of the user submitting the job	Integer
Dependency	Jobs to wait for completion before execution	String
Group id	Group of the user submitting the job	Integer
Requested nodes	Specific nodes requested	List[String]
Num tasks per socket	Number of tasks to invoke on each socket	Integer
Partition	Name of the assigned partition	String
Time limit	Maximum allowed run time in minutes or infinite	Integer
Qos	requested quality of service	String
Num cpu	Number of requested CPUs	Integer
Num nodes	Number of requested nodes	Integer
Num gpus	Number of requested GPUs	Integer
Submit time	Time of job submission	Timestamp

description. Jobs submitted by the same user and close in time tend to be similar because in a production HPC, users often submit jobs in batches referring to similar experiments and jobs in the same batch tend to have similar names and command. Thus, we believe that all these features are useful for our purposes. We note that user name and similar private data are omitted in the public dataset. However, CINECA granted us access under a non-disclosure agreement.

Job Exit State Labels. For the training data, we need to assign a label to each job, indicating whether it has failed or not. In Sect. 3.1, we presented the job ES labels as they are present in the dataset, which are assigned by Slurm based on job EC. According to the Slurm official documentation, the labels assigned by the scheduler may not be coherent with the actual EC, due to lack of proper synchronization between the signal emitted by the job exit and the data collected in the database. We therefore inspect the data and identify any possible discrepancy, e.g., a job with an ES label *completed* and an EC $\neq$ 0. Our analysis reveals that more than 70K jobs labelled differently than *completed* have an EC value of 0. This is confirmed by the difference between the percentage of the completed jobs (83%) and the jobs having an EC of 0 (89%). As a consequence, we discard the original labels and create new labels based on the job EC.

Despite the discrepancy between the original ES labels and EC, the highly unbalanced nature of the entire dataset (see Sect. 3.1) is observed also in the subset data we use in this study. In particular, while the percentage of jobs with EC = 1 is 9%, the percentage with EC > 1 is 2%. We therefore group all types of failures under the same category; discriminating among different fail modes is outside the scope of this work. Moreover, we are interested in failure caused by the workload itself, so we remove from the dataset all the jobs originally

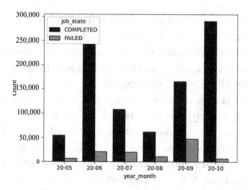

Fig. 1. Job ES label distribution throughout the months in the final dataset.

labelled as *cancelled* (failure due to user) and *node fail* (failure due to hardware). Eventually, we re-label the remaining data according to the following policy: for every job, we assign an ES label of *completed* if its EC is 0, *failed* otherwise. The final dataset after the relabelling is composed of 924,252 (89%) completed and 113,027 (11%) failed jobs. The distribution of the labels, throughout the months, is reported in Fig. 1. We can observe that imbalance between the two classes of jobs appears in all the months, while the ratio between them changes considerably, showing that the workload is highly variable across time.

4.2 Job Failure Prediction

Feature Encoding. In order to compute a prediction for a job, we need to represent it suitably to feed into the classification models presented in Sect. 3.2. We achieve that by relying on job feature values, and we propose two different ways to encode them. In the first (INT), we assign an integer to the values which are not numerical, i.e. *name, command, account, dependency, requested nodes, partition, qos, submit time*, while setting all the missing values in the other fields (*num tasks per socket, time limit*) to a default value of 0. In the second encoding (SB), we first concatenate all the feature values into a comma divided string, e.g. *job1, run_job1.sh, [1, 10], 2020-10-01 15:30:00, account_1, partition_1, 0, normal, 4, 100, 2, etc.*. Then we encode the string with SBERT, obtaining a 384-dimensional floating-point array.

We believe that with SBERT we can extract more fine-grained insights about job features expressed in natural language (e.g. *name, command, account*). This is because SBERT is designed to result in similar encodings with sequences with semantically similar contents. As we discussed in Sect. 4.1, jobs with similar names and command could belong to the same submission batch running similar operations. Therefore, features like *submit_time, name, account, command* could reveal important patterns on the nature of the job and its workload. This is hard to recognize with the INT encoding, since similar natural language values will be mapped to different integer values, while they would have similar representation in SB, due to semantic similarity.

Classifier Training and Testing. In our prediction task, it would not be realistic to do inference on a job by learning from the data of the future jobs submitted at a later time. We thus create the training and test sets by considering the timeline of the job data, keeping in the training set the data that comes before in chronological order the data of the test set.

We identify two settings in which a classifier can be trained and tested on a dataset. The first is the *offline* setting, where we consider the job data as a whole, train the model once on one portion of it, and test it using the data of the other portion in chronological order. To do this, we sort the jobs based on their submission time, split them into two, use the first split preceding in time as the training set, and the other as the test set.

The second setting, which we refer to as *online*, is more suitable to our context. We treat the job data as live and streaming in time, retrain the model periodically on a fixed size of recent data, and test it on future data that comes later (but near) in time. As we discussed in Sect. 4.1, the workload of an HPC system can be very similar in a short period, while may vary in the long term. As our experimental results confirm, a model trained once on data which slowly gets further in time to the test data could classify poorly compared to a model which is retrained continuously on data closer in time to the test data.

In the *online* setting, we use the time information provided by the *submit_time, start_time and end_time* features in order to simulate job submission and execution on a machine, and add the *day* feature as the submission date by extracting it from *submit_time*. We consider as the first training set all the jobs that were submitted in the first α days and not finished after the date of the first test set. Starting from the submission time of the first job not present in the first training set, we divide the data in batches in chronological order, where each batch contains the jobs submitted in the next ω days. We then iterate over each batch, considering it as a new test set. At every iteration, the training set is updated with the data of the last α days and the supervised models are retrained. With the unsupervised models, no actual re-training takes place, however the training set is extended for each new job in the test set with the jobs that finished before the submission time of the new job (with negligible overhead).

5   Experimental Study

In this section, we report our experimental study and discuss our results.

Experimental Setting. All the experiments are conducted on a node of a small cluster equipped with two Marvell TX2 CPUs with 32 cores and 256 GB of RAM. No accelerator, such as GPU, is used in the experiments.

The classification algorithms are implemented with *scikit-learn* Python library. The sequence encoder model is provided by the *sentence transformers* library[6], while the weights for SBERT are pulled from huggingface[7]. We use

---

[6] https://www.sbert.net.

[7] https://huggingface.co.

Table 3. Results in the offline setting, for both classes (T), completed class (C) and failed class (F) using precision (Prec), f1 and recall (Rec). In (T), we consider the macro averaged metrics ($F1_m$, $Prec_m$, Rec_m). The model name is composed of the feature encoding and the classification algorithm/distance metric. Best results are highlighted in bold.

Model	T $F1_m$	T $Prec_m$	T Rec_m	C F1	C Prec	C Rec	F F1	F Prec	F Rec
Supervised									
INT+DT	0.30	0.50	0.48	0.55	0.96	0.38	0.06	0.03	**0.57**
INT+LR	0.54	0.62	0.53	**0.98**	0.97	0.99	0.10	0.26	0.06
INT+RF	**0.71**	**0.72**	**0.69**	**0.98**	**0.98**	0.98	**0.43**	**0.47**	0.39
SB+DT	0.38	0.50	0.50	0.70	0.97	0.55	0.06	0.03	0.45
SB+LR	0.66	0.70	0.63	**0.98**	**0.98**	0.99	0.34	0.43	0.28
SB+RF	0.55	0.54	0.61	0.95	0.97	0.92	0.16	0.11	0.30
Unsupervised									
INT+CD	0.52	0.52	0.58	0.92	0.97	0.87	0.11	0.07	0.28
INT+MWD	0.39	0.50	0.50	0.72	0.97	0.58	0.06	0.03	0.42
SB+CD	0.42	0.50	0.52	0.76	0.97	0.63	0.07	0.04	0.42
SB+MWD	0.42	0.50	0.52	0.76	0.97	0.63	0.07	0.04	0.42
Majority	0.49	0.50	0.48	**0.98**	0.97	**1.00**	0.00	0.00	0.00
Random	0.36	0.50	0.50	0.66	0.97	0.50	0.06	0.03	0.49

the pre-trained model *all-MiniLM-L6-v2*[8], since it is the best trade-off between prediction performance and speed [12]. All the models are instantiated with the default setting provided by the library.

We set the hyperparameters as follows after an initial empirical evaluation. We use MWD of order $p = 2$ and set $k = 5$ in the KNN algorithm. As discussed in Sect. 4, the testing period strictly follows the training period. For the offline setting, we take the first 70% of the data as the training set and the remaining 30% as the test set. For the online, we fix the training interval α to 30 days, based on the trade-off between prediction performance and training/inference time. The time-span of data in each test set is $\omega = 1$ day. The implementation is available in a GitHub repository[9].

The results are reported in Tables 3 and 4, where we distinguish between the job feature encodings (INT and SB), the supervised algorithms (DT, LR, RF), and the distance metrics of the KNN algorithm (CD and MWD). Each classification algorithm is evaluated using the two feature encodings and are compared with two simple baselines, namely majority and random. Both baselines ignore the input feature values. The majority returns the most frequent label observed in the training data, while the random generates predictions uniformly from the list of unique labels, so each class has equal probability. The results reported in Table 4 are averaged over 5 months between June 2020 and October 2020.

---

[8] https://huggingface.co/sentence-transformers/all-MiniLM-L12-v2.
[9] https://github.com/francescoantici/job-failure-predictor/.

Table 4. Results in the online setting, presented similarly to Table 3. The time (in sec) is the avg. training time per day and the avg. inference time per job (including the SB encoding time where applicable – "N.A." indicates the cases where SB is not applicable).

Model	T F1$_m$	T Prec$_m$	T Rec$_m$	C F1	C Prec	C Rec	F F1	F Prec	F Rec	Time
Supervised										
INT+DT	0.60	0.64	0.63	0.80	0.84	0.79	0.41	0.44	0.46	1.27 + 0.005
INT+LR	0.46	0.53	0.51	0.85	0.79	0.95	0.06	0.26	0.06	78 + 0.3
INT+RF	0.64	0.69	0.64	0.84	0.84	0.87	0.43	0.54	0.41	25 + 0.12
SB+DT	0.61	0.62	0.63	0.80	0.84	0.78	0.41	0.39	0.47	455 + 0.09
SB+LR	0.60	0.66	0.60	0.85	0.82	0.89	0.34	0.50	0.30	84 + 0.4
SB+RF	0.64	0.70	0.63	0.86	0.83	0.91	0.41	**0.57**	0.35	922 + 0.4
Unsupervised										
INT+CD	0.68	0.69	0.69	0.84	0.86	0.82	0.52	0.52	0.56	**N.A. + 0.3**
INT+MWD	0.68	0.69	0.69	0.84	**0.87**	0.83	0.52	0.51	0.55	**N.A. + 0.3**
SB+CD	0.69	0.70	0.71	0.84	**0.87**	0.83	**0.54**	0.54	**0.59**	N.A. + 0.7
SB+MWD	**0.70**	**0.71**	**0.71**	0.85	**0.87**	0.83	**0.54**	0.54	**0.59**	N.A. + 0.7
Majority	0.44	0.40	0.50	**0.87**	0.79	1.00	0.00	0.00	0.00	N.A.
Random	0.44	0.50	0.50	0.61	0.79	0.5	0.28	0.21	0.5	N.A.

Results. We evaluate our models with metrics typically used for classification tasks, namely f1, precision and recall. Table 3 reports the results of the offline setting. The model that gives the best results overall is INT+RF. It achieves a f1 score of 71% and is very good at classifying the completed jobs, as the f1 score computed over such jobs is 98%. The prediction of the failures is somewhat harder, with a f1 score of 43%.

Overall, we observe that the supervised techniques perform better, but all the models struggle with the classification of the failed jobs, as most of them (with the exception of INT+DT) have lower recall than the random baseline in the failed class. Conversely, the classification of completed jobs is much easier, with the precision being ≥96%; this is probably due to the imbalance in the dataset (completed jobs are more abundant). This is compounded with the proportion between the completed and failed jobs varying significantly across different periods, as shown in Fig. 1. Thus, with the offline setting, the model has a high risk of overfitting on the completed job examples (being more numerous) and of spectacularly underperforming when tested on jobs that fail.

This behaviour can be mitigated by retraining the models to adapt them to the workload and the class distribution shift over time. Indeed, Table 4 shows the results of the online setting, with notable improvements in the classification of the failed jobs. The SB encoding coupled with the clustering classifier using the Minkowski distance (SB+MWD) yields the best results overall, suggesting that properly extracting meaningful job information from textual data is beneficial. In terms of the f1 score, SB+MWD reaches 70%, outperforming all the supervised models, which arrive to a maximum of 64% with SB+RF and INT+RF.

The classification of the completed jobs is good for all the models and their f1 scores are always above the 80%; the clustering methods have the highest precision (87%), while SB+RF has better recall (91% with respect to 83%). There is some minor drop in performance in the completed class compared to the offline setting (less overfitting), but the results are still solid. In the failed class, the clustering methods (SB+CD, SB+MWD) obtain a f1 score of 54% outperforming all the supervised algorithms. We observe a significant improvement with respect to the offline setting. Indeed, the best f1 score obtained over failed jobs in the offline setting (INT+RF) is increased by 20% by the best model in the online setting (SB+MWD and SB+CD); clearly, retraining the models helps to classify job failures.

As can be observed in both tables, the use of the SB encoding has a marginal impact with the supervised models, while the training time increases significantly in the online context (e.g., the training time of INT+RF is 25 s, while SB+RF requires 922 s). The increase in training time is not surprising, as the extraction of the text features through NLP involves the usage of a computationally hungry DN. We note, however, that the inference time remains very small and this is the operation that needs to be performed in real time without affecting the machine's normal workload (the retraining can be scheduled in less busy periods). On the other hand, in the case of the unsupervised models, SB improves the performance by 1–2% in almost every metric while no training time is incurred and the inference time always remains under a second. As we discussed in Sect. 4, with these models retraining is simply extending the training set (with negligible overhead) and classifying a new job requires a simple inference step (i.e., the new job is compared with those in the training set, projected in the feature space).

6   Conclusions and Future Work

We presented an ML-based classification approach to predict endogenous job failures in HPC systems, using only the information available at job submission time. The methodology can be deployed in an *online* context where jobs are continuously submitted by users to a real production system. We thoroughly validated our approach with a two-fold battery of test using supervised and unsupervised learning algorithms. In the first, we considered an *offline* setting and split the job data in time-consecutive sets for training and testing. We showed that in this setting the models poorly classify the failed jobs – which is what we are more interested in – while they are pretty accurate in predicting the completion. We then deployed our approach *online*, where we treated the job data as live and streaming in time, retrained the model periodically on recent (past) data, and tested it on (future) data that comes later (but near) in time. We observed an improvement in prediction accuracy by the use of this setting, especially in predicting the job failures. We also showed that an unsupervised technique like KNN is more suitable in the online setting, and the use of an NLP-based encoding to represent job features improves the classification accuracy.

Our contribution can be seamlessly integrated into the existing operational data analytic frameworks deployed in modern systems. The marginal overhead increase is not worrying, as adopting hardware accelerators (GPUs, TPUs, etc.) or deploying the models to scalable architectures will make the inference time almost negligible. In future work, we want to study continuous learning techniques and investigate different retraining strategies. We also plan to take into account the uncertainty of the ML models and investigate policies to handle jobs with high failure risk (in accordance to the Service-Level-Agreements (SLAs) between the HPC provider and the users). For instance, the workload deemed to be at high risk of failure can be postponed or directly discarded if the confidence of the classifier surpasses a threshold defined by the SLA. The employment of job power prediction models would allow to leverage such decisions also on the power required by the job, for instance by distributing the power budget of the system coherently with the power required by the jobs and their likelihood to fail.

References

1. Antici, F., Yamamoto, K., Domke, J., Kiziltan, Z.: Augmenting ML-based predictive modelling with NLP to forecast a job's power consumption. In: Proceedings of the Workshops of the International Conference on High Performance Computing, Network, Storage, and Analysis. The 1st International Workshop on the Environmental Sustainability of High-Performance Software. IEEE (2023, to appear). https://doi.org/10.1145/3624062.3624263
2. Banjongkan, A., Pongsena, W., Kerdprasop, N., et al.: A study of job failure prediction at job submit-state and job start-state in high-performance computing system: using decision tree algorithms. JAIT **12**, 84–92 (2021)
3. Borghesi, A., et al.: M100 dataset (2023). https://gitlab.com/ecs-lab/exadata
4. Carpenter, P.M., et al.: ETP4HPC's SRA 5 strategic research agenda for high-performance computing in Europe 2022: European HPC research priorities 2023–2027 (2022)
5. Chen, X., Lu, C.D., Pattabiraman, K.: Failure prediction of jobs in compute clouds: a Google cluster case study. In: 2014 IEEE ISSRE Workshops, pp. 341–346 (2014)
6. Devlin, J., Chang, M.W., Lee, K., et al.: BERT: pre-training of deep bidirectional transformers for language understanding. In: Proceedings of the 2019 NAACL: Human Language Technologies (Volume 1: Long and Short Papers), Minneapolis, Minnesota, pp. 4171–4186. Association for Computational Linguistics (2019)
7. Di, S., Guo, H., Pershey, E., Snir, M., Cappello, F.: Characterizing and understanding HPC job failures over the 2k-day life of IBM Blue Gene/Q system. In: 2019 49th Annual IEEE/IFIP DSN, pp. 473–484. IEEE (2019)
8. Fadishei, H., Saadatfar, H., Deldari, H.: Job failure prediction in grid environment based on workload characteristics. In: 2009 14th CSICC, pp. 329–334. IEEE (2009)
9. Islam, T., Manivannan, D.: Predicting application failure in cloud: a machine learning approach. In: 2017 IEEE ICCC, pp. 24–31. IEEE (2017)
10. Jassas, M.S., Mahmoud, Q.H.: Analysis of job failure and prediction model for cloud computing using machine learning. Sensors **22**(5), 2035 (2022)
11. Li, J., Wang, R., Ali, G., Dang, T., Sill, A., Chen, Y.: Workload failure prediction for data centers. arXiv preprint arXiv:2301.05176 (2023)

12. Reimers, N., Gurevych, I.: Sentence-BERT: sentence embeddings using Siamese BERT-networks. arXiv preprint arXiv:1908.10084 (2019)
13. Rojas, E., Meneses, E., Jones, T., Maxwell, D.: Analyzing a five-year failure record of a leadership-class supercomputer. In: 2019 31st SBAC-PAD, pp. 196–203. IEEE (2019)
14. Vaswani, A., et al.: Attention is all you need. In: NeurIPS, vol. 30 (2017)
15. Yoo, W., Sim, A., Wu, K.: Machine learning based job status prediction in scientific clusters. In: 2016 SAI, pp. 44–53 (2016)

Enhancing Supercomputer Performance with Malleable Job Scheduling Strategies

Jonas Posner[1]([⊠]) [ID], Fabian Hupfeld[1], and Patrick Finnerty[2] [ID]

[1] University of Kassel, Kassel, Germany
jonas.posner@uni-kassel.de, fabian.hupfeld@student.uni-kassel.de
[2] Kobe University, Kobe, Japan
finnerty.patrick@fine.cs.kobe-u.ac.jp

Abstract. In recent years, supercomputers have experienced significant advancements in performance and have grown in size, now comprising several thousands nodes. To unlock the full potential of these machines, efficient resource management and job scheduling—assigning parallel programs to nodes—are crucial. Traditional job scheduling approaches employ rigid jobs that use the same set of resources throughout their lifetime, resulting in significant resource under-utilization.

By employing malleable jobs that are capable of changing their number of resources during execution, the performance of supercomputers has potential to increase. However, designing algorithms for scheduling malleable jobs is challenging since it requires complex strategies to determine when and how to reassign resources among jobs while maintaining fairness.

In this work, we extend a recently proposed malleable job scheduling algorithm by introducing new strategies. Specifically, we propose three priority orders to determine which malleable job to consider for resource reassignments and the number of nodes when starting a job. Additionally, we propose three reassignment approaches to handle the delay between scheduling decisions and the actual transfer of resources between jobs. This results in nine algorithm variants.

We then evaluate the impact of deploying malleable jobs scheduled by our nine algorithm variants. For that, we simulate the scheduling of job sets containing varying proportions of rigid and malleable jobs on a hypothetical supercomputer. The results demonstrate significant improvements across several metrics. For instance, with 20% of malleable jobs, the overall completion time is reduced by 11% while maintaining high node utilization and fairness.

Keywords: Malleability · Job Scheduling · High Performance Computing

1 Introduction

High Performance Computing (HPC) systems, also known as *supercomputers*, play a crucial role in addressing complex societal challenges across various scientific domains. In recent years, supercomputers have become increasingly powerful

© The Author(s), under exclusive license to Springer Nature Switzerland AG 2024
D. Zeinalipour et al. (Eds.): Euro-Par 2023 Workshops, LNCS 14352, pp. 180–192, 2024.
https://doi.org/10.1007/978-3-031-48803-0_14

and are often composed of several thousand nodes. Users do not execute their programs directly on the supercomputer, but submit them as *jobs* via batch scripts. Jobs specify not only how a program is executed but also the resources it requires, such as the number of nodes, and the job duration. A *resource manager* decides when to start which job on which nodes, aiming to maximize the overall supercomputer performance while maintaining fairness between users and jobs. Typically, this resource management is accomplished in a *static* way, i.e., jobs are *rigid* in that they retain their assigned resources throughout their entire lifetime.

This static approach limits the flexibility of the resource manager and may result in a suboptimal resource utilization of the supercomputer. For example, unassigned nodes remain idle until new jobs are submitted, rather than being assigned to currently running jobs. Additionally, jobs might not need all assigned nodes during their entire runtime, leading to idle nodes that could be assigned to other running jobs or used to launch waiting ones.

If resources are managed in an *elastic* way, running jobs can integrate new nodes (*grow*) and release nodes (*shrink*), either on the initiative of the job itself or the resource manager. While these resource changes incur adaptation costs for the job, they offer great potential to significantly increase node utilization and thus the overall performance of a supercomputer. Figure 1 illustrates a compact yet striking scenario in which jobs are executed rigidly (*left*) or elastically (*right*). In short, the overall completion time of four jobs is reduced from around 1200 minutes to around 1000 minutes.

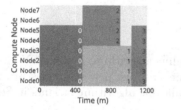 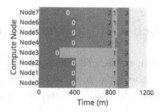

Fig. 1. Scheduling of rigid only jobs (*left*) and elastic only jobs (*right*)

Feitelson and Rudolph [6] classify jobs based on who determines the number of nodes they run with and when this decision is made. *Moldable* jobs see the number of nodes they use determined by the resource manager at job start. *Evolving* jobs can initiate resource changes at runtime. *Malleable* jobs do not initiate resource changes, but adapt to changes initiated by the resource manager.

In this work, we consider malleable jobs, but focus on the resource manager side, i.e., on algorithms for scheduling malleable jobs. Designing algorithms for scheduling malleable jobs is challenging, as they demand complex strategies to effectively determine to reassign nodes among jobs while maintaining fairness.

We extend a recently proposed malleable job scheduling algorithm [12] by introducing new strategies. These strategies include a) three priority orders to determine which malleable job to consider next for resource changes as well as the number of nodes for starting a malleable job; and b) three approaches to determine which resource to reassign from one job to another while handling the delay between decisions and the actual transfer of resources between jobs. Since both a) and b) are required for scheduling malleable jobs, we combine these strategies into nine variants, with one resembling [12] and eight new ones.

We then evaluate the impact of deploying malleable jobs scheduled by our nine algorithm variants. We simulate the execution of artificial job sets with varying proportions of rigid and malleable jobs on a hypothetical supercomputer. We use the open-source simulation software *ElastiSim* [14] and extend its source code to implement our nine algorithm variants. We compare our nine variants with the EASY-backfilling algorithm commonly used to schedule rigid jobs [19].

The simulation results demonstrate that malleable jobs scheduled by one of our proposed algorithm variants enhance the overall supercomputer performance. We evaluate this performance enhancement regarding several metrics, including the overall completion time of a job set, which could be reduced by up to 13% compared to rigid only jobs while maintaining high resource utilization and fairness. In general, as the proportion of malleable jobs increases, so does the performance. No single malleable job scheduler variant consistently outperforms others across all scenarios.

This work is organized as follows. Section 2 describes backfilling, the recently proposed malleable algorithm, and our new strategies. Section 3 covers the simulation environment, while Sect. 4 presents and analyzes the simulation results. Section 5 discusses related work, and Sect. 6 concludes.

2   Job Scheduling Algorithms

In this section, we describe the job scheduling algorithms: rigid EASY-backfilling in Sect. 2.1, the base malleable algorithm and our new strategies in Sect. 2.2. Finally, we provide an overview of all malleable algorithm variants in Sect. 2.3.

2.1   Rigid EASY-Backfilling (backfill)

We consider rigid EASY-backfilling job scheduling [19], referred to as `backfill`, as a baseline for comparison with our new malleable algorithm variants, given it is well-known and widely-used in practice. `backfill` deploys a *First Come First Served strategy (FCFS)* to order jobs in a queue based on their submission time.

The scheduling procedure is typically started when new jobs are submitted and when jobs are finished. First, if sufficient idle nodes are available, the first job in the queue is started. Otherwise, backfilling is initiated: the queue is scanned for smaller jobs that can be started on the available nodes *without* delaying the start of the first job in the queue. This way, node utilization may be improved while preserving the FCFS scheduling order.

2.2 Malleable Job Scheduling Algorithms

2.2.1 Base (mallBase)

We build upon a recently proposed malleable job scheduling algorithm, referred to as mallBase [12], and extend it with new strategies. To enable malleable jobs, users no longer define the exact number of nodes required as for rigid jobs, but *minimum* and *maximum* nodes instead. The scheduling procedure of mallBase executes the following steps in sequence:

1. Waiting jobs are started using backfill. The original mallBase utilizes back-filling without ensuring fairness, which may result in badly delaying the start of the first waiting job. The number of nodes for starting a malleable job is determined using the strategies described in Sect. 2.2.2.
2. If there are waiting jobs and not enough idle nodes, nodes from running malleable jobs are extracted so that waiting jobs can be started. This step requires a priority order strategy to determine which malleable job(s) should be shrunk, which we discuss in Sect. 2.2.2. Freed nodes need to be assigned to waiting jobs, which is discussed in Sect. 2.2.3.
3. Any remaining idle nodes are assigned to running malleable jobs. This step again requires a priority order to determine which malleable job(s) to consider.

In the initial study of mallBase [12], multiple strategy variants were proposed. However, due to their minimal performance differences, we have chosen to focus on just one of them, as detailed in Sect. 2.3.

2.2.2 Malleability Priority Order Strategies

Step 2 of mallBase requires an ordering of all running malleable jobs to determine which one should be shrunk to start waiting jobs. In the following, we introduce three priority order strategies. While in step 2, the job with the highest priority is always considered first; in step 3 the opposite is true. If several jobs have the same priority, the job submission time is used to break ties (older jobs are given precedence).

Minimum Number of Nodes. This strategy calculates priority as follows:

$$priority_{job} = current\text{-}nodes_{job} - min\text{-}nodes_{job} \qquad (1)$$

Jobs currently running with a lot more nodes than their given minimum nodes are more likely to be a fair target for shrinking. In step 1, jobs are always started with their minimum number of nodes. In steps 2 and 3, as few jobs as possible are resized to maximize node utilization. mallBase uses this strategy.

Preferred Number of Nodes. For this strategy, we use a job attribute previously introduced in the literature [15] but currently not used in practice—*preferred nodes*. The job priority is calculated as follows:

$$priority_{job} = current\text{-}nodes_{job} - preferred\text{-}nodes_{job} \qquad (2)$$

Since the number of preferred nodes is usually higher than the minimum number of nodes, this strategy typically extracts fewer nodes than Eq. 1. In step 1, jobs are attempted to be started with their preferred nodes. However, if it is not possible, a smaller number of nodes is utilized. Again, in steps 2 and 3, as few jobs as possible are resized to maximize node utilization.

Average Number of Nodes. This strategy calculates priority as follows:

$$priority_{job} = \frac{current\text{-}nodes_{job} - min\text{-}nodes_{job}}{max\text{-}nodes_{job} - min\text{-}nodes_{job}} \tag{3}$$

Jobs are prioritized based on their node proportion rather than the absolute number of nodes, promoting a more equitable node distribution among jobs of varying sizes, enhancing fairness. Again, in step 1, jobs always start with their minimum nodes. In contrast, in steps 2 and 3, all jobs may be considered for resizing to maintain a balanced node allocation among them.

2.2.3 Node Reassignment Strategies

In step 2, running malleable jobs are shrunk to free nodes that are then used to start waiting jobs. In step 3, idle nodes are assigned to running malleable jobs, allowing them to expand. `mallBase` assumes these node reassignments occur *instantaneously*, meaning that shrinking requires no time and the freed nodes can be used immediately to start waiting jobs. In practice, programs need some time to release nodes without data loss and can often only adapt to resource changes at discrete points during their execution. For instance, programs divided into several phases may be capable of adapting to resource changes only between such phases [9].

In this work, we consider phase-based jobs and introduce the following three strategies as practical and realistic alternatives to instantaneous reassignments.

Agreement. This strategy resembles `mallBase`'s instantaneous reassignment of but incorporates *agreements* to account for the time required to release nodes. In step 2, an agreement is established for each node that is to be reassigned, specifying which waiting job will receive the nodes upon their availability. Nodes become available only when a malleable job releases them between two phases. In a new *step 0*, waiting jobs that see all their agreements fulfilled—all the nodes that they are waiting on are available—are started, while those with unfulfilled agreements—at least one node is not yet available—are not. In steps 1–3, jobs and nodes with any agreement are excluded. This strategy enables precise node reassignment and accounts for the time required to release nodes.

Stealing + Agreement. To reduce the time spent waiting for node releases, this strategy introduces *node stealing*. In step 0, if a waiting job has unfulfilled agreements, it may start using other available nodes. These nodes may come from other agreements whose associated jobs cannot start due to other unfulfilled agreements. When nodes from another agreement are *stolen*, the job that lost these nodes receives a new agreement from the started job using the stolen nodes. This allows for more flexibility in agreements without completely discarding the initially planned reassignments.

Common Pool. In step 2, jobs to be started and nodes to be reassigned are gathered into a *common pool*. Again, running malleable jobs are instructed to release their respective nodes. In step 1, jobs are attempted to be started in the order of their pool entry, using both the nodes from the pool and those freed after other jobs finish. If there are insufficient idle nodes to start a job, the next job in the pool is considered. Consequently, there are no fixed reassignments of nodes and free nodes can be quickly assigned to waiting jobs.

2.3 Overview of Malleable Algorithm Variants

The combination of all strategies results in a total of nine malleable job scheduling algorithm variants, see Table 1. `minAgree` is an implementation of `mallBase`, but with `backfill` incorporating fairness and reassignment agreements instead of instant reassignments. The other eight variants are introduced in this work.

Table 1. Malleable job scheduling algorithm variants

Reassignment	Priority Order		
	Minimum Nodes	Preferred Nodes	Average Nodes
Agreement	`minAgree`	`prefAgree`	`avgAgree`
Stealing + Agreement	`minSteal`	`prefSteal`	`avgSteal`
Common Pool	`minPool`	`prefPool`	`avgPool`

3 Simulation Environment

3.1 Simulation Software

We used the OSS simulator *ElastiSim* [14] as it supports the simulation of scheduling malleable jobs. *ElastiSim* takes a job set as input and simulates their execution on an artificial supercomputer using a given scheduling algorithm. We implemented our scheduling algorithms in Python, and extended *ElastiSim* to introduce the *preferred number of nodes* attribute and the estimated job completion time. Our source code is entirely available online.[1]

3.2 Setup and Input

Supercomputer. We configured a hypothetical supercomputer composed of 128 homogeneous nodes. Each node have a computing power of 1 TeraFLOPS and node can either be free or assigned to a single job, with no node-sharing (co-scheduling) allowed. Other factors such as network bandwidth are ignored.

---

[1] https://github.com/ProjectWagomu/MalleableJobScheduling.
https://doi.org/10.5281/zenodo.8227473.

Scheduler. The scheduling algorithm is triggered every 60 s, when a job is submitted, when a job finishes, and when a job reaches its next phase.

Application Model. In practice, jobs do not scale linearly with the number of nodes. Thus, we use the following application model to describe artificial jobs. We calculate the required *flops* for each phase of a job as follows:

$$flops_{phase} = \frac{flops_{job}}{num\text{-}phases_{job}} \cdot \frac{1}{speedup(nodes)} \tag{4}$$

$$speedup(nodes) = \frac{1}{(1-p) + \frac{p}{nodes}} \tag{5}$$

Recall that the number of nodes can be changed for each phase, but the total *flops* for the job remain constant. The speedup is based on Amdahl's Law [1], which describes the performance of programs with a parallelizable portion p. Specific values for p will be outlined below.

Job Sets. We generated 10 job sets using a fixed-seed pseudo-random generator until a *theoretical* overall completion time of 30 days is reached. We then varied the percentage of malleable jobs in each job set from 0% to 100% in 10% increments. The theoretical overall completion time denotes the time in which all jobs could be *hypothetically* executed with their preferred number of nodes, disregarding submission times and scheduling.

For each job, its submission time is determined with a random uniform distribution and p is randomly selected in the interval $[0.95, 0.995]$ (discretized in 0.05 steps). Costs for adapting to resource changes are set to zero; however, adaptation is only possible between phases. On average, each job set contains 2,292 jobs, with each job requiring a total number of flops between 5 TeraFLOPS and 400 PetaFLOPS, the number of nodes ranges between 1 and 128, and each phase of a job taking one minute.

Concrete job values for the minimum, maximum, and preferred number of nodes are determined using the heuristic proposed by [15]. This heuristic is based on the well-known concept of program efficiency, defined as $efficiency = speedup(nodes)/nodes$. The minimum is defined as the largest number of nodes for which the efficiency is ≥ 0.95, preferred ≥ 0.8, and maximum ≥ 0.5. Additionally, the number of nodes is always a power of two. Rigid jobs are always started with their preferred number of nodes.

4 Evaluation

Figure 2 presents the results of the simulations, each data point representing the average of the corresponding 10 job set simulations. With the exception of Fig. 2c, `backfill` is shown as a gray horizontal line representing the baseline with rigid jobs only. Note that except for Fig. 2c, the y-axes do not start at 0. For rigid jobs only, all malleable variants behave like `backfill`. The complete experimental results can be found online.[2]

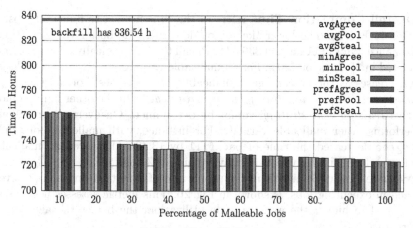

(a) Overall completion time

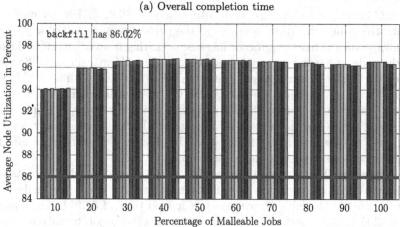

(b) Average node utilization

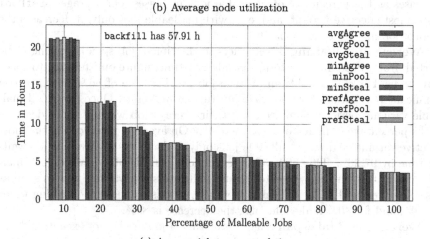

(c) Average job turnaround times

Fig. 2. Simulation results

Overall Completion Time refers to the time needed to finish all jobs; as depicted in Fig. 2a. The lower the completion time, the better the algorithm's performance. backfill needed 836.54 h. Recall that theoretically a job set can be completed in 30 days, or 720 h. For all malleable variants, the overall completion time decreases as the percentage of malleable jobs increases. For most settings, the most effective *priority strategy* is *preferred nodes*. On the other hand, a most effective *reassignment strategy* cannot be determined. On average, prefSteal outperforms other malleable variants. For instance, with malleable jobs only, prefAgree decreased the time of backfill by 13.49%. However, all malleable variants perform similarly, consistently within a 1% margin.

Average Node Utilization, the proportion of time that nodes are actively engaged in executing jobs, is shown in Fig. 2b. This metric assesses node usage efficiency. The higher the average node utilization, the better the algorithm's performance.

backfill yields an average node utilization of 86.02%. For all malleable variants, the node utilization increases as the percentages of malleable jobs rise up to 40%, with the most significant increase occurring from 0% to 10%. Beyond 40%, the node utilization remains consistent within a 1% margin and differences between the malleable variants are quite small. For instance, with malleable jobs only, avgPool is most effective leading to 96.25% node utilization and prefAgree is "worst" effective leading to 96.22% node utilization. However, it is important to note that while high node utilization is generally beneficial, it may come at the expense of other metrics. For instance, the efficiency of jobs can be affected due to the non-linear scaling application model we use.

Average Job Turnaround Time refers to the time a job takes from its submission to completion, including both its waiting time and makespan; as depicted in Fig. 2c. backfill yields an average job around time of 57.91 h. Once again, all malleable variants perform similarly, and their average job turnaround times decreases as the percentage of malleable jobs increases. On average, prefPool is the most effective variant, and, e.g., with malleable jobs only, it decreases the average job around time by 93.76%.

Average Job Waiting Time refers to the time a job spends waiting to be started, from its submission to its actual start time; figure omitted due to space limitations. backfill yields an average job waiting time of 56.98 h, which is a significant portion of above average job turnaround time. Once again, all malleable variants perform similarly, and their average job waiting times decrease as the percentage of malleable jobs increases. On average, prefPool is the most effective variant, and with malleable jobs only, it decreases the average job waiting time by 97.28%. This high value reflects one considerable advantage of malleability, as the scheduler tries to free up nodes to start waiting jobs as soon as possible. Even with 10% malleable jobs, all variants decrease the waiting times by 64%, and for 40% malleable jobs, the decrease is 89%.

Average Job Makespan refers to the time a job needed for execution, from its start to completion; figure omitted due to space limitations. backfill yields an average job makespan of 0.93 h, which consequently constitutes only a minor proportion of the above average job turnaround time. Although all malleable variants perform similarly once again, this time, their average job makespan increases as the percentage of malleable jobs increases, in contrast to the other metrics. For instance, with malleable jobs only, `minPool` is closest to `backfill`, with an average job makespan of 2.03 h. However, such an increase is expected, as malleable jobs run on a range of number of nodes, including those with lower program efficiencies compared to `backfill`, which consistently uses the preferred number of nodes for job execution.

Average Number of Shrink/Grow Events refers to the number of resource changes; figure omitted due to space limitations. `backfill`, understandably, does not incur any events. The malleable variants yield, on average, around 0.7 *shrink* events per job, with each event releasing around 16 nodes. Similarly, there are also around 0.7 *grow* events per job on average, but with each event adding around 21 nodes. For both event types, there are only minor variations between the malleable variants. The notably low number of events per job underscores that even a few malleability actions can still create a significant impact, as demonstrated by the metrics discussed above. These numbers become more relevant when adaptation costs are defined in the application model.

Discussion. The results confirmed the expectation that the more malleable jobs there are, the more flexible the scheduling can be, and that this flexibility impacts positively to supercomputer performance. Interestingly, we observed that a mere 10% of malleable jobs lead to significant enhancements.

A survey of the US Exascale Computing Project [2] reports that 39% of programs could change their number of processes by restarting from a checkpoint, while 16% could dynamically change the number of processes at runtime. Utilizing these nearly 40% of jobs, `prefAgree` could decrease the overall completion time by 12% and increase the node utilization by 12%. This substantial supercomputer performance enhancement could also increase energy efficiency.

The job attribute *preferred nodes* often proved to be the most effective strategy, but the impact compared to other strategies was minor. Thus, it is questionable whether this additional job attribute would gain traction in practice. Furthermore, we initially expected that the pool reassignment strategy would be most efficient one. However, in most cases, it was not, albeit the differences were minor. Instead, the results show that our direct adaption of the *agreements* to phase-based jobs performs well.

In summary, the results demonstrated the most important aspect is that the malleable jobs are supported, even if they remain a minority of the submitted jobs. The specific strategy is secondary and can be tailored to the needs of the supercomputer and its users.

This article lacks a precise definition for *fairness*. We understand fairness as treating every job equitably, regardless of required resources. For malleable jobs, fairness should prevent assigning all resources to one job and avoid resource stripping. We can assert that fairness is maintained since, on average, the number of *shrink* and *grow* events affecting jobs is less than 1. However, further refinement of fairness definition may be necessary. Developing malleable programs is more challenging than rigid ones, so offering rewards may be the key to user acceptance. Determining the appropriate reward system is a subject for future research.

5 Related Work

Malleability is rarely used in HPC, with only a minority of programs capable of changing their number of processes at runtime. This can be attributed to the extra programming effort required for elasticity. Consequently, resource managers offer limited support for malleable jobs, creating a chicken-and-egg dilemma. Nevertheless, several studies have investigated scheduling algorithms for malleable jobs to improve overall completion time and reduce energy consumption, e.g., [3,11,17,18]. Additionally, several extensions for Slurm [3,11] and Torque [17] have been proposed, but widespread adoption has yet to occur.

This work focuses on malleable jobs, where resource changes are initiated by the resource manager. In contrast, *evolving* jobs initiate resource changes by either releasing or requesting additional resources [6]. Further research is needed on scheduling algorithms that can determine whether to grant requests for additional resources from evolving jobs or to allocate more resources to malleable jobs [16,17]. Performance models for elastic jobs could assist schedulers making reasoned decisions about resource reassignments, with the reliance on profilers or user feedback remaining open.

Various studies aim to facilitate the implementation of elastic programs. Often, elasticity derives from program resilience, i.e., the ability to recover following runtime failures. Resilience is achieved either by incorporating support directly into the runtime system [9] or via *checkpoint and restart* [13]. While MPI remains prevalent in HPC, most research focuses on this distributed program model [5,10] In contrast, some studies target newer programming models such as (A)PGAS [8,15].

6 Conclusion

In this work, we extended a recently proposed algorithm for scheduling malleable jobs by introducing new strategies. These include three priority orderings to determine which malleable job is considered next for resource changes as well as the number of nodes for starting a malleable job; and three reassignment approaches to handle the delay between scheduling decisions and the actual transfer of resources between jobs.

Simulation results demonstrated that malleable jobs scheduled by one of our proposed algorithm variants enhance supercomputer performance. With 100% malleable jobs, the overall completion time of a job set was reduced by up to 13%, while maintaining a high resource utilization and fairness between jobs.

Future research might focus on studying different application models, e.g. [4], and supercomputer log traces, e.g., [7]. In addition, plans include investigating the cost of program adaptation to resource changes, evaluating our proposed algorithms with Slurm, and analyzing more metrics such as energy consumption.

Acknowledgements. We would like to thank Taylan Özden for his work on *ElastiSim* and for the valuable discussions during our personal meetings.

References

1. Amdahl, G.M.: Validity of the single processor approach to achieving large scale computing capabilities. In: Proceedings of Spring Joint Computer Conference (SJCC). ACM (1967). https://doi.org/10.1145/1465482.1465560
2. Bernholdt, D.E., et al.: A survey of MPI usage in the US exascale computing project. Concurr. Comput. Pract. Exp. (CCPE) **32**(3) (2020). https://doi.org/10.1002/cpe.4851
3. Chadha, M., John, J., Gerndt, M.: Extending slurm for dynamic resource-aware adaptive batch scheduling. In: Proceedings of International Conference on High Performance Computing (HiPC). IEEE (2020). https://doi.org/10.1109/HiPC50609.2020.00036
4. Downey, A.B.: A parallel workload model and its implications for processor allocation. In: Proceedings of International Symposium on High Performance Distributed Computing (HPDC) (1997). https://doi.org/10.1109/HPDC.1997.622368
5. Fecht, J., Schreiber, M., Schulz, M., Pritchard, H., Holmes, D.J.: An emulation layer for dynamic resources with MPI sessions. In: Anzt, H., Bienz, A., Luszczek, P., Baboulin, M. (eds.) High Performance Computing (ISC). LNCS, vol. 13387, pp. 147–161. Springer, Cham (2022). https://doi.org/10.1007/978-3-031-23220-6_10
6. Feitelson, D.G., Rudolph, L.: Toward convergence in job schedulers for parallel supercomputers. In: Feitelson, D.G., Rudolph, L. (eds.) JSSPP 1996. LNCS, vol. 1162, pp. 1–26. Springer, Heidelberg (1996). https://doi.org/10.1007/BFb0022284
7. Feitelson, D.G., Tsafrir, D., Krakov, D.: Experience with using the parallel workloads archive. Parallel Distrib. Comput. (JPDC) **74**(10) (2014). https://doi.org/10.1016/j.jpdc.2014.06.013
8. Finnerty, P., Takaoka, L., Kanzaki, T., Posner, J.: Malleable APGAS programs and their support in batch job schedulers. In: Zeinalipour, D., et al. (eds.) Euro-Par 2023. LNCS, vol. 14352, pp. 89–101. Springer, Cham (2023). https://doi.org/10.1007/978-3-031-48803-0_8
9. Gupta, A., Acun, B., Sarood, O., Kalé, L.V.: Towards realizing the potential of malleable jobs. In: International Conference on High Performance Computing (HiPC). IEEE (2014). https://doi.org/10.1109/HiPC.2014.7116905
10. Huber, D., Streubel, M., Comprés, I., Schulz, M., Schreiber, M., Pritchard, H.: Towards dynamic resource management with MPI sessions and PMIx. In: Proceedings of EuroMPI. ACM (2022). https://doi.org/10.1145/3555819.3555856
11. Iserte, S., Mayo, R., Quintana-Ortí, E.S., Peña, A.J.: DMRlib easy-coding and efficient resource management for job malleability. Trans. Comput. (TC) **70**, 1443–1457 (2020). https://doi.org/10.1109/TC.2020.3022933
12. Lina, D.H., Ghafoor, S., Hines, T.: Scheduling of elastic message passing applications on HPC systems. In: Klusacek, D., Julita, C., Rodrigo, G.P. (eds.) JSSPP 2022. LNCS, vol. 13592, pp. 172–191. Springer, Cham (2023). https://doi.org/10.1007/978-3-031-22698-4_9
13. Moody, A., Bronevetsky, G., Mohror, K., de Supinski, B.R.: Design, modeling, and evaluation of a scalable multi-level checkpointing system. In: Proceedings of International Conference for High Performance Computing, Networking, Storage and Analysis (SC). ACM (2010). https://doi.org/10.1109/SC.2010.18

14. Özden, T., Beringer, T., Mazaheri, A., Mohammadi, H.F., Wolf, F.: ElastiSim: a batch-system simulator for malleable workloads. In: Proceedings of International Conference on Parallel Processing (ICCP). ACM (2023). https://doi.org/10.1145/3545008.3545046
15. Posner, J., Fohry, C.: Transparent resource elasticity for task-based cluster environments with work stealing. In: Proceedings of International Conference on Parallel Processing (ICPP) Workshops (P2S2). ACM (2021). https://doi.org/10.1145/3458744.3473361
16. Prabhakaran, S., Iqbal, M., Rinke, S., Windisch, C., Wolf, F.: A batch system with fair scheduling for evolving applications. In: Proceedings of International Conference on Parallel Processing (ICPP). IEEE (2014). https://doi.org/10.1109/icpp.2014.44
17. Prabhakaran, S., Neumann, M., Rinke, S., Wolf, F., Gupta, A., Kale, L.V.: A batch system with efficient adaptive scheduling for malleable and evolving applications. In: Proceedings of International Parallel and Distributed Processing Symposium (IPDPS). IEEE (2015). https://doi.org/10.1109/IPDPS.2015.34
18. Sudarsana, R., Ribbens, C.J.: Combining performance and priority for scheduling resizable parallel applications. Parallel Distrib. Comput. (JPDC) **87**, 55–66 (2016). https://doi.org/10.1016/j.jpdc.2015.09.007
19. Wong, A.K., Goscinski, A.M.: Evaluating the EASY-backfill job scheduling of static workloads on clusters. In: Proceedings of International Conference on Cluster Computing (CLUSTER) (2007). https://doi.org/10.1109/CLUSTR.2007.4629218

Minisymposia

Applications and Benefits of UPMEM commercial Massively parallel Processing-In-Memory (PIM) Platform (ABUMPIMP) Minisymposium

The Applications and Benefits of UPMEM commercial Massively parallel Processing-In-Memory (PIM) Platform (ABUMPIMP) 2023 Minisymposium, held on August 29, 2023, brought together leading experts, researchers, and industry professionals to explore the capabilities and potential of UPMEM breakthrough processing-in-memory technology.

With the rise of data intensive applications in various fields, such as genomics, analytics and AI, the classical compute centric architecture reaches its limits. Communication between main memory and CPUs happens through a narrow bus with high latency, limited bandwidth, and most of the energy in the compute node is related to DRAM data-movement. The solution for this is to integrate powerful computing capabilities on the DRAM memory die, that is Processing-in-memory (PIM) DRAM.

As the first PIM architecture to be commercialized in real hardware, PIM architecture designed by UPMEM has received interest from many researchers, both academic and industrial. UPMEM PIM are pluggable in place of a regular DIMM. They offer massively parallel compute capabilities thanks to 8 simple processors (DPU) sitting on each DRAM chip that have extremely fast access to DRAM banks. A typical configuration totalises 2560 DPUs and can speed up applications up to tens of times.

This minisymposium gave the opportunity to understand how the technology can be used, how different applications can benefit from it, and the process of developing a PIM application, to anyone with a data intensive application to accelerate. Attendees benefited from feedback from industrial and academic researchers on their experiences in porting applications in genomics, analytics and AI. They left with a better understanding of the value of the technology to them and their ability to use it.

We would like to express our sincere gratitude to the Euro-Par organisers for hosting the ABUMPIMP 2023 Minisymposium and for their invaluable support. Special thanks to Demetris Zeinalipour and Dora Blanco Heras, the Co-Chairs of the Workshops and Minisymposia, for their dedicated efforts to ensure the success of our event.

Steering Committee

Yann Falevoz   UPMEM, Grenoble, France
Denis Makoshenko   UPMEM, Moscow, Russia
Renaud Ayrignac   UPMEM, Grenoble, France

Symposium Description

Agenda

TIME	TITLE	SPEAKER(S)
09:00 09:05	Session welcome and aims	UPMEM
09:05 10:00	Keynote: UPMEM PIM platform for Data-Intensive Applications	Yann FALEVOZ (UPMEM)/Julien LEGRIEL (UPMEM)
10:00 10:30	Invited talk: Understanding the potential of real processing-in-memory for modern workloads	Juan GOMEZ LUNA (ETHZ)
10:30 11:00	Coffee break	-
11:00 11:30	Research paper: pimDB: From Main-Memory DBMS to Processing-In-Memory DBMSEngines on Intelligent Memories	Arthur BERNHARDT (Reutlingen University)
11:30 12:00	Invited talk: A Fast Processing-in-DIMM Join Algorithm Exploiting UPMEM DIMMs	Chaemin LIM (Yonsei University)
12:00 12:30	Invited talk: PIM Performance and Economics for In-Memory Databases	Hanna KRUPPE (SAP)
12:30 14:00	Lunch Break	-
14:00 14:30	Research paper: Banded Dynamic Programming Algorithms on UPMEM PIM Architecture	Meven MOGNOL (Univ. Rennes, CNRS-IRISA, Inria & UPMEM)
14:30 15:00	Research paper: Protein Alignment on UPMEM PIM Architecture	Dominique LAVENIER (Univ. Rennes, CNRS-IRISA & Inria)
15:00 15:30	Research paper: Harnessing the Power of PIM for Machine Learning: An Evaluation of KMeans and Decision Tree Training on UPMEM System	Juan GOMEZ LUNA (ETHZ)/Sylvan BROCARD (UPMEM)
15:30 16:00	Coffee break	-
16:00 16:30	Research paper: Implementation and Evaluation of Deep Neural Networks in Commercially Available Processing in Memory Hardware	Purab SUTRADHAR (RIT)
16:30 17:00	Research paper: Privacy-Preserving Computing on UPMEM	Elaheh SADREDINI (UCR)
17:00 17:15	Closing	UPMEM

Welcome and Aims: The symposium opened with a warm welcome from Yann Falevoz, Head of Lab Relations at UPMEM. The overall aim of the symposium was to showcase the vast potential of UPMEM's PIM technology, foster meaningful discussions and encourage collaboration among participants.

UPMEM PIM Platform for Data-Intensive Applications: The keynote session[1], presented by Yann Falevoz and Julien Legriel of UPMEM, provided an insightful overview of the UPMEM PIM platform. Attendees gained a comprehensive understanding of the hardware architecture, programming intricacies[2] and real-world applications[3] of this revolutionary technology.

The keynote session highlighted the support provided by the European Commission and the French government. In particular, UPMEM was distinguished as a beneficiary of the highly selective EIC Accelerator programme. Three projects were presented (BioPIM, SustainML and STRATUM), illustrating the diverse impact of UPMEM active involvement in a number of collaborative research projects.

The keynote session was also an opportunity to look at the exciting future with a preview of the UPMEM roadmap. UPMEM's next-generation modules, with higher frequency and lower power consumption, are set to improve performance and efficiency. UPMEM server journey continues with partnerships with major server manufacturers, the transition from Skylake SP to Ice Lake SP, and the delivery of production-grade servers with increased memory slots and channels. Ongoing explorations include a dedicated AI chip, and efforts to simplify system integration continue with open firmware implementation and CXL to minimize the need for BIOS modifications.

Understanding the Potential of Real Processing-in-Memory for Modern Workloads: Juan Gomez Luna gave an invited talk highlighting recent research using UPMEM PIM architecture at ETH Zurich. The presentation focused on the practical implications and benefits of real processing-in-memory for modern workloads.

Research Papers and Insights: Throughout the symposium, attendees were treated to a series of research papers and insights from distinguished speakers:

- pimDB[4] - Arthur Bernhardt (Reutlingen University) presented a research paper that explored the transition from traditional main-memory database management systems to innovative Processing-In-Memory DBMS engines.
- A Fast Processing-in-DIMM Join Algorithm Exploiting UPMEM DIMMs[5] - Chaemin Lim (Yonsei University) introduced PID-Join, a high-performance processing-in-DIMM join algorithm optimized for UPMEM DIMMs.
- PIM Performance and Economics for In-Memory Databases - Hanna Kruppe (SAP) offered insights into datacenter hardware's role in enhancing in-memory analytics, with a specific focus on UPMEM PIM technology.

---

[1] https://youtu.be/xsTp6raY6fE.
[2] https://sdk.upmem.com/.
[3] https://github.com/upmem.
[4] https://dl.acm.org/doi/abs/10.1145/3592980.3595312.
[5] https://dl.acm.org/doi/abs/10.1145/3589258.

- Banded Dynamic Programming Algorithms on UPMEM PIM Architecture - Meven Mognol (Univ. Rennes, CNRS-IRISA, Inria & UPMEM) presented research on adapting alignment algorithms to UPMEM's Processing-in-Memory architecture, combining hardware, parallelization, and bioinformatics.
- Protein Alignment on UPMEM PIM Architecture - Dominique Lavenier (Univ. Rennes, CNRS-IRISA & Inria) discussed advancements in protein alignment using UPMEM PIM architecture.
- An Experimental Evaluation of Machine Learning Training on a Real Processing-in-Memory System[6] - Juan Gomez Luna (ETH Zurich) and Sylvan Brocard (UPMEM) explored the practical aspects of machine learning training on the UPMEM PIM system, showcasing its potential for Machine Learning (ML) workloads.
- Implementation and Evaluation of Deep Neural Networks in Commercially Available Processing in Memory Hardware[7] - Purab Sutradhar (RIT) presented research on implementing and evaluating convolutional neural networks on UPMEM PIM, emphasizing high-performance, energy-efficient AI acceleration.
- Privacy-Preserving Computing on UPMEM - Elaheh Sadredini (UCR) discussed her work on privacy-preserving computing, highlighting its relevance in data-centric computing.

Conclusion: The ABUMPIMP 2023 Minisymposium was a resounding success, illuminating the transformative power of UPMEM's Processing-In-Memory technology. Attendees were encouraged to envision the potential of PIM for their own work and industries. As the symposium concluded, we look forward to further exploration, collaboration, and innovation on the path paved by UPMEM revolutionary PIM technology. Thank you to all participants for making this symposium a remarkable event.

For more information and updates, please visit:

- UPMEM website: https://www.upmem.com
- ABUMPIMP 2023 webpage: https://www.upmem.com/abumpimp-2023/

---

[6] https://arxiv.org/abs/2207.07886.
[7] https://ieeexplore.ieee.org/abstract/document/9908126/.

Adaptive HPC Input/Output Systems

Jesus Carretero[1]([⊠]), Javier Garcia-Blas[1], André Brinkmann[2], Marc Vef[2],
Jean-Baptiste Besnard[3], Massimo Torquati[4], Yi Ju[5], and Raffaele Montella[6]

[1] Universidad Carlos III de Madrid, Leganes, Spain
`jesus.carretero@uc3m.es`
[2] Johannes Guttenberg University-Mainz, Mainz, Germany
[3] ParaTools SAS, Bruyères-le-Châtel, France
[4] University of Pisa, Pisa, Italy
[5] Max Planck Computing and Data Facility, Rosenheim, Germany
[6] University of Naples "Parthenope", Naples, Italy

Abstract. ADAPIO symposium was a forum to discuss how to create adaptive I/O systems through the creation of an active I/O stack
that dynamically adjusts computation and storage requirements through
intelligent coordination, malleability of computation and I/O, and the
scheduling of storage resources along all levels of the storage hierarchy.
Moreover, ADAPIO shows examples of co-designing applications and
I/O.

Keywords: Malleability · Ad-Hoc file systems · Workflows ·
Resources Management

HPC is on the verge of a revolution. With the new computational capabilities,
such as GPUs and FPGAs, the landscape of parallel programming abstractions
is getting more and more complex, with differentiated hardware (CPU, GPU)
materializing in differentiated software interfaces (OpenMP, MPI, CUDA, HIP),
eventually leading to inefficiencies in parallel programs. Moreover, the growing
need to process extremely large data sets is one of the main drivers for building
Exascale HPC systems. However, the input/output (IO) efficiency of the applications is not improving at the same pace, and the storage capacities remain
constrained as the flat storage hierarchies found in classic HPC architectures no
longer satisfy the performance and cost requirements of data-processing applications. Moreover, "old habits" such as POSIX I/Os, monolithic allocations, poor
software composition, and low-level languages still exists making currently I/O
the largest blocker materializing the monolithic nature of current HPC workloads.

The need to cope with more dynamic workloads in HPC is a good chance for
malleability techniques to be applied, as proposed in ADMIRE project. Possible

This project has received parcial funding from the European Union's Horizon 2020
JTI-EuroHPC research and innovation programme, with grant Agreement number:
956748.

solutions to mitigate those problems could be the upcoming availability of the MPI ABI, the democratization of malleability, and the implementation of in-situ use of higher-level languages. Another possible solution are emerging adaptive multi-tier storage hierarchies, which come with the potential to remove this barrier by deploying ad-hoc file systems for each application.

1   Adaptive Multi-tier I/O Hierarchies

In HPC systems the storage backend is driven by large distributed file systems, such as Lustre, GPFS, or BeeGFS. These file systems are built to work for all applications. Ad-hoc file systems are a new type of file system within the HPC storage stack that combines the available flash-based storage on the compute nodes to provide a job-temporal file system. To improve I/O performance and better accommodate the application while taking the HPC system's resources into account, such file systems can be *malleable*. In the ADAPIO mini-symposium, we discussed the **challenges and benefits of designing a malleable ad-hoc file system**. First, we showed the difficulties of the available I/O interfaces and concluded that a malleable file system should run entirely in user space. However, these file systems must be preloaded with an interposition library to provide applications with the standard POSIX interface. Next, we discussed the challenges of using the preloading mechanism on the GekkoFS [7] example to implement a file system that also offers a framework for client and server-side malleability mechanisms, e.g., node expansion or dynamic consistency guarantees that fit the application's access pattern. To overcome various challenges for user space file systems, we introduced the GekkoFS proxy component. Moreover, we presented the Hercules [1] ad-hoc file system and how malleability benefits I/O performance. In this case, we focused on adding nodes to the file system instance while it is running via external means or by relying on heuristics. We presented the performance results for both file systems. Finally, we concluded and presented an outlook on the next steps for ad-hoc file system malleability.

Enhancing workflows I/O is another major challenge in HPC. **CAPIO (Cross-Application Programmable I/O)** [4] is an open-source middleware[1], developed within the ADMIRE project, capable of injecting transparent I/O streaming functionalities into traditional loosely-coupled file-based workflows. It seeks to optimize the I/O used to implement the communications among distinct application modules in scientific workflows where the FS is used to allocate files used as communication buffer, and it is not possible (or convenient in terms of development cost) to modify the source code to introduce explicit communications among them. CAPIO promotes portability by supporting the POSIX standard and targeting workflows whose I/O backend uses POSIX I/O system calls (SCs). It intercepts POSIX SCs of processes composing the different workflow application components and bents their execution according to the user-provided semantics information provided through an I/O-tailored *coordination language* based on the JSON syntax. Users can specify input/output file dependencies of

---

[1] CAPIO git: https://github.com/High-Performance-IO/capio.

steps and annotate them with synchronization semantics information to enable (or improve) pipeline execution between steps. During the talk, the CAPIO middleware design, its runtime system, and the I/O coordination language.

2 Applications Co-design Using Adaptive Techniques

The imbalance between computing and I/O in HPC systems poses notable obstacles for applications like Molecular Dynamics (MD), which produce extensive data for subsequent visualization, analysis, or checkpointing for restart. In-situ techniques process data while it still resides in memory rather than post-mortem, a llwviating the aforementioned imbalance [2]. Quantum-Espresso (QE) suite includes a Car-Parrinello (CP) MD simulation package, optimized for both, CPUs and GPUs. We applied **in-situ techniques to perform data compression** QE and studied the performance and resource allocation of in-situ techniques on both CPU-based and GPU-accelerated QE. We further derived performance models for the in-situ techniques, using performance models of the MD simulation and data compression. These models are generated with Extra-P. The accuracies of the in-situ techniques' performance model have been verified with other case studies consisting of simulations (e.g. Nek5000) and in-situ tasks (e.g. data compression and image generation with Paraview). We also investigated the use of these performance models for dynamic resource allocation with dynamic resource management implemented with MPI sessions and PMIx.

Another application used was WaComM ()Water Community Model), a particle-based Lagrangian technique to simulate marine dynamics [5]. M-WaComM++, is a specialized version of WaComM++ for distributed memory scenarios, making it an excellent fit for high-performance cloud computing environments. It achieves superior performance by **leveraging WaComM++ CPU adaptability via FlexMPI** [3], which enables it to fine-tune resources according to workload demands dynamically, optimizing particle processing efficiency and responsiveness to computational requirements while featuring dynamic load balancing and performance-aware capabilities. The system dynamically regulates the process count in response to workloads through CPU malleability, ensuring efficient particle processing. When particle processing exceeds a specific threshold, the CPU malleability mechanism intelligently reduces processes to prevent overload and maintain desired performance levels. Conversely, when particle processing rates decrease, the CPU malleability feature increases process counts, ensuring resource utilization matches demand. This dynamic adjustment assures optimal resource allocation and responsiveness to computational variations, enhancing efficiency and proficiently managing particle processing.

Simulation of Malleable Workloads

As experiments on production systems are time consuming and expensive, simulations are indispensable to evaluate novel scheduling algorithms. To evaluate novel scheduling algorithms that support malleable jobs, we developed

ElastiSim [6], a batch-system simulator for malleable workloads. ElastiSim is a discrete-event simulator, distributed as open-source project[2], that supports the combined scheduling of rigid, moldable, and malleable jobs. It employs SimGrid to simulate platform activities and provides a high-level interface to specify the simulated workload. ElastiSim's workload model comprises jobs and application models. While jobs define attributes such as the required number of nodes, application models specify the application executed on the simulated platform. Our proposed application model comprises phases that, in turn, hold tasks representing activities such as computation or I/O. In malleable applications, we introduce scheduling points between phases, allowing applications to expand or shrink safely upon reaching such a point. As malleable (and moldable) applications have to support multiple configurations, our application model leverages performance models, allowing users to describe adaptive workloads. ElastiSim further provides a Python interface to forward scheduling decisions to the simulator process, facilitating the development of novel scheduling policies.

References

1. Garcia-Blas, J., Sanchez-Gallegos, G., Petre, C., Martinelli, A.R., Aldinucci, M., Carretero, J.: Hercules: scalable and network portable in-memory ad-hoc file system for data-centric and high-performance applications. In: Cano, J., Dikaiakos, M.D., Papadopoulos, G.A., Pericás, M., Sakellariou, R. (eds.) Euro-Par 2023. LNCS, vol. 14100, pp. 679–693. Springer, Cham (2023). https://doi.org/10.1007/978-3-031-39698-4_46
2. Ju, Y., Perez, A., Markidis, S., Schlatter, P., Laure, E.: Understanding the impact of synchronous, asynchronous, and hybrid in-situ techniques in computational fluid dynamics applications. In: 2022 IEEE 18th International Conference on e-Science (e-Science), pp. 295–305. IEEE (2022)
3. Martin, G., Marinescu, M.C., Singh, D.E., Carretero, J.: FLEX-MPI: an MPI extension for supporting dynamic load balancing on heterogeneous non-dedicated systems. In: Wolf, F., Mohr, B., an Mey, D. (eds.) Euro-Par 2013. LNCS, vol. 8097, pp. 138–149. Springer, Heidelberg (2013). https://doi.org/10.1007/978-3-642-40047-6_16
4. Martinelli, A.R., Torquati, M., Colonnelli, I., Cantalupo, B., Aldinucci, M.: CAPIO: a middleware for transparent I/O streaming in data-intensive workflows. In: 2023 IEEE 30th International Conference on High Performance Computing, Data, and Analytics (HiPC) (2023, to appear)
5. Montella, R., et al.: A highly scalable high-performance lagrangian transport and diffusion model for marine pollutants assessment. In: 2023 31st Euromicro International Conference on Parallel, Distributed and Network-Based Processing (PDP), pp. 17–26. IEEE (2023)
6. Özden, T., Beringer, T., Mazaheri, A., Fard, H.M., Wolf, F.: Elastisim: a batch-system simulator for malleable workloads. In: Proceedings of the 51st International Conference on Parallel Processing, ICPP 2022. Association for Computing Machinery, New York (2022). https://doi.org/10.1145/3545008.3545046
7. Vef, M., et al.: Gekkofs - a temporary burst buffer file system for HPC applications. J. Comput. Sci. Technol. **35**(1), 72–91 (2020)

---

[2] https://elastisim.github.io.

Demos and Posters

Dynamic Allocations in a Hierarchical Parallel Context

A Study on Performance, Memory Footprint, and Portability Using SYCL

Aymeric Millan[✉], Thomas Padioleau, and Julien Bigot

Université Paris-Saclay, UVSQ, CNRS, CEA, Maison de la Simulation,
91191 Gif-sur-Yvette, France
`aymeric.millan@cea.fr`

Abstract. This poster investigates the challenges of dynamic memory allocation in a hierarchical parallel context for the GYSELA code, a gyrokinetic simulation tool for studying plasma turbulence. Using the SYCL 2020 programming model and extensions, the study explores memory management using different parallelism paradigms.

Keywords: Hierarchical parallelism · Dynamic allocations · SYCL

1 Introduction

GYSELA [1] is a global full-f nonlinear gyrokinetic code designed to simulate electrostatic plasma turbulence and transport in Tokamak devices' cores using a semi-Lagrangian scheme. It evolves the 5-dimensional (3 space coordinates, 2 velocity coordinates) guiding-center distribution function in the electrostatic limit in a entire portion of the torus.

The code has several requirements: (1) **hierarchical parallelism:** parallelism is available at multiple levels of the algorithm and can be nested; (2) **dynamic memory requirements:** memory requirements vary along execution, requiring dynamic memory allocations; (3) **memory footprint:** huge arrays are manipulated, which require in-place updates to limit the memory footprint.

In this work, we study dynamic memory allocations within a hierarchical parallel context (i.e., nested *parallel for* loops) in a *performance-portable* environment (i.e. high-level programming model targeting various hardware architectures [2,3]). The study concentrates on the SYCL 2020 programming model [4] – a cross-platform abstraction layer based on modern C++ – and explores the trade-off between memory footprint depending on the choice of the parallelization strategy.

2 1D Advection Problem

For the purpose of this work, we have developed[1] a mini-app extracted from GYSELA. It implements a 1D advection operator that solves a one-dimensional

---

[1] https://github.com/Maison-de-la-Simulation/parallel-advection.

D. Zeinalipour et al. (Eds.): Euro-Par 2023 Workshops, LNCS 14352, pp. 205–209, 2024.
https://doi.org/10.1007/978-3-031-48803-0_17

advection in space (i.e., x) for each discrete velocity (i.e., vx), leveraging n_{vx} independent 1D advection problems of size n_x.

The general advection algorithm for one time-step is as follows: for each vx, (1) a temporary buffer `ftmp` of size n_x is allocated; (2) for each x, the associated foot of the characteristic is computed; (3) a Lagrange interpolation over the input distribution function at the foot coordinate is calculated, which may require values at any x_i coordinate depending on the foot value. The result is stored in `ftmp`; (4) the `ftmp` buffer is copied to replace the input in `fdist`.

For the interpolation phase, we use a Lagrange polynomial of degree 5 within the advection kernel. This simplifies the calculations compared to the splines of degree 3 used in the GYSELA code, but still provides a faithful representation of the underlying memory issues.

The distribution function is stored in a 2D SYCL `buffer` (namely `fdist`) with the second dimension representing the space discretization (the advected dimension, x) and associated velocities (first dimension, vx). In the real 5D GYSELA use case, the x dimension has typically 10^3 elements, and the 4 remaining dimensions (that we accumulate in vx) sum up to about 2.10^6 elements per node in the form of nested *for each* loops. This study focuses on exploring the limits of shared memory across various hardware platforms.

3   Implementation

This work explores different forms of parallelism in SYCL and experiments various methods to dynamically allocate memory, such as using the `local_accessor`. To this end, we use the functor interface `IAdvectorX` and define the `operator()` function in each implementation using a different SYCL parallelism paradigm. Notably, the code executes with the advected dimension (x) stored contiguously in memory because we used a `sycl::range<2>(nvx, nx)` to create the `fdist` `buffer` and adhere to the memory layout specified by SYCL [4, Section 3.11.1].

The following describes the properties of each implementation, particularly we describe how in-place is done, i.e., how we allocate the temporary buffer `ftmp` of size n_x. Implemented kernels are:

Sequential using C++ language `for` loops. `ftmp` is allocated only once and re-used for each independent 1D advection problem in vx

Basic Range (BR) using a classical `parallel_for` with a `sycl::range`. There are two implementations of the basic range kernels: using a 2D range, iterating over the `get_range()` function of the buffer, which is a `range<2>(nvx, nx)`, or using a 1D range along the vx dimension: `range<1>(nvx)`. With basic range kernels, one cannot control the degree of parallelism, these two kernels are thus **not** done in-place. Instead, we use a temporary buffer of the same size as the global buffer (i.e., $n_{vx} \times n_x$) stored in the global memory of the device, see "Out-of-place" from Table 1

ND-Range by specifying *global* and *local* sizes for the iteration spaces. The number of work-groups is deduced by the SYCL implementation

Table 1. Theoretical memory footprint (f) depending on the parallelism strategy. Where p is the degree of parallelism, p_x and p_{vx} the parallelism along x and vx, respectively; n_x and n_{vx} the number of points in x and vx, respectively. The value 8 corresponds to `sizeof(double)`.

Sequential	Along x	Along x and y	Along y	Out-of-place
$f = 8\, p_y\, n_x$ and $p = p_y\, p_x$ (e.g., $p_{GPU} = 10^5$ and $p_{CPU} = 64$, $n_x = 10^3$, $n_y = 2.10^6$)				
$p = p_y = 1$	$p = p_x, p_y = 1$	$p_x = n_x,\ p = p_y\, n_x$	$p = p_y$	
		$f = 8p$	$f = 8\, p\, n_x$	$f = 8\, n_x\, n_y$
$f = 8\, n_x$	$f = 8\, n_x$	CPU $\approx$ 512 B	CPU $\approx$ 512 kB	$\approx$ 16 GB
$\approx$ 8 kB	$\approx$ 8 kB	GPU $\approx$ 800 kB	GPU $\approx$ 800 MB	

Hierarchical by specifying the *number* of work-groups and their *local sizes*. These types of kernels provide a finer control on optimization by allowing to specify *physical group sizes* and *logical group sizes* (see [3] for more details) **Scoped** is an hipSYCL's extension to the hierarchical parallelism in SYCL aiming to be more flexible for the user and implementer [3]. This type of kernel is primarily oriented towards compile-time allocations.

The latter three kernels (ND-Range, Hierarchical and Scoped) allocate the temporary buffer `ftmp` using a SYCL `local_accessor` [4, Section 4.7.6.11], which allocates a shared memory between work-items of a same work-group. These three execution policies provide control over the degree of parallelism.

Table 1 presents the theoretical memory footprint for the 1D advection code based on different parallelisation strategies. In most kernel implementations, we use the parallel resources to parallelize along x and v_x.

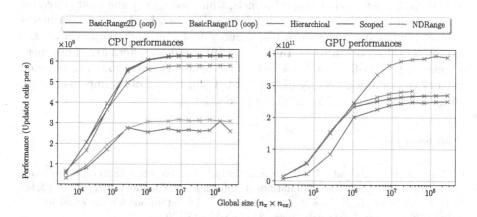

Fig. 1. Code performance for CPU and GPU. The in-place kernels are parallelized along x and vx. BR kernels are done out-of-place (oop).

4 Discussion

The primary objective of this study is to achieve optimal performance while adhering to the aforementioned memory constraints. To this end, we started a benchmark on the performance of each kernel implementation.

Figure 1 shows the performance of the 1D advection operator for an Intel CPU (Xeon Gold 6230) and NVIDIA GPU (A100 40GB). Note that the implementation has been optimized for the GPU, except for the BasicRange1D kernel, which is parallelized along vx and includes an inner sequential loop iterating over x (contiguous in memory), thus not complying with CUDA's best practice of coalescent access. The memory layout in SYCL cannot be redefined at compile time as it can with Kokkos' `LayoutRight` or `LayoutLeft` template arguments, which is a missing feature in SYCL. In the CPU plot, outliers can be observed for the BR kernels, this can be attributed to the chosen memory layout and the out-of-place algorithm, which requires storing a second buffer of size $n_{vx} \times n_x$. BR kernels do not have the same behavior on the GPU, meaning the performance portability is not guaranteed. In our experiments, the Hierarchical kernel achieved the best results as it allowed a finer tuning of hardware parameters such as work-group sizes.

In conclusion, it is not trivial to be able to finely control memory allocations in a hierarchical parallel context while guaranteeing code portability and performance across different vendor architectures. SYCL still lacks certain features to fulfill this objective, such as the ability to modify the memory layout.

BasicRange kernels, the default and simplest way to write parallel loops in SYCL does not allow managing work-groups nor writing hierarchical nested *for each* loops, resulting in a poor performance as well as a large memory footprint in our experiments. This emphasizes the need of other ways to express parallelism, such as the Hierarchical or Scoped kernels, which seem to be the most suited for our needs although we loose the ease-of-use of BR kernels. Ongoing experiments involve: (1) monitor *in practice* the memory footprint and compare with the theoretical values obtained in Table 1 and (2) exploring alternative implementations, such as utilizing `alloca` instead of the `local_accessor`, a distributed memory version using Celerity (SYCL + MPI) [5], and a Kokkos implementation using `ScratchSpace` and `TeamPolicy` [2, Section 8].

References

1. Grandgirard, V., et al.: A 5D gyrokinetic full- f global semi-Lagrangian code for flux-driven ion turbulence simulations. Comput. Phys. Commun. **207**, 35–68 (2016)
2. Trott, C.R., et al.: Kokkos 3: programming model extensions for the exascale era. IEEE Trans. Parallel Distrib. Syst. **33**(4), 805–817 (2022)
3. Deakin, T., et al.: Benchmarking and extending SYCL hierarchical parallelism. In: 2021 IEEE/ACM International Workshop on Hierarchical Parallelism for Exascale Computing (HiPar), pp. 10–19 (2021)

4. SYCL^{TM} 2020 Specification (revision 6) (2020)
5. Salzmann, P., et al.: Celerity: how (well) does the SYCL API translate to distributed clusters? In: International Workshop on OpenCL, ser. IWOCL 2022. Association for Computing Machinery, New York (2022)

Designing a Sustainable Serverless Graph Processing Tool on the Computing Continuum

Reza Farahani[1]([✉])(ID), Sashko Ristov[2](ID), and Radu Prodan[1](ID)

[1] Alpen-Adria-Universität Klagenfurt, Klagenfurt, Austria
reza.farahani@aau.at
[2] University of Innsbruck, Innsbruck, Austria

Abstract. Graph processing has become increasingly popular and essential for solving complex problems in various domains, like social networks. However, the processing of graphs on a massive scale poses critical challenges, such as inefficient utilization of resources and energy. To bridge such challenges, the *Graph-Massivizer* project, funded by the Horizon Europe research and innovation program, conducts research and develops a high-performance, scalable, and sustainable platform for information processing and reasoning based on the massive graph (MG) representation of extreme data. This paper presents an initial architectural design for the `Graph-Choreographer`, one of the five *Graph-Massivizer* tools. We explain `Graph-Choreographer`'s components and demonstrate how `Graph-Choreographer` can adopt the emerging serverless computing paradigm to process *Basic Graph Operations* (BGOs) as serverless functions across the computing continuum efficiently. We also present an early vision of our federated Function-as-a-Service (FaaS) testbed, which will be used to conduct experiments and assess the tool's performance.

Keywords: Computing Continuum · Serverless · FaaS · Massive Graph

1 Graph-Massivizer Platform

Graph processing involves different methods that encompass a range of algorithms and datasets. Therefore, processing graphs at scale requires significant considerations, particularly in terms of resource utilization and sustainability. Despite the availability of various graph processing systems, *e.g.*, the open-source and Hadoop-based Apache Giraph [3], none support sustainable and serverless graph processing across the computing continuum [1]. Therefore, the *Graph-Massivizer* project aims to explore, integrate, deploy and validate a novel integrated toolkit for sustainable serverless development and operation of MG processing in extreme data [4]. *Graph-Massivizer* also selects four real-world use cases with complementary economic, social, and environmental sustainability profiles: (1) Green AI for Sustainable Automotive Industry, (2) Global Foresight

D. Zeinalipour et al. (Eds.): Euro-Par 2023 Workshops, LNCS 14352, pp. 210–214, 2024.
https://doi.org/10.1007/978-3-031-48803-0_18

for Environment Protection, (3) Data Centre Digital Twin for Sustainable Exascale Computing, (4) Green and Sustainable Finance. The conceptual architecture of the *Graph-Massivizer* is depicted in Fig. 1.

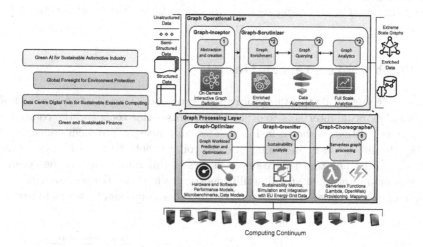

Fig. 1. *Graph-Massivizer* architecture.

1. **Graph-Inceptor:** This tool enables graph creation by translating data from static and event streams or generating synthetic data using heuristics. This data is then stored and published in a graph structure, allowing for interactive graph definition on demand. With its ability to handle large-scale input data, Graph-Inceptor is capable of producing extreme-scale graphs.
2. **Graph-Scrutinizer:** It realizes three crucial BGOs, *i.e.*, graph enrichment, querying, and analytics. These capabilities empower users to analyze and expand massive datasets using probabilistic reasoning and machine learning algorithms to discover graph patterns. Additionally, the system ensures efficient graph generation with minimal memory usage and provides query responses with low latency and controlled errors.
3. **Graph-Optimizer:** This tool takes, analyzes, and expresses graph-processing workloads and then transforms them into a *function choreography* (FC) or workflow of BGOs. It then leverages parametric BGO performance and energy models along with hardware models to accurately predict the performance and energy consumption of the workload on a heterogeneous infrastructure consisting of CPUs and GPUs.
4. **Graph-Greenifier:** This tool collects, studies, and archives performance and sustainability data from operational data centers and national energy suppliers on a large scale. It also provides features to analyze sustainability and promote energy awareness. Indeed, it emphasizes sustainability metrics (*e.g.*, CO_2, methane, GHG emissions), simulation techniques, digital twinning, and integration with the European Union energy grid data.

5. **Graph-Choreographer:** Finally, Graph-Choreographer uses performance and sustainability models and data provided by the above-mentioned tools to enable serverless BGOs/FCs processing. This tool orchestrates the entire platform and decides *where* and *how* to run BGOs/FCs on the computing continuum. The following section discusses the architectural design of this tool.

2   Graph-Choreographer Design

The architecture of Graph-Choreographer tool, consisting of seven core components and external interfaces to other *Graph-Massivizer* tools and the computing continuum testbed, is shown in Fig. 2. The *monitoring* component continuously checks the life cycle of incoming and outgoing events to record observations. In addition, it monitors the resource usages of different nodes in the computing continuum and their sustainability metrics to feed the *Graph-Greenifier* and Graph-Choreographer tools. Details of the other components are as follows.

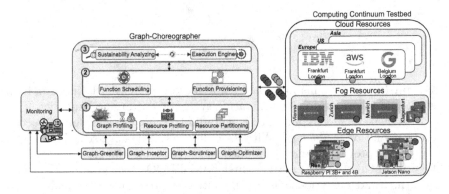

Fig. 2. Graph-Choreographer architecture.

1. **Graph Profiling:** It utilizes the interfaces of Graph-Inceptor and Graph-Scrutinizer tools to obtain essential information about raw input graphs, sampled graphs, and the analyzed data. It then categorizes the graph BGOs based on the received data, *e.g.*, the graph use case requirements and the time or resources (*i.e.*, CPU, memory) required for processing each BGO/FC, and sends this information to the *Function Scheduling* component.

2. **Resource Profiling:** It first retrieves the data monitored from the computing continuum nodes, *e.g.*, computational resources (*i.e.*, CPU and RAM), processing cores, storage, network bandwidth, the number and type of functions deployed, the providers' function concurrency limitations, and sustainability parameters. It also employs the interface of the Graph-Optimizer to

identify the resource usage patterns of BGOs/FCs, and estimate BGOs consuming excessive resources. It categorizes the gathered information and feeds the *Resource Partitioning* component.

3. **Resource Partitioning:** Graph processing in a heterogeneous environment, including cloud, fog, and edge servers with diverse resources, requires a method that handles resource diversity and network structures. Thus, the *Resource Partitioner* uses the data of the *Resource Profiling* component to form a multilayered graph of resources and applies multilayer techniques to cluster the computing continuum nodes and sends clusters' information to the *Function Scheduling* component. Indeed, each resource cluster is in disjoint resource partitions of nodes with similar resource types, including operational delay, sustainability, and energy consumption.

4. **Function Scheduling:** This component receives Graph Profiling and Partitioning information and employs the Graph-Optimizer interface to get the BGOs/FCs. It then parses received BGO/FCs, requests the *Sustainability Analyzing* component for providing feedback, and runs an scheduling model. This model defines groups of constraints considering resource utilization and cloud/fog/edge nodes limitations and decides whether the current nodes holding the required BGOs, achieve the lowest round-trip time (RTT) or new BGOs must be provisioned on other nodes with higher available resources. If the latter is decided, it triggers the *Function Provisioning* component; otherwise, it asks the *Execution Engine* to invoke the pre-deployed BGOs from the determined provider/region/instance.

5. **Fucntion Provisioning:** The Function Scheduling triggers it to determine the most suitable nodes with the highest available resources to deploy new BGOs. It then informs the Execution Engine component to run newly deployed BGOs, leading to overall lower RTT than pre-deployed ones.

6. **Sustainability Analyzing:** This component uses the information provided by the Monitoring and Graph-Greenfier tools to check the sustainability evaluation criteria (based on linear formulation) and inform the Function Scheduling and Execution Engine to make precise decisions.

7. **Execution Engine:** It considers all decisions made by Function Scheduling or Function Provisioning components and feedback of Sustainability Analyzing to invoke the providers' invokers for running or deploying/running BGOs and their required libraries on the computing continuum nodes.

We extend C^3 [2] testbed to support horizontal and vertical federated FaaS capability. The cloud layer contains cloud-based serverless platforms (*e.g.*, Amazon Lambda) on multiple continents and multiple regions. The fog layers use multiple instances of European Exoscale cloud providers in multiple regions, plus the University of Klagenfurt's OpenStack services, which are equipped with open-source serverless platforms like OpenFaaS. Furthermore, within the edge layer are tens of physical devices, such as Raspberry Pi or Jetson Nano, each equipped with open-source serverless platforms. Note that we use a Kubernetes-based method to orchestrate all resources and enable running/deploying BGOs of FCs horizontally on each layer or vertically between layers.

3   Conclusion and Future Work

This work explained the architecture of the *Graph-Massivizer* project, including five tools. We mainly focused on the `Graph-Choreographer` tool, presented its architecture, and described its connections with other *Graph-Massivizer* tools. We also discussed the early vision of our federated FaaS testbed design.

Acknowledgments. Graph-Massivizer is funded by the Horizon Europe program of the European Union, grant management number 101093202.

References

1. Farahani, R., et al.: Towards sustainable serverless processing of massive graphs on the computing continuum. In: Companion of the 2023 ACM/SPEC International Conference on Performance Engineering (2023)
2. Kimovski, D., et al.: Cloud, fog, or edge: where to compute? IEEE Internet Comput. **25**(4), 30–36 (2021)
3. Martella, C., et al.: Practical Graph Analytics with Apache Giraph, vol. 1. Springer, Cham (2015). https://doi.org/10.1007/978-1-4842-1251-6
4. Prodan, R., et al.: Towards extreme and sustainable graph processing for urgent societal challenges in Europe. In: 2022 IEEE Cloud Summit. IEEE (2022)

Diorthotis: A Parallel Batch Evaluator for Programming Assignments

Alexandros Karakasidis^(✉)

Department of Applied Informatics, University of Macedonia, Thessaloniki, Greece
a.karakasidis@uom.edu.gr

Abstract. One of the most time consuming, yet important tasks in academia is assessing and correcting student assignments. When it comes to programming, this task becomes even more complicated, as the evaluation involves compilation and execution correctness. In this demo, Diorthotis, a parallel, language-agnostic batch evaluator is presented which has the capacity to exploit the multiple cores available in modern processors so as to quickly compile, execute and evaluate assignments for hundreds of students only in a few seconds.

Keywords: Batch Evaluation · Multiprocessing · Parallel Execution

1 Introduction

Recently, there has been a blossom in systems for online evaluation of programming assignments. One of the reasons is the development of online education, made available through Massive Online Open Courses. This tendency towards acquiring new skills has become even more evident during the recent COVID-19 pandemic. More people decided to spend their time during lockdowns for self-development on a variety of topics with one of them being programming.

Despite the significant efforts towards such systems focusing on user experience and personalized feedback for a single user, there have not been corresponding developments in the area of batch evaluation of programming assessments, an area of particular interest to the academia. In this case, instead of focusing on a single user learning individually through an online system, the goal is to assess batches of submissions, also providing feedback, in a timely manner.

Towards this direction, this paper demonstrates *Diorthotis*, a batch programming assessment tool[1] designed for large academic audiences so as to be used by the instructors to quickly evaluate programming assignments. It has been in operation for three academic years in real conditions for evaluating assignments for two courses, namely Procedural Programming and Data Structures, at the Department of Applied Informatics at the University of Macedonia, Greece, featuring high result accuracy.

What makes *Diorthotis* unique is the combination of the following characteristics. First of all, it is open-source and written in Python 3, so that it can

---

[1] Diorthotis is available at https://github.com/akarakasidis/diorthotis.

D. Zeinalipour et al. (Eds.): Euro-Par 2023 Workshops, LNCS 14352, pp. 215–218, 2024.
https://doi.org/10.1007/978-3-031-48803-0_19

be used and modified by everyone to adapt to any specific needs. Second, it is language-agnostic, meaning that it can operate with any interpreted or compiled programming language. Last, and most important of all, it has been designed to be highly performant by employing a three-stage data elimination approach, reducing workload for the most resource demanding tasks and by exploiting multicore architectures of modern processors.

Automatic programming assessment tools may be considered within two major categories [2]: The dynamic ones, which perform the evaluation after execution, and the static ones, which do not execute the code, extracting metrics, assessing programming style etc. *Diorthotis* is a dynamic assessment tool with static assessment characteristics. This means that evaluation for each assignment is primarily based on the execution results, while there is also evaluation of code quality characteristics. It is evident that, executing a student's code may jeopardize a system's security and stability. To this end, *Diorthotis* has been designed for Unix-line environments, so as to exploit the operating system's inherent security features.

An important aspect of automatic evaluators regards their output. *Diorthotis* produces data as output in csv files, compatible with the Learning Management System deployed at the University of Macedonia, to allow for post-processing, as these results may be used for student feedback and for producing learning analytics. Having introduced the highlights of *Diorthotis* we will delve into more details in the rest of this paper which is organized as follows. Section 2 provides the architecture and the operational workflow of *Diorthotis*, while conclusions and future work are presented in Sect. 3.

2   Architecture

In this section, first, the architectural components and the workflow of *Diorthotis* are described. Then, its operation is briefly presented.

2.1   Components

The operation of *Diorthotis* consists of three stages, as illustrated in Fig. 1. At each stage a distinct evaluation component is activated. The main idea is that, the source code of each assignment under evaluation goes through these stages. Then, based on the result of each stage, it either continues to the next one or the evaluation process is finished, depending on certain criteria. These stages form a workflow and they have been arranged considering resource requirements, with the former ones comprising less resource intensive tasks. Assignments not fulfilling certain criteria of a stage are eliminated and evaluated accordingly, not proceeding to the later ones. As at each stage submissions are eliminated, the final, most resource intensive stages will cope with a reduced load. Each of these stages relies on components executed in parallel using multiple processes. Let us now describe each of these components.

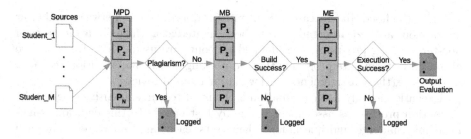

Fig. 1. Operation of *Diorthotis*.

Multiprocess Plagiarism Detector (MPD). The role of MPD, as illustrated in the left part of Fig. 1, is to identify identical or similar submissions among students per assignment. Detection of identical submissions has been implemented internally by means of a hash table. Source files from all students for a particular assignment are hashed using SHA256. For each hash, there is a list holding the identifiers of the students with that specific hash. If a list has length greater than one, then these assignments are eliminated from the rest of the workflow and logged accordingly as exact copies. Hashing of files is performed in parallel using a process pool. Apart from the native hashing mechanism, MPD also employs the option of using JPLAG, a sophisticated external plagiarism detector [3].

Multiprocess Builder (MB). MB maps an input file to the corresponding binary file and, after linking, to an executable. As compiling is independent for each student's submission, this task is inherently parallelizable. MB, in the central part of Fig. 1, considers only the submissions not eliminated by MPD. The executable of each submission is built within its own folder. Submissions failing to build, i.e. not producing an executable file, are removed from the workflow so that they are graded accordingly. In cases of building with warnings, where an executable is eventually produced, the corresponding submissions are not eliminated, but logged accordingly so that they are assessed based on user-defined rules.

Multiprocess Executor (ME). ME, in the right part of Fig. 1 runs the executables created by MB and harvests their outputs. It supports both interactive and non-interactive execution, meaning that, based on its configuration, it can execute programs either requiring user input or programs that simply produce an output. Furthermore, it can also handle programs that use files for input, output or both. File-based programs can be either interactive or non-interactive. For all these cases, multiple executions might take place per user and per assignment.

In the case of non-interactive programs, output is simply retrieved in order to be evaluated. For interactive programs, inputs are consecutively provided according to the description of the assignment in the corresponding configuration file. This means that for *Diorthotis* to be used, the sequence of all interactions should be strictly defined. In this case, all outputs produced, before, between, and after interactions are concatenated so as to be evaluated at a whole. To avoid cases of non-terminating programs, user-defined timeouts are used. These timeouts are also used to terminate programs that do not align with the execution scenario. In this case, these assignments are logged for manual review.

Execution and dynamic evaluation is the most resource intensive stage of the evaluation process, as assessment is mainly test-based. To this end, an assignment may undergo multiple independent tests, each rated separately. For each of these tests, the user indicates different inputs, if any, and the desired outputs in form of strings, either console or file based. There are two modes for locating these strings, ordered, which is the strictest, mandating for the desired outputs to be found in the respective order, and unordered where these strings may appear in any order within the output. For the evaluation of each student's submission a separate process out of a process pool is used.

2.2   Operation

Diorthotis can be easily launched through command line or through its web interface. Two configuration files are used. One for the programming language and one per assignment. Student submissions, used as its input, are organized in a directory. Within it there are subdirectories, one per student, each of them containing one or more source files, as a student's submission may regard more than one assignments. Configuration through text files allows *Diorthotis* to either run independently on a server or as part of a service, as in [1]. Multiprocessing significantly benefits execution time since, on a Core i7 processor using 8 processes for the same target program, *Diorthotis* evaluates 200 real-world student submissions in under 15 seconds, on average. On the other hand, using a single process for the same task requires 90 seconds.

3   Conclusions

In this demo, the architecture and capabilities of *Diorthotis*, a time efficient programming batch evaluator were illustrated. Plans for future work include extensions for supporting execution in distributed environments and generation of detailed learning analytics.

References

1. Nerantzis, O.R., Tselios, A., Karakasidis, A.: MI-OPJ: a microservices-based online programming judge. In: 2021 IEEE International Conference on Big Data (Big Data), pp. 5969–5971. IEEE (2021)
2. Paiva, J.C., Leal, J.P., Figueira, Á.: Automated assessment in computer science education: a state-of-the-art review. ACM Trans. Comput. Educ. (TOCE) **22**(3), 1–40 (2022)
3. Prechelt, L., Malpohl, G., Philippsen, M., et al.: Finding plagiarisms among a set of programs with JPlag. J. Univers. Comput. Sci. **8**(11), 1016 (2002)

Experiences and Lessons Learned from PHYSICS: A Framework for Cloud Development with FaaS

George Kousiouris[1] , Marta Patiño[2](✉) , Carlos Sánchez[3], and Luis Tomás[4]

[1] Harokopio University of Athens, Athens, Greece
gkousiou@hua.gr
[2] Universidad Politécnica de Madrid, Madrid, Spain
mpatino@fi.upm.es
[3] Atos, Madrid, Spain
carlos.sanchez@atos.net
[4] Red Hat, Madrid, Spain
ltomasbo@redhat.com

Abstract. The PHYSICS European project aims at developing a set of tools for application developers, system administrators and cloud providers that ease the development, deployment and optimization of resources in Function-as-a Service (FaaS) environments in the cloud. PHYSICS provides a visual development framework for abstracting cloud application development, an optimized platform level FaaS toolkit for the deployment of FaaS applications in the cloud and back-end optimization toolkit for local resource management. In this paper we present the main experiences and lessons learned during the project execution as well as some of the solutions adopted in the project.

1 Introduction

The PHYSICS European project [1] targets at exploiting the Function as a Service (FaaS) model in the continuum (multi-)cloud/edge interplay [2]. The PHYSICS stack consists of:

- a FaaS application design environment for the creation of functions and function workflows, designed and reused through intuitive visual flow programming tools (based on Node-RED).
- Platform-level services to translate the application workflows into deployable functional sequences, optimizing their placement across available (e.g., OpenWhisk) FaaS clusters
- Cluster-level resource management mechanisms tailored to the FaaS execution model and offering local fine grained optimization at the container level, based on Kubernetes.

This research has been partially funded by the European Commission under project PHYSICS (H2020 grant 101017047).

The original version of this chapter was previously published without open access. A correction to this chapter is available at
https://doi.org/10.1007/978-3-031-48803-0_41

D. Zeinalipour et al. (Eds.): Euro-Par 2023 Workshops, LNCS 14352, pp. 219–223, 2024.
https://doi.org/10.1007/978-3-031-48803-0_20

This paper presents a summary of the limitations of open source FaaS platforms (Sect. 2) and the challenges we have faced in the PHYSICS project when dealing with the development and deployment of multi-cluster(cloud)/edge FaaS applications and associated infrastructure, as well as an overview of the solutions for these challenges (Sect. 3).

2   Open Source FaaS Platforms Limitations

One of the most important decision we made in the project was the selection of the Faas platform. We compared pure serverless open source platforms, Kubeflow[1]), and others that also offer function management (FaaS), such as OpenWhisk and OpenFaaS[2]. Kubeflow also portrays significant features at the application logic layer and applies Knative[3] as execution model. The following key characteristics of interest were examined.

Run Any Type of Container. Goal: support easier legacy code inclusion. Both OpenWhisk and OpenFaaS have a process for registering an arbitrary container image and trigger it as a result of events. Kubeflow has the ability to include arbitrary scripts as executables, based on the Argo notation.

Support for Sequences of Functions/Workflows. Goal: complex and on demand application logic. Only OpenWhisk provides native sequences (functions invoked one after the other). The other frameworks do not support a native workflow definition. Extensions can be used in OpenFaaS (FaaS-flow), Kubeflow (Elyra).

Different Endpoints for Triggering Events. Goal: better flexibility and reuse. OpenWhisk provides a variety of endpoints such as triggers, rules and actions while OpenFaaS has only HTTP based triggers. Kubeflow through Knative also supports different eventing mechanisms.

Size/Activity of the Community. Goal: sustainability. All tools have a large community. Kubeflow and OpenWhisk are also backed by major companies (Google AI Hub and IBM Cloud Functions, respectively).

Maximum Execution Time for a Function. Goal: use of FaaS with any application. OpenFaaS and Kubeflow do not have any limitation on function execution time. OpenWhisk has a maximum limit. Alternative mechanisms, such as the Function Chain pattern, are needed to overcome this limitation.

Ability to Change Runtime Management Parameters. Goal: fine grained and optimized resource management. OpenFaaS can be configured with different scaling parameters at the function level, including a REST API to change them during runtime. OpenWhisk has similar parameters but it needs to be restarted.

Based on these features we selected OpenWhisk as FaaS platform. However, the PHYSICS architecture is generic enough to be used with other platforms.

---

[1] https://www.kubeflow.org/..

[2] https://www.openfaas.com/.

[3] https://knative.dev/docs.

3   Experiences and Lessons Learned

A number of key take-aways are highlighted from the work in PHYSICS across the various layers of the project.

3.1   FaaS Applications and Workflow Design

In the application design layer, one of the initial outcomes was that significant workflow assistance needs to be given to the developer, in order to be able to create more complex function flows. For this reason, supporting structures should be created, not only for common workflow primitives but also for simple tasks such as retrieving the result of an async function activation. Many developers are not used to the functional and event-driven programming style hence, relevant helper flows and recipes should be created as examples and starting points.

To this end, wrapping functionality around generalized patterns, that can be parameterized per case can help reusability. The low code approach (using Node-RED as workflow), followed by the project, helped developers that are not hard-core programmers, such as data scientists and scientific engineers, to better understand and quickly migrate legacy code [4,5].

Another significant aspect is the ability of developers to customize their environment. Very rarely the native runtime images of OpenWhisk would only be needed. The number and range of dependencies can be significant. Some of them (e.g., npm packages) are easy to be included in the native environments, others like Tensorflow or other AI libraries require more Dockerfile-like extensions. Thus, a design framework should offer full customization at the docker image level, as well as complex DevOps pipelines in order to create the baseline images and move any local dev environment dependencies to the production image.

Error management and distinction is crucial for assisting the testing process. Errors in a distributed FaaS model are frequent and may be due to numerous reasons. Function time-outs, function input limitations, function invocation limits, image pull errors, internal function errors etc. create a daunting debugging case and proper filtering and categorization should be applied. Operation retries should be a common ground across all levels of function creation and invocation.

3.2   Infrastructure Management for FaaS Clusters

FaaS workflows generated in the previous step may be executed in different clusters from edge/fog to cloud. This required the coordination of different clusters. For this, we used open cluster management[4] (OCM), a platform for Kubernetes cluster orchestration. In OCM, the Hub is the multi-cluster control plane, which manages the different clusters. The manifestWork object in OCM allows to embed any kind of Kubernetes objects to be deployed in selected clusters.

One of the issues we faced in a multi-cluster scenario was to easy enable the registration of (OpenWhisk) functions. A new operator (WorkflowCRD) was

---

[4] https://open-cluster-management.io/concepts/manifestwork/.

implemented to extend the Kubernetes API with a new object with all the information required to register a function in a cluster, and make that easily consumable from OCM Hub. The information includes the function itself and also annotations added in the design environment, such as the need for specific hardware (e.g., a GPU) or from other components in the PHYSICS platform that characterize the use of resources of functions based on offline benchmarking. This information is used to avoid the interference in shared resources of different functions in a given cluster. The WorkflowCRD operator is in charge of parsing that new object and call the OpenWhisk API for executing the needed actions for properly registering the function(s) and assigning labels to pods to be used for avoiding interference of functions based on interpod affinity/anti-affinity rules.

Some work was required to automate the on-boarding of new clusters. We used Knative[5] functionality to implement a Knative APIServerSource that detects the creation of new managed cluster object (OCM) and sends the event to a Knative service that runs the needed logic. In this case it deploys the PHYSICS components on the new cluster (leveraging OCM ManifestWork objects).

3.3 Dynamic Multi-cluster Orchestration

An application in the PHYSICS platform may consist of one or more workflows (function sequences and/or service invocations). The deployment of an application is preceded by an optimization process that based on the workflow annotations defined during development phase and the resources available at each cluster decides the optimal placement. This information is processed and converted into Kubernetes manifestWork/workflow object in order to register and deploy the associated functions in the corresponding cluster.

However, changes during operation may require changes on the initial deployment of functions. For instance, a cluster may become overload. To adapt to changes by routing invocations to an alternative location or redeployment of a function in a different cluster, a feedback loop based on OpenWhisk Prometheus metrics was designed to quickly adapt applications based on cluster load. The function waiting time metrics was selected as an indicator of the load of a cluster.

References

1. PHYSICS: Optimized Hybrid Space-Time Continuum in FaaS. https://physics-faas. eu/
2. Kousiouris, G., Kyriazis, D.: Functionalities, challenges and enablers for a generalized FaaS based architecture as the realizer of cloud/edge continuum interplay. In: International Conference in Cloud Computing and Service Science (CLOSER), pp. 199–206 (2021)
3. Kousiouris, G.: A self-adaptive batch request aggregation pattern for improving resource management, response time and costs in microservice and serverless environments. In: IEEE International Performance Computing and Communications Conference (2021)

---

[5] https://cloud.google.com/knative.

4. Kousiouris, G., Pnevmatikakis, A.: Performance experiences from running an e-health inference process as FaaS across diverse clusters. In: Companion of the 2023 ACM/SPEC International Conference on Performance Engineering (2023)
5. Fatouros, G., Kousiouris, G., et al.: Enhancing smart agriculture scenarios with low-code, pattern-oriented functionalities for cloud/edge collaboration. In: International Workshop on IoT Applications and Industry 5.0 (2023)

Improved IoT Application Placement in Fog Computing Through Postponement

Aisha Aljohani$^{(\boxtimes)}$ and Rizos Sakellariou

Department of Computer Science, University of Manchester, Manchester, U.K.
`aisha.aljohani@postgrad.manchester.ac.uk`

Abstract. In fog computing, to ensure Quality of Service (QoS), we need to specify a placement plan for distributing IoT applications among computing devices for processing; this is the IoT application placement problem. With a potentially huge number of computing devices and applications, solving the IoT application placement problem can be decentralized, i.e., independent optimization can be performed in parallel across diverse clusters, thus mitigating the networking and computing overhead and enhancing the QoS consequently. However, deploying applications in clusters based on available resources at the time of placement decision may lead to the propagation of undeployed applications among clusters, in which case ensuring the QoS constraints of those applications is not guaranteed. This paper proposes an algorithm that can be integrated into any existing placement algorithm to enhance the QoS of undeployed applications through postponement rather than immediate propagation among clusters. Initial experimental results from integrating this algorithm into an existing placement algorithm show an improvement in the percentage of applications satisfying QoS.

1 Introduction

Fog Computing (FC) aims to deploy computational devices, known as fog devices, in proximity of the IoT environment to ensure high QoS for IoT applications with pre-defined QoS constraints, e.g., delay-bound. The IoT application placement problem (APP), which is how to distribute applications among devices, plays a crucial role in FC. A centralized approach to solve APP has drawbacks such as increased networking overhead and longer computing time, particularly as the number of devices and applications increases, which can potentially cause IoT applications to fail [5]. To alleviate these issues, various studies propose decentralized solutions where fog devices within a geographical region are grouped into clusters and independent optimization is performed in parallel in each cluster [4]. However, in the majority of studies, the number of applications deployed in a cluster is determined based on the resources available at the time of making the placement decision [3,6]. As a result, undeployed applications may be distributed among clusters in search of resources where QoS constraints are not guaranteed.

D. Zeinalipour et al. (Eds.): Euro-Par 2023 Workshops, LNCS 14352, pp. 224–228, 2024.
https://doi.org/10.1007/978-3-031-48803-0_21

Given the significance of this problem, this work proposes the *Postp* algorithm which postpones the placement of undeployed applications within a cluster rather than propagating them if such postponement guarantees the QoS constraints. Experimental results of integrating *Postp* into the *MaxFog* algorithm [6], which maximizes fog device utilization, show an improvement in the percentage of applications satisfying QoS (PQSA) and the average QoS violation time (AQVT).

2   A Proposed Postponement Algorithm

In this work, an IoT device sends an application placement request to a control device C along with the initial input, followed by a stream of inputs and a release request after the final input. A two-step algorithm is run by C, where the first step identifies placement plans, i.e., a fog device f that delivers an application a_i within its QoS constraint, while the second step assures that assigning a_i on f does not violate the QoS constraints of applications already deployed on f. Unlike *MaxFog* [6], *Postp* prioritizes applications with the most critical QoS constraints during the placement process.

Step 1: The algorithm finds an available fog device f for each application a_i that meets its QoS constraint. The response time $T_r(a_i)$ is calculated as follows:

$$T_r(a_i) = T_w(a_i) + T_e(a_i) + T_c(a_i), \qquad (1)$$

where $T_w(a_i)$ is the waiting time of a_i until it is deployed at f, $T_e(a_i)$ is the time for executing an input of a_i, and $T_c(a_i)$ is the communication time from IoT device to f. $T_e(a_i)$ and $T_c(a_i)$ are calculated as in [6], with the computation capacity of f assigned proportionally to applications based on their sizes.

If $T_r(a_i)$ on f meets a_i's QoS constraint, the algorithm records the time slot at which the first input k of a_i keeps acquiring the assigned resources for execution, denoted by $[T_{ra}(a_i^k), T_{rr}(a_i^k)]$, where $T_{ra}(a_i^k)$ is the resource acquiring time at which the input starts executing and $T_{rr}(a_i^k)$ is the resource release time at which the input releases the resources. $T_{ra}(a_i^k)$ is computed as follows:

$$T_{ra}(a_i^k) = \begin{cases} T_a(a_i) & \text{if } \forall a_j \in A^f, \ T_{rr}(a_j^k) <= T_a(a_i) \\ T_a(a_i) + T_w^f(a_i) & \text{otherwise} \end{cases} \qquad (2)$$

where $T_a(a_i)$ denotes the arrival time of a_i at f and $T_w^f(a_i)$ denotes the remaining processing time for the inputs at $T_r(a_i)$ for reallocating resources among the assigned applications A^f. $T_{rr}(a_i^k)$ is computed as follows.

$$T_{rr}(a_i^k) = T_{ra}(a_i^k) + T_e(a_i^k) \qquad (3)$$

If no fog device f is currently available, the algorithm checks if the placement of a_i can be postponed by searching for an application a_j with a submitted release request and estimates $T_w^f(a_i)$ based on $T_{rr}(a_j^k)$ of the last received input

k. Estimating $T_w^f(a_i)$ considers $T_w^{'f}(a_i)$, which is the time a_i waits for a_j to release the resources, i.e., to reach $T_{rr}(a_j^k)$, and $T_w^{''f}(a_i)$ which is the time a_i waits after $T_{rr}(a_j^k)$ until it acquires the resources. These are calculated as follows.

$$T_w^{'f}(a_i) = \begin{cases} T_{rr}(a_j^k) - T_a(a_i) & \text{if } T_a(a_i) < T_{rr}(a_j^k) \\ 0 & \text{otherwise} \end{cases} \tag{4}$$

$$T_w^{''f}(a_i) = \begin{cases} R - T_{rr}(a_j^k) & \text{if } T_a(a_i) < T_{rr}(a_j^k) \\ R - T_a(a_i) & \text{if } T_a(a_i) > T_{rr}(a_j^k) \end{cases} \tag{5}$$

where R denotes the waiting time for inputs under processing at time $T_{rr}(a_j^k)$, if a_i arrives before $T_{rr}(a_j^k)$. If a_i arrives after $T_{rr}(a_j^k)$, R denotes the waiting time for inputs under processing at time $T_a(a_i)$.

Step 2: As assigning a_i to f changes the computation capacity assigned to the applications in A^f, this step ensures that the QoS constraints of those applications are not affected. For each application $a_z \in A^f$, the algorithm checks if any of the received inputs will have its execution delayed and its QoS affected. In case the first condition of Eq. (5) is met and if there is k that has $T_{ra}(a_z^k)$ earlier than $T_{rr}(a_j^k)$ or in case the second condition is met and if there is k that has $T_{ra}(a_z^k)$ earlier than $T_a(a_i^k)$, then there is no delay. Otherwise, all the unprocessed inputs at $T_{rr}(a_j^k)$ or $T_a(a_i^k)$ (depending on the condition met) will be delayed to reallocate the resources. The delay $T_d(a_z^k)$ is computed as follows.

$$T_d(a_z^k) = \begin{cases} R - T_{ra}(a_z^k) & \text{if } T_{ra}(a_z^k) < R \\ 0 & \text{otherwise} \end{cases} \tag{6}$$

where R is computed according to which condition is met in Eq. (5). $T_r(a_z^k)$ is recomputed using Eq. (1) considering the computed delay and the new assigned computational capacity, and compared with the QoS constraint. If there are no violations, the placement of a_i is confirmed and the values T_{ra} and T_{rr} of the delayed inputs are recomputed to keep records for next placement decisions.

3   Evaluation

The algorithm is evaluated in iFogSim [1] using the datasets of fog devices and IoT applications from [2], with two extra parameters: IoT device input frequency (2–4 input/s) and random allocation of release requests. We consider a cloud server combined with two 6-fog device clusters: a main and a neighbour.

As shown in Fig. 1, *Postp* outperforms *MaxFog* [6] in terms of PQSA as the number of applications submitted to the main cluster increases. For example, when the number of applications is 50, PQSA is 57.8% for *Postp* and 33.8% for *MaxFog*. Note that in *Postp*, 41% of applications are deployed in the main cluster (28% of these are immediately deployed and 13% are postponed until resources are released) and 16.8% are satisfied at the neighbour whereas in *MaxFog* only

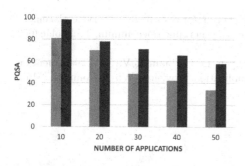

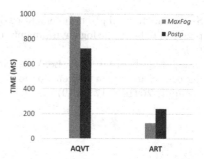

Fig. 1. Percentage of applications satisfying QoS

Fig. 2. Average QoS violation time and average response time

22% are immediately deployed in the main cluster and 11.8% are satisfied at the neighbour. The results depend primarily on the number of release requests sent, with better performance observed if a larger number of requests are present at the placement decision time. As shown in Fig. 2 (with 20 applications), *Postp* achieves a lower average QoS violation time (AQVT) than *MaxFog* [6]. This is due to the high number of applications experiencing QoS violations at propagation. *Postp* gets a higher average response time (ART) as more applications are postponed, meaning longer waiting times.

4 Conclusion

In this work, an algorithm is proposed to enhance the QoS of the undeployed IoT applications through postponement rather than propagation which risks violations of QoS constraints. Integrating this algorithm in *MaxFog* shows an improvement in terms of PQSA and AQVT. This study suggests that more work is needed to assess the trade-off between postponement and immediate propagation to achieve good QoS properties in fog computing.

References

1. Gupta, H., Dastjerdi, A.V., Ghosh, S.K., Buyya, R.: iFogSim: a toolkit for modeling and simulation of resource management techniques in the Internet of Things, Edge and Fog computing environments. Software Pract. Exp. **47**(9), 1275–1296 (2017)
2. Hassan, H.O., Azizi, S., Shojafar, M.: Priority, network and energy-aware placement of IoT-based application services in fog-cloud environments. IET Commun. **14**(13), 2117–2129 (2020)
3. Liu, C., Wang, J., Zhou, L., Rezaeipanah, A.: Solving the multi-objective problem of IoT service placement in fog computing using cuckoo search algorithm. Neural Process. Lett. **54**(3), 1823–1854 (2022)
4. Mann, Z.A.: Decentralized application placement in fog computing. IEEE Trans. Parallel Dist. Syst. **33**(12), 3262–3273 (2022)

5. Sulimani, H., et al.: Reinforcement optimization for decentralized service placement policy in IoT-centric fog environment. Trans. Emerging Telecommun. Technol. e4650 (2022)
6. Tran, M.Q., Nguyen, D.T., Le, V.A., Nguyen, D.H., Pham, T.V.: Task placement on fog computing made efficient for IoT application provision. Wirel. Commun. Mob. Comput. **2019**, 1–17 (2019)

High-Performance Distributed Computing with Smartphones

Nadeem Ishikawa[1]([✉]), Hayato Nomura[1], Yuya Yoda[1], Osamu Uetsuki[2],
Keisuke Fukunaga[2], Seiji Nagoya[2], Junya Sawara[2], Hiroaki Ishihata[1],
and Junsuke Senoguchi[1]

[1] Tokyo University of Technology, 1404-1 Katakuramachi, Hachioji City, Tokyo,
Japan
nadeemishikawa@gmail.com

[2] ITOCHU Techno-Solutions Corporation, Kamiyacho Trust Tower, 4-1-1,
Toranomon, Minato-ku, Tokyo, Japan

Abstract. The demand for large-scale computing, such as the application of AI in big data analytics and engineering simulations, has been steadily increasing. Meanwhile, many companies and individuals now own smartphones and PCs, but a significant portion of these IT assets remains underutilised, especially overnight or utilised as computing resources. This paper solves these issues by proposing to use these resources in a distributed system. This system highlights the opportunities for cost-effective and resource-efficient high-performance computing(HPC) solutions by utilising underutilised resources. The original distributed computing system framework SMPDG will be described in this paper.

Keywords: Distributed Computing · Parallel Computing · High Performance Computing

1 Introduction

In recent years, the demand for computing resources has increased rapidly due to advances in AI and simulation technologies. This demand has increased device density in data centres to process large volumes of data [1]. The efficient utilisation of these high-density devices generates a significant amount of heat, thus requiring cooling and increasing power consumption [2]. Meanwhile, many companies and individuals own IT assets such as smartphones and PCs, but their use is inefficient. They rarely use them overnight or utilise them as computing resources. A distributed computing framework named SMPDG, which uses these devices, will solve these problems. Notably, smartphones demonstrate more energy efficiency than traditional hardware like servers [3].

This system allows us to achieve low-cost, high-performance computing (HPC). However, smartphones are typically considered unsuitable for HPC applications due to their limited processing power, memory, and storage capacity. Nevertheless, the widespread availability of smartphones and the advancements

D. Zeinalipour et al. (Eds.): Euro-Par 2023 Workshops, LNCS 14352, pp. 229–232, 2024.
https://doi.org/10.1007/978-3-031-48803-0_22

in their processing capabilities necessitate a reconsideration of their role in the realm of HPC. This paper focuses on the system description and evaluation of SMPDG.

2   Related Work

Effective use of smartphones is expected to require the execution of small applications that require minimal memory, data and little interaction. Applied to tasks that meet these limitations, it is expected to maximise output within the constraints of the device. For example, applications to tasks such as stock price prediction, optimising hyperparameters using grid search in random forest models, and models requiring frequent updates are expected to maximise their potential.

Projects such as World Community Grid [4], BOINC [5] and Folding@Home [6] have managed to use smartphones and PCs as distributed computing resources. However, these projects requiring specific software installation, the limited range of supported platforms, such as operating systems and devices, and the restrictions on the types of tasks that can be executed constrain these systems' potential.

3   System Description

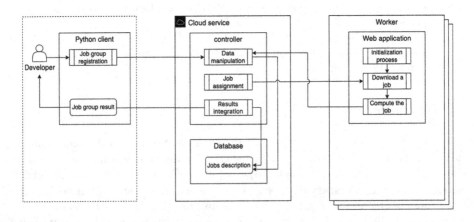

Fig. 1. SMPDG framework.

This research proposes a distributed computing system using AWS as the controller of the distributed computing system and smartphones, PCs and containers as workers. The system is designed to be practical for performing many similar computations, for instance, repeatedly performing the same function with different parameters and data (Fig. 1).

3.1   Job Registration

To register a job, a developer wishing to parallelise a job first writes a function with parameters and data as arguments on a Python client such as JupyterNotebook, which describes the process the developer wants each worker to perform in parallel. The parameters of these functions are specified for each job. The function is common to the job group, which is registered simultaneously, and the parameters and data for each job are registered in the system.

In order to make it easy for users to register jobs, Python is used in the implementation, and the jobs can be registered in the job management database on the system using an originally developed parallelisation Python library. It is also possible to define the Python libraries to be installed in the initialisation process before the worker processes the job when registering the job.

3.2   Control of Jobs

To ensure that the controller is not bottlenecked in controlling jobs, AWS lambda, a serverless, event-driven computing service, controls the job management database on the system.

Whenever a job is registered, it sends a job with a ready status to a device on standby and changes the job status in the job management database to running. If there is no job with a ready status, a job with a running status is distributed to deal with the case where the job has not finished successfully. When all groups of jobs registered in the database have been returned from workers, the processing results are integrated, and the results are returned to the developer who requested the job processing.

3.3   Process Flow at Each Worker

Each worker computes a function and returns the result to the controller. When implementing the system, it was considered that in other existing systems, workers needed to download specified software when participating in distributed computing and were restricted by platforms, such as the operating system. In this system, each worker uses a browser as an environment with few platform restrictions to execute the processing. On the browser, jobs can be executed as Python functions via an originally created web application that uses a library called Pyodide. It makes it possible to easily execute processes in the web browser without depending on the operating system or installing a custom application. The browser first performs the initialisation process, then obtains the function and parameters from the controller, and finally executes the job and sends the results to the controller. This process, from parameter acquisition to transmission of computation results, is repeated until all jobs are completed. This process, from parameter acquisition to transmission of computation results, is repeated until all jobs are completed.

3.4 System Evaluation

The stock price prediction simulator was applied to this system. The simulator is a backtesting that learns a decision tree and predicts the logarithmic rate of change of the stock index futures in the following 5,000 days. The simulator is a walk-forward model, and each day's processing is independent. In this experiment, each day's predictions were processed as one job. Distribute jobs with 5000 smartphone-equivalent workers; Each equivalent is the container provided by AWS Fargate, similar or lower performance than one smartphone. As a result, a processing time of 1662 s was obtained. This processing time compares with 627 s for the same simulation with 5000 threads on the supercomputer system Oakbridge-CX provided by the University of Tokyo's Centre for Information Infrastructure. It is a result of the fact that smartphones are still an underutilised computing resource and that the performance of the built-in CPU is constantly improving indicates its potential as a low-cost HPC [7].

Past validations have also shown that even when distributed on a small scale across two actual smartphones, the computational performance is higher and more cost-effective than a single container, Amazon EC2 M4.large [8].

4 Conclusion

SMPDG is distinctive in that developers can easily register distributed computing, devices can contribute to distributed computing on a web browser without installing specific software, and the potential to realise HPC at a low cost.

This system allows limited resources to be used effectively, and large scale computations can be executed at low cost and low power consumption. It is expected to promote research by enterprises and individuals.

Commercial use and large-scale evaluation experiments using real smartphones are to be discussed in future research.

References

1. Davis, J., et al.: Uptime Institute Global Data Center Survey 2022. Uptime Institute, New York (2022)
2. Bizo, D.: Silicon Heatwave: The Looming Change in Data Center Climates. Uptime Institute, New York (2022)
3. Mamchych, O., Volk, M.: Smartphone based computing cloud and energy efficiency. In: 12th International Conference on Dependable Systems, Services and Technologies (DESSERT), pp. 1–5. IEEE Press, New York (2022)
4. World Community Grid. https://www.worldcommunitygrid.org. Accessed 20 May 2023
5. BOINC. https://boinc.berkeley.edu. Accessed 20 May 2023
6. Folding@home. https://foldingathome.org. Accessed 20 May 2023
7. Ishikawa, N., et al.: Project for Grid Computing with Smartphones 2022 - distributed computing with 10,000 units. In: Proceedings of the 85th National Convention of IPSJ, pp. 383–384. IPSJ, Japan (2023)
8. Kotani, Y., et al.: Project for Grid Computing with Smartphones - Large-scale computing with your smartphones. In: Proceedings of the 84th National Convention of IPSJ, pp. 405–406. IPSJ, Japan (2022)

Blockchain-Based Decentralized Authority for Complex Organizational Structures Management

Kamil Jarosz[✉][ID], Patryk Wojtyczek, and Renata G. Słota[ID]

AGH University of Krakow, Krakow, Poland
{kamil.jarosz,renata.slota}@agh.edu.pl

Abstract. Collaboration based on data sharing within global networks of autonomous organizations requires complex user and group structures. Decentralized group management provides greater resilience and independence compared to classical approaches with centralized architectures. We propose a blockchain-based solution that ensures consistency of global user and group structures, allowing them to be updated collectively by a set of authorized organizations. The evaluation showed the blockchain-related costs of performing changes to the structures.

Keywords: data sharing · decentralized management · collaborative systems · blockchain

1 Introduction

Nowadays, conducting research requires sharing data on a global scale. Collaborative data sharing systems aim to achieve collaboration within global networks of autonomous organizations [7]. The classical approach is to deploy a centralized or a semi-decentralized architecture, where each organization is a central point of failure regarding users and groups originating from it. Decentralization discards the central authority allowing greater resiliency and independence [3]. The organizational structures required for the aforementioned collaboration may be relatively complex, for instance, containing nested groups which require computing and maintaining a transitive closure for feasible membership queries [5]. The complexity of these structures pose a challenge for their decentralization, and so the concept of peer-sets was introduced as a solution for decentralizing authority using consensus and atomic commitment to synchronize state [4].

The emergence of smart contracts brought a new perspective for decentralization, allowing data to be managed on a distributed, cryptographically secure public ledger. Blockchain-based solutions are increasingly popular, e.g. for access control [2] or general data sharing [1,6].

In this paper, we propose a blockchain-based solution for decentralizing authority over users and groups for collaborative data sharing, considering complex organizational structures, as an alternative to [4]. Decentralized authority provides greater resiliency and independence compared to centralized architectures.

© The Author(s), under exclusive license to Springer Nature Switzerland AG 2024
D. Zeinalipour et al. (Eds.): Euro-Par 2023 Workshops, LNCS 14352, pp. 233–236, 2024.
https://doi.org/10.1007/978-3-031-48803-0_23

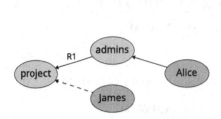

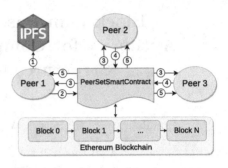

Fig. 1. An example complex organizational structure. *Alice* is able to add *James* to group *project*, because she inherits a right to do so through group *admins*, which is encoded in relation *R1*.

Fig. 2. Interactions between the smart contract and peers. Peers 1–3 form a peer-set.

2 Blockchain-Based Decentralized Authority

When authority over organizational structures is decentralized, a set of organizations in the form of a peer-set oversees a given set of users and groups, called entities. The set of entities as vertices and a set of permissions as edges form a graph called an entity graph. Connections in the graph represent the collaboration between users and may be modified as shown in Fig. 1. Blockchain simplifies the process of decentralization, however storing and processing data on it may be costly. Maintaining complex organizational structures on blockchain requires both large storage (to accommodate the structures themselves) and heavy computations (in case of changes, to verify correctness; cf. Fig. 1). In order to minimize blockchain-related costs, off-chain resources are used for storage and heavy computations. We provide a smart contract which performs changes off-chain to the structures taking into consideration decentralized authority and peer-sets.

Each peer-set is realized by a smart contract (called `PeerSetSmartContract`; cf. Fig. 2). The deployment of the smart contract is equivalent to creating a peer-set and the smart contract itself stores and manages a URI which identifies the entity graph managed by the peer-set. The URI is provided by an external storage, e.g. IPFS. When using IPFS it is t To modify the entity graph, an organization (Peer 1) serializes the new version of the graph and stores it in the external storage (1). Then, it proposes this version to the smart contract (2), which in turn sends notifications to all peers from the peer-set (3). Peers now may verify the correctness of the new version and vote on it (4). If enough votes are positive, the smart contract accepts the changed version, updates the URI, and notifies peers about the new version (5).

In cooperation on a global scale, users from different peer-sets may collaborate with each other. The global entity graph's edges span across both peer-sets, and the smart contract atomically modifies both subgraphs, necessitating separate votes from each peer-set.

3   Evaluation

We have evaluated our smart contract mainly from two perspectives: the time spent on blockchain operations and the monetary costs related to it. Evaluation was carried out in a local environment using Foundry[1]—a toolkit for Ethereum application development and simulating blockchain transactions.

Figures 3–4 show costs of deployment of the smart contract and performing a modification to the entity graph in terms of gas[2]. The cost of deployment and performing a single modification for 3 peers is 1 623 290 gas and 319 494 gas respectively. The cost of deployment is increasing with number of peers, due to storage requirements of the smart contract, which stores information about the peers. The cost of modification is increasing not only due to storage requirements, but also due to an increasing number of transactions required to perform it.

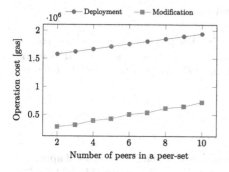

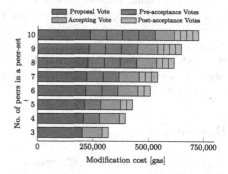

Fig. 3. Costs of deploying the smart contract and performing a single modification to the entity graph.

Fig. 4. Costs of performing a single modification divided into votes. Each vote is realized within a blockchain transaction.

The deployment of the smart contract requires one transaction in the blockchain, whereas performing a modification with n peers requires a number of transactions equal to the minimal positive vote count, in our case $\lfloor \frac{n}{2} \rfloor + 1$ transactions. Assuming a block time of 15 s, the optimistic time of performing a modification is 15–30 s regardless of the number of peers. The optimistic time is constant with respect to the number of peers because all votes performed by peers are included in the next nearest block. In practice, the time may be arbitrarily high when peers respond slowly or do not respond at all. By choosing the percent of required positive votes, one may balance between the rate of acceptance and reliability. The expected number of peers in a peer-set is around 3–5, and the system scales with the number of peer-sets, and not their size.

---

[1] Foundry—https://github.com/foundry-rs/foundry.

[2] Gas is a unit measuring the amount of computational work on Ethereum.

4   Conclusions

We have presented a blockchain-based solution for decentralizing authority over users and groups for collaborative data sharing. Our solution stores subgraphs of organizations' user structures on an external storage and uses blockchain to ensure consistent structure of the global graph. The proposed smart contract allows performing modifications of the subgraph and managing votes by the peers. Increasing the number of peers in a peer-set improves availability of the system, but also increases blockchain-related costs of performing changes. The presented costs are related to a single organization, however further research will focus on scalability related to the number of peer-sets and off-chain costs. Future work will also concentrate on further minimizing blockchain-related costs by moving out of blockchain operations related to performing modifications to the entity graph, leaving only operations related to peer and peer-set identification and management. This will also reduce the complexity of the smart contract and limit potential vulnerabilities resulting from it.

Acknowledgments. The research presented in this paper has been supported by the funds of the Polish Ministry of Education and Science assigned to AGH University of Krakow. The authors are grateful to Łukasz Opioła and the Onedata team for cooperation.

References

1. Athanere, S., Thakur, R.: Blockchain based hierarchical semi-decentralized approach using IPFs for secure and efficient data sharing. JKSUCI **34**(4), 1523–1534 (2022). https://doi.org/10.1016/j.jksuci.2022.01.019
2. Di Francesco Maesa, D., Mori, P., Ricci, L.: Blockchain based access control. In: Chen, L.Y., Reiser, H.P. (eds.) DAIS 2017. LNCS, vol. 10320, pp. 206–220. Springer, Cham (2017). https://doi.org/10.1007/978-3-319-59665-5_15
3. Ihle, C., Trautwein, D., Schubotz, M., Meuschke, N., Gipp, B.: Incentive mechanisms in peer-to-peer networks - a systematic literature review. ACM Comput. Surv. (2023). https://doi.org/10.1145/3578581
4. Jarosz, K., Opioła, Ł., Dutka, Ł., Słota, R.G., Kitowski, J.: Increasing data availability and fault tolerance for decentralized collaborative data-sharing systems. In: FedCSIS, pp. 563–566 (2022). https://doi.org/10.15439/2022F183
5. Opioła, Ł., Jarosz, K., Dutka, Ł., Słota, R.G., Kitowski, J.: Group membership management framework for decentralized collaborative systems. Comput. Sci. **23**(4) (2022). https://doi.org/10.7494/csci.2022.23.4.4642
6. Wang, S., Zhang, Y., Zhang, Y.: A blockchain-based framework for data sharing with fine-grained access control in decentralized storage systems. IEEE Access **6**, 38437–38450 (2018). https://doi.org/10.1109/ACCESS.2018.2851611
7. Wrzeszcz, M., Dutka, Ł., Słota, R.G., Kitowski, J.: New approach to global data access in computational infrastructures. Futur. Gener. Comput. Syst. **125**, 575–589 (2021). https://doi.org/10.1016/j.future.2021.06.054

Transparent Remote OpenMP Offloading Based on MPI

Ilias K. Kasmeridis[✉][iD], Spyros Mantelos[iD], Apostolos Piperis[iD],
and Vassilios V. Dimakopoulos[iD]

Department of Computer Science and Engineering, University of Ioannina,
Ioannina, Greece
{i.kasmeridis,s.mantelos,cs04475,dimako}@uoi.gr

Abstract. In this work, we present an efficient mechanism which allows unmodified OpenMP applications to leverage the computational resources of any node in a cluster through the OpenMP device interface. Remote CPUs and remote accelerators such as GPUs are all available to offload code portions to, completely transparently, as if they belonged to the host node that executes the application. This is possible by virtualizing remote resources to appear as local devices and introducing a device-agnostic communication mechanism that forwards data requests to/from the remote nodes. The communication layer is based on MPI, eliminating the need for custom request servers, while providing excellent portability and optimized performance for a variety of network fabrics. Moreover, our implementation allows concurrent offloading to any combination of local and remote devices.

Keywords: OpenMP · Cluster computing · GPUs · Offloading

1 Background and Contribution

OpenMP has long been the programming model of choice for shared-memory systems, utilizing the multiplicity of CPU cores, and more recently attached accelerator devices. When in a cluster environment, it provides the means for intra-node parallelism either exclusively or as part of a hybrid MPI+OpenMP application. Because of the versatility and the inherent intuitiveness of OpenMP, it had been considered for cluster-level programming, i.e. to generate intra-node as well as inter-node parallelism, mostly through software DSM (sDSM) libraries.

This work was supported by the project "Dioni: Computing Infrastructure for Big-Data Processing and Analysis" (MIS No. 5047222) which is implemented under the Action "Reinforcement of the Research and Innovation Infrastructure", funded by the Operational Programme "Competitiveness, Entrepreneurship and Innovation" (NSRF 2014–2020) and co-financed by Greece and the European Union (European Regional Development Fund). It was also supported by computational time granted from the National Infrastructures for Research and Technology S.A. (GRNET S.A.) in the National HPC facility–ARIS–under project ID pa221202-ROMPIC.

D. Zeinalipour et al. (Eds.): Euro-Par 2023 Workshops, LNCS 14352, pp. 237–241, 2024.
https://doi.org/10.1007/978-3-031-48803-0_24

While the mileage of such approaches varied, they did not catch on and were only demonstrated for early and outdated versions of OpenMP.

Recently, there has been a revived interest in using OpenMP to exploit the computational resources of a cluster, albeit in a different way, through its *device* interface. Jacob et al. [1] first proposed using remote CPU cores as OpenMP devices and gave some insights on an implementation in the context of the LLVM compiler; a bioinformatics, loop-based application was used to demonstrate the potential of their proposal. Yviquel and Araújo [6] treat an entire cluster as a single device using map-reduce Spark nodes and remote communication management. Kleftakis and Dimakopoulos [2] presented a concrete implementation of offloading onto remote CPU cores for the OMPi compiler; they elaborated on what modifications are needed for task-based applications to exploit the infrastructure and utilize multiple cluster nodes as offloading devices. Finally, Patel and Doerfert [4] implemented remote GPU offloading in Clang/LLVM as a plugin. Their implementation is based on either gRPC or UCX and requires manually starting custom request servers at the participating nodes for every application execution. Communication optimizations were discussed in [3].

In this work we present a full implementation of the OpenMP offloading model that is capable of employing CPU cores and accelerators in remote nodes as if they were local devices to the node that executes the main part of the application. Building on our previous work, that offered offloading only to remote CPU cores, our OMPi OpenMP compiler can now support seamlessly any accelerators installed on remote nodes. In contrast to [4] we based our design on MPI for two main reasons. First, it provides portability and is available everywhere; our system is self-contained and can be trivially deployed on commodity clusters. Second, it can offer excellent performance on a wide variety of network fabrics. Furthermore, our system a) avoids setting up remote custom request servers, b) allows repeated and parallel use of different remote CPUs and accelerators within the same program, c) offers automated configuration and d) provides runtime calls to index remote devices by location and/or class.

2   Organization and Operation

The node where an application starts its execution in is called *primary*. The rest of the cluster nodes execute a copy of the application binary and constitute the *workers*. However, workers never reach user code; they block awaiting for commands from the primary, to execute kernels on specific local devices.

Runtime Organization. The runtime system of OMPi consists of ORT which provides OpenMP facilities for the host (CPU), and the device *modules* which are implemented as shared libraries (plugins) and are loaded on demand; a module provides support for offloading to a particular class of physical devices. To access remote devices, a new module (RDEV) was implemented; for each remote module, RDEV creates a *virtual* one locally at the primary node, containing the exact same devices. The sole purpose of these virtual modules is to forward all

ORT requests, such as data transfers and offloads, to the corresponding remote devices, through the network. Figure 1 demonstrates the operation of the RDEV module and the path an offloading request takes to reach a remote device. It is important to highlight that the offloaded kernel is embedded into the application image and thus it is not actually transferred; only its arguments are. Requests regarding local devices continue being served at the primary node.

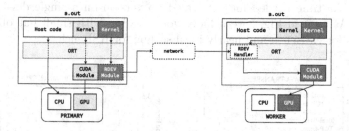

Fig. 1. Kernel offloading to a remote GPU device using the RDEV module

Configuration and Initialization. Setting up remote offloading in OMPi is a simple one-time procedure based on a configuration file which enlists participating nodes along with their devices. Automated scripts connect to each of the nodes to build and install all enlisted OMPi device modules by employing the corresponding device toolchains; nothing else is required from the user's part. When an application runs, MPI processes are created in participating nodes when needed, using `MPI_Comm_spawn`, eliminating the need for custom servers or daemons in worker nodes. Since `MPI_Comm_spawn` is not supported fully in all implementations, we also provide a portable static initialization option whereby processes are created in all participating nodes from the start of the execution.

3   Evaluation

We experimented on ARIS, a national HPC facility. The partition we used consists of 44 nodes, each equipped with two Intel Xeon E5-2660v3 CPUs and two NVIDIA Tesla K40 GPUs. Nodes are interconnected via InfiniBand FDR (56Gbps). The system software includes Intel ICC compiler v18.0.5, Intel MPI v2018.0 and CUDA toolkit 10.1.168. We report average times for 10 executions.

To assess communication overheads we measured the time to execute a target enter (exit) data directive with a `map(to:array[:N])` (`map(from:array[:N])`) clause, which copies a variable-size array to (from) the target GPU. We compare transfer times using two MPI fabrics: TCP (over InfiniBand) and DAPL (which uses native IB primitives and achieves minimal latency). The DAPL fabric had negligible overheads, giving comparable times with local GPU transfers, save very large sizes; the rest of our experiments use DAPL exclusively.

The protein alignment application from the Barcelona OpenMP Tasks Suite was modified to utilize `target` instead of `task` directives, so as to utilize multiple

CPUs from remote nodes. The communication requirements of the application allow for quite scalable performance as shown in Fig. 2, for 100 protein sequences.

For the performance of remote GPU offloading we used two proxy applications, XSBench and RSBench, which model the most computationally intensive part of OpenMC Monte Carlo neutron and photon transport code [5]. Two different input sizes were used (small and large), and weak scaling was determined: device workload was kept constant and execution time was normalized by dividing it by the time needed for the scaled up version on a single device at the primary. As seen in Fig. 2 we achieve good scaling with small but observable overheads for XSBench and nearly ideal scaling for RSBench.

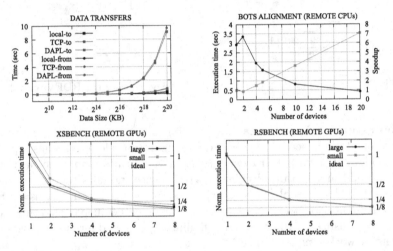

Fig. 2. Performance evaluation of our remote offloading mechanism

References

1. Jacob, A.C., et al.: Exploiting fine- and coarse-grained parallelism using a directive-based approach. In: Proceedings of the IWOMP 2015, 11th International Workshop on OpenMP, pp. 30–41. Aachen, Germany (2015)
2. Kleftakis, I., Dimakopoulos, V.V.: Experiences with task-based programming using cluster nodes as OpenMP devices. In: HPCS 2020/2021, 18th Int'l Conference on High Performance Computing and Simulation. Barcelona, Spain (2021). also arXiv:2205.10656
3. Lu, W., et al.: Towards efficient remote OpenMP offloading. In: Proceedings of the IWOMP 2022, 18th International Workshop on OpenMP, pp. 17–31. Chattanooga, TN, USA (2022)
4. Patel, A., Doerfert, J.: Remote OpenMP offloading. In: Proceedings of the PPoPP 2022, 27th ACM SIGPLAN Symposium on Principles and Practice of Parallel Programming, pp. 441–442. Seoul, Republic of Korea (2022)

5. Romano, P.K., Horelik, N.E., Herman, B.R., Nelson, A.G., Forget, B., Smith, K.: OpenMC: a state-of-the-art Monte Carlo code for research and development. Ann. Nucl. Energy **82**, 90–97 (2015)
6. Yviquel, H., Araújo, G.: The cloud as an OpenMP offloading device. In: Proceedings of the ICPP 2017, 46th Int'l Conference on Parallel Processing, pp. 352–361. Bristol, UK (2017)

DAPHNE Runtime: Harnessing Parallelism for Integrated Data Analysis Pipelines

Aristotelis Vontzalidis[1], Stratos Psomadakis[1], Constantinos Bitsakos[1],
Mark Dokter[2], Kevin Innerebner[3], Patrick Damme[4], Matthias Boehm[4],
Florina Ciorba[5], Ahmed Eleliemy[5], Vasileios Karakostas[6], Aleš Zamuda[7],
and Dimitrios Tsoumakos[1(✉)]

[1] ICCS–National Technical University of Athens, Athens, Greece
`dtsouma@mail.ntua.gr`
[2] Know-Center GmbH/TU Graz, Graz, Austria
[3] Graz University of Technology, Graz, Austria
[4] Technische Universität Berlin, Berlin, Germany
[5] University of Basel, Basel, Switzerland
[6] University of Athens, Athens, Greece
[7] University of Maribor, Maribor, Slovenia

Abstract. Integrated data analysis pipelines combine rigorous data management and processing, high-performance computing and machine learning tasks. While these systems and operations share many compilation and runtime techniques, data analysts and scientists are currently dealing with multiple systems for each stage of their pipeline. DAPHNE is an open and extensible system infrastructure for such pipelines, including language abstractions, compilation and runtime techniques, multi-level scheduling, hardware accelerators and computational storage. In this demonstration, we focus on the DAPHNE runtime that provides the implementation of kernels for local, distributed and accelerator-enhanced operations, vectorized execution, integration with existing frameworks and libraries for productivity and interoperability, as well as efficient I/O and communication primitives.

Keywords: Machine Learning Systems · High Performance Computing · Vectorized Execution · Distributed Systems

1 Introduction

Complex end-to-end analysis requirements of modern analytics create a definite trend towards integrated pipelines where data management, high-performance computing and ML tasks are arbitrarily "mixed-and-matched". Distinctive such use-cases or domains include ML-assisted simulations, exploratory query processing and data cleaning, etc. The DAPHNE project[1] is building an open and extensible system infrastructure for such integrated data analysis pipelines. DAPHNE

---

[1] https://daphne-eu.eu/.

D. Zeinalipour et al. (Eds.): Euro-Par 2023 Workshops, LNCS 14352, pp. 242–246, 2024.
https://doi.org/10.1007/978-3-031-48803-0_25

[1] is built on top of MLIR [2], allowing seamless integration with existing applications and runtime libraries while also enabling extensibility for specialized data types, hardware-specific compilation chains and custom scheduling algorithms. Its technical contributions are available as open source[2] under the Apache-2.0 license. In this demonstration, we present an overview of the current design and implementation of the DAPHNE execution engine and describe the demonstration scenarios and level of interaction with the participants.

2 DAPHNE Runtime Overview

The DAPHNE Runtime system [3] (DR henceforth) is a crucial component of DAPHNE. It supports the execution of user-defined workflows and operations specified in DaphneDSL (a high-level scripting language) or DaphneLib (high-level Python API). The system utilizes a multi-level compilation chain based on the MLIR infrastructure to convert DaphneDSL scripts into DaphneIR, an intermediate representation. Multiple optimization passes allow for cost-based, pipelined and efficient execution of kernels, i.e., code that implements the logical operations on specific hardware in standalone or distributed mode. The runtime system is designed hierarchically. The coordinator receives DaphneDSL user code and generates an execution plan. The compiler determines whether each workload should be executed locally or across multiple worker nodes. The local runtime system handles execution on a single compute node, while the distributed runtime system coordinates the distribution of work among worker nodes and collects the results.

DR includes local and distributed kernels for executing computational, I/O and combined operations, supporting heterogeneous hardware devices (CPUs, GPUs and FPGAs). DR supports data structures such as matrices (both dense and sparse formats) and frames that have a schema and rely on column-oriented storage. DR's vectorized execution works by fusing multiple operations together and exploiting data parallelism. Data is split across multiple processing units (e.g., CPUs) and each processing unit works on a chunk of data (local runtime case). In distributed execution mode, DR uses distribution primitives (such as broadcast, all-reduce, ring-reduce, scatter/gather, etc.) to distribute data and code to worker nodes, similarly to the local runtime. Instead of CPUs, there are multiple distributed nodes that receive chunks of data and perform computations on them. Each worker locally compiles the received code fragment in order to optimize the code generation targeting its available resources (CPUs, accelerators, etc.), and executes the generated code through the local runtime system via the vectorized execution engine. This is pictorially described in Fig. 1 for the Connected Components algorithm.

Communication between cluster nodes is facilitated by utilizing common frameworks. DR's design allows for easy integration with different frameworks. Currently, DR can successfully utilize gRPC and the MPI library. I/O support is significant, currently allowing CSV, Arrow and Matrix Market formats. It is

---

[2] https://github.com/daphne-eu/daphne.

also noteworthy to mention that DR implements a DAPHNE-specific file format along with custom (de)serialization support to enable more efficient I/O and network communication.

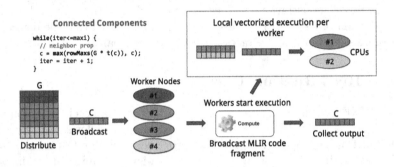

Fig. 1. Example of distributing work hierarchically with the DAPHNE Runtime.

Overall, the DAPHNE Runtime plays a central role in executing integrated data analysis pipelines and optimizing performance through parallelism in heterogeneous hardware settings. DR uniquely allows researchers to experiment with different modules and subsystems (integration with different storage, communication and serialization protocols), as its extensible design allows for deployment combinations otherwise impossible by a single system.

3   Demonstration Description

In this demonstration we showcase the capabilities of DR, providing participants with a comprehensive understanding of the runtime's functionality and versatility via different scenarios and configurations. While DR's contributions and parameters that affect its performance are manifold, in this demonstration we focus on the following important features-dimensions: a) Execution mode (standalone vs. distributed modes and scalability to available resources), b) communication frameworks (gRPC vs. MPI), c) I/O features (distributed filesystem integration and serialization support) and d) hardware-specific execution (utilization of accelerator resources).

Participants will be able to interact with DR via a comprehensive web-based GUI. The GUI controls two deployments, namely an in-house 16-node cluster and a Vega-bound deployment. Vega[3] is a powerful supercomputer infrastructure that boasts impressive processing power and a high-performance network, making it an ideal platform for showcasing the capabilities of DR. Three algorithms (Connected Components, PageRank and Principal Component Analysis) that utilize diverse inputs (real and synthetic data of various sizes and types) and kernels will be available for execution. The UI will integrate both textual

---

[3] https://www.izum.si/en/vega-en/.

and graphical execution feedback in order to visually inspect the quality and quantity of specific features under inspection. As such, our demonstration will showcase the following DR functionalities:

Execution Mode: We will showcase the ability of executing a workload on a single machine versus distributing it across a cluster of variable size and configuration. Participants can choose between different pipelines, input sizes and cluster resources in order to study the performance trade-offs induced in each case. Moreover, they can compare the execution speed and efficiency of vectorized and non-vectorized computations, demonstrating DAPHNE's ability to leverage vectorization for performance. This functionality is shown in Fig. 2, including a screenshot of our Grafana-based DR metrics visualizer.

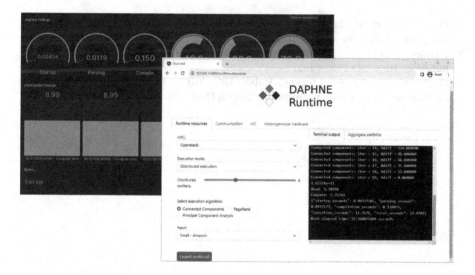

Fig. 2. Use of the DAPHNE Runtime UI.

Communication Frameworks: We will allow workflow execution with both gRPC and MPI in different scenarios, such as latency-sensitive tasks and large-scale data transfers, so as to provide insights into their suitability for different algorithms currently implemented within DR.

I/O Features: We will demonstrate how DR currently integrates with HDFS, showcasing its ability to efficiently read data of variable sizes by leveraging data locality in large-scale I/O compared to using the local file system. The participants can also observe the enhanced performance that the DAPHNE serialization protocol brings forth compared to a default (protobuf) serialization protocol.

Hardware-Specific Execution: We will showcase how DR efficiently manages the workload distribution and data movement using different hardware components. Specifically, for the Connected Components algorithm (with available accelerator-aware kernels), the DR will offload computational tasks to accelerators assuming their availability. By comparing the execution times and throughput of tasks on a cluster with accelerators versus a cluster without, the audience can witness the speedup achieved through heterogeneous hardware execution.

Acknowledgements. ▣ The DAPHNE project is funded by the European Union's Horizon 2020 research and innovation program under grant agreement number 957407 from 12/2020 through 11/2024.

References

1. Damme, P., et al.: DAPHNE: an open and extensible system infrastructure for integrated data analysis pipelines. In: CIDR (2022)
2. Lattner, C., et al.: MLIR: scaling compiler infrastructure for domain specific computation. In: CGO 2021 (2021)
3. D4.2: DSL Runtime Prototype. Public EU Project Deliverable (2022). https:// daphne-eu.eu/wp-content/uploads/2022/12/D4.2-DSL-Runtime-Prototype.pdf

Exploring Factors Impacting Data Offloading Performance in Edge and Cloud Environments

Gap-Joo Na[1], Youngwoo Jang[2], Harin Seo[2], Byungchul Tak[2], and Young-Kyoon Suh[2(✉)]

[1] Electronics and Telecommunications Research Institute, Daejeon, South Korea
funkygap@etri.re.kr
[2] Kyungpook National University, Daegu, South Korea
{jangscon6568,rinyo0126,bctak,yksuh}@knu.ac.kr

Abstract. Recently, the deployments of smart IoT devices, such as wearable devices and drones, have risen at an unprecedented pace. But these edge devices typically have limited computing and storage resources, thus making it hard to perform compute-intensive jobs on their acquired data despite growing demands. In this paper, we uncover five major factors and present our empirical evaluation results in an offloading environment utilizing external servers. From the findings, we present a taxonomy of factors that should be considered along with different data types for offloading the data of edge devices to external nodes more efficiently.

Keywords: Edge Device · Data Offloading · Cloud · Factor Taxonomy

1 Introduction

Widely deployed in real-world environments, various Internet-of-Thing (IoT) edge devices monitor and collect a large volume of streamed data in various formats, such as text, images, and videos. But edge devices typically have limited computing and storage capacity due to various constraints of size, cost, and battery capacity.

Existing works have been conducted to leverage more powerful servers connected to edge devices to realize resource augmentation. Specifically, researchers have been actively studying the task offloading [1] and the data offloading [2] schemes on edge or cloud servers to perform more complex tasks on the data collected from edge devices. But, there has been *little* research to explore the impact of various factors on offloading performances from a data-centric viewpoint.

This paper analyzes empirical results on the impact of 5 key factors—*network connection type, communication protocol type, data compression type, offloading*

G.-J. Na and Y. Jang—These authors contributed equally to this work.

D. Zeinalipour et al. (Eds.): Euro-Par 2023 Workshops, LNCS 14352, pp. 247–251, 2024.
https://doi.org/10.1007/978-3-031-48803-0_26

site location, and *load distribution type*—on the offloading performances between IoT devices and their associated edge (or cloud) servers. Also, we establish and present a taxonomy of factors that needs to be considered for efficient offloading of edge devices.

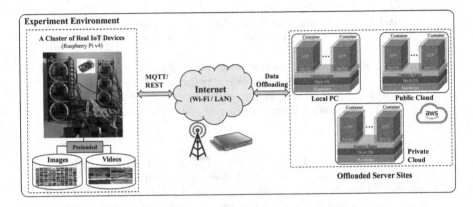

Fig. 1. The established testbed for our empirical evaluation

2 Experiment Design

Testbed: As shown in Fig. 1, our testbed used Raspberry Pi version 4 as an IoT device. Also, we used three kinds of offloading sites: a local PC, a private cloud, and a public cloud (Amazon AWS). Both local and remote edge servers were equipped with $i7$-11700 processor, NVIDIA RTX 3090, 64 GB RAM, 500 GB SSD, and 1 TB HDD, running Ubuntu 18.04. Each server ran as many containers as the number of IoT devices so that every device was mapped to its container for offloading. For a cloud server, we utilized an AWS EC2 instance [3]. The instance type was m5a.4xlarge, running Ubuntu 18.04, with $i7$-11700 processor, 64 GB RAM, and 500 GB SSD.

Datasets: We used two types of public datasets. One was an *image* dataset, called *ImageNet* [4]. We created four sub-datasets: a sub-dataset (*IMG-A*) with 20,000, another (*IMG-B*) with 40,000, another (*IMG-C*) with 80,000, and the other (*IMG-D*) with 160,000 files, each totaling 2.5 GBytes, 5 GBytes, 10 GBytes, and 20 GBytes, respectively. Another was a *video* dataset, called *VIRAT* [5]. We created three sub-datasets: one (*VD-A*) with a 20-GByte volume of 288, another (*VD-B*) with a 40-GByte volume of 365, and the other (*VD-C*) with an 80-GByte volume of 882 files.

3 Empirical Evaluation Results

Network Connection Type: We considered Wi-Fi and LAN. In our experiments offloading to the remote edge node, when LAN was used, its offloading latency was about 1255 secs, which was lower than Wi-Fi by about 10% for the IMG-C image dataset. For the VD-B video dataset, LAN took 327 secs, which was about 10× faster than Wi-Fi (about 2998 s). These results are certainly because LAN has a larger bandwidth than Wi-Fi. For better offloading, nevertheless, we emphasize considering the network characteristics as well.

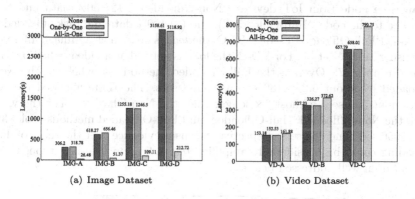

(a) Image Dataset   (b) Video Dataset

Fig. 2. Impact of data compression on the data offloading performance

Communication Protocol Type: We experimented with MQTT and REST protocols. In our offloading experiments to the remote edge node through LAN, for the image IMG-C dataset, it took about 6090 secs via MQTT and 1274 secs via REST. Also, REST outperformed MQTT on the VD-B video dataset by about 12×. Since MQTT is suitable for sending and receiving short text data, REST appears more appropriate to offload a larger volume of data.

Data Compression Type: We investigated three types of compression: 1) *no compression* (denoted 'None'), 2) *per-file compression* ('One-by-one'), 3) *whole compression* of the entire data to be offloaded ('All-in-One'). For the image datasets, 'All-in-one' was about 11.8× faster for IMG-A, 12.4× for IMG-B, 11.5× for IMG-C, and 14.8× for IMG-D, than the other two (Fig. 2(a)). This implies that if small files are numerous, they must be compressed as one package and offloaded as the number of REST API calls can be significantly reduced. This finding has *not* been well addressed previously. For the video datasets, on the other hand, the 'All-in-One' method took longer, up to 20% (for VD-C), compared with the other two (Fig. 2(b)). This result implies that when offloading a few large files in low-end IoT devices with poor processor performance, it is better to compress one at a time or never compress ('None') to lower the latency. This also has not been addressed before.

Offloading Server Location: For the IMG-C dataset, the offloading latencies to the public cloud, the private cloud, and the local PC were about 6939 secs, 3159 secs, and 213 secs. For the VD-C dataset, the public cloud took 856 secs, while the private cloud and the local PC took 327 s and 313 secs, respectively. These features are consistent with the purpose of edge computing to perform computing where data is generated, and they can be seen as the shortcomings of cloud-based data storage.

Load Distribution: We considered 3 scenarios: (1) no data and task offloaded to an edge node from IoT devices ('Non-Offloaded'), (2) 50% data and task offloaded to the node ('Half-Offloaded'), and (3) 100% data and task offloaded to the node ('Full-Offloaded'). For IMG-C, the *load* is defined as an image inference task using MobileNet [6]. For VD-B, the load is defined as a video reduction task using FFmpeg [7]. Overall, the Full-Offloaded method overwhelmed the Non-Offloaded by about 6.2×: 189 secs vs. 1188 secs. The Half-Offloaded method took about 597 secs, almost 2× longer than the Non-Offloaded. For the video data, the Non-Offloaded, Half-Offloaded, and Full-Offloaded methods took 8398 secs, 3656 secs, and 362 secs, respectively. This is evidence that the effect of data offloading could be considerably amplified depending on the data type, which has *not* been well addressed before.

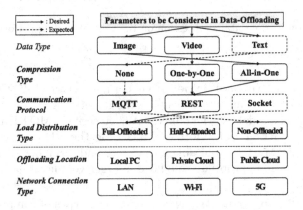

Fig. 3. A Taxonomy of the Parameters that Need to Be Considered in Data-Offloading

Data-Offloading Parameter Taxonomy: Figure 3 depicts a taxonomy of parameters that should be considered in data offloading derived from our evaluation results. (The dashed boxes and arrows will be verified in future work.)

4   Conclusion and Future Work

In this paper, we empirically studied key factors influencing performance on data offloading in edge/cloud environments. We plan to explore additional factors.

Acknowledgments. This work was supported by the ETRI grant funded by the Korean government [23zs1300, Research on High Performance Computing Technology to overcome limitations of AI processing].

References

1. Yao, S., et al.: Deep compressive offloading: speeding up neural network inference by trading edge computation for network latency. In: SenSys 2020, pp. 476–488 (2020)
2. Wang, P., et al.: Task-driven data offloading for fog-enabled urban IoT services. IEEE Internet Things J. **8**(9), 7562–7574 (2020)
3. Amazon: Amazon EC2 (2023). https://aws.amazon.com/ec2/
4. Deng, J., et al.: ImageNet: a large-scale hierarchical image database. In: IEEE Conference on Computer Vision and Pattern Recognition, pp. 248–255 (2009)
5. VIRAT: VIRAT Video Dataset (2023). https://viratdata.org/
6. Howard, A.G., et al.: MobileNets: efficient convolutional neural networks for mobile vision applications. arXiv preprint arXiv:1704.04861 (2017)
7. FFMpeg: FFMpeg: A Complete, Cross-platform Solution to Record, Convert and Stream Audio and Video (2023). https://ffmpeg.org/

HEAppE Middleware: From Desktop to HPC

Jakub Konvička⬤, Václav Svatoň(✉)⬤, and Jan Křenek⬤

IT4Innovations, VSB Technical University of Ostrava, Ostrava, Czech Republic
info@it4i.cz , vaclav.svaton@vsb.cz
https://www.it4i.cz/en

Abstract. HEAppE Middleware is IT4Innovations' in-house implementation of HPC-as-a-Service concept. It is being continuously developed for a more than a 10 years taking into account the user requirements and security policies and constraints of different HPC or Data centres while supporting a number of widely used HPC workload managers. Via simple and easy-to-use REST API the end-users can manage the complete HPC job life cycle, file transfers, and HEAppE-specific functionality. HEAppE provides a user-friendly, secure, and cost-effective solution for the end-users or third-party applications on how to remotely access supercomputing resources without the HPC-specific know-how.

Keywords: HEAppE Middleware · HPC-as-a-Service ·
High-Performance Computing · Remote Execution · Secure Access

1 Introduction

HPC-as-a-Service concept is well know term in the domain of High-Performance Computing. It offers remote access to supercomputing infrastructure in a service-like manner offering HPC capabilities to users or third party applications and services while encapsulating most of the HPC specific functionality behind an easy-to-use interface.

IT4Innovations also adopted this approach more than 10 years ago when it was apparent that there is a growing community of users that wants to integrate HPC capabilities in their own solutions or just need a simple interface to utilize the power of supercomputers within their specific domains.

Throughout its existence HEAppE Middleware[1] was successfully integrated into a number of national and international projects [3] under the header of Horizon 2020, Horizon Europe, and European Space Agency projects and many others and also deployed at several major HPC infrastructure or data centre providers.

---

[1] https://heappe.eu.

2   From Desktop to HPC

This chapter describes the HEAppE's basic features and focuses mainly on the latest version enabling the users to test HEAppE in a simulated cluster environment on their own local computer. For more technical details, see the official HEAppE documentation[2].

Main Features and Security

HEAppE Middleware implements several concepts in terms of remote and secure access to computational resources. In terms of security, HEAppE recognizes two types of credentials: *external user accounts* and *internal service accounts*. External user accounts do not have direct access to the HPC infrastructure itself. They are used only to authenticate the external user via HEAppE middleware to access only HEAppE's provided functions via its REST API.

Service accounts are used to submit jobs to the actual HPC cluster queue. These service accounts are usually non-personalized standard cluster accounts bound to a specific computational project. The service accounts are generated specifically to be used within HEAppE Middleware on the request of *Primary Investigator (PI)* of a given computational project. This way the PI of the project agrees with the creation of service accounts and their usage within HEAppE.

HEAppE provides the mapping between an external user accounts and internal service accounts. It keeps track of which service account was used for the submission of which compute job and which user made the job submission.

HEAppE also enables the users to run only a pre-prepared set of so-called *Command Templates*. Each template defines a script or executable binary, that will be executed on the cluster together with any dependencies or third-party software it might require.

Simulated HPC Cluster Environment

The simulated HPC cluster feature within the HEAppE Middleware allows users to create a virtual representation of an HPC environment directly on their computer. This *simulated cluster* runs in a Docker container, leveraging containerization technology for easy deployment and management.

With the simulated HPC cluster running on a Docker container, users can establish a *self-contained and regulated environment* on their personal computer. This eliminates the necessity for dedicated physical infrastructure or remote access to an HPC system for development purposes. Users can set up and configure the simulated cluster on their local machine, allowing them to efficiently test and experiment with HPC workflows through the HEAppE's REST API in the *sandbox mode*.

---

[2] https://heappe.it4i.cz/docs.

Users have the ability to manage jobs by creating, submitting, monitoring, cancelling, and deleting them on the simulated HPC cluster. Job specifications, such as the number of tasks, task dependencies, and job arrays, can be defined to simulate real-world HPC job scenarios.

After completing the testing of HEAppE on the simulated HPC cluster, it is straightforward to change the configuration and start using HEAppE in the same way, but with the difference that HPC computational jobs will be executed on a real HPC infrastructure.

3   Summary and HEAppE's Showcases

This chapter contains a list of the most important projects where HEAppE has been integrated as an integral part of the developed solution. Infrastructures' list illustrates that HEAppE Middleware is mature enough to be adopted also by other HPC infrastructure providers apart of IT4Innovations' HPC systems.

Projects and Use-Cases

- **DHI**: First version of HPC-as-a-Service Middleware; Integration of HPC into hydrological domain. https://www.mikepoweredbydhi.com
- **Floreon**: FLOod REcognition On the Net; Web-based map interface integrating data visualizations and HPC on-demand analysis from different thematic domains [4]. https://www.floreon.eu
- **UrbanTEP**: Urban Thematic Explotation Platform; ESA funded TEP platform providing data hosting and data processing services from the area of urbanisation [2]. https://urban-tep.eu
- **LEXIS Platform**: Large-scale EXecution for Industry and Society; H2020 project that is building an advanced engineering platform at the confluence of HPC, Cloud and Big Data. https://lexis-project.eu
- **Fiji**: Fiji is an open source image processing package based on ImageJ2; Plug-in for Fiji to access HPC for advance image processing. https://imagej.net/plugins/hpc-workflow-manager
- **LIGATE**: H2020 Drug discovery solutions for HPC; Urgent computing workflows for drug discovery. https://www.ligateproject.eu
- **EVEREST**: H2020 dEsign enVironmEnt foR Extreme-Scale big data analyTics on heterogeneous platforms; HEAppE execution workflows via LEXIS platform running at IBM infrastructure. https://everest-h2020.eu/
- **BLENDED**: BLockchain Enabled Deep learning Data analysis; ESA funded project created a peer-to-peer deep learning training platform for decentralised processing [1].
- **BioDT**: Biodiversity Digital Twin for Advanced Modelling, Simulation and Prediction Capabilities; Horizon Europe project creating the Biodiversity Digital Twin. https://biodt.eu

Infrastructures

- **LRZ**: Leibniz Supercomputing Centre (DE); HEAppE used to integrate LRZ's HPC systems into the LEXIS platform. https://www.lrz.de
- **EPCC**: Centre of Excellence at the University of Edinburgh; Providing access to EPCC's Cirrus cluster for LEXIS platform. https://www.epcc.ed.ac.uk
- **IBM**: IBM HPC solutions; HEAppE is used to access IBM's cluster in the scope of H2020 EVEREST project.
- **CINECA**: Operating the largest computing centre in Italy; HEAppE deployment under preparation to integrate selected CINECA clusters to be utilized in H2020 LIGATE project. https://www.cineca.it
- **LUMI**: One of the pan-European pre-exascale supercomputers under the head of EuroHPC JU. HEAppE deployment under preparation as part of BioDT project. https://lumi-supercomputer.eu

Acknowledgement. This work was supported by the Ministry of Education, Youth and Sports of the Czech Republic through the e-INFRA CZ (ID:90254). This work was also supported by the EVEREST project - the European Union's Horizon 2020 research and innovation programme under grant agreement No. 957269. This work was also supported by the LIGATE project. This project has received funding from the European High- Performance Computing Joint Undertaking (JU) under grant agreement No 956137. The JU receives support from the European Union's Horizon 2020 research and innovation programme and Italy, Sweden, Austria, the Czech Republic, Switzerland. This project has received funding from the Ministry of Education, Youth and Sports of the Czech Republic (ID: MC2102).

References

1. Valentin, B., et al.: BLENDED - using blockchain and deep learning for space dada processing (2021)
2. Bachofer, F., et al.: UrbanTEP - EO data processing, integrative data analysis and monitoring for SDG reporting (2021)
3. Svaton, V., Martinovic, J., Krenek, J., Esch, T., Tomancak, P.: HPC-as-a-Service via HEAppE platform. In: Complex, Intelligent, And Software Intensive Systems, pp. 280–293 (2020)
4. Svatoň, V., et al. Floreon+: integration of different thematic areas. In: Proceedings of the GisOstrava 2018 (2018)
5. Golasowski, M., et al.: The LEXIS platform for distributed workflow execution and data management. In: HPC, Big Data, and AI Convergence Towards Exascale: Challenge and Vision, pp. 17–35 (2022). ISBN 978-1-03-200984-1

Towards Energy-Aware Machine Learning in Geo-Distributed IoT Settings

Demetris Trihinas[1]([✉])(iD) and Lauritz Thamsen[2](iD)

[1] Department of Computer Science, University of Nicosia, Nicosia, Cyprus
`trihinas.d@unic.ac.cy`
[2] School of Computing Science, University of Glasgow, Glasgow, UK
`lauritz.thamsen@glasgow.ac.uk`

Abstract. As the Internet of Things (IoT) increasingly empowers the network extremes with in-place intelligence through Machine Learning (ML), energy consumption and carbon emissions become crucial factors. ML is often computationally intensive, with state-of-the-art model architectures consuming significant energy per training round and imposing a large carbon footprint. This work, therefore, argues for the need to introduce novel mechanisms into the ML pipelines of IoT services, so that energy awareness is integrated in the decision-making process for when and where to initiate ML model training.

Keywords: Machine Learning · Internet of Things · Distributed Systems · Energy Profiling · Carbon Footprint · System Orchestration

1 Introduction

With recent advancements in IoT hardware, we are seeing the use of ML on IoT devices for highly responsive and intelligent services. However, ML is compute-hungry. In fact, the computational power required for training new state-of-the-art model architectures has been doubling every 4 months [2]. This computational effort results in higher and higher energy consumption and, in turn, increasing carbon emissions, contributing to global warming. Already, ICT organizations report that approximately 15% of their energy consumption can be attributed to AI/ML and this ratio is expected to rise considerably [3]. With Gartner [1] indicating that 75% of enterprise data will be created and processed outside of data centers, and the climate crisis demanding a rapid reduction in carbon emissions, a key emerging challenge is to adequately support the migration to sustainable AI-driven cloud edge IoT solutions [5].

This work discusses the challenges of deploying AI-driven IoT services in geo-distributed settings with a focus on energy consumption and carbon footprint. During the session we will broaden the discussion towards the need for extending ML orchestration frameworks so that their decision-making mechanisms cover energy-awareness by recommending *when* and *where* ML models should be trained and elaborate why these two inter-related challenges are not easy to overcome.

© The Author(s), under exclusive license to Springer Nature Switzerland AG 2024
D. Zeinalipour et al. (Eds.): Euro-Par 2023 Workshops, LNCS 14352, pp. 256–259, 2024.
https://doi.org/10.1007/978-3-031-48803-0_28

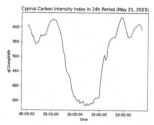 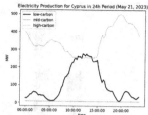 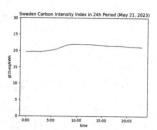

Fig. 1. Cyprus 24 h carbon intensity

Fig. 2. Cyprus 24 h power production

Fig. 3. Sweden 24 h carbon intensity

2 Reference Use Case

To drive the discussion, let us consider a realistic ML-driven IoT application. This application features several road-side IoT units, using cameras and object detection for traffic monitoring. Several Mobile Edge Computing nodes (MECs) are scattered across the city and employed for local coordination as well as recurrent model training at a neighborhood level. For the evaluation we consider a MEC to be powered by a DELL PowerEdge R610 server and equipped with a Nvidia T4 GPU. The ML pipeline employs the TensorFlow benchmark suite[1] to output a CNN model for object detection, trained with the ImageNet dataset[2] (144 GB, 1.3 M images) for a duration of approximately 5 h, when it reaches a satisfactory MLPerf accuracy.

3 When to Train a ML Model?

Deciding when to initiate repeated ML model training can highly impact the carbon footprint of an ML-based application. In particular, an application's operational carbon footprint depends on the energy mix powering the compute resources used. An illustrative example is given in Fig. 1, where for a given day in the country of Cyprus, the carbon intensity of the energy grid shows significant volatility. This is attributed to the mix of energy sources powering the grid (Fig. 2), where the low-carbon energy sources solar and wind generate to the greatest extent during the day, while high-carbon sources (i.e., oil) dominate production during the evening hours.

Taking this into account, power utilization data is extracted from the CNN model training runs over the use case testbed. Figure 4 (red palette) showcases the estimated carbon footprint for model training with the training process initiated at different times in Cyprus. Specifically, it shows that initiating model training at mid-day versus 6 pm reduces the carbon footprint by 1.93 kg, while the carbon footprint is reduced even by 2.61 kg in comparison to 9 pm.

---

[1] https://github.com/tensorflow/benchmarks.
[2] https://www.image-net.org/.

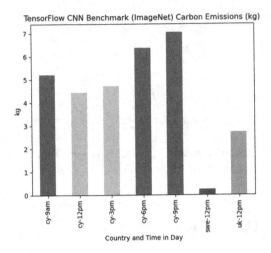

Fig. 4. Carbon footprint in kg for different periods of the day and countries. (Color figure online)

4 Where to Train a Model?

Arguably, a country or region that uses high-carbon energy sources, such Cyprus, may not be ideal for ML model training. In contrast, let us consider the country of Sweden, with Fig. 3 showing its carbon intensity measured over the same day. We can observe that the intensity is relatively stable across the day. This is ideal. First, when the model is trained does not make a huge difference. Second, the intensity is significantly lower, with Sweden usually being the EU state reporting the lowest carbon intensity. Considering now also the UK with a moderate carbon intensity that would rank it in the middle of the EU, let us go back to Fig. 4 and compare this with the training rounds initiated at different times in Cyprus. We can see that migrating an ML application to a different country can yield a significantly different environmental footprint, with model training in Sweden and the UK promising a 93% and 38% reduction in carbon emissions, respectively, in contrast to the Cyprus-based training, even during mid-day.

5 Energy-Aware Support for ML Workflow Orchestrators

Figure 5 depicts a high-level overview of the PowerML tool for aiding the decision-making of ML orchestration frameworks as to when and where to train ML models. To design such a tool the following steps are required. First, resource utilization must be mapped into energy consumption with different power models embraced for processors, memory, graphic and AI accelerators, as well as network links. In large-scale heterogeneous deployments this can easily become a configuration nightmare. To aid with this, we are building an open repository for power models that can be shared among users. Second, energy consumption must be used for estimating carbon emissions, which are dependent on the

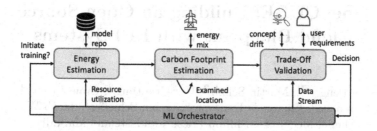

Fig. 5. The PowerML tool for aiding energy-aware orchestration of ML training

energy mix currently powering the power grid. Several grids provide live and historic data but this is either through websites or APIs, without a common data model. PowerML overcomes this challenge by providing an abstraction layer for accessing energy mix data from energy grids.

Moreover, there are many trade-offs to consider for the decision-making, commonly requiring human input as to which strategies should be explored. This is an inhibitor to a fully automated processes. One such trade-off is between accuracy and energy saving when postponing model training. That is, waiting for a low-carbon energy time window may come with a huge accuracy hit if the data distribution changes (concept drift) in the meantime [4]. Other trade-offs come with moving the workload to a different location. Moving large volumes of training data introduces delays and has a carbon cost of its own to consider. Moreover, moving data across regions is not a simple process with potential legal and privacy requirements, contradicting key arguments for in-place processing and edge intelligence.

Acknowledgements. This work is partially supported by the University of Nicosia Seed Grant Scheme for the FlockAI project.

References

1. Gartner: What Edge Computing Means for Infrastructure and Operations Leaders (2018). https://www.gartner.com/smarterwithgartner/what-edge-computing-means-for-infrastructure-and-operations-leaders
2. OpenAI: AI and Compute (2021). https://openai.com/blog/ai-and-compute/
3. Patterson, D., et al.: The Carbon Footprint of Machine Learning Training Will Plateau. Then Shrink (2022)
4. Trihinas, D., Pallis, G., Dikaiakos, M.D.: Monitoring elastically adaptive multi-cloud services. IEEE Trans. Cloud Comput. **6**(3), 800–814 (2018)
5. Trihinas, D., Thamsen, L., Beilharz, J., Symeonides, M.: Towards energy consumption and carbon footprint testing for AI-driven IoT services. In: 2022 IEEE International Conference on Cloud Engineering (IC2E) (2022)

OpenCUBE: Building an Open Source Cloud Blueprint with EPI Systems

Ivy Peng[1]([✉]), Martin Schulz[2], Utz-Uwe Haus[3], Craig Prunty[4],
Pedro Marcuello[5], Emanuele Danovaro[6], Gabin Schieffer[1], Jacob Wahlgren[1],
Daniel Medeiros[1], Philipp Friese[2], and Stefano Markidis[1]

[1] KTH Royal Institute of Technology, Stockholm, Sweden
ivybopeng@kth.se
[2] Technical University of Munich, Munich, Germany
[3] Hewlett Packard Enterprise, Zürich, Switzerland
[4] SiPearl, Maisons-Laffitte, France
[5] Semidynamics, Barcelona, Spain
[6] ECMWF, Bologna, Italy

Abstract. OpenCUBE aims to develop an open-source full software stack for Cloud computing blueprint deployed on EPI hardware, adaptable to emerging workloads across the computing continuum. OpenCUBE prioritizes energy awareness and utilizes open APIs, Open Source components, advanced SiPearl Rhea processors, and RISC-V accelerator. The project leverages representative workloads, such as cloud-native workloads and workflows of weather forecast data management, molecular docking, and space weather, for evaluation and validation.

Keywords: Open-source · Converged HPC and Cloud · Computing continuum · EPI · RISC-V

1 Introduction

OpenCUBE is a project funded by the European Commission and initiated in January 2023. Its primary aim is to create, implement, and validate a full software stack for enabling a European Cloud computing blueprint deployed on European hardware infrastructure and cater to industrial and consumer cloud workloads. Additionally, the project aims to prioritize power and energy efficiency by incorporating power awareness at all levels. OpenCUBE will support the diverse requirements of the entire computing continuum, spanning from edge to cloud and high-performance computing (HPC).

OpenCUBE involves designing and installing a prototype hardware infrastructure composed of SiPearl processors and Semidynamics RISC-V accelerators, which are outcomes of the European Processor Initiative (EPI). Heterogeneous compute nodes will be interconnected with a high-performance

OpenCUBE is funded by European Commission Horizon Project 101092984.

Ethernet network to support the exploration of emerging memory and storage disaggregation. OpenCUBE will create a unified software stack encompassing various best practices and open-source tools at the operating system, middleware, and system management levels. The OpenCUBE software stack for cloud services will be open-source and leverage industry-standard Open APIs and Open Source components.

In line with the European Green Deal initiative, OpenCUBE is designed to enable energy awareness as a fundamental feature across the entire stack. Through software-hardware co-design, the OpenCUBE software stack will provide API access to various site levels, from core, socket, node, and even to the electricity grid. The project will utilize representative workloads, such as weather forecast data management, molecular docking, and space weather workflows, to inform the design and deployment of the OpenCUBE system.

2 Approach

OpenCUBE takes an approach focusing on close hardware and software interfaces and is organized into four thrusts – hardware platform, middleware, heterogeneous data center (DC), and applications (Fig. 1).

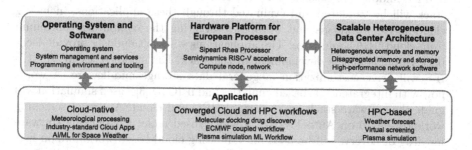

Fig. 1. An overview of the OpenCUBE approach with a focus on close interface between software and hardware.

- **The Hardware Platform** is designed for hosting EPI systems, e.g., SiPearl Rhea and Semidynaimcs RISC-V processors. The design is adapted for catering to both cloud-native and HPC workloads' requirements. Also, the hardware platform provides inputs to the design of the operating system and middleware for a heterogeneous data center. As in the early phase, a prototype platform is built to exploit ARM-based processors available in commercial cloud systems, high-performance Ethernet-based interconnects, and the EPAC RISC-V accelerator.
- **Operating Systems and Software** will leverage and extend open-source components to support newly released hardware features for monitoring and

resource management on the hardware platform. Extensions to system management services and OS will be designed to utilize the high-performance Ethernet network and enable power awareness at various system levels to achieve energy efficiency and performance. Open-source profiling tools will be adapted to the new CPU architecture to improve performance tuning and debugging.

- **A Scalable Heterogeneous Data Center** architecture will be deployed through open-source middleware specifically adapted to the hardware platform and targeted workloads. In particular, the OpenCUBE middleware will focus on improving the utilization of heterogeneous compute and memory resources on node. Also, extensions are to be developed to enable memory disaggregation over the fast network for either memory expansion or data staging in workflows. High-performance network software is designed to enable the efficient execution of applications in cloud-based containerized environments. For instance, MPI is the dominant communication API for traditional HPC applications. However, its relatively static model, which was developed for conventional HPC setups and schedulers, needs to be revised for and adapted to cloud-based application deployment, for example, using the recently introduced MPI Sessions concept [2].
- **Driver Applications & Workflows** will interact with hardware, software, and DC middleware thrusts to input workload requirements. The OpenCUBE stack will be validated and evaluated through these applications, including cloud-native workloads and workflows targeting the computing continuum from cloud, HPC, and edge. The applications will continuously provide feedback throughout the development of the stack. For instance, ECMWF [1]'s IFS will drive customization of general data storage middleware. A workflow with integrated ML-based analytics and iPIC3D [3]-based simulation will guide the software stack for converged HPC and cloud. A virtual screening workflow based on AutoDock [7], a widely used molecular docking software for drug discovery, will be used for validating cloud-based workflows on heterogeneous resources.

3   Preliminary Results and Roadmap

In the first phase, we are deploying a prototype hardware platform of one rack of four HPE ProLiant RL300 servers with 256 GB DDR4 memory and a minimum of 1 TB NVMe SSD for provisioning fabric-attached memory. An FPGA emulator is employed to integrate EPAC RISC-V processors for acceleration. The platform is equipped with Slingshot interconnects, including one Cassini Switch GB Ethernet and the Cassini network interface card.

To enable cloud-native workflows, we investigate a popular workflow management software, Apache Airflow. As a case study, we used a virtual screening software in drug discovery, AutoDock, to enable a workflow of automatic elastic molecular docking on the cloud [4]. Our preliminary results confirm the feasibility of deployment into the containerized environment. We investigated the state-of-the-art disaggregated memory technologies such as Compute Express Link (CXL) for the scalable heterogeneous data center architecture. We developed a memory-centric profiling tool and a software emulation framework to explore design space [9] quantitatively.

To enable converged computing between Cloud and HPC, we developed a framework atop the open-source container orchestrator Kubernetes that enables the reuse of already provisioned infrastructure. This capability enables automatic horizontal scaling for tightly coupled MPI-based applications, which is cumbersome to realize on traditional HPC systems [5]. In analyzing application requirements for input to OpenCUBE stack design, we also identified a scalability bottleneck in reduction operation due to a large number of synchronization points. We proposed a matrix-based multi-dimensional reduction algorithm for accelerating the local search of the scoring function and explored a tensor-based implementation for optimizing the molecular docking process [8]. The results show an over 25% improvement in average docking time for a real-world docking scenario.

On the roadmap towards an open-source cloud blueprint, the OpenCUBE project employs an approach focusing on close interaction between software and hardware development to create an open-source cloud blueprint on EPI systems. The prototype implementation in OpenCUBE will be validated and evaluated with industrial and consumer cloud applications. Development in enabling adaptive MPI communication setup, e.g., session, will also provide feedback to standardization bodies [6]. OpenCUBE's roadmap aligns the major upgrade of the prototype hardware infrastructure with chips produced from EPI. Meanwhile, insights and findings learned during the design and development of the Open-CUBE stack based on the Sipearl Rhea and Semidynamics RISC-V processors are feedback to the Open Source, EPI, and Computing Continuum communities.

Acknowledgment. OpenCUBE is funded by EU Horizon Project 101092984.

References

1. Bauer, P., Thorpe, A., Brunet, G.: The quiet revolution of numerical weather prediction. Nature **525**(7567), 47–55 (2015)
2. Holmes, D., et al.: MPI sessions: leveraging runtime infrastructure to increase scalability of applications at exascale. In: Proceedings of the 23rd European MPI Users' Group Meeting, pp. 121–129 (2016)
3. Markidis, S., Lapenta, G., et al.: Multi-scale simulations of plasma with iPIC3D. Math. Comput. Simul. **80**(7), 1509–1519 (2010)
4. Medeiros, D., Schieffer, G., Wahlgren, J., Peng, I.: A GPU-accelerated molecular docking workflow with kubernetes and apache airflow. In: Bienz, A., Weiland, M., Baboulin, M., Kruse, C. (eds.) International Conference on High Performance Computing, pp. 193–206. Springer, Heidelberg (2023). https://doi.org/10.1007/978-3-031-40843-4_15
5. Medeiros, D., Wahlgren, J., Schieffer, G., Peng, I.: Kub: enabling elastic HPC workloads on containerized environments. In: 35th International Symposium on Computer Architecture and High Performance Computing (SBAC-PAD). IEEE (2023)

6. The MPI Forum: The MPI Standard, v4.0 (2021)
7. Santos-Martins, D., Solis-Vasquez, L., Tillack, A.F., Sanner, M.F., Koch, A., Forli, S.: Accelerating AutoDock4 with GPUs and gradient-based local search. J. Chem. Theory Comput. **17**(2), 1060–1073 (2021)
8. Schieffer, G., Peng, I.: Accelerating drug discovery in AutoDock-GPU with tensor cores. In: Cano, J., Dikaiakos, M.D., Papadopoulos, G.A., Pericás, M., Sakellariou, R. (eds.) Euro-Par 2023: Parallel Processing: 29th International Conference on Parallel and Distributed Computing, Proceedings, pp. 608–622. Springer, Heidelberg (2023). https://doi.org/10.1007/978-3-031-39698-4_41
9. Wahlgren, J., Schieffer, G., Gokhale, M., Peng, I.: A quantitative approach for adopting disaggregated memory in HPC systems. In: International Conference for High Performance Computing, Networking, Storage and Analysis (2023)

BDDC Preconditioning on GPUs
for Cardiac Simulations

Fritz Göbel[1], Terry Cojean[1]([✉])[iD], and Hartwig Anzt[1,2][iD]

[1] Karlsruhe Institute of Technology, Karlsruhe, Germany
{fritz.gobel,terry.cojean,hartwig.anzt}@kit.edu
[2] ICL, University of Tennessee, Knoxville, USA

Abstract. In order to understand cardiac arrhythmia, computer models for electrophysiology are essential. In the EuroHPC MicroCARD project, we adapt the current models and leverage modern computing resources to model diseased hearts and their microstructure accurately. Towards this objective, we develop a portable, highly efficient, and performing BDDC preconditioner and solver implementation, demonstrating scalability with over 90% efficiency on up to 100 GPUs.

Keywords: BDDC preconditioning · Sparse Linear Algebra · High Performance Computing · GPUs · Cardiac simulations

1 Introduction

Cardiovascular diseases are the most frequent cause of death worldwide, and half of them are due to cardiac arrhythmia. To understand these disorders of the heart's electrical system very sophisticated and widely used, but currently, they are not powerful enough to take the heart's individual cells into account. Rather than simulating at or below the cell level, the base units of the simulations are groups of hundreds of cells prevents from representing several events in aging and structurally diseased hearts.

Moving towards a cell-by-cell model of the heart increases the size of the problem by 10,000 while making it harder to solve. For this, exascale computers are required, and software leveraging these new architectures, like GPUs, must be developed. The EuroHPC MicroCARD project [1,8] was started to tackle these challenges. In this paper, we provide efficient, portable, GPU-enabled, and scalable solvers and a BDDC preconditioner tailored for the MicroCARD project. This is implemented within the Ginkgo portable linear algebra framework [3] which is the numerical backend selected for the MicroCARD project.

This work was supported by the European High-Performance Computing Joint Undertaking EuroHPC under grant agreement No 955495 (MICROCARD).

2   Background and Implementation

In the Cell-by-Cell model, individual cells and extracellular space provide a natural division of the simulation domain into subdomains making domain decomposition preconditioners attractive. Considering discontinuous Galerkin discretizations that are required to approximate discontinuous potentials, Huynh et al. identified Balancing Domain Decomposition by Constraints (BDDC) as a well-suited preconditioner for this type of problem [6].

In a BDDC preconditioner as introduced in [4], we consider the individual contributions A_i of each subdomain Ω_i to the global stiffness matrix A locally: $A = \sum_{i=1}^{N} R_i^T A_i R_i$ where R_i are adequate restriction matrices. Global coupling is achieved with a coarse problem $A_c = \sum_{i=1}^{N} R_{ci}^T A_{ci} R_{ci}$ where $A_{ci} = \Phi_i^T A_i \Phi_i$ with Φ_i arising from the solution of saddle point problems of the form

$$\begin{bmatrix} A_i & C_i^T \\ C_i & 0 \end{bmatrix} \begin{bmatrix} \Phi_i \\ \Lambda_i \end{bmatrix} = \begin{bmatrix} 0 \\ I \end{bmatrix}. \tag{1}$$

Here, C_i are constraint matrices on the subdomain boundaries. While different constraint approaches exist, we use the popular simple approach of averaging over subdomain faces and edges while taking full values on corners. Redistributing the solution of the coarse system into the subdomains requires weights for each dof in the subdomains. Here, we use $w_i = \frac{1}{\|\kappa\|}$ where κ is the number of subdomains sharing the global dof i. In 2D, it will be 1 for interior nodes, $\frac{1}{2}$ on subdomain edges and $\frac{1}{k}$ on subdomain corners cornering k subdomains.

The preconditioned residual $M^{-1} = v_1 + v_2 + v_3$ has three parts [4]: 1) **coarse grid correction:** as in Eq. (2) with the coarsened residual $r_c = \sum_{i=1}^{N} R_{ci}^T \Phi_i^T W_i R_i r$; 2) **local subdomain correction:** as in Eq. (3) with z_i extracted from solving Eq. (4); 3) **static condensation correction:** as in Eq. (5), where R_{Ii} restricts to the inner dofs of subdomain Ω_i, we compute a new residual $r_1 = r - A(v_1 + v_2)$ with the coarse grid and local subdomain corrections.

$$v_1 = \sum_{i=1}^{N} R_i^T W_i \Phi_i R_{ci} A_c^{-1} r_c \tag{2}$$

$$v_2 = \sum_{i=1}^{N} R_i^T W_i z_i \tag{3}$$

$$\begin{bmatrix} A_i & C_i^T \\ C_i & 0 \end{bmatrix} \begin{bmatrix} z_i \\ \lambda_i \end{bmatrix} = \begin{bmatrix} W_i R_i r \\ 0 \end{bmatrix} \tag{4}$$

$$v_3 = \sum_{i=1}^{N} R_i^T R_{Ii}^T (R_{Ii} A_i R_{Ii}^T)^{-1} R_{Ii} R_i r_1 \tag{5}$$

The implementation of the BDDC preconditioner in Ginkgo is individually configurable, the linear solvers used in Eqs. (1), (2), (4) and (5) can be tuned independently. For the results we show in this paper, we solve the coarse system

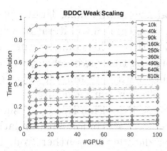

(a) Weak scaling a 2D-Poisson problem. Local problems: GPU sparse direct solver (solid) or AMG+GMRES (dashed).

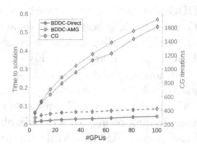

(b) Weak scaling for BDDC preconditioned vs. plain CG with a local size of 10k dofs per subdomain.

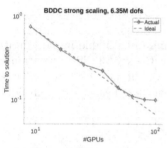

(c) Strong scaling results for a 2D-Poisson stiffness matrix with 6.35 million dofs.

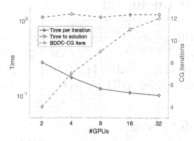

(d) Strong scaling results for a Bidomain simulation stiffness matrix with 120k dofs.

Fig. 1. Results for the BDDC preconditioned CG.

in (Eq. (2)) with a plain CG solver and leverage recently developed GPU-resident sparse direct solvers for the solution of the local problems. The direct solvers are used to factorize the complete linear systems in Eqs. (1), (2) and (5) or in the coarsest level of an Algebraic Multigrid (AMG) preconditioner inside a GMRES solver. In both cases, we pre-process the local matrices with MC64 [5] for numerical stability and AMD [2] for fill-in reduction.

3   Experimental Results

Figures 1a to 1c show scaling results for a 2D-Poisson equation on the unit square, subdivided into equal-sized square subdomains, solved with BDDC preconditioned CG on AMD MI250X GPUs on the Frontier Supercomputer. Figure 1a highlights good weak-scaling of our BDDC. When comparing AMG preconditioned GMRES for local problems (dashed lines) against GPU-resident sparse direct solvers (solid lines), we see that AMG is slower for small problems, but gives significant benefits for larger problems. Figure 1b compares CG with a

BDDC preconditioner and without using a local size of 10k dofs. Unlike plain CG, we are able to solve the Poisson equation with one global CG iteration when using BDDC leading to almost constant execution time. This confirms that our BDDC implementation is highly effective in improving the convergence and time to solution. Figure 1c shows strong-scaling results with 6.35 million dofs. The time to solution scales down until around 9 subdomains in each direction (81 GPUs) where we are no longer able to saturate the GPUs. Finally, Fig. 1d shows strong-scaling results for a matrix obtained from a realistic bidomain simulation of the openCARP [7]. While the preconditioner deteriorates further from the true inverse of the matrix when increasing the number of subdomains, the timer per iteration scales down for small GPU counts and due to the rather small problem size flattens out earlier than for the larger Poisson example.

4 Conclusion

In this paper, we show a portable, high-performance, scalable implementation of the BDDC preconditioner and solvers within Ginkgo [3]. This solution can be combined with the ongoing implementation of the new Cell-by-Cell model within OpenCARP [7] to target Exascale simulations of heart electrophysiology.

References

1. The MICROCARD Project. http://microcard.eu/. Accessed 23 Apr 2022
2. Amestoy, P.R., Davis, T.A., Duff, I.S.: An approximate minimum degree ordering algorithm. SIAM J. Matrix Anal. Appl. **17**(4), 886–905 (1996). https://doi.org/10.1137/S0895479894278952
3. Anzt, H., et al.: Ginkgo: a modern linear operator algebra framework for high performance computing. ACM Trans. Math. Softw. **48**(1) (2022). https://doi.org/10.1145/3480935
4. Dohrmann, C.R.: A preconditioner for substructuring based on constrained energy minimization. SIAM J. Sci. Comput. **25**(1), 246–258 (2003). https://doi.org/10.1137/S1064827502412887
5. Duff, I.S., Koster, J.: On algorithms for permuting large entries to the diagonal of a sparse matrix. SIAM J. Matrix Anal. Appl. **22**(4), 973–996 (2001). https://doi.org/10.1137/S0895479899358443
6. Huynh, N.M.M., Chegini, F., Pavarino, L.F., Weiser, M., Scacchi, S.: Convergence analysis of BDDC preconditioners for hybrid DG discretizations of the cardiac cell-by-cell model (2022)
7. Plank, G., et al.: The openCARP simulation environment for cardiac electrophysiology. Comput. Methods Programs Biomed. **208**, 106223 (2021). https://doi.org/10.1016/j.cmpb.2021.106223
8. Potse, M.: Microscale cardiac electrophysiology on exascale supercomputers. In: SIAM Conference on Parallel Processing (PP22). SIAM (2022)

PhD Symposium

Exploring Mapping Strategies
for Co-allocated HPC Applications

Ioannis Vardas[(✉)] [iD], Sascha Hunold [iD], Philippe Swartvagher [iD],
and Jesper Larsson Träff [iD]

TU Wien, 1040 Vienna, Austria
{vardas,hunold,swartvagher,traff}@par.tuwien.ac.at

Abstract. In modern HPC systems with deep hierarchical architectures, large-scale applications often struggle to efficiently utilize the abundant cores due to the saturation of resources such as memory. Co-allocating multiple applications to share compute nodes can mitigate these issues and increase system throughput. However, co-allocation may harm the performance of individual applications due to resource contention. Past research suggests that topology-aware mappings can improve the performance of parallel applications that do not share resources. In this work, we implement application-oblivious, topology-aware process-to-core mappings via different core enumerations that support the co-allocation of parallel applications. We show that these mappings have a significant impact on the available memory bandwidth. We explore how these process-to-core mappings can affect the individual application duration as well as the makespan of job schedules when they are combined with co-allocation. Our main objective is to assess whether co-allocation with a topology-aware mapping can be a viable alternative to the exclusive node allocation policies that are currently common in HPC clusters.

Keywords: High Performance Computing · Parallel Computing · Performance Optimization · Process Mapping · Co-allocation

1 Introduction

HPC systems are typical multi-user systems, where users submit batch jobs that request compute resources for a specified amount of time. Many CPU-based supercomputers are composed of compute nodes that feature a large number of cores. Parallel applications that run on these compute nodes cannot always efficiently use all allocated cores as some resources become saturated at high core counts, such as the memory or I/O bandwidth [3]. Under these circumstances, HPC systems strive to maintain a high job throughput and low makespan while also keeping the job duration short to meet users' needs. Therefore, two important metrics for HPC systems are: (1) the makespan which is the time difference between the start and finish of a sequence of jobs and, (2) the individual

The original version of this chapter was previously published without open access. A correction to this chapter is available at
https://doi.org/10.1007/978-3-031-48803-0_41

D. Zeinalipour et al. (Eds.): Euro-Par 2023 Workshops, LNCS 14352, pp. 271–276, 2024.
https://doi.org/10.1007/978-3-031-48803-0_31

job duration. Co-allocating multiple applications to share the compute nodes can reduce the makespan of a job schedule. Even though previous research has shown promising results for co-scheduling [2,3], it is rarely used in production systems for multi-node CPU applications. A drawback of co-allocation is that it can increase the duration of jobs [1] if jobs conflict over shared resources such as the L3 cache, memory controllers, or the network interface.

To address this issue, applying efficient process mappings can improve the performance of applications by reducing their communication time [4]. Mapping is the assignment of processes of a parallel application to the processing units (cores) of the system. Due to the deeper memory hierarchies, the higher core-density nodes, and the increased number of compute nodes of HPC systems, the mapping of parallel applications can significantly affect their performance. Most works that improve the mapping of applications are not concerned with co-allocated applications, and they often require an extra profiling run, which renders them impractical for production systems [5].

In the present work, we explore different process-to-core mappings for co-allocated applications similar to the work of Breslow et al. [2], which proposes a method for co-allocating applications called job striping. With job striping, two jobs share a set of nodes where half of the cores of each node run one job and the other half run the other. In our work, we go beyond job striping by devising several topology-aware and application-oblivious process-to-core mappings using different enumerations of the compute cores for co-allocated applications. We analyze the effects of our mapping strategies and show that they affect the available memory bandwidth of a parallel application. In our evaluation, we employ typical HPC applications to explore the impact of mapping and co-allocation. We compare our strategies combined with an allocation policy that is common in HPC systems.

2   Experimental Environment and Methods

As an example of an HPC system with a deep resource hierarchy, we use the Vienna Scientific Cluster 5 (VSC-5). Each of its 770 compute nodes consists of two packages (sockets), and each socket has an AMD EPYC^{TM} 7713 processor with 64 cores. Figure 1a depicts the hierarchical topology of one VSC-5 compute node, showing the four levels of hierarchy, which are: (1) compute node, (2) package, (3) NUMA node, and (4) the core. Each package has four NUMA nodes and each NUMA node comprises 16 cores. Each compute node has 512 GiB of RAM and eight memory channels per socket (2 per NUMA node). This deep and complex hierarchy motivates us to explore various mapping strategies that leverage the resources of such hierarchies differently. Our strategies take into account three levels of the node's hierarchy: the package, the NUMA node, and the core. In multi-node scenarios, we make three assumptions: (1) the scheduler distributes an equal number of processes to each node; (2) each compute node is shared between applications; and (3) the mapping is replicated to each node.

We produce different process-to-core mappings by varying core enumerations. With $n!$ possible enumerations of n elements, directly exploring all of them is

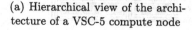

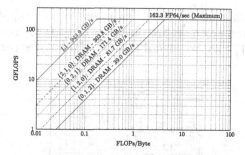

(a) Hierarchical view of the architecture of a VSC-5 compute node

(b) Roofline models: DRAM lines show the available bandwidth with different mappings

Fig. 1. Overview of a single VSC-5 compute node: (a) Hierarchical view of the architecture, and (b) the Roofline models of eight processes.

impractical. Our mappings leverage the machine's hierarchical topology to narrow this search space. We represent core enumerations in a mixed-radix numerical system, based on an ordered set of the hierarchy $h = \{2, 4, 16\}$, which denotes two sockets, four NUMA nodes per socket, and 16 cores per NUMA node. First, we decompose the core IDs into digit sets using Algorithm 1. These sets of digits are the indices to the different levels defined by the hierarchy. Second, we compute the new core IDs via Algorithm 2, employing the decomposed digits from Algorithm 1, hierarchy h, and order o of hierarchy. The order o denotes the sequence of hierarchy levels considered by Algorithm 2. Using order $o = \{0, 1, 2\}$, we produce the enumeration in Fig. 1a. By permuting o, we produce different mappings, e.g., $o = \{2, 1, 0\}$ enumerates the core IDs as $\{0, 64, 16, 80, ...\}$, that is, we first cyclically assign processes between packages and then cyclically assign processes between NUMA nodes. Since this hierarchy has three levels, o is a set of three elements, therefore, six permutations and thus six different mappings are possible. We focus on four out of six mappings, which differ significantly in terms of bandwidth.

Algorithm 1. Decompose core ID	**Algorithm 2.** Compute core ID
Input: h: hierarchy, id: core id	**Input:** h: hierarchy, d: digits, o: order
Output: d: decomposed digits	**Output:** nid: new core id
1: $d \leftarrow []$	1: $nid \leftarrow 0, s \leftarrow 1$
2: **for** $i \leftarrow 0$ to length(h) $- 1$ **do**	2: **for** $i \leftarrow 0$ to length(h) $- 1$ **do**
3: $d[i] \leftarrow id$ mod $h[i]$	3: $nid \leftarrow nid + d[o[i]] \times s$
4: $id \leftarrow id // h[i]$ ▷ Integer division	4: $s \leftarrow s \times h[o[i]]$
5: **end for**	5: **end for**

Figure 2 shows the mappings of four co-allocated MPI applications using orders $\{0, 1, 2\}, \{1, 2, 0\}, \{2, 1, 0\}$, and $\{0, 2, 1\}$, where each application is allotted 32 cores in a VSC-5 compute node. We name the mappings after the orders that they are derived from. From Fig. 2, we notice that different applications use different resources: For example, when applications are mapped with {1, 2, 0} the processes are placed in one NUMA node per package, whereas with {0, 2, 1} they are placed in two NUMA nodes per package.

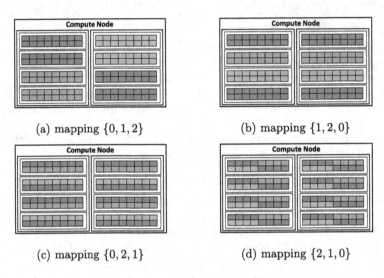

(a) mapping {0, 1, 2}

(b) mapping {1, 2, 0}

(c) mapping {0, 2, 1}

(d) mapping {2, 1, 0}

Fig. 2. Process-to-core mappings of four co-allocated MPI applications each with 32 processes sharing one compute node. Different colors denote cores that are allotted to different applications.

Figure 1b illustrates the distinct memory bandwidths offered by the four mappings, each with eight processes. The arithmetic intensity is on the x-axis and the performance on the y-axis. We notice that mapping {2, 1, 0} yields a maximum bandwidth of 304 GB/s, in contrast to {0, 1, 2} at 39 GB/s. Consequently, an application with 1 FLOP/Byte arithmetic intensity, for example, can attain 162 GFLOPS and 39 GFLOPS at the respective bandwidths. Moreover, our mappings influence the resource contention of co-allocated applications by affecting their shared resources. The least amount of shared resources between applications is achieved by the {0, 1, 2} mapping in Fig. 2a, whereas Fig. 2d shows that more resources are shared with {2, 1, 0} mapping. We categorize mappings {0, 1, 2} and {1, 2, 0} as *compact*, whereas, {2, 1, 0} and {0, 2, 1} are categorized as *spread*.

3 Evaluation and Results

We conducted our experiments on the VSC-5 using a typical HPC workload of eight MPI applications: LAMMPS, CG from NAS Parallel Benchmarks, GROMACS, FFT, and four ECP Proxy applications, all compiled with OpenMPI 4.1.3. In the first scenario, we measure the impact of the mappings

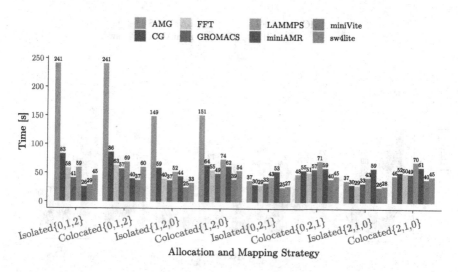

Fig. 3. The impact of mapping and co-allocation on performance, applications run with 8 × 16 processes, either in isolation or co-allocation with four mappings.

on the application performance when run either in isolation or co-allocation. Figure 3 shows the duration of each application running with 8 nodes and 16 processes per node in either co-allocation or isolation mode using all four different mappings. In co-allocated runs, all eight applications run concurrently and share a different part of the nodes, similar to Fig. 2. In isolated runs, applications run exclusively on compute nodes while using the same mapping as with co-allocation. We notice that *spread* mappings improve the performance of most applications in this set. However, there is no mapping that benefits every application. We also notice that the negative impact of co-allocation on applications with *compact* mappings is lower than that of *spread*. This is because with *spread* mapping more resources are shared, which can increase resource contention. Finally, *spread* mappings, show better performance, outweighing the negative effect of co-allocation in this application set. In the second scenario, we focus on the makespan and the sum of job durations. We compare our mapping methods with co-allocation against the common allocation and mapping policy of Slurm on VSC-5, which performs an exclusive allocation with round-robin mapping, denoted as `exclusive.RR`. When applying the `exclusive.RR` strategy, one node is exclusively allotted to each application, where it runs with 128 cores with a round-robin mapping. We show these results in Fig. 4, where we observe that our mapping strategies outperform the `exclusive.RR` for most applications. Mappings {2, 1, 0} and {0, 2, 1} show the best performance in terms of makespan. Strategy `colocated{2,1,0}` offers an improvement of 2.4× and 1.4× over `exclusive.RR` in terms of makespan and the sum of job durations, respectively.

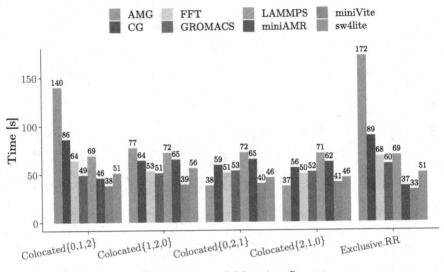

Allocation and Mapping Strategy

Fig. 4. Comparison between our mapping strategies with co-allocation against `exclusive.RR` where each application runs in one node exclusively.

4   Conclusion

We have explored the effects and benefits of different process-to-core mappings coupled with co-allocation. We have devised application-oblivious and topology-aware process-to-core mapping strategies using different core enumerations. Our preliminary results show that co-allocation coupled with *spread* mappings can improve both individual job performance and makespan for workloads consisting of eight HPC applications compared to the exclusive allocation. We plan to implement more dynamic mappings using additional HPC applications and scenarios with diverse numbers of processes, and perform experiments on additional HPC systems with different architectures.

Acknowledgements. This work was partially supported by the Austrian Science Fund (FWF): project P 31763-N31 and project P 33884-N.

References

1. de Blanche, A., Lundqvist, T.: Terrible twins: a simple scheme to avoid bad co-schedules. In: Proceedings of the 1st COSH Workshop, pp. 25–30 (2016)
2. Breslow, A.D., et al.: The case for colocation of high performance computing workloads. Concurr. Comput.: Pract. Exper. 232–251 (2016)
3. Frank, A., Süß, T., Brinkmann, A.: Effects and benefits of node sharing strategies in HPC batch systems. In: IEEE IPDPS, pp. 43–53 (2019)
4. von Kirchbach, K., Lehr, M., Hunold, S., Schulz, C., Träff, J.L.: Efficient process-to-node mapping algorithms for stencil computations. In: CLUSTER (2020)
5. Vardas, I., Hunold, S., Ajanohoun, J.I., Träff, J.L.: mpisee: MPI profiling for communication and communicator structure. In: IEEE IPDPSW, pp. 520–529 (2022)

A Polynomial-Time Algorithm for Detecting Potentially Unbounded Places in a Petri Net-Based Concurrent System

Marcin Wojnakowski[(✉)] [iD], Remigiusz Wiśniewski [iD], and Mateusz Popławski [iD]

Institute of Control and Computation Engineering, University of Zielona Góra,
65-516, Zielona Góra, Poland
m.wojnakowski@issi.uz.zgora.pl

Abstract. This paper deals with the preliminary verification of the Petri net-based concurrent system. In particular, a novel algorithm aimed at the identification of the potentially unbounded places in a system is proposed. The idea is based on the structural analysis of the system, and it involves the linear algebra technique. Contrary to the most popular techniques, which are exponential in the general case, the proposed algorithm is bounded by a polynomial with the number of places and transitions of a Petri net. The efficiency and effectiveness of the presented solution were examined through the experimental setup performed on 247 test cases (benchmarks). The obtained results were compared with the most popular Petri net-oriented tools, such as GreatSPN and PIPE.

Keywords: Petri net-based systems · unbounded places · analysis of Petri nets

1 Introduction and Related Work

Petri nets have become especially popular in specification of concurrent control systems [1], including manufacturing systems [2], distributed systems [3], and cyber-physical systems (CPS) [4]. Modelling such a system can be a real challenge to the designer due to its complexity and the need for adequate reflection of parallelism [4]. Petri nets seem to fit perfectly since they are parallel from their nature, and additionally offer a graphical and intuitive way to represent the dynamic of concurrent processes [5]. They are especially useful in the specification of integrated systems to be implemented within programmable devices (e.g., field programmable gate arrays, FPGAs), as well as distributed systems, such as programming language controllers, PLCs) [5]. Moreover, modelling of a Petri net-based system is strongly supported by formal verification techniques [6]. Such mathematical analysis methods permit the examination of the concurrent system at the early prototyping stage. One of the crucial properties that is usually verified is boundedness [7]. This feature assures a finite number of reachable states and prevents the consuming of the redundant resources of the system [8].

© The Author(s), under exclusive license to Springer Nature Switzerland AG 2024
D. Zeinalipour et al. (Eds.): Euro-Par 2023 Workshops, LNCS 14352, pp. 277–283, 2024.
https://doi.org/10.1007/978-3-031-48803-0_32

There exist several techniques that permit for boundedness analysis of the Petri net-based systems. The most popular are based on the structural analysis, or, state-space analysis [8]. The first one involves linear algebra, and usually is based on the computation of place invariants (also named "p-semiflows") in the system [9, 10]. Such an idea is relatively efficient and allows for obtaining the results in a reasonable time. However, it has a serious drawback related to the exponential computational complexity [3]. This means that the solution can never be found within the assumed time (we will show such cases later, cf. Sect. 3). In contrast, state-space analysis concerns the exploration of all possible (reachable) states in order to determine whether the Petri net is bounded. Unfortunately, this technique is also restricted by the so-called "state explosion problem". Briefly stated, computation of state-space for a given system is also exponential in the general case. Let us underline that complexity of the system does not only depend on places and transitions, but on the number of reachable states [11]. Concluding, Petri net-based systems, especially those that strongly utilize concurrency, may be extremely hard to analyse and verify. In such a situation, examination of the system may even fail, while existing methods and tools are not able to compute the results (due to the exponential computational complexity).

In this paper, we propose a polynomial-time algorithm that allows for detection of the potentially unbounded places in the system. Such an initial verification is especially useful at the early-stage design process to detect the possible malfunctions in the system. The technique is based on the linear algebra, and it utilizes mathematical operations performed on the incidence matrix of a Petri net. Contrary to the existing techniques, the method does not compute place invariants in a Petri net. Therefore, the verification is performed polynomially. Note that the initial idea of the proposed method was shown in other authors' works [11, 12]. Nevertheless, let us point out that previous versions have serious limitations, especially related to the obtained results and computational complexity. In contrast, the algorithm shown in this paper is a pure polynomial.

The main contributions of this work are summarized as follows:

- Proposition of a polynomial-time algorithm for the preliminary examination of the boundedness of the Petri net-based system.
- Experimental verification of the method with the set of 247 benchmarks.
- Comparison of the efficiency and effectiveness of the proposed algorithm with the other Petri net tools (GreatSPN and PIPE).

2   The Proposed Algorithm for Boundedness Verification

Let us firstly introduce definitions and notations necessary to present the proposed idea [3, 8, 11–13]. Then, we will move on to the main idea of the proposed technique.

Definition 1. *A Petri net* is a 4-tuple $N = (P, T, F, M_0)$, where $P = \{p_1, \ldots, p_n\}$ is the finite set of places, $T = \{t_1, \ldots, t_m\}$ is the finite set of transitions, $F \subseteq (P \times T) \cup (T \times P)$ is the finite set of arcs. A marking (a system state) $M : P \to \mathbb{N}$ can be considered as a distribution of tokens in the Petri net places, and M_0 is the initial marking.

Definition 2. A place $p \in P$ of a Petri net N is bounded if for every reachable marking $M : M(p) \le k$, where $k \in \mathbb{N}$. A Petri net N is *bounded* if every place $p \in P$ is bounded.

Definition 3. An *incidence matrix* $A_{|T| \times |P|} = [a_{ij}]$ of a Petri net N is a matrix of integers, given by $a_{ij} = -1$ if $(p_j, t_i) \in F$; $a_{ij} = 1$ if $(t_i, p_j) \in F$; $a_{ij} = 0$, otherwise.

Definition 4. A *place invariant (p-invariant)* is a vector $\overrightarrow{x} : P \to \mathbb{N}$ such that $A\overrightarrow{x} = \overrightarrow{0}$, where A is the incidence matrix of the Petri net N. The set of places corresponding to nonzero entries in a p-invariant $\overrightarrow{x}$ is called a *support* of a place invariant.

Definition 5. A Petri net N is *covered* by p-invariants if every place $p \in P$ belongs to at least one support of a p-invariant.

Theorem 1. A Petri net N is (structurally) bounded if it is covered by p-invariants [9].

Definition 6. A matrix A is in the *reduced row echelon form* (RREF) [13], if (1) any rows consisting entirely of zeros are grouped together at the bottom; otherwise, the first nonzero number in the row is 1 (*leading one*); (2) each column containing a leading one has zeros everywhere else; (3) in any two successive non-zero rows, the leading one in the lower row occurs farther to the right than the leading one in the higher row.

Algorithm 1 shows a simplified pseudo-code of the proposed technique oriented on the initial verification of boundedness in the Petri net-based concurrent system. In general, the presented technique includes two main stages. The first one transforms the incidence matrix into the RREF. Such a procedure involves elementary row operations (including *Gauss-Jordan* elimination). Once the reduced matrix is obtained, the algorithm searches for the unbounded places in the Petri net. This operation is executed by including into account Definitions 4–6 and Theorem 1.

Algorithm 1. Detection of potentially unbounded places in a Petri net-based system

---

Input: incidence matrix $A_{|T| \times |P|}$ of the Petri net $N = (P, T, F, M_0)$
Output: the set of possible unbounded places U
//Circular shifting input matrix by one column left:
for each column $c \in P$:
    set $B = A$;
    //Transformation of matrix B into the reduced row echelon form:
    for each row $r \in T$:
        find row $r_i \in T$ with the leftmost non-zero entry v;
        swap rows r_i and r;
        divide row r by v;
        for each row $r_j \in T - \{r\}$:
            for each column $c \in P$: $r_i = r_i - r_n \cdot B[r][p]$;
        end for
    end for
    //Searching for the unbounded places in the reduced matrix:
    for each row $r \in T$ that contains a leading one $l \in P$:
        set $u \leftarrow \emptyset$;
        for each column $c_{\geq l} \in P$:
            if $[B[r][c] = 1$ and $\nexists_{s \in R \setminus \{r\}} : B[t][c] < 0]$ **then** $u = u \cup \{c\}$;
            else $u \leftarrow \emptyset$; $c = |P|$;
        end for
        if $[u \neq \emptyset]$ **then** $U = U \cup \{u\}$;
    end for
    shift A by one column left (circularly);
end for
return U

In particular, the algorithm searches for rows that contain only positive entries, and additionally, those entries are not annulled by any other row. Existence of such values determine that places corresponding to those entries cannot form a proper p-invariant, and thus they are potentially not bounded (based on Definition 5 and Theorem 1). The above steps (transformation and examination of RREF) are executed circularly, by shifting columns in the initial matrix. Such an additional examination permits the avoiding of the influence of column order in the matrix.

Proposition 1. Algorithm 1 runs in a polynomial time.

Proof. The proposed method includes one main *for each* loop, which is executed at most $|P|$ times. The loop includes two further *for each* loops, related to the transformation of the matrix into RREF, and to its examination, respectively. The first one is executed at most $|T|$ times, and it includes two further nested *for each* loops, bounded by the number of transitions $|T|$, and number of places $|P|$. Thus, the transformation of the matrix into RREF is bounded by $O(|T|^2|P|)$. Further searching for the unbounded places includes two nested *for loops*, while the first is executed at most $|T|$, and the second $|P|$ times. However, the second loop additionally contains a condition that examines all the remaining rows in the matrix ($\nexists_{s \in R \setminus \{r\}}$), thus the complexity of this part is bounded by $O(|T|^2|P|)$. To summarize, the computational complexity of the whole method is bounded by $O(|T|^2|P|^2)$, hence Algorithm 1 runs in a polynomial time.

3   Experimental Results

The efficiency (runtime) and effectiveness (correctness of results) of the proposed algorithm were verified experimentally. The presented algorithm was implemented physically (C++ code) and included within the authors' system Hippo. The set of benchmarks includes 247 Petri net-based systems, their detailed descriptions are available at: http://www.hippo.uz.zgora.pl. The results were compared with the two most popular tools aimed at the modelling and analysis of Petri net-based systems. The first one, *PIPE* (Platform Independent Petri net Editor 2), is an intuitive tool used by, for example, mechanical engineers [2, 11, 12]. The second tool, *GreatSPN*, is constantly being developed and widely cited in the Petri net world [14]. The experiments for all tools (including our method) were performed on the same computational server (Intel Xeon @2.2 GHz, 128 GB memory). The interruption (break) time was set to one hour.

Table 1 shows the results for the representative tests (full results are available online: https://hippo-cps.issi.uz.zgora.pl/download/europar2023_results.xlsx). The subsequent columns of the table include the name of the benchmark, results gained by a particular method, and its runtime. Value "TRUE" means that potentially unbounded places are detected, while "FALSE" indicates that no unbounded places are found. The experiments were conducted as follows. Firstly, the runtime of the proposed algorithm was performed. The method returns results for all tested 247 cases. It should be underlined that even for highly-complex systems (*oil_separator_cover_s_net*, *inv_exp_4_layers* or *crossroadSM_FPGA*) the algorithm was able to find the solution. This confirms the theoretical assumptions presented in Proposition 1. In contrast, *PIPE* was not able to complete the tasks within the assumed time. In particular, the tool could not finish the computations for 25 benchmarks (above 10% of all tested cases) within one hour. Let us also underline that the tool may compute incorrect results. For 33 cases, PIPE produced wrong results (that differ from GreatSPN and the proposed method, additionally the referential algorithm [10] was used to confirm that results obtained by PIPE are inaccurate). Finally, comparison with GreatSPN was performed. Such a tool was able to obtain results for 244 (98.79%) benchmarks. This is a very high value; however, it should be noted that GreatSPN was not able to compute results for three cases. One of them is presented in Table 1 - *inv_exp_4_layers* (200 places and 4 transitions). In contrast, the proposed algorithm obtained the result in 11.407 ms.

Table 1. Sample of experimental results (comparison of the method with PIPE and GreatSPN)

Concurrent system (Petri net)	Proposed method		PIPE		GreatSPN	
	Result	Time [ms]	Result	Time [ms]	Result	Time [ms]
oil_separator_cover_s_net ($|P| = 29, |T| = 25$)	FALSE	8.877	timeout (>1 h)		FALSE	191.028
inv_exp_4_layers ($|P| = 200, |T| = 4$)	TRUE	11.407	timeout (>1 h)		timeout (>1 h)	
transfer ($|P| = 7, |T| = 5$)	TRUE	10.508	TRUE	0.140	TRUE	159.601
exOR ($|P| = 10, |T| = 7$)	TRUE	8.849	TRUE	90.721	TRUE	203.298
crossroadSM_FPGA ($|P| = 32, |T| = 12$)	FALSE	10.102	timeout (>1 h)		FALSE	192.229

4 Conclusions

A novel algorithm dedicated to the detection of potentially unbounded places in a Petri net-based concurrent system is proposed in the paper. The idea is mainly aimed at practitioners, and facilitates the indication of errors and mistakes during the early prototyping and analysis process. Contrary to the existing solutions, the proposed method is bounded by $O(|T|^2|P|^2)$ by the number of places and transitions of a Petri net. The experimental results confirm extremely high efficiency and effectiveness of the presented technique. The method was successfully compared with the most popular tools oriented toward the Petri net-based concurrent systems, such as PIPE and GreatSPN. The obtained results show that the proposed algorithm correctly computed results for all tested cases, while PIPE and GreatSPN were not able to finalize all required tasks.

Beside the advantages presented above, it should be noted that the proposed method is aimed at the initial verification of the system. The obtained result indicates *potentially* unbounded places, thus the designer ought to perform additional verification/validation. Such a limitation is the main motivation for future research. Moreover, it is planned to include liveness analysis of the system. Initial experiments show that the proposed method can be useful in detection of deadlocks in Petri net-based systems.

Acknowledgements. This work is supported by the National Science Centre, Poland, under Grant number 2019/35/B/ST6/01683.

References

1. Girault, C., Valk, R.: Petri Nets for Systems Engineering: A Guide to Modeling, Verification, and Applications. Springer, Heidelberg (2003). https://doi.org/10.1007/978-3-662-05324-9
2. Patalas-Maliszewska, J., Posdzich, M., Skrzypek, K.: Modelling information for the burnishing process in a cyber-physical production system. Int. J. Appl. Math. Comput. Sci. (AMCS) **32**, 345–354 (2022). https://doi.org/10.34768/amcs-2022-0025

3. Wojnakowski, M., Wiśniewski, R., Bazydło, G., Popławski, M.: Analysis of safeness in a Petri net-based specification of the control part of cyber-physical systems. Appl. Math. Comput. Sci. (AMCS) **31**, 647–657 (2021). https://doi.org/10.34768/amcs-2021-0045

4. Lee, E.A., Seshia, S.A.: Introduction to Embedded Systems: A Cyber-Physical Systems Approach. The MIT Press, Cambridge (2016)

5. Wiśniewski, R., Wojnakowski, M., Li, Z.: Design and verification of Petri-net-based cyber-physical systems oriented toward implementation in field-programmable gate arrays—a case study example. Energies **16**, 67 (2023). https://doi.org/10.3390/en16010067

6. Diaz, M.: Applying Petri net based models in the design of systems. In: Voss, K., Genrich, H.J., Rozenberg, G. (eds.) Concurrency and Nets, pp. 23–67. Springer, Heidelberg (1987). https://doi.org/10.1007/978-3-642-72822-8_7

7. Murata, T.: Petri nets: properties, analysis and applications. Proc. IEEE **77**, 541–580 (1989). https://doi.org/10.1109/5.24143

8. Wojnakowski, M., Wiśniewski, R.: Verification of the boundedness property in a Petri net-based specification of the control part of cyber-physical systems. In: Camarinha-Matos, L.M., Ferreira, P., Brito, G. (eds.) DoCEIS 2021. IAICT, vol. 626, pp. 83–91. Springer, Cham (2021). https://doi.org/10.1007/978-3-030-78288-7_8

9. Reisig, W.: Nets consisting of places and transistions. In: Reisig, W. (ed.) Petri Nets. EATCS Monographs on Theoretical Computer Science, vol. 4, pp. 62–76. Springer, Heidelberg (1985). https://doi.org/10.1007/978-3-642-69968-9_6

10. Martínez, J., Silva, M.: A simple and fast algorithm to obtain all invariants of a generalised Petri net. In: Girault, C., Reisig, W. (eds.) Application and Theory of Petri Nets. Informatik-Fachberichte, vol. 52, pp. 301–310. Springer, Heidelberg (1982). https://doi.org/10.1007/978-3-642-68353-4_47

11. Patalas-Maliszewska, J., Wiśniewski, R., Topczak, M., Wojnakowski, M.: Modelling of the effectiveness of integrating additive manufacturing technologies into Petri net-based manufacturing systems. In: 2022 IEEE International Conference on Fuzzy Systems, pp. 1–9 (2022)

12. Wiśniewski, R., Patalas-Maliszewska, J., Wojnakowski, M., Topczak, M.: Interpreted Petri nets in modelling and analysis of physical resilient manufacturing systems. In: 2022 IEEE International Conference on Systems, Man, and Cybernetics (SMC), pp. 1096–1102 (2022)

13. Yuster, A.T., Yuster, T.: The reduced row echelon form of a matrix is unique: a simple proof. Math. Mag. (1984)

14. Amparore, E.G., Balbo, G., Beccuti, M., Donatelli, S., Franceschinis, G.: 30 years of Great-SPN. In: Fiondella, L., Puliafito, A. (eds.) Principles of Performance and Reliability Modeling and Evaluation. SSRE, pp. 227–254. Springer, Cham (2016). https://doi.org/10.1007/978-3-319-30599-8_9

Data Assimilation with Ocean Models: A Case Study of Reduced Precision and Machine Learning in the Gulf of Mexico

Daniel Voss[1]([✉]), Gary Tyson[1], Olmo Zavala-Romero[1], Alexandra Bozec[1], and Ashwanth Srinivasan[2]

[1] Florida State University, Tallahassee, FL 32304, USA
{dvoss,gtyson,osz09,abozec}@fsu.edu
[2] Tendral, LLC, Key Biscayne, FL 33149, USA
a.srinivasan@tendral.com

Abstract. The deployment of increasingly higher resolution environmental observation systems along with higher resolution geophysical models has caused operational data assimilation systems to explore techniques to increase computational performance while maintaining numerical accuracy. Recent research efforts have explored implementing reduced or mixed-precision in geophysical circulation models and data assimilation schemes to validate their numerical accuracy versus full-precision models, or using Machine Learning techniques to enhance and speed up model simulations and data assimilation. In this paper, we combine the two techniques by examining the effects of coupling a modified, reduced-precision data assimilation system, the Tendral Statistical Interpolation System (T-SIS) version 1.0, with a Machine Learning model using the HYbrid Coordinate Ocean Model (HYCOM) outputs for a Gulf of Mexico experiment. A Unet type Convolutional Neural Network (CNN) was trained with two years, 2009–2010, of T-SIS reduced-precision assimilation runs. It was tested on two different years, 2002 and 2006, with unique ocean circulation properties. For sea-surface height, the ocean modeling variable, an optimal, reduced-precision trained CNN was capable of predicting the full-precision 2002 and 2006 data assimilation increment with an analysis root mean square error (RMSE) reduction of the same order versus the full-precision trained CNN version.

Keywords: reduced precision · machine learning · ocean modeling · high-performance computing · data assimilation · environmental big data

1 Introduction

Assimilation of observational data into geophysical models greatly enhances their forecast accuracy [1,6]. Sophisticated data assimilation (DA) techniques are computationally more expensive than the models they are coupled with, often by one

© The Author(s), under exclusive license to Springer Nature Switzerland AG 2024
D. Zeinalipour et al. (Eds.): Euro-Par 2023 Workshops, LNCS 14352, pp. 284–289, 2024.
https://doi.org/10.1007/978-3-031-48803-0_33

or two orders of magnitude [8, 10, 12]. The amount and diversity of high resolution environmental data observations are growing along with the development of higher-resolution geophysical models. Because operational ocean forecast models run on supercomputers with a finite time to release the forecasts, methods to reduce the time and increase the performance are vital. Since we have reached the limit of performance gains provided by Moore's law, new optimizations and software approaches are required to continue the gain in performance. Some techniques are utilizing specialized vector units, GPGPUs, TPUs, and Machine Learning (ML) methods instead of relying on chip frequency speed increases. Research from Voss et al. produced comparable results to full-precision DA experiments using performance-targeted reduced-precision [13]. The challenge is both developing and validating these new techniques to assimilate data into geophysical models with greater performance and reduced computational cost.

Recent research efforts have focused on developing data-driven models with ML that use geophysical model simulations and observations as their training datasets [7, 9, 11, 14]. New methods and techniques from ML are being applied in the geophysical modeling and assimilation domain. These data-driven models, once they are trained, can be orders of magnitude more computationally efficient than classic, large-scale numerical models and might better represent the underlying physical processes when mathematical equations are insufficient in modeling these dynamic processes [2, 5]. ML struggles when there are sparse and uncertain data. Brajard et al. [3] integrated DA with ML using a two-step process of training a neural network with the analysis to predict the model error.

In this paper, we studied the effects of combining the two techniques of reduced-precision DA with ML in a parallel, distributed, HYbrid Coordinate Ocean Model (HYCOM), for multi-year Gulf of Mexico hindcast experiments. The outputs of the reduced-precision DA experiments were then coupled with a ML model for training and then tested on a different time-series dataset with unique ocean circulation properties. With the two techniques, there was considerable opportunity to increase the performance for DA. We evaluated the error and estimated the performance speedup for both the reduced-precision DA model runs and the ML training and prediction versus the full-precision runs.

2 Methodology

The rpe Fortran library from Dawson and Düben was used with the DA software, the Tendral Statistical Interpolation System (T-SIS) version 1.0, to simulate reduced-precision variables [4]. Floating point variables are replaced with a special Fortran type, the rpe_var, which can define the number of bits used in calculations. The emulator rounds to zero or infinity if the number is above or below the specified bit range.

An encoder-decoder Convolutional Neural Network (CNN) model, based on the Unet architecture, was used to assimilate sea-surface height (SSH) observations in the Gulf of Mexico. Unet is a deep learning architecture with a U-shape that consists of a contracting and an expansive path. Previous experiments with different grid sizes in the Gulf of Mexico domain showed larger grids improved the predictability of the CNN and the percent of ocean coverage in the training showed no effect [15].

Table 1. The performance and error of the reduced-precision experiment runs and ML model experiments with their best training loss.

Reduced-Precision Experiments: T-SIS & HYCOM Model Runs			Machine Learning Experiments			
Name	Restart Days	Mean RMSE (1×10^{-4}) m	Epoch	MSE Training Loss (1×10^{-4})	Mean RMSE Predict (1×10^{-4}) m	Mean Time Predict 1 day (1×10^{-2}) s
32-bit reference run	0	0	44	3.0	47 ± 130	6.6 ± 9.3
28-bit run	14	7 ± 4	76	2.0	39 ± 77	6.1 ± 26.7
24-bit run	14	7 ± 4	63	2.2	43 ± 91	6.5 ± 3.7
20-bit run	14	8 ± 3	49	1.9	42 ± 108	6.8 ± 9.6
16-bit run	14	15 ± 4	57	1.7	43 ± 105	6.0 ±28.4
16-bit run	7	13 ± 4	59	2.5	67 ± 100	6.7 ± 11.5
16-bit run	0	175 ± 78	54	1.8	38 ± 86	6.1 ± 28.9

2.1 Experimental Setup

The Gulf of Mexico was chosen as the model domain because of its complex ocean dynamics and importance to the region for extreme-weather and natural hazards forecasting, fisheries management, and offshore oil and gas. The dynamic nature makes the Gulf of Mexico a compelling environment to test assimilation and prediction schemes. Seven simulations were run (Table 1) to create different training sets to test 32-bit (full-precision) versus 28-bit, 24-bit, 20-bit, and 16-bit reduced-precision DA with ML. The default forecast time period tested for the reduced-precision simulations was 14 days (simulations were restarted with 32-bit restart files after 14 days).

Machine Learning Setup. The first 574 days (80%) were selected for training, from the beginning of January, 2009, through the end of July, 2010. The following 73 days were used for validation and the last 73 days were used for initial testing of the model. The years 2002 and 2006 were chosen to test how well the ML model will generalize to different ocean circulation characteristics in the Gulf of Mexico versus 2009 and 2010.

Targeted Reduced-Precision Setup. The T-SISv1.0 Fortran source code was modified with rpe to evaluate the impact of reduced-precision calculations on DA for a multi-year experiment. Our previous research evaluated identifying the most computationally expensive, time-consuming portion of the software and using targeted reduced-precision [13]. The research showed a noticeable reduction in the RMSE of using targeted reduced-precision, while focusing on the portion of the code with the highest computational impact on performance.

3   Error Evaluation and Results

3.1   Reduced-Precision DA Experimental Results

The assimilated SSH increment file (in meters) from the reduced-precision run was compared to the assimilated SSH from the full-precision run. The RMSE was calculated (the square root of the mean of the squared errors). An RMSE zero value is a perfect fit and the closer the RMSE is to zero indicates the experimental run results are very close to the reference run. The mean RMSE results of these experiments for the 2002 and 2006 model runs are listed in the left side of Table 1. The 28-bit, 24-bit, and 20-bit runs for 2002 and 2006 are nearly identical with a mean RMSE (m) of 7×10^{-4}, 7×10^{-4}, and 8×10^{-4}, respectively, compared to the 32-bit reference run.

3.2   Results of Deep Learning Using CNN

The CNN training was evaluated with different number of images from the 2009 - 2010 T-SIS/HYCOM ocean modeling runs to assess the overall fit of the model. The times series with the best fit (minimum loss function and lowest prediction error) was trained with 574 days from the beginning of January, 2009, through the end of July, 2010. The results of the 2D-Unet CNN training and prediction runs are summarized in Table 1. The mean RMSE for the reduced-precision experiments from 28-bit to 16-bit with 14 day restarts are within the standard deviation of each other so we will concentrate our analysis on the lowest tested reduced-precision experiment, 16-bit with 14 day restart. Figure 1 is a daily plot of the RMSE of the 2002 and 2006 ML prediction for the 32-bit training data experiment versus the 16-bit, 14 day restart training data experiment. The mean RMSE (m) for the 32-bit experiment was $(47\pm130)\times10^{-4}$ and $(43\pm105)\times10^{-4}$ for the 16-bit experiment. The trends in the data with spikes in increased error prediction are similar, with outliers for both experiments.

3.3   Performance Analysis

T-SIS and HYCOM. The T-SIS and HYCOM model 32-bit reference run experiment ran for an average total run-time of 2.46 min/day using 92 cores on 3 cluster nodes on HPC cluster. The maximum number of cluster nodes (randomly assigned based on scheduling availability) for a 92-core run was 12 nodes with an average of 2.55 min/day. Both T-SIS and HYCOM utilize MPI for inter- and intra-node communication. Increasing the inter-node communication has minimal impact on the run-time performance. Although the reduced-precision experiments cannot be used for timing due to the overhead of the rpe library, for reference, the average run-time per day was 3.59 min, 46% longer than the 32-bit reference run.

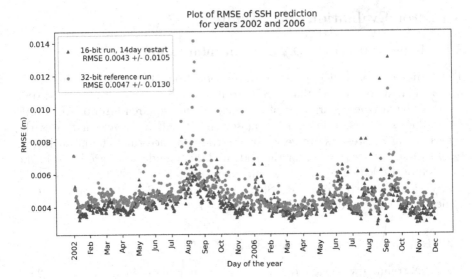

Fig. 1. RMSE plot of the 2002 and 2006 ML prediction using the 32-bit training data versus the 16-bit, 14 day restart training data.

Machine Learning. For testing the model predicting 2002 and 2006, the average total run-time was 67 min, an average of 5.5 s/day. Column 7 in Table 1 lists the mean time in seconds for 1 day of SSH prediction, an average of 6.4×10^{-2} seconds across the experiments. This timing is specific to the model predict function to separately account for its performance timing.

4 Conclusions and Discussion

The results of the reduced-precision multi-year simulations with an RMSE of a fraction of a centimeter ($(15 \pm 4) \times 10^{-4}$ (m) for the 16-bit 14 day restart) support the theory that assimilating sparse, noisy observational data may not require full-precision arithmetic. Further testing and implementing coupled parallel models with DA code that can take advantage of specialized architectures such as TPUs and GPUs or newer generation CPUs with support for bfloat16, provides the opportunity for a minimum of double the speed up of the functions which can fully utilize reduced-precision. Native bfloat16 instruction sets double the compute throughput versus float32 and memory bandwidth can also be twice as fast with half the memory footprint of a bfloat16 number.

Our experimental results show both DA and ML can produce comparable results to full-precision with reduced-precision computation and training datasets. For DA and ML, the RMSE reduction is of the same order versus the full-precision reference runs and training. The reduced-precision experimental results support future research for exploring and testing reduced-precision in the ML algorithm to increase the performance.

Acknowledgment. This research was supported in part by the Office of Naval Research under grant N00014-20-1-2023 (MURI ML-SCOPE).

References

1. Bauer, P., et al.: A digital twin of earth for the green transition. Nat. Clim. Chang. **11**(2), 80–83 (2021)
2. Boukabara, S.A., et al.: Outlook for exploiting artificial intelligence in the earth and environmental sciences. Bull. Am. Meteor. Soc. **102**(5), E1016–E1032 (2021)
3. Brajard, J., et al.: Combining data assimilation and machine learning to emulate a dynamical model from sparse and noisy observations: A case study with the Lorenz 96 model. J. Comput. Sci. **44**, 101171 (2020)
4. Dawson, A., Düben, P.D.: RPE v5: an emulator for reduced floating-point precision in large numerical simulations. Geoscientific Model Dev. **10**(6), 2221–2230 (2017)
5. Dueben, P.D., Bauer, P.: Challenges and design choices for global weather and climate models based on machine learning. Geoscientific Model Dev. **11**(10), 3999–4009 (2018)
6. Gettelman, A., et al.: The future of earth system prediction: advances in model-data fusion. Sci. Adv. **8**(14), eabn3488 (2022)
7. Gottwald, G.A., Reich, S.: Supervised learning from noisy observations: combining machine-learning techniques with data assimilation. Physica D **423**, 132911 (2021)
8. Isaksen, L.: Data assimilation on future computer architectures. In: ECMWF Seminar on Data Assimilation for Atmosphere and Ocean, pp. 301–322. ECMWF (2011)
9. Lee, S., et al.: Air quality forecasts improved by combining data assimilation and machine learning with satellite AOD. Geophys. Res. Lett. **49**(1) (2022)
10. Menemenlis, D., et al.: NASA supercomputer improves prospects for ocean climate research. Eos Trans. Am. Geophys. Union **89**(9) (2005)
11. Schneider, T., et al.: Earth system modeling 2.0: a blueprint for models that learn from observations and targeted high-resolution simulations. Geophys. Res. Lett. **44**(24), 12396–12417 (2017)
12. Smedstad, O.M., O'Brien, J.J.: Variational data assimilation and parameter estimation in an equatorial Pacific ocean model. Prog. Oceanogr. **26**(2), 179–241 (1991)
13. Voss, D. et al.: Evaluation of reduced-precision computation on the tendral statistical interpolation system (T-SIS) for ocean modeling. In: World Congress in Computer Science, Computer Engineering, & Applied Computing (CSCE). Springer, Cham (2022)
14. Wikner, A., et al.: Using data assimilation to train a hybrid forecast system that combines machine-learning and knowledge-based components. Chaos (Woodbury, N.Y.) **31**(5), 53114–053114 (2021)
15. Zavala-Romero, O., et al.: Data assimilation by convolutional neural networks on ocean circulation models. Ocean Sciences Meeting (2022)

Massively Parallel EEG Algorithms for Pre-exascale Architectures

Zeyu Wang$^{(\boxtimes)}$ ⓘD and Zoltan Juhasz ⓘD

University of Pannonia, Veszprem, Hungary
{zeyu.wang,juhasz.zoltan}@mik.uni-pannon.hu

Abstract. High-density EEG is a non-invasive measurement method with millisecond temporal resolution that allows us to monitor how the human brain operates under different conditions. The large amount of data combined with complex algorithms results in unmanageable execution times. Large-scale GPU parallelism provides the means to drastically reduce the execution time of EEG analysis and bring the execution of large cohort studies (over thousand subjects) within reach. This paper describes our effort to implement various EEG algorithms for multi-GPU pre-exascale supercomputers. Several challenges arise during this work, such as the high cost of data movement and synchronisation compared to computation. A performance-oriented end-to-end design approach is chosen to develop highly-scalable, GPU-only implementations of full processing pipelines and modules. Work related to the parallel design of the family of Empirical Mode Decomposition algorithms is described in detail with preliminary performance results of single-GPU implementations. The research will continue with multi-GPU algorithm design and implementation aiming to achieve scalability up to thousands of GPU cards.

Keywords: EEG · Pre-exascale computing · GPU

1 Introduction

Bioelectrical imaging, such as Electroencephalography (EEG) has superior temporal resolution when compared to traditional brain imaging modalities (CT, MRI, PET) enabling us to track changes in brain activity with millisecond accuracy. Consequently, EEG is the method of choice in epilepsy diagnosis, sleep studies and cognitive task execution analysis. Unfortunately, state-of-the-art EEG signal processing is a highly compute and data-intensive task. The combination of long recording times, large number of electrodes (64, 128 or 256), high sampling rates (1 kHz and higher) and sophisticated processing methods can easily lead to unmanageably large execution times when used for large subject cohorts.

The European Union have been executing an ambitious programme under the coordination of EuroHPC Joint Undertaking[1] to deploy several petascale and pre-exascale

---

[1] https://eurohpc-ju.europa.eu/.

D. Zeinalipour et al. (Eds.): Euro-Par 2023 Workshops, LNCS 14352, pp. 290–295, 2024.
https://doi.org/10.1007/978-3-031-48803-0_34

supercomputing facilities within the EU[2]. The bulk of the computing power of these systems is provided by GPU accelerators using computing cores in the order of millions. These supercomputers would be ideal devices to speed up long-running EEG data processing and analysis jobs. However, developing algorithms that run efficiently on systems of this size is a great challenge as (*i*) most of our existing algorithms were designed with moderate-level parallelism in mind and (*ii*) in modern supercomputers, not computation but data movement cost dominates execution time.

2 Problem Statement

Traditionally, parallel EEG algorithm research focused on the design and efficient implementation of individual algorithms. While this is very important, it only provides a partial solution. To minimise data movement, application-level, end-to-end performance-oriented design is required [1].

Fortunately, EEG data processing is well suited to this type of optimisation; analysis pipelines contain multiple algorithms and EEG datasets exhibit a high degree of parallelism. An experiment may contain one or more groups, groups include multiple subjects, subject recordings are partitioned into trials/segments, which in turn contain multiple channels and samples, and at the lowest level, many operations can be executed with fine-grain instruction-level parallelism (e.g. FFT).

Our research is focusing on how this data hierarchy and the potential billion-degree parallelism can be exploited for fast and scalable implementations on GPU-accelerated supercomputers. Our work will cover a variety of algorithms used in pre-processing steps (filtering, baseline removal, artefact detection and removal, bad channel interpolation), frequency domain analysis (power spectral density calculation, time-frequency analysis methods), decomposition methods (Independent Component Analysis /ICA/ [2], Empirical Mode Decomposition /EMD/ [3]), cortical imaging, source localization and brain connectivity calculation and analysis.

Parallel implementations for EEG signal and data processing algorithms are scarce. Independent Component Analysis (FastICA [4] and Infomax ICA [5]) received most of the attention resulting in various CPU and GPU implementations [6, 7]. GPU-accelerated versions of various EMD-based algorithms have also been reported [8, 9]. However, there is still a lot of room for optimization in these existing parallel implementations, and especially at the full application (processing pipeline) level. The known implementations are not suitable for multi-GPU supercomputers, nor do they provide a parallel solution for the EEG processing pipeline.

This paper describes the results of one section of our research, that is the design and performance optimisation of efficient single-GPU algorithms for the family of Empirical Mode Decomposition algorithms.

---

[2] LUMI: 375 petaFLOPS , Leonardo: 249 petaFLOPS, Meluxina: 10 petaFLOPS, Vega: 6.9 peta-FLOPS, Karolina: 9.13 petaFLOPS, Discoverer: 4.5 petaFLOPS and Deucalion: 7.22 petaFLOPS.

2.1 Signal analysis Using Empirical Mode Decomposition

Traditionally, EEG time-frequency analysis is based on either the Short-Time Fourier Transform (STFFT) or the Continuous Wavelet Transform (CWT). Both methods assume pre-determined basis functions and assume signal stationarity. However, EEG signals – as most natural signals – are non-periodic and non-stationary, hence violate these basic assumptions.

Empirical Mode Decomposition (EMD) is an alternative, data-driven, adaptive signal decomposition algorithm [3] that can separate a signal into a finite number of so-called Intrinsic Mode Functions (IMFs). IMFs are narrow band signals that contain only one dominant oscillatory mode of the signal. The advantages of EMD over the Fourier or Wavelet transforms are that (*i*) the method can be used *without* a pre-determined set of basis functions, (*ii*) the extracted narrow band oscillatory modes (IMFs) carry *amplitude and frequency modulation* information, and (*iii*) can be used to extract *instantaneous frequency and phase* information. The EMD algorithm has a filter-bank property [10] and as a result, the signal can be easily analysed in a multi-resolution fashion.

The EMD algorithm automatically extracts the intrinsic mode functions from the signal starting with the highest frequency components and progressing to the lower

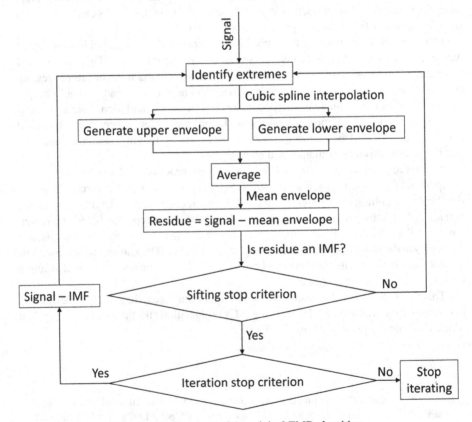

Fig. 1. The flowchart of the original EMD algorithm

frequencies. First the local minima and maxima of the signal are located, then signal envelopes are computed using the extrema by cubic spline interpolation. Then, the mean envelope is extracted from the signal to create a new signal, and the process continues until no oscillation can be detected. The exact steps of the algorithm are shown in Fig. 1.

Since the original EMD algorithm suffers from the *mode mixing* phenomenon [11], several noise-assisted – ensemble – variants were developed: Ensemble EMD (EEMD) [11], Complete EEMD (CEEMD) and Improved Complete EEMD with Additive Noise (CEEMDAN) [12]. Multivariate EMD (MEMD) [13] and Noise Assisted MEMD (NA-MEMD) [14] were proposed to solve the *mode alignment* problem arising in the analysis of multi-channel signals.

3 Parallel EMD Algorithms

The fundamental steps of any EMD algorithm variant are the (1) extrema detection, (2) cubic spline interpolation for envelope generation, (3) mean envelope calculation and subtraction, and (4) convergence checks. The main challenge here is that the algorithm is iterative, and steps 1 and 3 have very low arithmetic intensity, while step 2 requires the solution of a tridiagonal system for each EEG signal channel. These steps are executed by CUDA kernels with maximum degree of parallelism.

In the extreme point detection kernel, each thread performs neighbour value comparisons for a single sample to find the local minimum and maximum, and produces a vector of boolean flags indicating the extrema locations. To avoid excessive data movements, each CUDA warp stores additional boundary values and warp shuffle functions are used to access neighbour values directly with a 1–2 clock cycle overhead. Finally, the generated position indexes are compacted using a parallel prefix sum operation.

We use the NVIDIA cuSPARSE library tridiagonal solver in the cubic spline interpolation step. Fortunately, the library contains a parallel cyclic reduction based solver - cusparseSgtsv2 - that can be used in a multi-right-hand-side tridiagonal fashion to calculate the spline coefficients for all channels in one step. This is followed by an interpolation kernel to generate the upper and lower envelopes that evaluates the polynomial for each sample point in parallel. Signal update (subtraction of the mean envelope and new input signal generation) is performed in one fused kernel to further reduce the number of memory operations.

The noise-assisted EMD versions (EEMD, CEEMDAN) and the multivariate EMD (MEMD) require further attention. EEMD and CEEMDAN relies on hundreds of noise-added signal realisations that must be processed by the EMD algorithm, which increases the computational cost significantly. The number of direction vectors in the multivariate EMD case increases workload similarly. EEMD can be trivially parallelised executing N copies of the EMD independently. CEEMDAN, however requires the execution of EMD on the added white noise signal as well, which increases the workload in the preparation phase of the implementation.

In each iteration of the EMD algorithms, a large number of small kernels will be executed causing a kernel launch performance bottleneck. Using the CUDA Graphs functions that can capture a set of kernels in a directed acyclic graph and hide individual kernel launches in subsequent iterations, we were able to achieve a 4.5× speedup in each iteration.

4 Results

We have finished the design and implementation of the single-GPU EMD, EEMD, CEEMDAN and MEMD algorithms using several optimisation techniques, such as warp shuffle functions, memory optimisation, kernel fusion, CUDA Graphs. As an example of this work, the achieved performance of the MEMD implementation is presented in Fig. 2. Tests were performed on different GPUs, and the execution times were compared with a MATLAB implementation running on an 8-core Intel i7 CPU. As the signal length increases, the implementation achieves higher performance. At a length of 20k samples per channel, the Tesla V100 GPU achieved over 250× speedup.

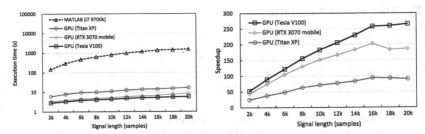

Fig. 2. The execution time and speedup of the MEDM implemented based on the proposed framework when processing signals of different lengths on different GPUs.

5 Conclusions and Future Works

This paper described the aims of our parallel EEG algorithm research and provided details of the parallel algorithm design and implementation effort for developing efficient and scalable algorithms for the family of Empirical Mode Decomposition methods. These algorithms are crucial in the time-frequency analysis of non-stationary, high-density EEG measurements and can create the basis for analyzing the dynamic properties of brain processes.

The work is part of our ongoing effort to create GPU-only EEG processing pipelines for pre-exascale systems, allowing the analysis of very large datasets (thousands of subjects) within minutes. Preliminary results of the single-GPU implementations show over 200× speedup values compared to MATLAB implementations.

In the future, we will focus on the end-to-end optimisation of the EEG pipeline and will use various state-of-the-art design and implementation techniques (e.g. latency hiding methods, mixed-precision computing and the use of Tensor core architectures, etc.) to minimise data movement and achieve maximum performance. We will also create scalable multi-GPU implementations using the NCCL and NVSHMEM NVLink-based inter-GPU communication libraries, which we plan to test and benchmark on the LEONARDO pre-exascale system.

References

1. Leiserson, C.E., et al.: There's plenty of room at the top: what will drive computer performance after Moore's law? Science (1979), 368 (2020)
2. Cardoso, J.F., Comon, P.: Independent component analysis, a survey of some algebraic methods. In: Proceedings of the IEEE International Symposium on Circuits and Systems, vol. 2, pp. 93–96 (1996)
3. Huang, N.E., et al.: The empirical mode decomposition and the Hilbert spectrum for nonlinear and non-stationary time series analysis. RSPSA **454**, 903–998 (1998)
4. Hyvärinen, A.: Fast and robust fixed-point algorithms for independent component analysis. IEEE Trans. Neural Netw. **10**, 626–634 (1999)
5. Bell, A.J., Sejnowski, T.J.: An information-maximization approach to blind separation and blind deconvolution. Neural Comput. **7**, 1129–1159 (1995)
6. Keith, D.B., Hoge, C.C., Frank, R.M., Malony, A.D.: Parallel ICA methods for EEG neuroimaging. In: 20th International Parallel and Distributed Processing Symposium, IPDPS 2006 (2006)
7. Raimondo, F., Kamienkowski, J.E., Sigman, M., Fernandez Slezak, D.: CUDAICA: GPU optimization of infomax-ICA EEG analysis. Comput. Intell. Neurosci. **2012** (2012)
8. Waskito, P., Miwa, S., Mitsukura, Y., Nakajo, H.: Parallelizing Hilbert-Huang transform on a GPU. In: Proceedings of the 2010 1st International Conference on Networking and Computing, ICNC 2010, pp. 184–190 (2010)
9. Mujahid, T., Rahman, A.U., Khan, M.M.: GPU-accelerated multivariate empirical mode decomposition for massive neural data processing. IEEE Access **5**, 8691–8701 (2017)
10. Wu, Z., Huang, N.E.: On the filtering properties of the empirical mode decomposition. Adv. Adapt. Data Anal. **2**, 397–414 (2010)
11. Wu, Z., Huang, N.E.: Ensemble empirical mode decomposition: a noise-assisted data analysis method. Adv. Data Sci. Adapt. Anal. **1**, 1–41 (2009)
12. Colominas, M.A., Schlotthauer, G., Torres, M.E.: Improved complete ensemble EMD: a suitable tool for biomedical signal processing. Biomed. Signal Process. Control **14**, 19–29 (2014)
13. Rehman, N.U., Aftab, H.: Multivariate variational mode decomposition. IEEE Trans. Signal Process. **67**, 6039–6052 (2019)
14. Zhang, Y., et al.: Noise-assisted multivariate empirical mode decomposition for multichannel EMG signals. Biomed. Eng. **16** (2017)

Transitioning to Smart Sustainable Cities Based on Cutting-Edge Technological Improvements

Andreas Andreou(✉) ⓘ and Constandinos X. Mavromoustakis ⓘ

Department of Computer Science, University of Nicosia and University of Nicosia Research Foundation, Nicosia, Cyprus
{andreou.andreas,mavromoustakis.c}@unic.ac.cy

Abstract. A smart city is a concept that has been gaining momentum in recent years as cities worldwide seek to improve their efficiency, sustainability, and quality of life for their residents. Smart cities are constructed atop smart data. Therefore, this research work focuses on the optimization of data acquisition, data sharing and data analysis. Aiming towards this evolution, the research elaborates on the advancement of smart healthcare, a novel approach for energy consumption, preparedness for a potential pandemic, innovative data encryption techniques, and vehicle-to-everything (V2X) connectivity to enable smart mobility. However, developing an intelligent ecosystem is paramount to providing citywide, reliable, high multi-Gbps peak data speeds with ultra-low latency. Hence, we finally focused our research on Unmanned Aerial Vehicles (UAV) assisted network optimization.

Keywords: Smart Cities · UAV · Healthcare · Consumption · V2X

1 Introduction

Developing smart communities is essential to creating more efficient, sustainable and environmentally friendly urban environments. The prerequisite for this transition incorporates integrating various innovative technologies and practices across different sectors, including energy, transportation, healthcare, public services etc. However, the contribution of cutting-edge technological advances will be the cornerstone for smart, sustainable cities [1].

Aiming to revolutionize the future of medical services in the upcoming smart cities, we investigate technology integration in healthcare, allowing the groundbreaking approach of smart healthcare [2]. By leveraging technology, data, and connectivity, smart healthcare is transforming how we approach healthcare, leading to improved patient outcomes, enhanced efficiency and a patient-centric approach. Throughout this research, we approach one of the fundamental pillars of smart healthcare, remote patient monitoring [3]. The objective is for wearable devices and remote monitoring systems to allow healthcare providers to monitor patients' vital signs and health parameters closely.

The research concentrates on confidentiality, integrity, and availability to ensure data exchange in smart cities, especially in healthcare. The fragmentation method achieved

D. Zeinalipour et al. (Eds.): Euro-Par 2023 Workshops, LNCS 14352, pp. 296–301, 2024.
https://doi.org/10.1007/978-3-031-48803-0_36

integrity by securely dissociating sensitive information and exchanging datasets. Confidentiality was performed by deploying polynomials and Newton-Gregory's divided difference interpolation [4]. Also, utility methods were employed to enable end-user availability [5]. In addition, innovative text encryption techniques based on fundamental mathematics were developed to improve Internet of Things (IoT) data privacy in smart cities [6].

Besides the integration of technological improvements in healthcare, we are working on integrating UAVs, commonly known as drones, into smart cities. The field has emerged as a transformative technology with enormous potential in many aspects of the urban ecosystem. UAVs offer a wide range of applications that can enhance urban environments' efficiency, safety, and sustainability [7], from infrastructure inspection and public safety to traffic management and environmental monitoring. With careful planning, regulatory frameworks, and public engagement, cities can fully embrace the potential of UAVs and unlock the benefits they bring to citizens and communities [8].

However, enabling interoperability in a smart city ecosystem is a prerequisite to achieving full network coverage, ensuring that every corner of the city is connected, and facilitating uninterrupted communication and data transmission. Therefore, we investigate the deployment of UAVs to expand the network's area [9]. By leveraging various wireless technologies and future advancements like UAV assistance, cities can overcome connectivity gaps and deliver ubiquitous internet access. Connectivity will empower residents, businesses, and public services to stay connected, access vital information, and utilize digital services seamlessly.

1.1 Motivation

The motivation to develop smart cities stems from a desire to create urban environments that are sustainable, efficient, and livable for residents. By leveraging technology, data, and innovative approaches, smart cities aim to enhance the quality of life, drive economic growth, and promote environmental sustainability. Furthermore, through improved urban efficiency, citizen empowerment, and resilient infrastructure, smart cities offer the potential to transform urban living, creating a future where cities are more connected, sustainable, and responsive to the needs of their residents.

1.2 Novelty and Contribution

The research done to date contributes to several key pillars that form the foundation for creating intelligent, connected, and sustainable urban environments. These pillars encompass various aspects, including network security, UAV integration, smart healthcare, and citywide network availability.

In the era of smart cities, where connectivity and data-driven decision-making reign supreme, achieving full network coverage is paramount. Therefore, utilizing UAVs and deploying Voronoi diagrams was innovative and promising. Notwithstanding, network security is attained using novel encryption approaches and the unique technique of partializing the dataset into fragments. In addition, novel algorithmic methods were used to promote real-time data evaluation for healthcare providers. Thus, ensuring the availability of health data involves guaranteeing uninterrupted access to Electronic Health

Records (EHRs) and real-time forecast of unpleasant situations such as heart failure, hypertension, and diabetes [10].

2 Proposed Framework

As urbanization continues to accelerate worldwide, the development of smart cities has emerged as a compelling solution to address the evolving needs and challenges of urban environments. Smart cities leverage technology, data, and innovative approaches to create more sustainable, efficient, and functional urban landscapes. This research framework explores the motivations behind the development of smart cities and the potential benefits they offer residents and communities.

2.1 Smart Healthcare

Confidentiality is paramount when it comes to health data exchange. Patients must have confidence that their sensitive information will remain private and secure. Robust security measures, such as encryption, access controls, and authentication mechanisms, must be implemented to safeguard data at rest, in transit, and during storage.

Therefore, we developed a novel cryptographic technique that uses the circulant matrix C, as presented in (1), to operate the confidential transmission of encrypted text messages. The encryption was implemented by assigning numerical values to Latin letters by modifying an archaic alphanumeric method called Gematria.

$$C = \begin{pmatrix} f_{11}(x)\,f_{12}(x)\,f_{13}(x) & \cdots & f_{1n}(x) \\ f_{12}(x)\,f_{13}(x)\,f_{14}(x) & \cdots & f_{11}(x) \\ f_{13}(x)\,f_{14}(x)\,f_{15}(x) & \cdots & f_{12}(x) \\ \ddots & \ddots & \ddots \\ f_{1n}(x)\,f_{11}(x) & \cdots & f_{1n-2}(x)\,f_{1n-1}(x) \end{pmatrix} \tag{1}$$

The assignment is applied by implementing (2),

$$\log[f(x)] = \frac{(x-1)}{9} + \log[((x-1)\,mod\,9) + 1] \tag{2}$$

where x denotes the initial assignment of the letter and $f(x)$ the assignment after the encryption.

Due to the triple nested loops, we concluded to $\mathcal{O}(n^3)$ time complexity. Thus, the algorithm does not require high CPU capacity to operate robust encryption.

2.2 Smart Mobility

One of the key drivers of smart mobility is sustainability. By promoting the use of alternative fuels, electric vehicles, and low-carbon modes of transportation, smart mobility initiatives aim to reduce emissions and combat climate change.

Based on this objective, innovative Pressure-Sensitive Panels (PSPs) were proposed to interpret the pressure exerted by the road and distribute the required energy among the wheels. Thus, torque will be operated with the appropriate energy consumption.

The research investigates the conservation form of Navier–Stoke's momentum equation given in (3). By implementing the equation, we achieve the main idea: to interpret pressure on a panel using pixels that depict how fluid flows after exerting pressure.

$$3\frac{\partial}{\partial t}(\varrho v) + 3\nabla(\varrho v \otimes v) = -3\nabla\varrho + 3\mu\nabla^2 v + \mu\nabla(\nabla v) + 3\varrho g \qquad (3)$$

where, $\frac{\partial}{\partial t}$ is the material derivative, μ denotes the dynamic viscosity, ∇v and $\nabla^2 v$ denotes the first and second tensor divergence, ∇v is the tensor gradient, and ϱ is the density. The external source $g = -\nabla\varphi$ as the external field is a conservative field.

The evaluation of the proposed methodology for energy consumption is proved in Table 1, where we compare using simulation three methods, the Active Torque, the Torque and Battery, and the proposed PSP. According to the results, the proposed methodology for torque distribution can effectively improve energy conservation and reduce energy consumption.

Table 1. Compare Energy Consumption

Strategy	Traction	Recovery	Overall
Active Torque	3752.31 kJ	756.64 kJ	3217.45 kJ
Torque and Battery	4143.14 kJ	664.21 kJ	3586.62 kJ
Smart Panel	4019.42 kJ	644.43 kJ	3231.69 kJ
Comparison	↓ 6.87%	↑ 12.42%	↓ 12.28%
	↓ 4.31%	↑ 11.35%	↓ 8.06%

2.3 Citywide Network-UAVs Integration

With citywide network coverage, intelligent cities can unlock a plethora of innovative services and technologies mentioned above. For example, it enables the deployment of autonomous vehicles, intelligent transportation systems, and mobility-as-a-service solutions, transforming how people move around urban areas. Additionally, it allows the implementation of smart grids, efficient energy management, and remote monitoring of utility infrastructure, leading to reduced energy consumption and improved sustainability.

Hence, we elaborated on integrating UAVs in the urban landscape to optimize network coverage, one of the main pillars of smart city development [11]. More precisely, the localization of areas without a network was studied and using circles; we constructed Voronoi diagrams. The centres were specified using Poisson Point Process. Each centre will be a base station or a UAV that will function as a transceiver. The flexibility of UAVs allows full network coverage, which was the research's objective.

Voronoi diagrams, $V(D_n)$ are determined by (4),

$$V(D_n) = \left\{ \begin{array}{c} x \in X : x \in e_{ij} \setminus \{d(x, S_i) = d(x, S_j)\} \leq d(x, S_n), \\ \forall n \neq (i, j), (i, j, n) \in N \end{array} \right\} \quad (4)$$

where a tuple of $(V_n)_{n \in N} \subseteq X$ and a set of sites S_n such that $\forall n \in N$, $S_n = \bigcup_{i \neq n} e_{in}$, are convex.

After implementing the appropriate iterations of the algorithm, the overlap circles representing the transceiver's coverage area, as presented in Fig. 1, cover the grey areas. The sides of the Voronoi diagram are constructed by the lines that connect their points of intersection. Simulation depicted in Fig. 2 presents the full coverage of the examine area.

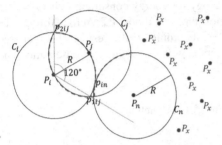

Fig. 1. Construct Voronoi Diagram　　　　　**Fig. 2.** Simulation

3　Conclusion and Future Work

Smart cities represent a transformative approach to urban development, leveraging technology and data-driven solutions to address pressing urban challenges. By integrating various components such as IoT, big data analytics, sustainable infrastructure, and citizen engagement, smart cities offer the potential for enhanced quality of life, sustainability, and economic prosperity. However, their successful implementation requires overcoming privacy, inclusivity, and collaboration challenges. As cities evolve and embrace technological advancements, the journey towards building smarter cities is well underway, paving the way for a more connected, sustainable, and resilient future.

Acknowledgement. This research work was funded by the Smart and Healthy Ageing through People Engaging in supporting Systems SHAPES project, which has received funding from the European Union's Horizon 2020 research and innovation programme under grant agreement No 857159.

References

1. Ullah, F., Al-Turjman, F.: A conceptual framework for blockchain smart contract adoption to manage real estate deals in smart cities. Neural Comput. Appl. **35**(7), 5033–5054 (2023)

2. Andreou, A., et al.: Cultivate smart and healthy ageing. In: Spinsante, S., Iadarola, G., Paglia-longa, A., Tramarin, F. (eds.) IoT Technologies for HealthCare, HealthyIoT 2022, vol. 456, pp. 136–147. Springer, Cham (2023). https://doi.org/10.1007/978-3-031-28663-6_11

3. Usmani, N.A., Ahmed, T., Faisal, M.: An IoT-based framework toward a feasible safe and smart city using drone surveillance. Smart Cities, 97–112 (2022)

4. Andreas, A., et al.: Towards an optimized security approach to IoT devices with confidential healthcare data exchange. Multimed. Tools Appl. **80**, 31435–31449 (2021)

5. Andreas, A., et al.: Robust encryption to enhance IoT confidentiality for healthcare ecosys-tems. In: 2021 IEEE 26th International Workshop on Computer Aided Modeling and Design of Communication Links and Networks (CAMAD), pp. 1–6. IEEE (2021)

6. Amrollahi, M., Hadayeghparast, S., Karimipour, H., Derakhshan, F., Srivastava, G.: Enhanc-ing network security via machine learning: opportunities and challenges. Handb. Big Data Priv., 165–189 (2020)

7. Andreou, A., Mavromoustakis, C.X., Batalla, J.M., Markakis, E.K., Mastorakis, G., Mumtaz, S.: UAV trajectory optimisation in smart cities using modified A* algorithm combined with haversine and vincenty formulas. IEEE Trans. Veh. Technol. (2023)

8. Hemmati, A., Zarei, M., Souri, A.: UAV-based internet of vehicles: a systematic literature review. Intell. Syst. Appl., 200226 (2023)

9. Andreou, A., Mavromoustakis, C.X., Batalla, J.M., Markakis, E.K., Mastorakis, G.: UAV-assisted RSUs for V2X connectivity using voronoi diagrams in 6G+ infrastructures. IEEE Trans. Intell. Transp. Syst. (2023)

10. Spargo, M., et al.: Shaping the future of digitally enabled health and care. Pharmacy **9**(1), 17 (2021)

11. Khayat, G., Mavromoustakis, C.X., Pitsillides, A., Batalla, J.M., Markakis, E.K., Andreou, A.: Enhanced redundant scheme based on weighted cluster-head selection for critical 6G infrastructures. In 2022 IEEE Globecom Workshops (GC Wkshps), pp. 1448–1453. IEEE (2022)

Algorithm Selection of MPI Collectives Considering System Utilization

Majid Salimi Beni[1]([✉]), Sascha Hunold[2], and Biagio Cosenza[1]

[1] Department of Computer Science, University of Salerno, Salerno, Italy
msalimibeni@unisa.it
[2] Faculty of Informatics, TU Wien, Vienna, Austria

Abstract. MPI collective communications play an important role in coordinating and exchanging data among parallel processes in high performance computing. Various algorithms exist for implementing MPI collectives, each of which exhibits different characteristics, such as message overhead, latency, and scalability, which can significantly impact overall system performance. Therefore, choosing a suitable algorithm for each collective operation is crucial to achieve optimal performance. In this paper, we present our experience with MPI collectives algorithm selection on a large-scale supercomputer and highlight the impact of network traffic and system workload as well as other previously-investigated parameters such as message size, communicator size, and network topology. Our analysis shows that network traffic and system workload can make the performance of MPI collectives highly variable and, accordingly, impact the algorithm selection strategy.

Keywords: High Performance Computing · MPI · Collectives · Broadcast · Algorithm Selection · Tuning

1 Introduction

MPI (Message Passing Interface) is a widely-used standard for programming parallel and high performance computing (HPC) systems that allows efficient communication among distributed processes over the network [2]. MPI collective communication operations are fundamental building blocks for developing parallel applications, and a big share of HPC applications' runtime is spent while performing collective communications [13].

In recent MPI implementations, several algorithms have been implemented for each collective operation, each of which owns distinct internal characteristics such as communication costs and scalability attributes. An efficient algorithm selection for MPI collectives is crucial in achieving optimal performance and significantly impacts the overall scalability, communication overhead, and resource utilization in a parallel application. Hence, researchers have explored different parameters that impact the algorithm selection [8,11]. Considering the network as a shared resource among jobs in supercomputers, network elements are subject to congestion, degrading performance reproducibility [12]. Collective algorithms, as the main communication primitives may also perform differently under diverse network conditions since they have distinct strategies for data transmission and message chunking. Therefore, network traffic is a key factor affecting the decision-making process for the best algorithm.

In this paper, we first analyze the behavior of different implementations of MPI_Bcast on a large-scale cluster and show the impact of network traffic on each algorithm's performance. Then, by monitoring the network, we propose a workload-aware algorithm selection method for MPI collectives that considers network conditions as well as data and communicator size. In the rest of the paper, we perform a preliminary analysis in Sect. 2. Related work is presented in Sect. 3, and Sect. 4 describes the proposed algorithm selection method. A summary of the current status and future directions are given in Sect. 5.

2 Motivation

Large-scale clusters are often utilized by many users at the same time, and several resources, including the network, are shared among them. Sharing the network with other users can degrade the communication performance of jobs and make it variable, especially in communication-intensive applications. It has been shown that collective operations may behave differently under heavy network traffic, and their performance can significantly vary from run to run [1,12].

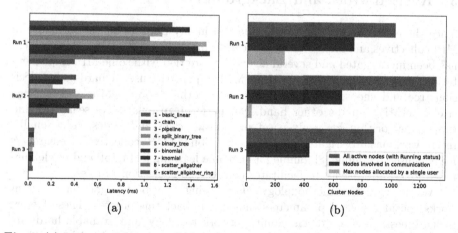

Fig. 1. (a) Latency of running all algorithms of MPI_Bcast three times with 512 processes on 16 nodes, allocated across different islands of Marconi100, with 10KB message size. (b) Cluster utilization data for the three runs extracted from SLURM's job queue.

The runtimes of the collective communications presented were obtained with the ReproMPI benchmark [7], and the collective algorithms are adopted from Open MPI 4.1. We conducted our analyses on Marconi100 compute cluster [10] at the CINECA supercomputing center, which comprises 980 nodes divided into 4 groups called islands. Each node comes with two 16 cores of IBM POWER9 AC922.

Figure 1a shows the latency of running different algorithms of MPI_Bcast on three different days. In each run, the runtime of each algorithm was measured, one after the other. Although the message size and process count are the same in this figure for the three runs, their behavior changes. First, there is high variability between runs: in run 3, algorithm 1 is 25x faster than in run 1. Second, the best algorithm is not the same for the three runs: algorithms 4, 3, and 8 are the best for the three runs, consecutively. Figure 1b presents the job scheduler's monitored data before the execution of the benchmark. We can observe that when there are users that allocated many nodes for their jobs or more nodes are allocated by single jobs (more nodes are involved in the communication), the latency of our benchmark is higher and the best algorithm changes.

From Fig. 1, it is clear that another factor is impacting the algorithm selection besides message size and the number of processes. Since the node allocation strategy has been the same for the three runs and nodes are allocated on different islands of the cluster in all runs, the only changing factor is the network condition and cluster utilization. In this paper, we quantify the network traffic between the currently allocated nodes and show which algorithms perform better under different network traffic.

3   Related Work and Background

Since the collective algorithm selection can highly improve the performance of MPI collectives and impacts communication-intensive applications, this problem has been investigated and several algorithms are tied with some MPI implementations, such as Open MPI and Intel MPI. Open MPI uses a hard-coded decision tree and chooses an algorithm based on the communicator and message size. Intel MPI, on the other hand, can perform an exhaustive search to find the best algorithm for a given set of message sizes and nodes. Additionally, recent work has investigated algorithm selection for MPI collectives. Researchers have focused on online [8], offline [3], machine learning [5,14,15], and modelling-based [6,11] approaches to facilitate the algorithm selection process.

Apart from the methodology of choosing the best algorithm, current works consider several parameters that can impact this process. These factors include message size, process count, network topology, and available hardware resources [9]. The message size determines whether a certain algorithm, such as a binomial tree or a ring-based algorithm, is more suitable for small or large messages, respectively. The process count affects the algorithm's scalability, ensuring efficient communication considering the number of processes involved. Network topology helps determine whether a hierarchical or non-blocking algorithm would be more suitable for minimizing communication overhead. Finally, considering the available hardware resources, such as specialized communication hardware or network features, can guide the selection of algorithms optimized for specific architectures.

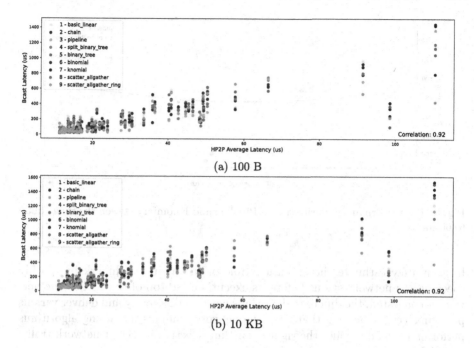

Fig. 2. The correlation between latencies of HP2P and Bcast

When running MPI jobs on supercomputers, selecting the best algorithm while ignoring the network traffic can lead to a non-optimal algorithm selection since the algorithms may perform differently whilst operating on a network with changing background traffic. Despite the above-mentioned parameters' impact on collectives algorithm selection, to the best of our knowledge, the literature does not investigate network traffic's effect.

4   Workload-Aware Algorithm Selection

In this section, we provide our preliminary results about the impact of network traffic on algorithm selection. In order to show the impact of network traffic on the performance variability of MPI collective algorithms, we use the HP2P benchmark [4] that measures the peer-to-peer latency and bandwidth between the pairs by exchanging asynchronous messages. In our experiments, and before running the main benchmark, we run HP2P for 1000 iterations with 4KB and monitor the network status.

Figure 2 shows the latency of different algorithms of Broadcast on 512 processes for two different message sizes correlated with HP2P's latency. Each set of algorithms is executed once, one after the other, and HP2P measures the latency before running each set. The figure includes 100 series of runs executed on different days and hours of the days, three runs per day. For the two sizes, the latencies of HP2P and Broadcast are highly correlated (92%), and it is possible

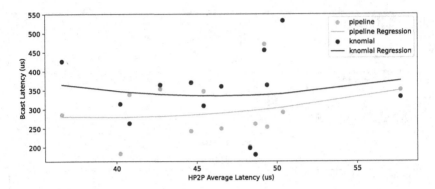

Fig. 3. The performance distribution of Pipeline and Knomial between the range of 35 to 60 μs.

to accurately estimate the execution time of the main benchmark by quickly checking the network status before its execution. On top of that, when the network is congested, the different algorithms perform differently and deliver various performances. Indicating that first, the network traffic is impacting algorithms performance, and second, the right algorithm selection in higher network traffic can highly improve the communication performance.

To highlight network traffic's impact on the algorithms, in Fig. 3, we focus on a subset of runs between 35–60 μs (average cases) of Fig. 2a. As shown for this subset, on average, Pipeline has shown a higher performance (around 15% on average) than Knomial (to which the Default algorithm is mapped). However, in cases where the HP2P average latency was found to be smaller than 35 μs, the average-best algorithm is a different one. Therefore, for each range of network traffic, different algorithms have diverse behavior, and the best algorithm may change.

5   Summary

In this work, we highlighted the impact of network traffic on the algorithm selection of MPI collectives. We proposed a workload-aware algorithm selection method for MPI collectives that monitors the network traffic and chooses the best algorithm according to the network traffic between the allocated nodes. For future work, we plan to collect data from the job scheduler as well as other microbenchmarks to better characterize the cluster's workload and network utilization. Then, combining the statistical with regression and machine learning methods to provide a more accurate algorithm selector for MPI collectives and automate the selection process.

References

1. Beni, M.S., Cosenza, B.: An analysis of performance variability on dragonfly+ topology. In: 2022 IEEE International Conference on Cluster Computing (CLUSTER), pp. 500–501. IEEE (2022)
2. Chunduri, S., Parker, S., Balaji, P., Harms, K., Kumaran, K.: Characterization of MPI usage on a production supercomputer. In: SC18: International Conference for High Performance Computing, Networking, Storage and Analysis, pp. 386–400. IEEE (2018)
3. Faraj, A., Yuan, X., Lowenthal, D.: STAR-MPI: self tuned adaptive routines for MPI collective operations. In: Proceedings of the 20th Annual International Conference on Supercomputing, pp. 199–208 (2006)
4. GitHub - cea-hpc/hp2p: Heavy Peer To Peer: a MPI based benchmark for network diagnostic. https://github.com/cea-hpc/hp2p. Accessed 25 Sept 2023
5. Hunold, S., Bhatele, A., Bosilca, G., Knees, P.: Predicting MPI collective communication performance using machine learning. In: 2020 IEEE International Conference on Cluster Computing (CLUSTER), pp. 259–269. IEEE (2020)
6. Hunold, S., Carpen-Amarie, A.: Autotuning MPI collectives using performance guidelines. In: Proceedings of the International Conference on High Performance Computing in Asia-Pacific Region, pp. 64–74 (2018)
7. Hunold, S., Carpen-Amarie, A.: Reproducible MPI benchmarking is still not as easy as you think. IEEE Trans. Parallel Distrib. Syst. **27**, 3617–3630 (2016)
8. Hunold, S., Steiner, S.: OMPICollTune: autotuning MPI collectives by incremental online learning. In: 2022 IEEE/ACM International Workshop on Performance Modeling, Benchmarking and Simulation of High Performance Computer Systems (PMBS), pp. 123–128. IEEE (2022)
9. Loch, W.J., Koslovski, G.P.: Sparbit: towards to a logarithmic-cost and data locality-aware MPI allgather algorithm. J. Grid Comput. **21**, 18 (2023)
10. Marconi100, the new accelerated system. https://www.hpc.cineca.it/hardware/marconi100. Accessed 25 Sept 2023
11. Nuriyev, E., Rico-Gallego, J.-A., Lastovetsky, A.: Model-based selection of optimal MPI broadcast algorithms for multi-core clusters. J. Parallel Distrib. Comput. **165**, 1–16 (2022)
12. Salimi Beni, M., Cosenza, B.: An analysis of long-tailed network latency distribution and background traffic on dragonfly+. In: Gainaru, A., Zhang, C., Luo, C. (eds.) Bench 2022. LNCS, vol. 13852, pp. 123–142. Springer, Cham (2023). https://doi.org/10.1007/978-3-031-31180-2_8
13. Beni, M.S., Crisci, L., Cosenza, B.: EMPI: enhanced message passing interface in modern c++. In: 2023 23rd IEEE International Symposium on Cluster, Cloud and Internet Computing (CCGrid), pp. 141–153. IEEE (2023)
14. Wilkins, M., Guo, Y., Thakur, R., Dinda, P., Hardavellas, N.: ACCLAiM: advancing the practicality of MPI collective communication autotuning using machine learning. In: 2022 IEEE International Conference on Cluster Computing (CLUSTER), pp. 161–171. IEEE (2022)
15. Wilkins, M., Guo, Y., Thakur, R., Hardavellas, N., Dinda, P., Si, M.: A fact-based approach: making machine learning collective autotuning feasible on exascale systems. In: 2021 Workshop on Exascale MPI (ExaMPI), pp. 36–45. IEEE (2021)

Service Management in Dynamic Edge Environments

Claudia Torres-Pérez[1](✉) , Estefanía Coronado[1,2] ,
Cristina Cervelló-Pastor[3] , and Muhammad Shuaib Siddiqui[1]

[1] i2CAT Foundation, Barcelona, Spain
{claudia.torres,estefania.coronado,shuaib.siddiqui}@i2cat.net
[2] High-Performance Networks and Architectures, Universidad de Castilla-La
Mancha, Albacete, Spain
estefania.coronado@uclm.es
[3] Department of Network Engineering, Universitat Politècnica de Catalunya,
Castelldefels, Barcelona, Spain
cristina.cervello@upc.edu

Abstract. Beyond 5G and 6G networks are foreseen to be highly
dynamic. These are expected to support and accommodate temporary activities and leverage continuously changing infrastructures from
extreme edge to cloud. In addition, the increasing demand for applications and data in these networks necessitates the use of geographically distributed Multi-access Edge Computing (MEC) to provide reliable services with low latency and energy consumption. Service management plays a crucial role in meeting this need. Research indicates
widespread acceptance of Reinforcement Learning (RL) in this field due
to its ability to model unforeseen scenarios. However, it is difficult for
RL to handle exhaustive changes in the requirements, constraints and
optimization objectives likely to occur in widely distributed networks.
Therefore, the main objective of this research is to design service management approaches to handle changing services and infrastructures in
dynamic distributed MEC systems, utilizing advanced RL methods such
as Distributed Deep Reinforcement Learning (DDRL) and Meta Reinforcement Learning (MRL).

Keywords: Service management · Dynamic environments · Edge
Computing

1 Introduction and Motivation

Multi-access Edge Computing (MEC) for beyond 5G and 6G networks enables
dynamic use cases and applications, necessitating flexible and scalable service
management to address them. Changes in service demands and dynamic infrastructures are crucial problems attracting dynamicity to the network. Increasing heterogeneous services, complex applications, and different user types carry
service demand changes. These users could request the same service but needing different Quality of Service (QoS) levels due to complex tasks consuming

D. Zeinalipour et al. (Eds.): Euro-Par 2023 Workshops, LNCS 14352, pp. 308–313, 2024.
https://doi.org/10.1007/978-3-031-48803-0_38

more edge server resources. On the other hand, network infrastructures become more dynamic when considering geographically distributed edge-enabled networks composed of multiple MEC systems and orchestrators. The network infrastructures turn complicated because it is necessary to consider a larger number of edge nodes, applications, administrative domains, and/or specific geographical areas. Therefore, distributed MEC systems with multiple orchestrators are utilized to handle its complexity. This approach enables localized management and control, interoperability, coordination across different domains, and efficient global load balancing. The information used by orchestrators to make informed decisions must be broad enough to avoid the need to design resource management algorithms specific to each type of application or location, and to avoid decisions made by some orchestrators being far from optimal if traffic patterns change.

However, it is still a problem to manage services, due to unpredictable services' patterns, the possibility of operators variation, connection and disconnection of nodes, changes in the range of applications' requirements, or catastrophic events. These cases lead to the need for variations in service management, resulting in increased computing time and potential non-compliance with the Service Level Agreements (SLA). Service management strategies must take into account the resources available at each node and the demands of different users to ensure robustness and availability.

Therefore, it is necessary to identify service management strategies to host and migrate services' requests, to assure SLA, optimize resource allocation and maximize revenue [7], considering providers' and services' needs to satisfy both sides. In these scenarios, there exists an increase of high-power demanding devices to support applications and training of Artificial Intelligence algorithms. Consequently, ensuring minimum energy consumption and avoiding resource fragmentation is crucial. Minimizing the number of active nodes reduces energy consumption, resulting in cost savings, increased network reliability, reduced risk of failure, and more likelihood to guarantee the high demand services hosting.

Service handling algorithms based on meta-heuristic and linear programming techniques in highly distributed scenarios are excessively time-consuming, making them impractical for managing services with a high likelihood of change. Machine Learning (ML) techniques such as Reinforcement Learning (RL) are utilized to improve service automation and network management, due to their ability to model unforeseen scenarios and decision-making policies [2,3,6]. RL variants are used iteratively in these processes to reach the optimal policy in training data, but they still face some issues with the online arrival of new requirements and constraints. They need to collect new samples through environment interaction and retrain to produce appropriate actions. Therefore, advanced RL-based algorithms have arisen to overcome the drawbacks. For instance, Distributed Deep Reinforcement Learning (DDRL) presents generalization capabilities through learning in different environments, with parameter variability in each of them [1,9]. In addition, RL algorithms are sensitive to hyperparameters such as discount factors, learning, and exploration rates. It is necessary to contemplate approaches that can quickly adapt to new tasks with a reduced number of samples and gradient updates, i.e. Meta Reinforcement Learning (MRL) [5]. It adapts baseline RL or Deep Reinforcement Learning (DRL) models to changing network characteristics [4,8], helps overcome challenges such as hyperparameters setting in neural networks, and deals with dynamic environments. MRL involves training agents on multiple tasks, using experiences from previous tasks to identify data priorities.

To discuss this Ph.D. research proposal, the paper is divided into different sections. The research problem and the research questions are introduced in Sect. 2. The initial results, work plan and methodology are provided in Sect. 3. The next research directions are exposed in Sect. 4. Finally, the conclusions are included in Sect. 5.

2   Research Problem

Available research is dedicated to specific use cases or optimization of a reduced number of parameters, but not much literature exists related to (i) management of different services to achieve required QoS depending on specific use cases, (ii) model adaptation to the dynamic changes of the environment considering a new range of services and resources in the network, (iii) energy minimization in distributed MEC systems managed by multiple orchestrators. Despite service management advances, there is a specific need to address the dynamically changing services and infrastructures in distributed edge networks with different orchestration, for efficient service placement and migration, while reducing power consumption. Therefore, we aim to develop network-aware methods that adapt to the effects of dynamicity while ensuring desired SLAs and minimizing energy consumption. We hypothesize that DDRL and MRL can effectively handle distributed MEC systems for beyond 5G and 6G networks, addressing dynamicity issues in changing infrastructures, online service requests, and constraint changes. Based on this research, the following research questions arise:

- How to develop a cognitive machine learning model aimed at resource provisioning that can efficiently assure SLA for different use cases in distributed MEC systems in beyond 5G and 6G networks?
- How to perform service management in multiple MEC systems managed by different orchestrators while minimizing power consumption?
- How to manage training-retraining in changing Edge Computing infrastructures?
- How to enable using MRL and DDRL to adapt to new tasks to optimize different requirements, depending on the needs of the service?

3   Initial Results

The main purpose of the research is to contribute to managing services in dynamic environments in distributed Edge Computing networks for service placement and migration. The methodology of each phase of the work plan and the first results are described below.

3.1   Work Plan and Methodology

This Ph.D. research is divided into four main phases: (i) study of the state of the art and related work for service management in dynamic MEC environments for beyond 5G and 6G networks, (ii) design of adaptable RL models for service management, (iii) development of the algorithms, and (iv) validation of the performed models with selected use cases. This Ph.D. is currently in the early stages of the second year. The duration of Phase (i) is nearly three years. It started with the beginning of the Ph.D. and is intended to continue until almost the end of the studies. Phase (ii) has a 6-month duration, which started in the second year, where the service requirements for distributed edge networks are being analyzed, and the overall operation of the RL models is established. Phase (iii) includes the implementation process of the RL methods. The term is 10 months and is carried out at the end of the second phase. The last phase (iv) is the validation of the designed models, which is intended to start at the beginning of the 3rd year with a duration of 10 months to describe the use cases and the validation performed. Phases from (ii) to (iv) include publishing ongoing research.

3.2   First Results

The first results described in this section are referred to as the ongoing phase (ii) and (iii) of the Ph.D. Ensuring reduced energy consumption is a crucial aspect of managing distributed MEC systems that require powerful devices for supporting multiple tasks, including ML model training. Therefore, the first results of this research are based on application placement in distributed MEC systems managed by several orchestrators to minimize the number of active nodes using a DDRL approach. DRL agents interact with a MEC system, sharing their experiences in order to consider the experiences of other agents. The model inputs are the application data requirements of storage, CPU, and RAM and the available capacity of each node to output the placement node action. The algorithm is tested with several MEC systems, nodes and different number of entry applications to determine its scope, it has demonstrated accurate performance in these cases. The results are currently under the publication process.

DDRL generalizes the diverse set of learnt experiences among agents, while MRL adapts to new experiences based on previous ones. Therefore, MRL is chosen for further work to handle unforeseen network variations. We envision the design of an MRL algorithm to place and migrate service requests in distributed edge computing environments. Figure 1 shows the proposed design. The overall operation and the ML models' processing sequence have been established. In service management, MRL usually bases its functionality on inner and outer models, trained in two loops. In general, the outer model is responsible for training the initial parameters and determining whether the environment changes the model parameters to adapt to them. Thus, the inner model can quickly adapt to the new tasks using RL techniques to find the optimal decision. A learning task is considered a Markov Decision Process, where all share the same action and state space, but may differ in reward functions or their dynamics.

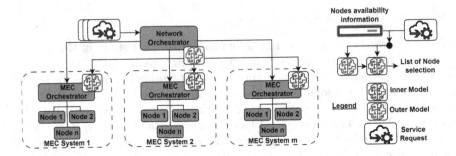

Fig. 1. MRL design in a Distributed MEC System architecture.

The outer model identifies and responds to new tasks related to reward changes depending on the service requirements. When a new service requirement arrives at the Network Orchestrator with a prioritized parameter to optimize, the model reacts and makes minimal configuration changes in the network to optimize processing time. A change in the requirements could be the need for hardware acceleration, an ultra-low latency requirement, or a resource demand not faced before. The inner model will take the outer model output, node availability information and service requests to provide a list of nodes for possible placement and migration activities. Currently, the first implementation of the MRL design includes service placement and migration, considering changes in the arrival distribution of requests, number of nodes, and active service time.

4   Next Research Directions

The activities described in Sect. 3 represent the first stage to address the research problem presented in this paper. The next research directions are oriented to continue with the response to the research questions. Within the scope of the next research purposes in the MRL model are the extension of selected requirements and constraints of services to develop service placement and migration. Regarding the DDRL algorithm in progress, we plan to enhance its capabilities to include migration activities. The MRL algorithm will be designed to operate in real-time. The system inputs are the service requirements and the availability of the network nodes. The output is the list of nodes with the best availability to perform the placement/migration, considering that some nodes can leave the network, thus always guaranteeing availability for the applications. The algorithms will be validated with use cases with the dynamicity included in the service requirements for different types of tasks. The MRL algorithm will be containerized in order to validate in a real testbed with multiple MEC systems managed by several orchestrators, considering: different number of nodes per MEC System, range of service requirements changing in real-time, unstable node connection and changing service lifecycle. We expect to compare the functionality of linear programming, RL, MRL and DDRL in this scenario in terms of accuracy, inference time, fulfilment of optimization objectives and average reward.

5 Conclusions

This paper has presented a research plan for service management in dynamic environments in distributed edge networks in beyond 5G and 6G. This research aims to adapt to scalable and dynamic networks with high variability in types of services and their requirements. The resulting design of ongoing research work has been presented. The idea of utilizing MRL and DDRL in an environment with several geographically distributed MEC systems is explained.

Acknowledgement. This work has been performed in the framework of the EU's H2020 project AI@EDGE (101015922). The authors would also like to acknowledge the CERCA Programme/Generalitat de Catalunya, the EU "NextGenerationEU/PRTR", MCIN and AEI (Spain) under project IJC2020-043058-I, and by MCIN/AEI/10.13039/501100011033 (FEDER, EU) under grant PID2022-142332OA-I00.

References

1. Goudarzi, M., Palaniswami, M.S., Buyya, R.: A distributed deep reinforcement learning technique for application placement in edge and fog computing environments. IEEE Trans. Mob. Comput. **22**(5), 2491–2505 (2023)
2. Li, M., Gao, J., Zhao, L., Shen, X.: Deep reinforcement learning for collaborative edge computing in vehicular networks. IEEE Trans. Cogn. Commun. Networking **6**(4), 1122–1135 (2020)
3. Park, S.W., Boukerche, A., Guan, S.: A novel deep reinforcement learning based service migration model for mobile edge computing. In: Proceedings of IEEE/ACM DS-RT, Prague, Czech Republic, pp. 1–8 (2020)
4. Qu, G., Wu, H., Li, R., Jiao, P.: DMRO: a deep meta reinforcement learning-based task offloading framework for edge-cloud computing. IEEE Trans. Netw. Serv. Manage. **18**(3), 3448–3459 (2021)
5. Saleh, H., Saber, W., Rizk, R.: Mobile computation offloading in mobile edge computing based on artificial intelligence approach: a review and future directions. In: Proceedings of Springer AMLTA, Cairo, Egypt, pp. 593–603 (2022)
6. Sami, H., Otrok, H., Bentahar, J., Mourad, A.: AI-based resource provisioning of IoE services in 6G: a deep reinforcement learning approach. IEEE Trans. Netw. Serv. Manage. **18**(3), 3527–3540 (2021)
7. Tabatabaee Malazi, H., et al.: Dynamic service placement in multi-access edge computing: a systematic literature review. IEEE Access **10**, 32639–32688 (2022)
8. Wang, J., Hu, J., Min, G., Zomaya, A.Y., Georgalas, N.: Fast adaptive task offloading in edge computing based on meta reinforcement learning. IEEE Trans. Parallel Distrib. Syst. **32**(1), 242–253 (2021)
9. Wei, D., Ma, J., Luo, L., Wang, Y., He, L., Li, X.: Computation offloading over multi-UAV MEC network: a distributed deep reinforcement learning approach. Comput. Netw. **199**, 108439 (2021)

Path Plan Optimisation for UAV Assisted Data Collection in Large Areas

Ruben Enrique Padilla Robles$^{(\boxtimes)}$ (ID) and Rizos Sakellariou (ID)

Department of Computer Science, University of Manchester, Manchester, UK
`ruben.padillarobles@postgrad.manchester.ac.uk`

Abstract. Integrated systems that combine wireless sensor networks (WSNs) and unmanned aerial vehicles (UAVs) are emerging as state-of-the-art solutions for large-scale remote sensing. In order to achieve an energy-efficient path plan, this paper highlights the importance of considering parameters from sensor nodes beyond just UAV travel distance. For example, residual battery and buffer size of sensor nodes are equally important in enhancing data collection, reducing energy consumption, minimising data loss and extending the lifetime of WSNs. The paper presents an extract from a proposed algorithm that demonstrates how to generate UAV path plans based on the dynamic resources of the WSN. This algorithm harnesses parallelism by dividing WSN into clusters. The path plans only include a subset of sensors that interact with the UAV, serving as waypoints in the traversal process. The cost of each path plan is assessed by our proposed system model, which considers the energy-consuming actions the sensors can perform. Graph theory is used to map the problem of UAV path plan generation to the Travelling Salesman Problem (TSP).

1 Introduction

Robust and efficient methods for collecting data are required for wide-area monitoring, utilising the full potential of different devices that make up a distributed remote-sensing system. To achieve this goal, WSNs on the ground and UAVs are combined to create cooperative environments [5].

A UAV-WSN system consists of the following components:

- **Sensor nodes (SNs)** refer to compact electronic devices specifically designed to monitor and collect data from the surrounding environment. These devices are capable of collecting various types of information, including temperature, humidity, pressure, light, sound, or motion. These devices are resource-constrained and battery-powered and generally lack the ability to recharge their batteries.
- **Unmanned Aerial Vehicles (UAVs)** are compact and lightweight aircraft that can be equipped with sensors, cameras, and communication devices to interface with the WSN system. They assist the WSNs by transporting data collected from ground sensor nodes to the base station.

© The Author(s), under exclusive license to Springer Nature Switzerland AG 2024
D. Zeinalipour et al. (Eds.): Euro-Par 2023 Workshops, LNCS 14352, pp. 314–320, 2024.
https://doi.org/10.1007/978-3-031-48803-0_39

- A **Base Station (BS)** functions as a central device that serves as a gateway between the sensor nodes and the external world. The base station is responsible for processing, collecting, aggregating, and storing data. It also serves as a starting and ending point for the path plan.

Numerous energy-efficient path planning strategies have been studied in existing literature for UAV-assisted data collection in WSNs. These strategies encompass various approaches such as optimising the path plan and wake-up schedule for sensor nodes simultaneously [10], addressing deadline-based WSNs with UAVs path plans [1], incorporating system activation scheduling into a border surveillance framework [4] and determining the minimum UAV distance required to create an effective path plan [8]. This short paper presents a model and a solution aimed at finding a suitable path plan for UAVs that considers sensor resources such as residual battery and buffer size. The proposed approach places significant emphasis on the sensor nodes, which are considered the common cause of failure in these systems. The paper makes the following contributions:

- Firstly, we formulate the UAV assisted data collection problem in large areas, which aims to minimise multi-hop routing on sparse networks to reduce sensor transmissions and minimise sensor energy consumption.
- Secondly, we establish a comprehensive system model that considers energy-consuming sensor operations and provide a cost equation to quantify the impact on energy for each operation in relation to the path plan.
- Thirdly, we propose an algorithm that determines a suitable trajectory to connect a subset of a sparse WSN based on parameters such residual energy, buffer size and distance between nodes.

2   Problem Definition

The aim of this study is to construct a cost-effective path plan for UAVs assisting WSNs in large areas. We assume that we deploy a WSN to monitor large agricultural plots that are spread over a large area. We also assume a network that contains low-cost sensor nodes that are divided into different clusters using the Low-Energy Adaptive Clustering Hierarchy (LEACH) clustering algorithm [7]. Communication between the BS and SNs is not feasible due to energy transmission and distance. Therefore, the UAV assumes the role of a data mule, enabling communication and data transfer among the BS and SNs. LEACH categorises the SNs into Cluster Members (CMs) and Cluster Heads (CHs), with the UAV exclusively communicating with the latter. Additionally, the CMs solely engage in communication and transfer data with the CHs. The WSN can be represented as a graph, G, where nodes represent the sensors and edges represent the distance between the sensors [6]. Considering that CHs form a subset of the WSN then it is concluded that $CHs \subseteq WSN \therefore G$. The path plans consist of the WSN subset comprising CHs and BS, and they form a graph. The traversal of this graph corresponds to a well-known problem, the Travelling Salesman Problem (TSP) [2]. The TSP builds upon the Hamiltonian Cycle Problem (HCP)

[9], where the base station serves as both the designated starting and ending point. In this paper, in order to address the TSP, we employ the Lin-Kernighan-Helsgaun (LKH) heuristic algorithm [3], which enables us to obtain the most cost-effective path plan in terms of energy consumption while also enhancing scalability.

3   System Model

The proposed system model is designed to capture various energy-consuming operations of sensor nodes in WSNs. These operations include *aggregation, sensing, sleep, data transfer* and *data reception*. In the context of UAV-assisted WSN systems, the term *round (R)* represents a specific time period dedicated to data collection activities. Each round is further divided into multiple *time slots (TS)*, during which sensor operations are performed by different system devices. Furthermore, between rounds, there exists an *IDLE (I)* period during which the BS processes plans for the next round. Meanwhile, the sensors maintain their operations and the UAV recharges its battery at the BS. Equation 1 calculates the priority value, P, for each cluster head within the WSN.

$$P = 1 - \frac{C_b}{R_b},\qquad(1)$$

where R_b represents the residual battery of the SNs, and C_b represents the value of the cost function calculated using Eq. 2. The priority value, P, is a numerical representation between -1 and 1. Positive values indicate the available resources of a sensor node on a given scale. A lower priority value indicates a lower number of resources in the node, while a higher value suggests a higher number of resources in the node. If the priority value is negative, it indicates that the sensor node either has exhausted its battery or will deplete it before the UAV can reach it and extract its data. Such nodes are automatically disqualified from the path plan. Priorities values are typically represented using a matrix, where rows and columns correspond to the vertices (nodes) of the graph.

The cost function is calculated as follows:

$$C_b = S\alpha + I\beta + T_x[\gamma + \lambda] + DA\omega\qquad(2)$$

The individual terms of the cost function in Eq. 2 are:

a) $S\alpha$ refers to the energy cost of the *sensing* operation.
b) The term $I\beta$ indicates the energy cost of the *sleeping* operation.
c) The term $T_x[\gamma + \lambda]$ represents *transmit* and *reception* of data operations; one assumption in our system model is that they have the same energy cost.
d) The final term, represented as $DA\omega$, corresponds to the cost of the *data aggregation* operation multiplied by the size of the data.

The proposed system model generates the cost matrix weight by summing the priorities of the connected nodes to determine the costs of edge weights. This matrix allows us to refine the initial path plan, transforming it into one that considers dynamic resources in WSN. The experiments of the proposed model will be simulated using MATLAB. The prototype emulates a WSN along with multirotor UAVs capable of visiting and exchanging data with SNs. Additionally, the prototype also incorporates the algorithm discussed in the following section.

4 Proposed Algorithm

Algorithm 1 harnesses parallelism by dividing wireless sensor networks (WSN) into clusters and further dividing each cluster into subsets of nodes (CMs and CHs). The overall complexity of Algorithm 1 and Algorithm 1 is $O(R \cdot N^2 \cdot 2^N) \cdot O(N \cdot D)$ where R is the number of iterations, N is the number of cluster heads and D is the number of data packages collected in each iteration. Table 1 displays the variables utilised in the algorithm, while Table 2 presents the functions and their corresponding descriptions.

Table 1. Summary of acronyms for variables used in the algorithms

Acronym	Definition	Acronym	Definition
CP	Cluster Plan	PP	Path Plan
CM	Cluster Member	CH	Cluster Head
R	Round	IDLE	Inactivity or non-operation
V_{CH}	Vector with cluster heads	V_{CM}	Vector with cluster members
$V_S D$	Vector with sensed information	$V_W I$	Vector with WSN information
$M_{d_{CH}}$	Distance matrix	$M_{b_{CH}}$	WSN information matrix
PP_I	Initial path plan	PP_F	Final path plan
C	Cluster	SD	Sensed data

Table 2. Overview of functions utilised in the algorithms

Function	Definition
getCoordNodes	Get coordinates of all sensors in WSN
getDMatrix	Get Euclidian distance matrix; returns array of nodes with their coordinates
getWIMatrix	Get System Model cost matrix; returns array of nodes with their residual battery and buffer size
CP.getCHs	Get array of cluster heads
LEACH-C.getCP	Get Cluster Plan; returns distance and/or cost matrix
LKH3.getPP	Get Path Plan; returns either distance and/or cost matrix and/or initial plan

Figure 2 illustrates an example of a UAV-WSN system, depicting the enumeration of sensor nodes within the WSN. The leftmost box presents a layout showcasing potential paths that can be traversed in the deployed WSN. The remaining boxes shown in Fig. 2 visually represent path plans created by Algorithm 1. The initial path plans are based only on UAV's travelled distance. However, the path plans generated by Algorithm 1 consider sensor residual battery and buffer size, which provide insight into the dynamic resources of the WSN. These considerations may have a positive impact on path plans, especially when sensors in the path plan face battery depletion or buffer overflown.

Algorithm 1 Main Controller (BS)

  Input WSN
  Output PP_F

Initialise System
$R \leftarrow 0$
$V_N \leftarrow getCoordNodes()$
$M_d \leftarrow getDMatrix(V_N)$
$CP \leftarrow LEACH.getCP(M_d)$
$V_{CH} \leftarrow CP.getCHs()$
while True **do**
    if $R == 0$ **then**
        $M_{d_{CH}} \leftarrow getDMatrix(V_{CH})$
        $PP_d \leftarrow LKH3.getPP(M_{d_{CH}})$
        $UAV \leftarrow CP \leftarrow PP_d$
        CALL Algorithm 2
    else if $R == 1$ **then**
        CALL Algorithm 2
        return M_{WI}, SD
    else if $R > 1$ **then**
        $PP_I \leftarrow LKH3.getPP(M_{d_{CH}})$
        $M_{b_{CH}} \leftarrow getWIMatrix(V_{CH}, M_{WI})$
        $PP_F \leftarrow LKH3.getPP(PP_I, M_{b_{CH}})$
        CALL Algorithm 2
        return M_{WI}, SD
    end if
    sleep until next round starts
    R++
end while

Algorithm 2 Traversing path plan (UAV)

  Input PP_F
  Output SD, WI
for all V_{CH} in PP_F **do**
    UAV starts path plan to collect SD and WSN information.
    if SD is not collected in CH_i **then**
        $UAV \leftarrow SD$
        Raise SD collected in CH_i flag
        Set SD collection timestamp
    else if WI is not collected in CH_i **then**
        $UAV \leftarrow WI$
        Raise WI collected in CH_i flag
        Set WI collection timestamp
    end if
end for
UAV signs-off and returns to Base Station

Fig. 1. Algorithms executing on the UAV-WSN system to collect data

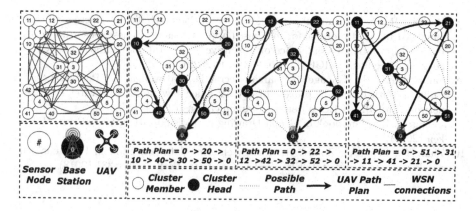

Fig. 2. UAV-WSN Path Plans

5   Conclusion

This paper presents a comprehensive system model addressing energy consumption in sensor operations and quantifying energy impacts on UAV path plans in WSNs. It utilises this model to refine path plans based on UAV travel distance through a generated cost matrix. An algorithm leveraging sensor parameters is introduced to identify suitable path plans. Initial findings indicate the potential benefits of the proposed algorithm in UAV-WSN scenarios, enhancing robustness, data collection, energy efficiency and reducing data loss. Future work involves prototype experiments and comparisons with state-of-the-art methods.

References

1. Albu-Salih, A.T., Seno, S.A.H.: Energy-efficient data gathering framework-based clustering via multiple UAVs in deadline-based WSN applications. IEEE Access **6**, 72275–72286 (2018)
2. Gutin, G., Punnen, A.P. (eds.): The Traveling Salesman Problem and Its Variations. Springer, New York (2006)
3. Helsgaun, K.: An extension of the Lin-Kernighan-Helsgaun TSP solver for constrained traveling salesman and vehicle routing problems. Technical report, Roskilde University 12, Roskilde (2017)
4. Lamine, L.M.: An efficient WSN based solution for border surveillance. IEEE Trans. Sustain. Comput. **6**(1), 54–65 (2021)
5. Martinez-De Dios, J.R.: Cooperation between UAS and wireless sensor networks for efficient data collection in large environments. J. Intell. Robot. Syst.: Theory Appl. **70**(1–4), 491–508 (2013)
6. Olivieri, B., Endler, M.: An algorithm for aerial data collection from wireless sensors networks by groups of UAVs. IEEE Int. Conf. Intell. Rob. Syst. **2017**, 967–972 (2017)

7. Ramya, R., Srinivasan, S., Vasudevan, K., Poonguzhali, I.: Energy efficient enhanced LEACH protocol for IoT based applications in wireless sensor networks. In: 5th International Conference on Inventive Computation Technologies, ICICT 2022 - Proceedings 1 (ICICT), pp. 953–961 (2022)
8. Samarakkody, P., Guruge, S., Samaradeera, D., Jayatunga, E., Porambage, P.: Enhance data collection process of a UAV-aided low power IoT wireless sensor network. In: 2021 IEEE Wireless Communications (2021)
9. Tamassia, R.: Handbook of Graph Drawing and Visualization. CRC Press, Hoboken (2013)
10. Zhan, C., Zeng, Y., Zhang, R.: Energy-efficient data collection in UAV enabled wireless sensor network. IEEE Wireless Commun. Lett. **7**, 328–331 (2018)

Efficiently Distributed Federated Learning

Gianluca Mittone$^{(\boxtimes)}$ [iD], Robert Birke [iD], and Marco Aldinucci [iD]

Computer Science Department, University of Turin, Turin, Italy
{gianluca.mittone,robert.birke,marco.aldinucci}@unito.it

Abstract. Federated Learning (FL) is experiencing a substantial research interest, with many frameworks being developed to allow practitioners to build federations easily and quickly. Most of these efforts do not consider two main aspects that are key to Machine Learning (ML) software: customizability and performance. This research addresses these issues by implementing an open-source FL framework named FastFederatedLearning (FFL). FFL is implemented in C/C++, focusing on code performance, and allows the user to specify any communication graph between clients and servers involved in the federation, ensuring customizability. FFL is tested against Intel OpenFL, achieving consistent speedups over different computational platforms (x86-64, ARM-v8, RISC-V), ranging from 2.5x and 3.69x. We aim to wrap FFL with a Python interface to ease its use and implement a middleware for different communication backends to be used. We aim to build dynamic federations in which relations between clients and servers are not static, giving life to an environment where federations can be seen as long-time evolving structures and exploited as services.

Keywords: Federated Learning · Distributed Computing · HPC

1 Introduction

Distributed Machine Learning. *Federated Learning* (FL) [13] is a *Machine Learning* (ML) paradigm in which different entities collaborate to train a ML model without sharing their data. In *Edge Inference* (EI), conversely, multiple entities participate in the inference over a dataset, each running the inference process independently with the local model. We refer to FL, EI, and other distributed approaches to ML as *Distributed Machine Learning* (DML) [20] approaches. In this paper, we focus primarily on FL and EI, which are also *federated approaches*, in which data is not shared among the clients.

This work receives EuroHPC-JU funding under grant no. 101034126, with support from the Horizon2020 programme (the European PILOT) and from the Spoke "FutureHPC & BigData" of the ICSC - Centro Nazionale di Ricerca in "High-Performance Computing, Big Data, and Quantum Computing", funded by European Union - NextGenerationEU.

D. Zeinalipour et al. (Eds.): Euro-Par 2023 Workshops, LNCS 14352, pp. 321–326, 2024.
https://doi.org/10.1007/978-3-031-48803-0_40

Limitation of Current Frameworks. Each DML paradigm can be described as a *communication graph*. For example, FL implies a directed cyclic graph, while EI requires a directed acyclic one. The majority of current FL frameworks are strict in this sense: each one implements a small subset of communication graphs, like FedML [8] and NVIDIA FLARE [18], and usually only one, like Intel OpenFL [17], and FLOWER [3]; this means that the federation structure is hard-coded in the framework itself, and a peer-to-peer federation created by HP Swarm Learning [21] cannot be replicated with Intel OpenFL, and vice-versa. Furthermore, users cannot create *customized communication graphs*, and not all frameworks allow *dynamic nodes* to join and leave the federation at will.

Another limitation of current FL frameworks is that many support only *Deep Neural Networks* (DNNs), with only a few supporting other ML models. The main non-deep ML models currently supported are Gradient Boosting Decision Tree (GBDT), like FATE [10], and eXtreme Boosting (XGBoost) of Decision Trees, like NVIDIA FLARE. Other *traditional ML models* could be federated due to their properties and performance, but merging different models may require different algorithms and communication protocols, and current FL frameworks hard-code these aspects of the DML process.

Finally, current FL frameworks do not consider *computational performance*. While major ML libraries offer a Python interface that covers the complexity of the underlying C/C++ high-performance implementation, current FL frameworks are written in plain Python. While it is true that the underlying ML library does the bulk of the computation, it is also necessary to take into account the distributed structure of a DML system and the subsequent waiting times and delays introduced by poor distributed programming. Efficient communication structures and data serialisation libraries will remove unnecessary waiting times and improve computational power usage, improving training times.

2   FastFederatedLearning

To address the above mentioned issues, we propose *FastFederatedLearning*[1] (FFL) [14], an open-source, high-performance, C/C++ based FL framework. FFL exploits the FastFlow [2] parallel programming framework for handling both single-node simulations and real-world distributed runtimes, the Cereal [7] library for data serialisation, and the PyTorch C++ interface [15] for training. In its current implementation, FFL already achieves faster execution times when compared to commercial FL software like Intel OpenFL, but it does not yet fully address all identified main issues of FL frameworks.

Custom Communication Graph. While already able to express various communication graphs, FFL still lacks a few features. Imitating most ML software on the market, we aim to hide the high-performance C/C++ code of FFL under a user-friendly Python-based hood. Using a Keras-like syntax, the user can specify a complete, full-scale federation with a small set of keywords and methods,

---

[1] https://github.com/alpha-unito/FastFederatedLearning.

just like is commonly done with DNNs in frameworks such as PyTorch and TensorFlow [12]. This high-level description will be translated into a formal representation based on the RISC-pb^{2}l [1] formal language, which can be mapped to FastFlow code in a one-to-one fashion. This formal representation can be simplified and optimized by an ad-hoc symbolic reasoner before being converted into code to improve the system's expected performance as much as possible. Such a *middleware* would also allow different backends to be used. By constructing an ad-hoc interpreter of RISC-pb^{2}l, users would have the possibility to use different parallel and distributed programming frameworks outside FastFlow. This feature opens the possibility of experimenting with different communication libraries. Commercial FL frameworks almost only rely on the gRPC+protobuf combo to handle communication. FastFlow instead supports MPI and TCP, and many other communication protocols, such as MQTT, could be envisioned.

Many studies [4, 6, 19] currently target the FL learning performance by applying clustering techniques to the clients involved in the process. In this case, the clients are often selected based on their data distribution, computational power, or even model architecture and are sorted out between different servers to obtain better aggregated models. Many of these approaches either require organizing clients in different clusters according to the state of the federation or having a hierarchical structure to handle the process better. To support these use cases, we plan to expand FFL by introducing a third entity in the structure other than server and clients, namely a *proxy node*. This new kind of node will be in charge of intermediating between server and clients, taking care of doing operations as partial aggregation, update encryption, supervising the federation process, storing the history of updates to back up in case of poisoning and other attacks, or just forwarding updates to the central server. Furthermore, as presented in the next paragraph, we will experiment with dynamic communication graphs. This way, we can manage the clusters at runtime, moving clients dynamically across different servers and proxies according to the algorithmic and federation needs.

Dynamic Communication Graph. FFL still cannot handle dynamic nodes due to FastFlow, which creates a static communication graph. We want to experiment with *dynamic communication graphs* in the DML scenario, allowing the movement of nodes across different servers. Such an approach would have a practical reflection in the IoT scenario, in which each sensor would then have the possibility to connect to the nearest server, or also in the automotive one, where moving across geographically distant zones could require changing the server connection. This dynamicity will open the door to experimenting with new types of FL algorithms, such as the clustering one mentioned in the previous paragraph, but also with long-living federations, in which different federations live over longer periods, merging, swapping nodes and being created and destroyed continuously according to the needs of the participating institutions.

Furthermore, having a dynamic communication graph will open the possibility of exploiting *FL-as-a-Service* (FLaaS) [9]. This new take on FL consists of offering the membership to the federation to a client as a possible service to the client itself. This approach can be exploited, for example, by large organisations federated together to share their FL model with smaller ones, thus making it exploit their high-quality ML model for the period agreed. After the closing of the service, the small organisation will be excluded from the federation, thus having no longer access to the updated shared model. Large dataset owners organised in federations can exploit this business model, and small organizations can exploit the shared knowledge without needing access to large datasets and huge computational power. Furthermore, organisations can not just share their model but also offer to train the client's model on their local dataset, thus offering data access and computational power as a service in a federated fashion.

Model Agnostic Federated Learning. Most current FL frameworks support only DNN models due to the very nature of those structures: being representable as tensors, they are easy to serialise, send over the network, and aggregate straightforwardly (e.g., calculating their mean). Also, DNNs usually offer high learning performance but require large datasets and high computational power to train efficiently. Traditional ML models, on the other side, provide a better complexity-to-learning performance trade-off and can thus be used where DNNs are not applicable. Recent research proposes an algorithm to allow the federation of any traditional ML model: AdaBoost.F [16]. AdaBoost.F is a federated extension of AdaBoost and, thus, is a *model-agnostic* algorithm: it can be applied using any ML model as a weak learner. Such a feature requires the use of advanced serialisation tools and also to consider the computation's communication costs more. Also, being different from the standard Federated Averaging (FedAvg) algorithm, AdaBoost.F requires a different communication protocol, which is usually hard-coded in current FL frameworks.

We implemented a Python-based, open-source version of AdaBoost.F into the Intel OpenFL FL framework: we called this software *OpenFL-extended*[2] (OpenFL-x). To our knowledge, OpenFL-x is the first FL framework to be model-agnostic, supporting both DNNs and traditional ML models. We have succeeded in optimising OpenFL-x by fine-tuning its distributed structure (e.g., refining the communication buffer sizes, the serialisation tool, and the sleeps present in the code) and also its internal structure (e.g., the internal tensor memorisation database) achieving a 5.5x speedup over the base software; however, it is still not able to scale over a large number of computational nodes efficiently due to its design architecture. We aim to implement the AdaBoost.F algorithm into the FFL framework, thus further empowering the possibilities offered by it, combining at the same time new and innovative ways of running FL with the additional benefit of a high-performance C/C++ implementation at scale.

High-Performance Federated Learning. As can be seen, our leitmotiv is *"high-performance C/C++ implementation"*. We believe that current Python-based FL frameworks introduce inefficiencies in the FL process, slowing down the

---

[2] https://github.com/alpha-unito/OpenFL-extended.

computation and convergence time of the models. All current widely exploited ML frameworks use the same strategy: masking the underlying complexity of a C/C++ implementation with a user-friendly Python interface, thus obtaining an excellent trade-off between the performance and usability of their software. From our perspective, FL frameworks are not different: they should not introduce more delays than the strictly necessary ones needed for communications. We thus aim to provide a Python-based, Keras-style interface to ease the use of FFL, making it more appealing and user-friendly, as discussed earlier.

Another contribution that we want to integrate into FFL are *asynchronous communications* between the different components of the federation. This approach is starting to get studied [5,11,22], but still lacks a mature FL framework allowing the user to choose whether or not to use asynchronous communications. The motivation behind this is clear: while asynchronous communication makes distributed computation faster, they are harder to manage and introduces ML-related issues, such as merging new and old updates from different sources. We aim to implement asynchronous FL algorithm(s) already validated by the literature into FFL and to test them in a real-world, distributed scenario.

We tested FFL on a heterogeneous cluster, successfully running FL training on a federation comprising x86-64, ARM-V8, and RISC-V devices: we assessed a 2.5x to 3.69x speedup with respect to OpenFL. This *real-world testing phase* is not trivial since most FL-related papers do not validate their methods in the wild but instead simulate them on small, homogeneous clusters, abstracting from issues like unstable internet connections, slow or delayed devices, high communication costs between long distances, differences in computation/communication capabilities, and different computational architectures. We aim to test FFL with different strategies available in the literature for exploiting such real-world federations at their best, e.g. not waiting for stragglers or slow devices.

3   Conclusions

We presented the current FL frameworks scenario, emphasising their limits and proposing possible solutions. We identify as significant research areas in this field the lack of dynamicity and customizability of the federation communication graph, the need to support traditional ML models other than DNNs, and the opportunities given by high-performance, asynchronous implementation of such frameworks. We propose FFL as an in-development research software for experimenting with these concepts.

References

1. Aldinucci, M., Campa, S., Danelutto, M., et al.: Design patterns percolating to parallel programming framework implementation. Int. J. Parallel Prog. **42**(6), 1012–1031 (2013)
2. Aldinucci, M., Danelutto, M., Kilpatrick, P., et al.: Fastflow: high-level and efficient streaming on multicore. Program. Multi-core Many-core Comput. Syst., 261–280 (2017)

3. Beutel, D.J., Topal, T., Mathur, A., et al.: Flower: a friendly federated learning research framework. arXiv preprint arXiv:2007.14390 (2020)

4. Briggs, C., Fan, Z., Andras, P.: Federated learning with hierarchical clustering of local updates to improve training on non-IID data. In: 2020 International Joint Conference on Neural Networks, pp. 1–9 (2020)

5. Chen, Y., Ning, Y., Slawski, M., et al.: Asynchronous online federated learning for edge devices with non-IID data. In: 2020 IEEE International Conference on Big Data, pp. 15–24 (2020)

6. Ghosh, A., Chung, J., Yin, D., et al.: An efficient framework for clustered federated learning. Adv. Neural. Inf. Process. Syst. **33**, 19586–19597 (2020)

7. Grant, S.W., Voorhies, R.: Cereal a c++11 library for serialization (2013). https://github.com/USCiLab/cereal

8. He, C., Li, S., So, J., et al.: FedML: a research library and benchmark for federated machine learning. arXiv preprint arXiv:2007.13518 (2020)

9. Kourtellis, N., Katevas, K., Perino, D.: FLaaS: federated learning as a service. In: Proceedings of the 1st Workshop on Distributed Machine Learning, pp. 7–13 (2020)

10. Liu, Y., Fan, T., Chen, T., et al.: FATE: an industrial grade platform for collaborative learning with data protection. J. Mach. Learn. Res. **22**(1), 10320–10325 (2021)

11. Lu, X., Liao, Y., Lio, P., et al.: Privacy-preserving asynchronous federated learning mechanism for edge network computing. IEEE Access **8**, 48970–48981 (2020)

12. Martín, A., Ashish, A., Paul, B., et al.: TensorFlow: large-scale machine learning on heterogeneous systems (2015). https://www.tensorflow.org/

13. McMahan, B., Moore, E., Ramage, D., et al.: Communication-efficient learning of deep networks from decentralized data. In: Proceedings of the 20th International Conference on Artificial Intelligence and Statistics, vol. 54, pp. 1273–1282 (2017)

14. Mittone, G., Tonci, N., Birke, R., et al.: Experimenting with emerging RISC-V systems for decentralised machine learning. In: 20th ACM International Conference on Computing Frontiers (2023)

15. Paszke, A., Gross, S., Massa, F., et al.: Pytorch: an imperative style, high-performance deep learning library. In: Advances in Neural Information Processing Systems 32, vol. 32, pp. 8024–8035 (2019)

16. Polato, M., Esposito, R., Aldinucci, M.: Boosting the federation: cross-silo federated learning without gradient descent. In: 2022 International Joint Conference on Neural Networks, pp. 1–10 (2022)

17. Reina, G.A., Gruzdev, A., Foley, P., et al.: OpenFL: an open-source framework for federated learning. arXiv preprint arXiv:2105.06413 (2021)

18. Roth, H.R., Cheng, Y., Wen, Y., et al.: Nvidia flare: federated learning from simulation to real-world. arXiv preprint arXiv:2210.13291 (2022)

19. Sattler, F., Müller, K.R., Samek, W.: Clustered federated learning: model-agnostic distributed multitask optimization under privacy constraints. IEEE Trans. Neural Netw. Learn. Syst. **32**(8), 3710–3722 (2020)

20. Verbraeken, J., Wolting, M., Katzy, J., et al.: A survey on distributed machine learning. ACM Comput. Surv. **53**(2), 1–33 (2020)

21. Warnat-Herresthal, S., Schultze, H., Shastry, K.L., et al.: Swarm learning for decentralized and confidential clinical machine learning. Nature **594**(7862), 265–270 (2021)

22. Wu, W., He, L., Lin, W., et al.: SAFA: a semi-asynchronous protocol for fast federated learning with low overhead. IEEE Trans. Comput. **70**(5), 655–668 (2020)

Parallel Auto-Scheduling of Counting Queries in Machine Learning Applications on HPC Systems

Pawel Bratek[1]([✉]) [iD], Lukasz Szustak[1] [iD], and Jaroslaw Zola[2] [iD]

[1] Czestochowa University of Technology, Dabrowskiego 69, 42-201 Czestochowa,
Poland
pawel.bratek@pcz.pl, lszustak@icis.pcz.pl
[2] University at Buffalo, Buffalo, NY 14260, USA
jzola@buffalo.edu

Abstract. We introduce a parallel mechanism for auto-scheduling data access queries in machine learning applications. Our solution combines the advantages of three individual strategies to reduce the time of query stream execution. Using bayesian network learning as a use case, we achieve several times speedup compared to the best possible strategy on two different computing servers.

1   Introduction and Problem Formulation

Counting queries are the most basic operation utilized by machine learning (ML) algorithms. Their task is to count data records with instances supporting specific configurations of the selected variables. This problem arises every time a probability distribution has to be estimated and hence applies to many applications, like evaluating a scoring function while training Bayesian network structure [5] or assessing support and confidence in association rule mining problems [1]. Other relevant application areas could be classification [6], deep learning [8] or information retrieval [7].

Consider a set of n categorical random variables $\mathcal{X} = \{X_1, X_2, \ldots, X_n\}$, where each variable X_i may be represented by different number of r_i states $[x_{i1}, \ldots, x_{ir_i}]$. Let $D = [D_1, D_2, \ldots, D_m]$ be a complete database containing m instances (observations) of $\mathcal{X}$, where each row D_i, records observed states of all n variables in $\mathcal{X}$. Given D, and a set of input query variables $\{X_i, X_j, \ldots\} \subseteq \mathcal{X}$, the counting query $\text{COUNT}((X_i = x_i) \wedge (X_j = x_j) \wedge \ldots)$ returns the number of instances of D that support the specific configuration $[x_i, x_j, \ldots]$ of variables $[X_i, X_j, \ldots]$. For instance, given the database D shown in Fig. 1, the answer to query $\text{COUNT}((X_1 = 2) \wedge (X_2 = 0) \wedge (X_3 = 1))$

	X_1	X_2	X_3
D_1	2	0	1
D_2	0	1	0
D_3	1	0	1
D_4	2	0	1
D_5	1	1	0
D_6	2	0	1
D_7	0	2	1

Fig. 1. Example of database with three variables

D. Zeinalipour et al. (Eds.): Euro-Par 2023 Workshops, LNCS 14352, pp. 327–333, 2024.
https://doi.org/10.1007/978-3-031-48803-0_12

is 3, as there are 3 records matching the query condition. In many practical scenarios, simple counting queries COUNT are issued in batches of consecutive queries over the same set of variables. We can perceive such a batch of queries with shared context as one query $COUNT(X_i, X_j, \ldots)$ in which the task is to retrieve all non-zero responses to queries COUNT for all possible configurations of query variables. For example, the result of executing query $COUNT(X_2, X_3)$ is the following list of counts: $[((0,1),4),((1,0),2),((2,1),1)]$, where each element is in the form $((x_i, x_j), COUNT((X_2 = x_i) \land (X_3 = x_j)))$. Finally, let $Pa(X_i)$ (called parent set) be a subset of $\mathcal{X} - \{X_i\}$ and consider query of type $COUNT(X_i \mid Pa(X_i))$, which details responses for query $COUNT(Pa(X_i))$ depending on possible states of given variable X_i. Figure 2 shows the answers to an example query $COUNT(X_1 \mid \{X_2, X_3\})$ in a contingency table containing only non-zero responses.

The importance of counting queries comes from the fact that in many applications, they account for more than 90% of the total execution time [4]. Therefore, improving the performance of counting can significantly boost the performance of multiple applications. At the same time, counting is usually treated as a black-box procedure and neglected by implementing it using simple but not necessarily efficient strategies, e.g. contingency

$Pa\{X_1\}=\{X_2, X_3\}$

	00	01	10	11	20	21
0			1			1
X_1 1		1	1			
2		3				

Fig. 2. Contingency table for query $COUNT(X_1 \mid \{X_2, X_3\})$

tables. While this approach may benefit from fast memory access, it often becomes impractical due to its sparse nature and prohibitive memory complexity. An alternative approach is to use a dictionary (e.g. hash table) that addresses the problem of sparsity and memory (it stores only assignments observed in D) but imposes non-trivial overheads of hashing and traversing scattered memory. More advanced techniques like ADTrees, which rely on data indexing, have limited applicability due to extensive preprocessing time and memory requirements.

A novel approach to the problem of counting, called SABNAtk, was proposed in the work [4]. SABNAtk is a framework which abstracts counting queries and their context such that the counts can be aggregated as a stream irrespective of the user-defined downstream processing. In addition to a simple contingency table strategy (ct), it implements two memory-efficient data traversing algorithms that outperform commonly used ADtrees and hash tables. First is the Bitmap strategy (bv), in which the idea is to represent query variables as bitmaps and reduce the counting process to performing logical AND operations on bitmaps and counting of resulting bits. The second is the Radix strategy (rad), which derives from the classic Radix sort algorithm and involves columnar data partitioning. Figure 3 shows two representative examples illustrating the performance of individual strategies depending on query size. From these plots, we can see that no single approach dominates the others, and for a given input data, the best method depends on query properties. At the same time, choosing the proper strategy could significantly reduce the query execution time, as we noticed for the first time in [3] and presented a preliminary idea of a mechanism for selecting strategy at runtime. This work describes a developed and implemented solution, including parallel support to enable deployment in large-scale multi-threaded environments. We also demonstrate substantial results achieved in real-world machine learning application on two different HPC architectures.

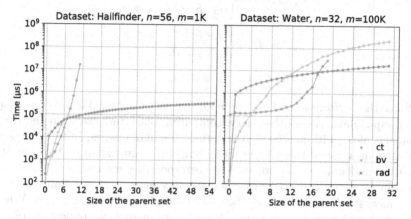

Fig. 3. The execution time of counting queries by different strategies depending on the size of the parent set (shorter is better). Each point represents an average time of one hundred randomly generated queries of a given size.

2 Proposed Approach

Our key idea is to develop a mechanism that selects the optimal strategy for each individual query from the stream based on its execution cost predicted by regression models. Apart from experimentally assessing the performance of individual strategies, we analyse their asymptotic average complexity. We consider a query $COUNT(X_i \mid Pa(X_i))$ and assume that each variable of $Pa(X_i)$ derives from a multinomial distribution with K equiprobable states. This simplifying assumption is necessary for the bv strategy as its complexity follows directly from the properties of input data due to implementing the DFS algorithm. While the cost of computing intersections in each DFS node is constant and equal to m, the number of nodes is challenging to assess a-prior. Therefore, we analyse a single tree node and determine the probability of not removing it during traversal. Next, we use the Bernoulli scheme and properties of expectation to establish the cost of bv as $m \times \sum_{L=0}^{N} K^L \cdot (1 - (1 - \frac{1}{K^L})^m)$. Based on this result and complexity analysis of the two remaining strategies, we formulate functions (1) - (3) that let us model query processing time. The independent variable x of these functions is the size of the query, and the remaining parameters λ, β and γ are regression coefficients, which we want to learn by executing queries. We omit the parameter m, as in typical deployment, it is constant due to processing a stream of queries for a given dataset. Furthermore, to enable the usage of linear regression, we model the cost of bv and ct strategies using piecewise functions dividing the domain at $x_0 = \log_\kappa(m)$. It is not necessary for the rad strategy, which is asymptotically linear relative to the number of query variables.

$$C_{ct}(x, \boldsymbol{\alpha}) = \begin{cases} \alpha_1 \cdot x + \alpha_2 & x \leq x_0 \\ \alpha_3 \cdot K^{\alpha_4 \cdot x} & x > x_0, \end{cases} \tag{1}$$

$$C_{bv}(x, \boldsymbol{\beta}) = \begin{cases} \beta_1 \cdot K^{\beta_2 \cdot x} & x \leq x_0 \\ \beta_3 \cdot x + \beta_4 & x > x_0, \end{cases} \tag{2}$$

$$C_{rad}(x, \boldsymbol{\gamma}) = \gamma_1 \cdot x + \gamma_2, \tag{3}$$

Since the performance of our methods depends on many factors (e.g. properties of input data, size of the query, computing platform), we train the models online, i.e. along with processing the actual stream of queries. Initially, we select strategies in a round-robin style. For each query, we measure the time of its execution and apply it to update the corresponding regression coefficient. As this is linear regression, we must calculate only mean, variance and covariance, which have stable and extremely fast incremental algorithms, e.g. [10]. When a given strategy handles some assumed number of queries, we remove it from the round-robin queue. We notice that this moment may come at a different time for each method. The reason is that depending on the input data, some approaches may be unable to process all assigned queries due to exceeding available memory (see ct in Fig. 3). In practice, we handle it by delegating problematic queries to the best available method. When all models (1) - (3) are trained, we start using them to estimate the performance of strategies. Specifically, for a given query, we choose an approach with the lowest predicted execution cost.

Furthermore, to enable the deployment of the developed mechanism in real-world large-scale scenarios, we implement it in a way that supports multi-threaded execution. The fact that each strategy within SABNAtk is stateless favours the execution of queries in the task-parallel model. However, the introduced mechanism must store the state (e.g. model parameters), causing potential race condition issues. Therefore, we protect all problematic procedures with mutexes, making the developed mechanism thread-safe.

Figure 4 shows two examples of applying the developed mechanism for handling a stream of random queries. From these plots, we see that our cost models quickly get an initial estimation of parameters, and as stream execution progresses, queries are handled by the strategies that offer the lowest cost of execution.

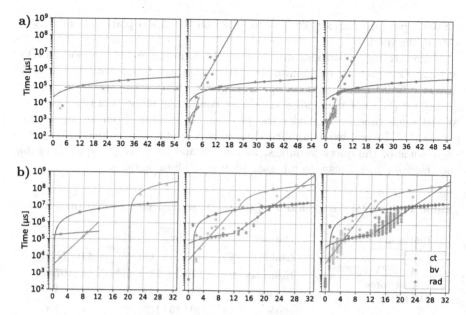

Fig. 4. The regression models for: a) Hailfinder ($n = 56$, $m = 1K$) and b) Water ($n = 32$, $m = 100K$) datasets after processing 10, 100 and 1000 queries. Each point represents the time of one query execution. X-axis is the size of the query.

3 Experimental Validation

We assess how our auto-scheduling mechanism performs in the actual real-world application related to Bayesian network structure learning. Specifically, we test the performance of the parent set assignment solver [4] using popular machine learning benchmark datasets [2] containing 100,000 instances. For given $\mathcal{X}$ and D, queries of the form $\mathrm{COUNT}(X_i \mid Pa(X_i))$ are performed for each X_i, where Pa iterates over all possible subsets of $\mathcal{X} - \{X_i\}$, starting from empty set. Consequently, at level $i = 0, \ldots, n-1$, we have that $|Pa| = i$, and there are total $\binom{n-1}{i}$ queries to execute, creating an interesting pattern of queries that grow in size as computations progress. Internally, the solver uses MDL [9] scoring function and implements several optimizations to reduce the number of queries based on the results from previous levels. It also leverages Intel TBB to execute multiple queries in parallel.

Table 1 shows that the performance of individual strategies (bv, rad or ct) depends not only on the given dataset but even on the computing platform. For instance, while bv is the fastest strategy for the Insurance dataset running on the AMD platform, it loses with rad on the Intel platform and the same dataset. Our auto-scheduling mechanism (called auto) addresses all these issues, becoming the best approach in all test cases. At the same time, it offers significant improvement, even compared to the best possible strategy. Depending on the dataset, speedup ranges from 5.84 to 11.26 on the AMD platform and 2.29 to 3.99 on the Intel.

Currently, we are working on adapting the counting process to modern HPC systems. Our preliminary results show that using the full potential of state-of-the-art ccNUMA architectures opens a way to enhance the speed of counting queries for the most demanding databases containing millions of records.

At the same time, we consider the problem of counting from an algorithmic perspective. In real-world applications, it is common that consecutive queries share some of the query variables. Hence, we aim to develop a query queuing and rewriting mechanism to mitigate redundant data accesses.

Table 1. The total execution time of the parent set assignment solver (in seconds)

Platform	Dataset	n	bv	rad	ct	auto
AMD EPYC 7763 2 × 64 cores 512 GB RAM	Child	20	167.13	135.97	65.44	11.20
	Insurance	27	1210.42	1461.15	*	107.46
	Mildew	35	1788.61	382.83	*	46.95
	Barley	48	7302.15	1256.18	*	202.47
Intel Xeon Gold 6240 2 × 18 cores 192 GB RAM	Child	20	838.00	290.42	166.36	74.32
	Insurance	27	6197.68	3175.13	*	796.70
	Mildew	35	9275.16	860.44	*	248.45
	Barley	48	38489.10	3091.74	*	973.32

* – strategy could not complete the test due to running out of system memory

Acknowledgements. This research was supported by the project financed under the program of the Polish Minister of Science and Higher Education under the name "Regional Initiative of Excellence" in the years 2019–2023 project number 020/RID/2018/19 the amount of financing PLN 12,000,000.

References

1. Agrawal, R., Imielinski, T., Swami, A.: Mining association rules between sets of items in large databases. In: ACM SIGMOD International Conference on Management of Data, vol. 22, issue 2, pp. 207–216 (1993)
2. Bayesian Network Repository. https://www.bnlearn.com/bnrepository
3. Bratek, P., Szustak, L., Zola, J.: Parallelization and auto-scheduling of data access queries in ML Workloads. In: Euro-Par 2021: Parallel Processing Workshops, pp. 525–529 (2022)
4. Karan, S., et al.: Fast counting in machine learning applications. In: Uncertainty in Artificial Intelligence (2018). arXiv: 1804.04640
5. Koller, D., Friedman, N.: Probabilistic Graphical Models: Principles and Techniques. MIT Press, Cambridge (2009)
6. Quinlan, J.R.: Bagging, Boosting, and C4.5. In: AAAI Innovative Applications of Artificial Intelligence Conferences, pp. 725–730 (1996)

7. Ramos, J.: Using TF-IDF to determine word relevance in document queries. In: Instructional Conference on Machine Learning, pp. 133–142 (2003)
8. Salakhutdinov, R., Hinton, G.: Deep Boltzmann machines. In: International Conference on Artificial Intelligence and Statistics, pp. 448–455 (2009)
9. Schwarz, G.: Estimating the dimension of a model. Ann. Stat. **6**, 461–464 (1978)
10. West, D.H.D.: Updating mean and variance estimates: an improved method. Commun. ACM **22**, 532–535 (1979)

Correction to: Euro-Par 2023: Parallel Processing Workshops

Demetris Zeinalipour(ID), Dora Blanco Heras(ID), George Pallis(ID),
Herodotos Herodotou(ID), Demetris Trihinas(ID), Daniel Balouek(ID), Patrick Diehl(ID),
Terry Cojean(ID), Karl Fürlinger(ID), Maja Hanne Kirkeby(ID), Matteo Nardelli(ID),
and Pierangelo Di Sanzo(ID)

Correction to:
D. Zeinalipour et al. (Eds.): *Euro-Par 2023: Parallel Processing Workshops*, LNCS 14352,
https://doi.org/10.1007/978-3-031-48803-0

The following chapters were originally published electronically on the publisher's internet portal without open access:

"Performance and Energy Aware Training of a Deep Neural Network in a Multi-GPU Environment with Power Capping", written by Grzegorz Koszczał, Jan Dobrosolski, Mariusz Matuszek, and Paweł Czarnul.

"GPPRMon: GPU Runtime Memory Performance and Power Monitoring Tool", written by Burak Topçu and Işıl Öz.

"Towards Resource-Efficient DNN Deployment for Traffic Object Recognition: From Edge to Fog", written by Dragan Stojanovic, Stefan Sentic, and Natalija Stojanovic.

"The Implementation of Battery Charging Strategy for IoT Nodes", written by Petar Rajković, Dejan Aleksić, and Dragan Janković.

"subMFL: Compatible subModel Generation for Federated Learning in Device Heterogeneous Environment", written by Zeyneddin Oz, Ceylan Soygul Oz, Abdollah Malekjafarian, Nima Afraz, and Fatemeh Golpayegani.

The updated versions of these chapters can be found at
https://doi.org/10.1007/978-3-031-48803-0_1
https://doi.org/10.1007/978-3-031-48803-0_2
https://doi.org/10.1007/978-3-031-48803-0_3
https://doi.org/10.1007/978-3-031-48803-0_4
https://doi.org/10.1007/978-3-031-48803-0_5
https://doi.org/10.1007/978-3-031-48803-0_6
https://doi.org/10.1007/978-3-031-48803-0_7
https://doi.org/10.1007/978-3-031-48803-0_13
https://doi.org/10.1007/978-3-031-48803-0_20
https://doi.org/10.1007/978-3-031-48803-0_31

© The Author(s) 2024
D. Zeinalipour et al. (Eds.): Euro-Par 2023 Workshops, LNCS 14352, pp. C1–C2, 2024.
https://doi.org/10.1007/978-3-031-48803-0_41

"Towards a Simulation as a Service Platform for the Cloud-to-Things Continuum", written by Wilson Valdez, Hamza Baniata, Andras Markus, and Attila Kertesz.

"Cormas: The Software for Participatory Modelling and Its Application for Managing Natural Resources in Senegal", written by Oleksandr Zaitsev, François Vendel, and Etienne Delay.

"Energy Efficiency Impact of Processing in Memory: A Comprehensive Review of Workloads on the UPMEM Architecture", written by Yann Falevoz and Julien Legriel.

"Experiences and Lessons Learned from PHYSICS: A Framework for Cloud Development with FaaS", written by George Kousiouris, Marta Patiño, Carlos Sánchez, and Luis Tomás

"Exploring Mapping Strategies for Co-allocated HPC Applications", written by Ioannis Vardas, Sascha Hunold, Philippe Swartvagher, and Jesper Larsson Träff.

Author Index

D. Zeinalipour et al. (Eds.): Euro-Par 2023 Workshops, LNCS 14352, pp. 335–337, 2024.
https://doi.org/10.1007/978-3-031-48803-0

Printed in the United States
by Baker & Taylor Publisher Services